The Modern History of
PERU

PRAEGER HISTORIES OF LATIN AMERICA

Editors: R. A. Humphreys and John Lynch

THE MODERN HISTORY OF PERU
by Fredrick B. Pike

The Modern History of
PERU

Fredrick B. Pike

FREDERICK A. PRAEGER, *Publishers*

New York · Washington

BOOKS THAT MATTER

Published in the United States of America in 1967
by Frederick A. Praeger, Inc., Publishers
111 Fourth Avenue, New York, N.Y. 10003

Second printing, 1969

Library of Congress Catalog Card Number: 67–23150

Printed in Great Britain

to Pachita

Contents

CONTENTS

Illustrations

(between pages 172 and 173)

Maps

Maps

Preface

PERU is often held up as an example of a conservative country that fanatically shuns change and adamantly refuses to make the slightest concessions to the twentieth century. Actually, the country has undergone profound changes in the present century. Some of the changes, if not for the best, have at least been for the better and certainly it is not necessarily true that the more Peru changes the more it remains the same. Nor is it true, as the stereotyped assertions of many writers tend to imply, that Peru affords a classic example of the social and economic retardation that results from rule by a selfish oligarchy. This is one of the more frequently advanced generalizations about Peru to which this book takes exception.

It is my belief that the Peruvian 'oligarchy' has been enlightened and progressive about as often as it has been selfish and reactionary. Moreover, as I argue in my final chapter, real political power in the Peru of the mid-1960's has fallen into the hands of not just a middle sector but of a group which, because of its self-consciousness and willingness to regard its present social status as permanent, is actually a middle class.

In the past, those who were in Peru's middle sectors did not regard themselves as constituting a class. The smallness of their numbers, combined with the willingness frequently demonstrated by élite groups throughout the nineteenth and twentieth centuries to open their ranks to new members, permitted middle-sector members the reasonable hope of rising to upper-class, aristocratic status.

Since the end of World War II, however, the unprecedented increase in the numbers of those who can claim middle-sector status has meant that they must begin to reconcile themselves to the fact that they cannot reasonably expect to rise to the aristocratic level; for no aristocracy could possibly accommodate so many new members and at the same time remain an aristocracy. Beginning to regard their status as permanent, not just a transition stage in their progress towards a vastly more exalted level, middle-group members are seeking ways to guard what they consider to be the rights and privileges of a permanent middle class. Often in this quest they are more selfish and unenlightened than ever the old-time oligarchy was, but often as well they are willing to work honestly and consistently for the welfare of the proletariat, hoping thus to establish a mutually-advantageous alliance in the search for dignity, security, and material comfort. In part because many members of what is becoming a Peruvian middle class, not just a middle sector, are willing to align themselves with the proletariat, rather than identifying themselves with the upper classes, significant changes are under way.

Perhaps the most hopeful aspect of the entire process is that many leaders of the middle class, even as they turn towards the proletariat, regard it as logical and feasible to co-operate with, rather than to try to exterminate, a traditional, upper, aristocratic class. They are not necessarily hostile to the continuing existence of a class that is above them on the social ladder. A generation ago when certain middle-sector leaders briefly repudiated the traditional alignment with the ruling classes and experimented with wooing the proletariat, they adopted in many instances an unfortunate commitment to eliminate the upper classes – in part because, given their attitudes, they could not abide the thought of having any group higher than themselves. This is one reason why the Peruvian *Aprista* Party, with its middle-sector leadership dedicated to wiping out the upper classes, was able to contribute little of a positive nature to the developments of the 1920's and 1930's.

In spite of all past forces for change and the actual trans-formations they have occasionally brought about, Peru has clung to many vestiges of the past, frequently to its very great advantage. Even with the new pressures for change, Peru seems likely to retain many of its traditional ways of life, and very probably an aris-tocracy will continue to exercise a strong, although not a dominant, influence upon events within the country. With all that has been written since the end of World War II about the need for every Latin American country to undergo total change, and the more rapidly the better, it is hoped that this book will help some readers to find it possible to regard with empathy certain features of Peruvian life as it has been and as it is – including the at times very capable leadership of its upper sectors. In many ways Peru and Peruvians in their history and in their present moment of development merit respect and admiration rather than the conviction that the country and its citizens must be radically altered.

A myth of Peruvian history I find particularly annoying is that the country has developed and achieved what progress it has only through revolutionary fits and starts. It is true that at least two generations of liberals in the nineteenth century tried to introduce drastic changes at a revolutionary pace; that following them a generation of positivists, then one of humanistic idealists, and then one of fascists, tried to foment sweeping changes. In the 1920's and 1930's, moreover, Marxian-influenced groups, including the *Apristas*, had their try at inducing revolution. Probably it is also true that the names of Peruvians most familiar to the general readers of English-language studies dealing with the fascinating land of the Incas are those of revolutionaries, from Gonzalo Pizarro, Manco Inca, and Túpac Amaru, to Manuel González Prada, José Carlos Mariátegui, and Víctor Raúl Haya de la Torre. Yet the revolutionaries in Peru have actually exercised little lasting influence, and men of moderation and a decided flair, sometimes even a genius, for compromise have directed the country towards its proudest achievements. These men of moderation and compromise, who have combined respect for the past with concern for a better future, are actually the most important figures of Peruvian history and deserve to be better known outside Peru.

In acknowledging the debts I have incurred in preparing this book, it is necessary first to express appreciation to the large number of genuinely distinguished historians, and undoubtedly Jorge Basadre should head the list, from whose works I have so frequently borrowed. Next, reference must be made to a distinguished English historian. I was busily at work in Lima doing research for a history of political and social ideology when honoured with a request from Professor R. A. Humphreys of University College London to attempt to write a general history of Peru since independence. As yet I do not know whether to be grateful to him or not. In any event, I acknowledge him as the man mainly responsible for this book. If in the years ahead continued research leads me to believe I can live happily with at least the greater portion of the conclusions and interpretations reached in it, then I shall decide to be grateful. Experience with my earlier publications, however, leads me to suspect that this will not be so.

Without qualification, I acknowledge my gratitude to the Social Science Research Council and the University of Notre Dame. Generous grants received from these two sources enabled me, my wife, and children to spend the period from August 1963 to September 1964 in Peru. For all of us it was a fascinating experience and we established an abiding devotion to the country and to many Peruvians.

In Peru the co-operation of Graciela Sánchez Cerro, the vivacious, knowledgeable, and extremely competent head of the Sala de Investigaciones of the Biblioteca Nacional, enormously facilitated my research. Among the historians who personally assisted me, not only by sharing something of their profound professional knowledge but by acting as warm-hearted friends, were Alberto Tauro, Félix Denegri Luna, Carlos Radicati, and Ella Dunbar Temple. Without the assistance of Alberto Vargas Yzaga and his wife Isabel, and many members of their family, who offered to help in every conceivable manner and then always delivered far more than offered, this book could scarcely have been written. Since the year spent with my family in Peru, Don Alberto has died. We have lost thereby an incomparable friend and Peru has lost one of those fine, talented, and largely unheralded gentlemen who in their direction of business and affairs of state have proved that social and economic progress can be made by modification rather than destruction of past customs and by working within the framework of, rather than by trying to eradicate, tradition.

Once again, as with a previous book, I have been fortunate in having Professor Donald W. Bray of the California State College at Los Angeles and his wife Marjorie as editorial readers. Owing to their painstaking efforts with the manuscript and to their vast knowledge of Latin America, innumerable errors have been corrected and new insights added. However much the reader may dislike this book, he would have found it ever so much worse had the Brays not laboured so assiduously upon it.

Because of the way in which they adjusted with enthusiasm and real devotion to life in Peru, my children, Paulita, June, and Federico, added vastly to my own pleasure in living in that country. And because of her patience and willingness to suffer long hours of neglect, her insights into Latin American culture, and her gracious ease in establishing invaluable friendships that I would otherwise not have been able to profit from, my wife Pachita made an altogether indispensable contribution to the preparation of this book. It could not in justice be dedicated to another person.

With all of the guidance and encouragement that so many have contributed to it, this should have been a better book. The faults and mistakes, however, the organization, interpretations, and value judgements to be found in it are mine and I must assume full responsibility for them.

PHILADELPHIA 1966   FREDRICK B. PIKE

Geographic, Ethnic, Historical Backgrounds, and the Continuing Quest for a Nation

GEOGRAPHIC BARRIERS TO THE EMERGENCE OF A PERUVIAN NATION

In the early 1960's a group of surprised tourists witnessed an incident that was typical of Peru's heroic efforts to transport goods over 496,223 square miles of often almost impassable terrain. Not far from the Ucayali River port of Pucallpa in the hot, tropical eastern reaches of Peru's central *selva* or jungle region, where tributaries of the Amazon still provide the best highway system, a truck loaded with logs had stopped on one side of a narrow bridge which traversed a small river to link two sections of muddy, dirt road. As the primitive structure which spanned the river was not sturdy enough to bear the weight of truck and cargo, many of the logs were unloaded on one side of the bridge, which the partially empty truck then crossed. The logs were dragged across the bridge and on the other side once again hoisted aboard the truck. The operation consumed the better part of half a day, delaying traffic on both sides of the bridge for hours.

Conventional surveys of Peru often mention that before the advent of aviation, weeks if not months were required to travel from the capital city of Lima to Iquitos, a *selva* outpost in the north situated on the Amazon. It is less frequently observed that until the late 1930's a traveller wishing to reach the more centrally located Cajamarca, the town lying in the relatively low, north-central Andes or sierra where Francisco Pizarro and Atahualpa had their historic confrontation, had to endure rigours of travel nearly as severe as those faced by the conquistadors. In the 1920's, for example, government troops trying to subdue a Cajamarca-centred rebellion had to undertake a most arduous three-day trek on muleback from the mining centre of Chilete, where the railroad originating on the coast at Pacasmayo terminated. Even towards mid-century when Cajamarca, beginning to emerge as an important dairy centre, had been connected to the coast by a road, transportation continued to be difficult. During the nearly six-month rainy season the unpaved road often became impassable. When rains washed parts of it away, traffic had to wait until pick-and-shovel crews, recruited from near-by hamlets and often made up of school-age children, could repair the damage.

Farther to the south in the majestic sierra of the Cuzco region dense vegetation and difficulties of terrain present formidable obstacles not only to road building, but even to exploration by intrepid mountaineers. Despite a four-hundred-year search by amateur and professional mountain climbers, by historians and archaeologists, it was only in 1964 that the fabled Vilcabamba, the last haven of Inca rulers, was finally rediscovered.[1] In the same year there was discovered, or perhaps rediscovered, in the central sierra a canyon considerably larger than the celebrated Grand Canyon of Arizona. What other archaeological treasures and natural wonders may yet be ferreted out can scarcely be imagined, for defiant geographic barriers jealously guard the secrets of the still unknown Peru.

The vast area of the Peruvian *montaña*, located between the eastern peaks of the sierra and the *selva*, with an altitude ranging from six to two thousand feet, has remained nearly as inaccessible as the hundreds of isolated high-mountain valleys of the central sierra. True, some areas of the *montaña* have been connected to the outside world, and here important coffee and other crops are harvested. A considerable amount of *montaña* land is dedicated to the production of the coca plant from which cocaine is derived. It is widely rumoured that many of the Peruvian sources of narcotics are controlled by international crime syndicates which operate in impunity because their *montaña* bases are beyond the reach of Peru's law-enforcement agencies. Even in a thoroughly charted locale of the *montaña*, such as the town of Tarapoto midway between the coast and Iquitos in northern Peru, transportation problems are considerable. During the early 1960's more air cargo was handled at Tarapoto than at Lima, while residents of the *montaña* community were handicapped by a road system that did not extend more than forty miles in any direction from their town and which could be safely travelled only in four-wheel-drive vehicles.

The 1400-mile-long coastal area of Peru is for the most part relatively flat desert land that presents fewer transportation problems than the sierra, *montaña*, and *selva*. Still, as late as the 1930's Lima did not enjoy land communications with near-by cities either to the north or south, and coastal traffic was almost exclusively by sea. Since then the situation has improved considerably. Even in the 1960's, however, travellers were impressed and often exhausted by the difficulties of transportation when they made the fourteen-to-seventeen hour automobile trip of just under five hundred miles between Lima and Arequipa, Peru's second largest city which is situated on the western slopes of the southern sierra and dominated by volcanic peaks rising nearly twenty thousand feet. They could readily understand why in 1880 during the War of the Pacific geographic obstacles prevented some eight thousand troops in the Arequipa region from getting to Lima to help to defend the capital against Chilean forces.

The geographic barriers that afflict Peru are among the most formidable in the American Hemisphere. It is not, then, surprising that land transportation systems have made slow progress. On the contrary it is remarkable that a country with a relatively small income at the disposal of the central government has been able to build as many roads, rudimentary though they may be, as now traverse the sharply differing regions of the country. More surprising than the fact that there is no railway system that comes even close to linking the northern with the southern frontiers, is the existence of railroad facilities between Lima and Huancayo, separated from the capital city by the towering crests of the western sierra in central Peru; between Arequipa at eight thousand and Puno at nearly thirteen thousand feet on Lake Titicaca; and between Puno and ten-thousand-foot high Cuzco. The railways and many roads of Peru are virtual miracles of engineering audacity, boldly defying the prohibitions against surface travel imposed by nature.

One result of the difficulties of transportation is that the majority of citizens living in Lima and other cities along the coast where the well-to-do can enjoy all modern conveniences are seldom tempted to travel within their own country. Among the wealthy sectors of Lima's approximately two million inhabitants in the early 1960's, scores could boast of being at home in London, Paris, Rome, New York, Washington or San Francisco, and at the same time admit to being total strangers to that part of their native country which lay appreciably beyond the immediate confines of the capital and a handful of other coastal cities. The vast capital-dwelling bureaucracy, often not sufficiently well-to-do to travel abroad, was in general as unfamiliar as the Limanean aristocracy with the Peru lying beyond the sprawling coastal metropolis.

In some Latin American republics the issue of centralism versus federalism has represented little more than an academic discussion between political philosophers. In Peru the issue has had real substance. At the heart of a very highly centralized political and economic system controlled by people who know little of and often care no more about the rest of Peru, Lima has been able to syphon off wealth from the country as a whole and to use it for the exclusive benefit of capital-city development programmes. The natives of Lima and of a few other large coastal cities, who, because of wealth or government posts, possess influence, have been uninterested in the country as a whole. All too often they agree with the adage, as commonplace as it is fallacious, that 'Lima is Peru'. It is little wonder that every reforming movement that has appeared in Peru since independence in 1821 has made decentralization a central plank of its platform.

Geographic barriers and the resulting isolation of population sectors, as well as regional rivalries and the bitterly-contested issue of centralism versus federalism, have exerted powerful influences in preventing Peru from becoming a nation, that is, a region in which different geographic, ethnic and cultural elements are to some appreciable degree integrated by the physical ties of a communications system and the spiritual, intellectual ties of broadly shared values. Peru has remained a heterogeneous collection of unconnected geographic and population sectors, either ignorant of or, even worse, hostile to one another. Serious though they have been, however, geographic difficulties and regionalism have not been the primary obstacles to the development of broadly shared national sentiments.

4

RACIAL PREJUDICES AS AN OBSTACLE TO PERU'S BECOMING A NATION

In preventing the emergence of a Peruvian nation, racial considerations have been more important determinants than geographic and regional problems. While it is unscientific to speak of racial considerations, especially in any sense implying superior and inferior races, or to attribute the characteristics of a people to race rather than to traditions, experiences, environment and cultural background, it is necessary to consider race in all of its most unscientific connotations in trying to understand Peru. Here there persists a strong tendency to attribute to different elements of the population characteristics, good or bad, and potentials, high or low, that are allegedly the result of racial determinants.

If Peruvians tend to accept that racial factors influence the habits and determine the potential of the diverse ethnic groups that comprise their population, they disagree heatedly as to whether specific racial influences have been positive or negative. There is absolutely no consensus among intellectuals as to whether the Indian 'race', the Spanish 'race', the Negro 'race', the Oriental 'race', and the mixed-blood *mestizo* or *cholo* 'race' are good or bad races. Unhappily, each of the 'races' has had skilful enough detractors to spread the belief in the inferiority of that particular race among a wide cross-section of the populace. On the other hand, champions of a Peruvian 'race' have tended to praise exclusively only one of the five 'races' said to make up the national population (Indian, Spanish, Negro, Oriental, mixed-blood) and disparage the other four. Many Peruvians have as a result come to accept the monotonously-repeated message that at least four of the country's 'races' are bad. Not infrequently they have reached beyond this to the conclusion that all five are without redeeming features.

Referring to the two most important ethnic elements that comprise his country's population, an eminent Peruvian statesman has said: 'To denigrate either the Hispanic or the Inca element is to denigrate Peru.'[2] This is, of course, profoundly true, and the fact that it is common practice for Peruvians to denigrate not one but perhaps four or even five of the population's ethnic groups has contributed to a widespread apathy. Peruvians often justify

5

listlessness in facing their country's problems by asking, 'Why work towards improvement when we are foredoomed to failure because of our population's racial inferiority?' This attitude is found not only among the mixed-blood masses, suffering from an inferiority complex, in part because they have absorbed the non-scientific notions of race broadcast for so long a time in their country, but also within the often proud, superior-feeling white minority that constitutes the Peruvian aristocracy. Members of this small group tend to believe with fatalistic resignation that their own elevated talent and capacity, like that of their white forbears and perhaps that of their progeny, has been and will be wasted because of the low potential of the majority of the population.

Widely accepted historical interpretations in which the majority of a people can agree as to who their heroes and who their villains have been, which events have been triumphs and which ones tragedies, can provide an indispensable cement in binding together disparate geographic and ethnic groups. In Peru there are no widely-accepted historical interpretations that consistently differentiate hero from villain and triumph from tragedy. Rather, as Peru's greatest twentieth-century historian Jorge Basadre (b. 1903) has said, the teaching and writing of history in his country have constituted a perpetual civil war.[3] Conflicting attitudes over all five of the Peruvian 'races' contribute to this civil war. But Basadre is certainly correct in asserting that the main battles are fought between one group of teachers and writers dedicated to exalting the Indian and denigrating all other racial units, and a second group set upon venerating the Spaniard and contemptuously dismissing all those of different ethnic origin. For the first group the Indians are heroes and the conquest is a tragedy. For the second, the Spaniards alone are heroes, and the conquest is a triumph of unmitigated glory.

Broadly shared agreement on the interpretation of historical events is an indispensable ingredient in constructing nations, for this agreement is the very substance of traditions; and no nation can come into being without traditions. In the 1930's one of Peru's most famous conservative literary and political figures, the historian José de la Riva Agüero y Osma (1885-1944), declared:

... we want to build upon what there is of value in our national traditions. To maintain that there are not traditions ... in Peru is an absurd blasphemy, because it is equivalent to saying there are no hereditary interests, ideals, or goals, in short, that there is no body or soul in the nation. However pessimistic we might be, we could never bring ourselves to advance such a monstrous contention.[4]

Yet overwhelming evidence attests that there are no traditions in Peru. At least there are not, and this is what really matters, interpretations in regard to the meaning and value of traditions on which a vast majority of Peruvians can agree. It is owing to this fact, which has resulted primarily from prejudices and misconceptions vis-à-vis the Indian, Spaniard, Negro, Oriental, and mixed-bloods, that Peru is not a nation. Unless this is taken into account, the history of Republican Peru is without meaning.

THE INDIAN IN PERU

The passage of centuries has neither contributed to a consensus nor appreciably raised the level of the debate over the nature of the Indian and his preconquest empire. Since the arrival of the conquerors and their chroniclers, with the outstanding exception of a very few writers, romantic attitudes and unfounded prejudices, glib exaggerations and superficial generalizations have provided the basis for either uncritical exaltation or contemptuous denigration of Peru's aborigines and their historical feats. About all that has been agreed upon by those concerned with the Indian past is that the Inca empire or confederation extended southward to central Chile and northward to include most of Ecuador, a territory that had been added to Inca holdings only shortly before the arrival of the Spaniards. The empire also included a portion of the northwestern territory of Argentina as well as most of Bolivia and had an over-all area of some 380,000 square miles. But, when it comes to so fundamental a point as the number of Indians who inhabited the empire, the lack of agreement is startling. Certain Spanish chroniclers estimated the Indian population at the time of the conquest to be in excess of thirty million. Although this estimate was from the outset dismissed by other observers as being considerably inflated, it was not until the nineteenth century that reasonably scientific investigations led to the conclusion that Inca agriculture could not have supported a population of more than eight million. More careful investigations carried out in the twentieth century have produced evidence that the Indian empire

7

might not have been able to produce enough food to sustain a population in excess of two to three million.[5]

Various chroniclers of the early conquest period found much to admire in the empire of Tahuantinsuyo,[6] as the Inca confederation was called, and in its citizens. One of the most reliable of all sixteenth-century chroniclers, Pedro Cieza de León, described the Indians as people of great intelligence and in many respects altogether admirable, 'because of their just customs and good laws'. Not unduly shocked because they occasionally resorted to human sacrifice, Cieza de León maintained that the Indians possessed a remarkable aptitude and could contribute effectively, along with their recently-arrived Spanish masters, to a new and notable civilization.[7]

Garcilaso de la Vega, 'El Inca', son of a Spanish conqueror and a maiden of the Inca nobility and most famous of the *mestizos* of the early conquest period, was born in Peru in 1539. In his old age when living in Spain Garcilaso undertook the writing of the famous *Comentarios Reales* in which he included a detailed description of preconquest aboriginal life in Peru. Praising the mildness and benevolence of the Inca system of government, Garcilaso poignantly evoked the happy, almost idyllic existence of the Indian populace. In particular Garcilaso paid homage to the *ayllu*. Originating as a nomadic social cell based upon consanguinity, the *ayllu* had come to be, as the Indian civilization advanced to the sedentary stage, a tribal group located permanently on a carefully delimited area. In each *ayllu* land was apportioned to the various inter-related families, while additional tracts were set aside for the support of the Inca ruler, his vast bureaucracy, and the priestly élite. According to Garcilaso, the best land was given to the humble *purics* or agricultural labourers who constituted the main portion of the *ayllu*'s population. Periodic redistribution of property was made in accordance with the changing number of members in each *puric*'s family. Property ownership was thus semi-communal, and in addition much of the labour was performed in common. Of particular importance was the system of labour known as the *ayni* in which *purics* carried out projects aimed at the betterment of the *ayllu* as a whole.

While highly favourable in his description of the social security and justice that resulted from the communal landownership and labour patterns of Inca times, Garcilaso also gave credit to many positive features introduced by the Spaniards. Even as Cieza de León, he saw the future of Peru in a continuing fusion of aboriginal and European usages.

In 1611, two years after Garcilaso in Spain had published the first volume of the *Comentarios Reales*, the Peruvian Indian Felipe Guamán Poma de Ayala (b. ? – d. 1613) completed the writing of his *La Nueva Crónica y el Buen Gobierno*. The fruit of thirty years' labour, this work represented the beginning of *indigenista* (rabidly pro-Indian or Indiophile) literature in Peru. Emphasizing the moral superiority of Indian over Spanish civilization, Guamán Poma preached a type of pre-Columbian patriotism and saw very little that was worthwhile in Spanish civilization, even though he did outwardly profess the Catholic faith. Disdaining both the *peninsulares* and creoles (Spaniards born in the motherland and in the colony, respectively), Guamán Poma pictured the Indians as the only worthy population element in Peru.

Many of Peru's most eminent literary and academic figures of the nineteenth and twentieth centuries have agreed with the early chroniclers in extolling at least some of the virtues of the civilization of Tahuantinsuyo. Historians such as Jorge Basadre and Raúl Porras Barrenechea (1877–1960), as well as Víctor Andrés Belaúnde (1883–1966), have attested that Tahuantinsuyo was far more than a physical aggregate of *ayllus*. These three concur that the Inca confederation possessed notable institutions and at least an incipient unifying sentiment that in some respects almost approached an emerging nationalism.[8]

More romantic and less scientific in lavishing praise upon the Incas, the novelist-essayist-poet, Abelardo Gamarra (1850–1924), wrote in the early twentieth century: 'With only the fecund power of knowledge and virtue, the emperor Manco made of Peru the first nation in the world: first in civic spirit, first in wealth, first in grandeur, first in the ideal of altruism.'[9] Many years before this Juan Espinosa (1804–71), one of the most influential exponents of nineteenth-century liberalism, had written in a similar vein:

The Peruvian conquered by the Spaniard was more civilized, possessed a higher morality, was less fanatical and better governed than his conqueror. He was more civilized if civilization consists in good habits, in living in conformity with laws and precepts arising from concern with the good of all, in enjoying freedom from the fear of violence in a political régime so regulated that respect for the rights of

9

others was almost a religion. ... Our Indian was docile, sweet, kind, hospitable, loving, humble, religious, pure in his customs, obedient to duty and religion, industrious, able, hard-working, intelligent, quick to learn, patient, scientific in his knowledge of botany and medicine. ... The Indian was happy because he was good, before the arrival of those fierce men from Spain who corrupted him and his nature.[10]

Lashing out in mid-twentieth century at those who criticize the Indian because of his addiction to the chewing of coca leaves, the geographer and economist, Emilio Romero (b. 1899), stated that mastication of the leaves has been no more harmful to the native of the sierra than the use of chewing gum to the North American. Like others of his persuasion, Romero lauded the obedience in pre-Columbian times to the Inca commandments: do not be lazy, do not steal, do not lie, do not kill. The preconquest aborigines of Peru were also alleged by Romero to have lived by a higher concept of love and marriage than their European conquerors:

Love for the Inca was based on co-operation and friendship, not concerned with the libidinous appetite. When this co-operation and friendship were not found, the marriage dissolved. For this reason it was logical that there be a trial period of a year to test a marriage. A similar custom in the hands of western people would be more dangerous to society than the atom bomb because of the abuses which would be committed with women. Only the Peruvian Indian, without prejudices about virginity, without mental caprices which are the fruits of an entirely different social organization, could utilize this custom with austerity and collective advantage.[11]

Peru's great essayist-journalist and highly unorthodox Marxist-Leninist José Carlos Mariátegui (1895–1930) admired the Incas because of the socialistic features of their empire. Mariátegui asserted that the Incas had created an ideal economy. Within its structure some elements of individual initiative had been suppressed, but this had been more than compensated for by the 'humble and religious obedience to social duty practised by the people. As a consequence, collective labour and common effort were employed towards social ends'.[12] In the opinion of another socialist *indigenista* writing in 1947, the 'equalitarian socialism' of the Incas had enabled them to reach a stage of civilization 'which the world until today has not been able to match: a height of civilization which was only imagined by the great philosophers of the Middle Ages, but never achieved'.[13]

To other Peruvian intellectuals this picture of the Tahuantin-suyo empire as an egalitarian socialistic Utopia is utterly absurd. A one-time fascist sympathizer, Carlos Miró Quesada Laos, has declared:

We should not picture the Indians as pacific egalitarians; what we should most admire in them is their system of élite rule. . . . Always élite groups make a state. The Inca élite of privilege was very small and limited, and the only ones not born into it who might gain access to it were the successful warriors. Given the existence of this sort of social system, it is impossible to describe Inca organization as socialist or communist.[14]

While many of these writers do not agree on the strengths and weaknesses or even the true features of the Inca empire, they all view with favour some aspect, real or imagined, of the Indian past and feel that the descendants of the pre-Columbian population possess a vast potential which can and must be utilized in shaping a modern Peru. Other observers, from the early stage of the conquest to the mid-twentieth century, have advanced only the most unflattering opinions of Peru's Indians and have longed for the day when the influence of this element could be totally eradicated. According to these observers, nothing of a worthwhile nature existed in the Inca past, not even in its human resources, which could be utilized as a foundation for building the Peru of the future.

A series of interviews conducted at the behest of Viceroy Francisco de Toledo (1569–81) with the Inca nobility who survived the Spanish conquest and with their immediate descend-ants yielded information depicting the Tahuantinsuyo empire as abounding in barbarian customs, violence, armed uprisings, and acts of unmitigated tyranny. These interviews, recorded by Spanish scribes and known collectively as the *Informaciones*, were the sources utilized by Pedro Sarmiento de Gamboa in writing his sixteenth-century history of preconquest Peru.[15] Consequently, the elements of terror and despotism were uppermost in his account. The majority of Indians, even when the empire of Tahuantinsuyo was at its peak, were described as totally lacking in ambition, as creatures who were in their abject resignation con-tent when the state gave to them a bare subsistence minimum of food and clothes. Another sixteenth-century chronicler, Juan de Matienzo, described the citizens of the recently conquered empire as timid, fatalistic, and indolent, and not endowed with intelligence equal to that of Spaniards.[16]

Repeating some of the earlier disparaging appraisals of the Indians and adding a few of his own, Luis Carranza in the nineteenth century argued that the lowly estate in which Peru's aboriginal elements then found themselves was not owing to the harsh treatment they had received from Spaniards, but to the psychological aberrations which were characteristic of the Indian race. These aberrations were said to have been as prevalent during the flourishing days of the Inca empire as in the nineteenth century. Carranza described the Indians as permanently cursed with a static nature which made it impossible for them ever to mix successfully with Europeans. Through the years, the Indians would always preserve unaltered 'their limited horizons of desires, their same enervated nature that typified them even in the epoch of the Tahuantinsuyo empire.... The same dim light which barely illuminated the understanding of their ancestors today paralyzes the intellectual ability of this singular and curious race'.[17]

Writing in 1894 Javier Prado (1871–1921), one of Peru's leading social, intellectual, and political figures, claimed that drunkenness and addiction to the coca leaf had destroyed the Indian both physically and psychologically. More damning still, Prado insisted that drunkenness and coca addiction were not the cause but rather the result of inferiority. According to him, the Indians, lacking the potential to rise to the level of civilization of superior people, had in frustration resorted to liquor and narcotics.[18]

Perhaps the most extreme disparagement of the Indian that Peru has produced came from Alejandro O. Deustua (1849–1945), a widely-admired and influential writer, politician and professor of philosophy and aesthetics, and, for a short period during the 1920's, rector of San Marcos University. As Deustua saw it, a misguided patriotism had induced many Peruvians to twist the truth and to picture the Inca empire as a noble human creation. Starting from such faulty premises, these writers had sung encomiums of the supposed frugality, artistic abilities, discipline, and hard-working habits of the Incas. But, in truth, the predominant characteristics of the Indian had always been his laziness and inferior intelligence. Asking then if there inhered in the Indian nature 'subconscious and psychic forces' which justified hope for the eventual improvement of the race, Deustua replied negatively. Peru's misfortune, he felt, arose from the fact that the Indians had already developed themselves to the full degree of their limited potential, and could never in the future evolve towards a higher level.[19]

In mid-twentieth-century Peru rabid indiophiles and indiophobes, and between them numerous spokesmen of somewhat less extreme schools, were not much closer to a consensus of opinion on the nature of the Indian and his proper place in Peru than had been Garcilaso de la Vega and Sarmiento de Gamboa, or Mariátegui and Deustua. Thus there remained, to an extreme degree, disagreement as to what the realities of Peruvian existence had been and should, or could, in the future become.

THE SPANIARD AND THE EFFECTS OF THE COLONIAL PERIOD IN PERU

If Peruvians have been unable to agree upon the relative virtues and vices of the Indian and his future rôle in the country, they have been equally divided in assessing the rôle of the Spaniard, past, present, and future, in their country's development.[20]

A rather typical *hispanista* (hispanophile) apologist for Spanish character and the culture which was transplanted from the peninsula to Peru has asserted:

It is necessary to recognize as the very essence of Peru its Hispanic nature. This Hispanic nature should be loved and venerated as the reason for our present existence and the source of our right to that existence; as the only foundation for our hopes of future development and salvation.... The knowledge that through our veins runs even a red globule, an atom of the blood of that formidable race of genius justifies our feeling superior to whatever people or whatever individual.[21]

The detractors of Spanish character and tradition have been just as lacking in circumspection as the defenders. Julio C. Tello (1880–1947), often referred to as the father of Peruvian archaeology, declared that the dagger was the only fitting symbol of Spanish culture; that Spaniards were moved to come to the New World exclusively by lust for wealth; and that the Indians were superior to Spaniards in the art of peace, inferior only in the baser art of war.[22] And Alberto Hidalgo (b. 1893), a Peruvian writer who in his long career has never been accused of moderation, captured the sentiment of many of his country's extreme hispanophobes when he wrote: 'I hate Spain because it has never done anything worthwhile for humanity. Nothing, absolutely nothing. In no order of activity has Spain contributed to the advance of the world. Its children lack inventiveness, imagination, and even intelligence. Spaniards are brutes by nature.'[23]

The effect of the Spaniards in Peru must be judged largely on the basis of the colonial system which the Iberian conquerors imposed upon the lands wrested from the aborigines. The differences of opinion about the main features of the Spanish character or 'race' have inevitably produced sharp conflicts of interpretation in assessing the entire colonial period. Happily, when it comes to population estimates there is at least greater agreement among those who debate the meaning and significance of the colonial period than among those who dispute the character of the Inca past. It is generally accepted that two censuses conducted near the end of the colonial period afford at least an approximate idea of the number of people who inhabited the Peruvian viceroyalty.

According to the calculation of Spanish authorities in 1796, out of a total population of 1,076,122 in the viceroyalty of Peru, there were 135,755 Spaniards (*peninsulares* and creoles), 608,894 Indians, 244,436 *mestizos*, 41,256 free Negroes and Negroid castes, and 40,336 slaves. According to another estimate of the population made in 1812, there were 1,509,551 inhabitants. This figure included 178,025 Spaniards living mainly on the coast, 954,799 Indians living almost exclusively in the sierra and *selva*, 287,486 *mestizos* interspersed throughout the area but concentrated mainly in the sierra, and 89,241 Negro slaves, almost all of whom inhabited the coastal region.[24] There are, of course, considerable discrepancies between the two sets of figures, but given the crude methods available at the time for conducting a census and allowing for some population increase between 1796 and 1812 it is surprising that the discrepancies are not greater.

When it comes to the vitally important issue of how Spain governed and in general treated its subjects in the viceroyalty of Peru, divergence of opinion is at once apparent. As is the case when dealing with the empire of Tahuantinsuyo, the teaching and writing of the history of the Spanish colonial period have always constituted a civil war, obstructing the emergence of broadly-shared values.

Bartolomé Herrera (1808–64), the leading clerical spokesman of nineteenth-century Peruvian conservatism, made a laudatory appraisal in 1846 of the Spanish colonial period that stands as a classic expression of the *hispanista* school:

> The work which the Spaniards accomplished ... was the greatest work which the Almighty has accomplished through the hands of men. To conquer nature, to master inward fears, to dominate far-off places through the formidable power of the intrepid heart, to accomplish all of this and to take as the trophy of victory a new section of the world with an immense population which for thousands of centuries had been lost to civilization, and then to infuse this world with Christianity, to introduce the fire of life into millions of moribund souls, to broaden by millions of leagues the sphere of human intelligence, was an accomplishment of unparalleled splendour.

Herrera went on to praise the centralized administration, the social hierarchy and stratification tempered by paternalism, the sense of authority, responsibility, and religious fervour which he alleged to have characterized the colonial period. He argued that by any deviation from colonial customs and values Peru was courting disaster and defying providence.[25]

Not a few writers of the twentieth century have continued to echo the sentiments of Herrera. Typical of their favourable summation of the colonial period is the view of the respected Catholic intellectual and statesman, Carlos Arenas y Loayza (1885–1955):

> When there did not exist an institution of higher learning in the English colonies, among us there already flourished the University of San Marcos and the school of San Fernando. . . . Centuries before social assistance would be widely urged or practised, already in Lima, owing to the charity of the religious communities and the generous donations of private persons, there existed twelve hospital establishments in a population of only sixty thousand. . . . These traditions are the noble fountain of our democracy, which only subsequently would be threatened through the fomenting of racial hatreds. Even slavery in Spanish America was suave in contrast with its harshness in the South of the United States.[26]

A marked contrast in interpretation is presented by the harsh critics of the pre-independence period who for generations have found in Spanish colonial institutions most of the reasons for Peru's subsequent backwardness. They contend that Peru cannot expect to progress until every lingering and pernicious effect of colonial customs and values has been totally eliminated from the intellectual, spiritual, economic, political and social milieu.

Typical of this school of thought are the conclusions of Alejandro O. Deustua. Not finding much more to admire in Spaniards than in Indians, Deustua contended that the colonial régime in America was 'an organism sick by nature', because:

In religion it favoured fanaticism, in Government a sorry mixture of weakness on the one hand and on the other a total lack of limits on the exercise of civil power; in politics, intrigue and anonymous accusations; in the moral order the perversion of customs, and in economics the most absurd practices of exclusivism, monopoly and ruinous privilege.[27]

From these differing expressions of opinion it is clear that the major areas of dispute between the defenders and detractors of the Spanish colonial period are those of political and economic administration, religion and culture, and the effects produced upon the Indians by Spanish domination.

Those who look with favour upon the colonial past, seeking in it useful lessons for the present and future political and economic ordering of their country, praise the principle of authority that infused Spain's overseas political institutions, the orderly system of hierarchy tempered with paternalism, and the carefully-maintained control over economic operations intended to curb individual greed in the interests of the common good. Frequently suspicious of broad participation in decision-making processes, the apologists for the colonial period find in it the wise acceptance by the majority of rule by an élite and the laudable endeavours of society's leaders, under the direction and encouragement of the government, to alleviate lower-class poverty through charity rather than by allowing the unreasoning masses to exercise their own initiative in self protection.

So far as its critics are concerned, Spanish colonial administration

... transmitted absolutism, the enemy of all social liberty, which has dried up the fountain of the citizen's dignity, weakened the political organism with rivalries, lack of confidence, jealousies and discords, all of which were systematically fomented in the pre-independence period by the Spanish sovereign. In public administration the colonial past has bequeathed to us a pattern of abuses perpetuated by incorrigible functionaries, of avarice nourished by impunity for malfeasance in office, extending to the highest public post.[28]

Instead of picturing Spanish economic supervision as a soundly-conceived and paternally-administered system aimed at serving the common good, nineteenth- and twentieth-century critics of the colonial past, many of them believers in the redeeming virtues of free enterprise and classical economic liberalism, have found only ruinous effects in the business and commercial regulations imposed by the motherland. A renowned Peruvian statesman, for example, observed in 1911:

The colonial régime ... supervised trade, raised prices, corrupted men, limited production, and thus encouraged contraband. ... Because of the misconceived colonial economic policies, the kingdom of Peru in the last years of the eighteenth century had governments without authority, ministers without prestige, treasuries without funds, militia without honour, citizens without patriotism. Integrity was considered madness and the people had become desperate.[29]

The rôle of religion in the colonial past has also evoked much divergence of opinion. Víctor Andrés Belaúnde, for example, believes that the Catholic faith, widely and successfully trans-mitted in colonial times, literally called Peru and the rest of Ibero America into being. 'Faith, introduced through the prodigious Hispanic culture which served as the worthy instrument of the Catholic doctrine, has created nationalities, has moulded coun-tries.'[30] To Belaúnde and a large school sharing this inter-pretation, the Catholic faith constitutes the main essence of 'Peruvianness' (*peruanidad*) and the great and transcending glory of the colonial period was the transmission of redeeming faith to the aboriginal hordes.

Critics of the Church's influence in colonial times generally claim that the missionaries brought only a few superstitions to the Indians, never a really vital and reasonably well understood faith. To the religious influence they also impute a large measure of the intellectual stagnation said to have prevailed in colonial times. The distinguished diplomat and lawyer, Felipe Barreda Laos (b. 1888), criticized the spirit of scholasticism, imposed uni-versally upon the educational structure by the purportedly all-dominant clergy, for having discouraged intellectual curiosity, and the empirical, scientific approach to investigation. As Barreda saw the situation:

The two great objectives of colonial education were to achieve political submission, that is outward submission in all actions, to the monarchy, and religious submission that is inward submission in all spiritual and intellectual matters. . . . The absolute subjection to the teacher, another characteristic of colonial education resulting from the insistence of the authoritarian-oriented clergy, necessarily impeded the development of individual intellectual initiative and generated incapacity for self government.[31]

Raúl Porras, a better historian than Barreda, has disagreed with this appraisal of colonial intellectual life and the effects of Church influence upon it:

All of the restrictions, the strait jacket of scholasticism, and prohibition of books, the principle of authority in education, never stamped out of the colonial university in Peru the spirit of objective investigation. The Spanish people always, no matter how much subjected to external restraints, have maintained their inward freedom for thinking; they have always clung to interior liberty. And thus it was with colonial education, out of which gradually emerged a unique and Peruvian culture, whose culminating expression would be the independence movement.[32]

The effect of the conquest and colonial period upon the Peruvian aborigine has also generated heated debate. This debate has contributed another facet to the continuing civil war that, according to Basadre, characterizes the teaching and writing of history in his country.[33]

Víctor Andrés Belaúnde has asserted: 'Inspired by the dictates of their faith, the Spaniards protected the primitive races, respecting their property and even their institutions. Because of the faith and the efforts of the missionary, the Indians were assimilated into Spanish culture.'[34] Related views have been expressed by Guillermo Lohmann Villena (b. 1915), who praised the Spaniards for having by their conquest 'redeemed the Indian and incorporated him into our civilization, granting to him all of the prerogatives corresponding to each human being *per se*, as insisted upon by our religion and kindly colonial legislation'.[35]

In contrast, Francisco García Calderón, an eminent nineteenth-century lawyer-statesman and for a short time President of Peru (1881) wrote:

The conquest opened to the Indian a new era of slavery, one that was more severe than the slavery he had previously endured. While despots, the Inca rulers had been solicitous for the welfare of their subjects; but the newcomers cared little for their wards. In spite of all legal attempts to protect them, the Indians were slaves. It did no good to concede legal rights to the Indians while at the same time leaving them totally uninstructed.[36]

In a similar vein, the Spanish-born historian, Sebastián Lorente, a long-time resident in nineteenth-century Peru, stated: 'The only reason the Indian does not today include among his customs that of being a robber is because he lacks sufficient spirit and courage. The robber must at least have the desire, the spirit for self-improvement. . . . This desire and spirit were crushed by Spanish colonial rule.'[37]

The debate over the true nature of the colonial period continues to influence and to reflect attitudes towards the Peruvian present and future. Concretely, the issues of current debate which are related to interpretations of the colonial epoch include: Church versus State; spiritual as against material values; economic liberalism versus government regulation and planning; charity as administered by social élites as against social pluralism and class competition; mass, as against limited, participation in the political decision-making process; treatment of ethnically different groups as equals in opposition to the establishment of some sort of masterward relationship; technical as opposed to 'liberal' education; mass versus limited, élite instruction; freedom and liberty versus authoritarianism as instruments of reform.

Each Peruvian who maintains a position in regard to these and related issues discovers or reads into the colonial past material which justifies his stand. Thus, the interpretation of colonial history continues as a source of intellectual warfare. Perhaps not until a modern consensus is reached upon these vital issues will Peru begin consistently to produce objective historical appraisals of the colonial period. Meantime, as has been true of the approach to the Inca past, colonial history will serve largely to prevent the emergence of widely shared values and sentiments, thus holding Peruvians back in their search for a nation. Events of the past will not be studied in the light of how they have contributed to or retarded the emergence of the securely-established main features of present-day life. Instead, they will be seized upon as justification for passionate crusades seeking to influence the still-to-be resolved character of modern existence.

THE NEGRO AND MIXED RACES IN PERU

Negro slaves were brought in large numbers to Peru during colonial times. Although conditions for obtaining manumission were fairly liberal, the Negro, slave or free, was generally regarded as an inferior being. Hipólito Unánue, a remarkable scientist in some respects and one of the fathers of Peruvian independence, was among the many men of his era who were convinced that the African-born Negro was definitely an undesirable character and that the Negro born in America was even 'more advanced in vices' than his counterpart of the Dark Continent.[38]

Although some Peruvian writers have defended the Negro, emphasizing his enthusiasm, spontaneity and dynamism, most have agreed with the contention of Javier Prado in 1894 that the Negro 'is a robber from the moment he is born, and forever the victim of the lascivious nature that is bequeathed by African blood'.[39] Related views were expressed by Alejandro O. Deustua, never one to be outdone in matters of racial prejudice. Writing of Peru's Negroes, Deustua proclaimed that 'they suffered from the vices of thievery, sensuality, superstitiousness, laziness, and shiftlessness. Because of the rapid manner in which they reproduced, they spread far and wide their pernicious influence in Peru'.[40]

Similar prejudices against the mixed races were deep-reaching and well-nigh universal in colonial times and constituted one of the most significant legacies of the era of Spanish domination. Among many others, José Varallanos (b. 1908), one of Peru's most careful students of racial questions, has compiled overwhelming evidence that from fairly early colonial times there emerged the conviction that the crossing of one race with another leads to 'psychic, spiritual, and physical degeneration'.[41]

Attitudes of disparagement towards the mixed-blood population have carried over into modern times. In the 1920's the economic historian, César Antonio Ugarte, accepted the 'inferiority of

Negro and mixed races',[42] while in 1931 Deustua observed:

Among us the problem of the *mestizo* is much more grave than in other countries. The product of the Indian is his period of moral dissolution and the Spaniard in his epoch of decadence, the *mestizo* has inherited all of the defects of each without being able to conserve the remains of the gentlemanly life of the conqueror. . . . The mixture has been disastrous to the national culture.[43]

The philosopher and politician, Antenor Orrego (1892–1960), shared Deustua's low estimate of the *mestizo*. Writing in 1939 Orrego affirmed:

The *mestizo* is never a stable and organic product. . . . He is a hybrid creature both in his psychic and spiritual structure. As *mestizaje* is a juxtaposition of bloods, so it is also a juxtaposition of states of mind out of which has never emerged a coherent and unified accord.

To the psychological instability which he imputed to the *mestizo*, Orrego attributed the turbulence of Peruvian history.[44]

The geographic deployment of ethnic groups that took place during the colonial era provided another obstruction to the ultimate emergence of an integrated nation. By the late eighteenth century the sierra region had acquired in addition to its Indian population a large number of *mestizos*, while the coast had become largely a Negroid area. The coastal Negroid castes generally manifested a prejudice against the Indian and *mestizo*, in part absorbed from their Spanish *patrones*. From this may be traced some of the strong dislike which even the extreme lower-class coastal elements of the mid-twentieth century continue to demonstrate towards the Indian or *serrano*. Racial considerations reaching back to colonial times have thus deepened the geographically-originated gulf between the sierra and the coast.

'MESTIZAJE' AND THE FUTURE

Happily, since the dawn of the twentieth century, there has been an increasing tendency among Peruvian intellectuals and statesmen to see the future of the country in *mestizaje*, the mixing and fusion of all Peru's racial groups and their cultural patterns. In this new intellectual ambient, the *cholo* has found his defender, particularly in José Varallanos. 'The *cholo*,' writes Varallanos, 'is the only true Peruvian. . . . The *cholo* is the new person, the

mixture of the streams of blood and culture and habits, the man
in whom the elements have combined in harmony. . . . He is the
symbol of the original affinity among men'.[45] Along similar lines
the widely-read journalist, Manuel Solari Swayne, states:

We think . . . that Peru is a *mestizo* country. We believe that if we
wish to destroy the prejudices, the complexes of superiority and
inferiority that drown us we should commence by exalting the eternal
Peruvian values, the indigeneous and Hispanic as fused in *mestizaje*.[46]

In spite of the tolerance, moderation, and good intentions of a
growing number of men, there is a frequent lack of agreement as to
what *mestizaje* really means. To some outspoken champions of the
cholo, particularly to Varallanos, virtue inheres almost exclusively
in the *cholo* who is infinitely superior to the Indian.[47] To men of
this persuasion *mestizaje* implies the desirability of the eventual
extermination of the Indian through miscegenation. Meanwhile,
they do not advocate mitigation of the suffering or elevation of the
living standards of the pure-blooded Indians making up some
40 per cent. of the present population.

On the other hand, one-time rabid *indigenistas* who now profess
faith in *mestizaje* often tend still to believe that the only Peru that
really matters is Indian Peru, the Peru of the sierra. The *mestizo* in
their estimate is an unstable, inferior element. *Mestizaje*, as they
envision it, will occur when the racially superior Indian acquires
the skills of the modern, western world, mixing them with his old
and traditional habits and virtues. To them *mestizaje* means not
racial mixture, but only some sort of cultural cross-pollenization
during which the Indian should be protected from the racial
contamination likely to result from miscegenation.

Finally, to a defender of the Hispanic race and culture *mestizaje*
does not imply a genuine give-and-take process of mixture bet-
ween two good and essentially equal racial and cultural groups.
Rather, it means the process by which the inferior Indians relin-
quish every vestige of their past traditions and accept the Spanish,
European way of life *in toto*. In this type of *mestizaje*, the Indian is
expected to cease being an Indian and to become 'assumed' by
Spanish culture. Thus, the conservative Catholic historian, José
A. de la Puente Candamo, has written, 'The supreme values which
Spain delivered to us . . . have been the badge and style of *mestizo*
Peru, the definitive Peru'.[48] In similar fashion V. A. Belaúnde

in his well-known work *Peruanidad* (1957), although asserting that Peru is an integral fusion of Spanish and Indian components, attached primary importance to the former. Given its unquestionable superiority, he argued, the Spanish element 'assumed' the aboriginal race and culture.

Problems of geography and questions of race determined many features of Peruvian life in the colonial period. In the mid-twentieth century, geographic, but above all, racial determinants continued to exercise an only slightly diminished power over all aspects of Peruvian development. Until Peruvians, enmeshed more deeply than some peoples in problems and dilemmas that are worldwide in dimension, advance more boldly and precipitously down some of the recently-opened paths towards a consensus of opinion and sentiment on the relative capacities and proper rôles in society of Europeans and Indians, Negroes, Orientals – who began to arrive in large numbers in the mid-nineteenth century – and mixed bloods, they will not approach success in their quest for a nation, regardless of the increasing construction of impressive communications systems that obliterate geographic barriers.

Meantime, in the mid-1960's, it is encouraging that Peruvian prejudices have come to be based much more on cultural than racial considerations. The discriminated-against Indian can look forward to acceptance and fair treatment in society if he 'ceases to be an Indian', and adopts the cultural outlooks, values, habits, and language of the white or *mestizo*, westernized way of life. Cultural prejudice is less vicious and permanent than racial, for people can, and in Peru increasingly do, change their cultures.

2

The Crisis of the Colonial Empire and the Birth

of a Republic: Peru to 1823

THE COLONIAL BACKGROUND

PERU was Spain's great treasure house in South America. During the nearly three-hundred-year span of the colonial period Peruvian mines yielded a bullion treasure estimated at nearly two and a half billion pesos.[1] In the sixteenth century most of Peru's metallic treasure came from the silver mines of Potosí in the area known as Upper Peru, today the republic of Bolivia. For many years after their discovery in 1545 the Potosí mines produced more than half of the world's output of silver. In the early seventeenth century, however, Upper Peru's silver output declined appreciably and the mines in Peru proper, especially one at Pasco in the central sierra, became the main silver producers of South America.

Almost as valuable to Spain as silver itself was mercury, an essential ingredient in the sixteenth and seventeenth-century processes whereby silver ore was processed and refined. Peru was richly endowed with this resource, for the mine at Huancavelica, also in the central sierra, was one of the world's largest producers of 'quicksilver'.[2] In addition, Peru produced a substantial amount of gold, although its value was insignificant in comparison with that of the silver that poured from the mines of the sierra.

Spain, whose economic policies rested upon the concepts of mercantilism then unchallenged throughout Europe, quite naturally regarded Peru as its most important South American colony. As a result the motherland, in an effort to supervise its treasure house effectively, inflicted upon Peru the largest, most powerful and

24

prestigious, and the best-paid bureaucracy to be found in all of South America. The first viceroy, the king's *alter ego*, endowed with most of the prerogatives of the Spanish monarch himself, reached Lima, or the City of the Kings as it was called in colonial times, in 1543. However, it was not until the arrival of the fifth viceroy, Francisco de Toledo, who governed from 1569 to 1581, that the viceregal administrative system was established on a firm and reasonably well-functioning basis. Around the viceroy and his attendants, living in opulence in the magnificent Lima palace which was begun by the city's founder, Francisco Pizarro, there developed a social life that was more refined, elegant and ostentatious than that of any other area of South America. To Lima and Peru in general, moreover, came the higher percentage of the best-born Spanish aristocrats who emigrated to the New World.

In theory, the viceroy governed from Lima a huge domain which had as two of its more important component parts Upper Peru and Quito, and which also included Chile. Mainly because of the formidable geographic barriers to communications, however, Upper Peru by the mid-seventeenth century was governed principally by its own *audiencia*, a high court of law with certain administrative prerogatives, situated in Chuquisaca (today the town of Sucre), while Quito too was administered by an *audiencia* of its own. Nevertheless, Peruvians from early colonial times came to regard both Upper Peru and Quito (the modern Ecuador) as belonging to them. This attitude, handed down from generation to generation, was to cause friction and intense rivalry once the colonial period came to an end and Bolivia and Ecuador emerged as separate, independent republics.

The fortunes that were accumulated in Peru rested not only upon the natural resources of the land but also upon artificial privileges conferred by the crown upon a favoured few. A small group of merchants, for example, who comprised the *consulado* (merchant guild) of Lima, together with their Spanish counterparts in the *consulado* of Seville, exercised monopolistic control over the trade and commerce of much of South America. Goods sent from Spain reached the main Peruvian port of Callao after being unloaded on the Caribbean side of the Panamanian isthmus, transported overland, and then reloaded on to ships on the Pacific side. Once arrived in Callao many of the goods were then transported all the way to Upper Peru and even to parts of what is today Argentina and sold at exorbitant prices which brought tremendous profits to the handful of men officially authorized by the crown to engage in commerce. Rebelling against this unjust commercial system, colonists resorted on a massive scale to contraband trade and thereby became accustomed to flaunting royal laws.

Much of the wealth of Peru, whether produced by natural resources or accumulated by a tiny élite because of artificial advantages, was used to support cultural and educational institutions. Founded in 1551 in accordance with a decree of the Emperor Charles v, the University of San Marcos had by the seventeenth century become an outstanding centre of higher education, possessing a distinguished faculty and producing many graduates who won reputations for erudition that extended far beyond the confines of the viceroyalty. Even in remote Chuquisaca a university was established which throughout the colonial period produced intellectuals of note. Well before the end of the sixteenth century a printing press had been brought to Lima and there was thus established an important industry which in the years to come would place in circulation many valuable studies by the area's prominent men of letters. Although scholasticism generally dominated the spirit of university instruction and the majority of books published dealt with theological matters, the intellectual life of the Peruvian viceroyalty often benefited from the activities of highly original thinkers and from books that shed much light on secular topics.

The ecclesiastical bureaucracy established in Lima soon came to rival in wealth and influence the civilian political administrators. Shortly after the conquest began Lima welcomed its first archbishop and a royal decree of 1569 established in the City of the Kings a branch of the Holy Office or Inquisition. By the early years of the following century the Church had come into possession of vast amounts of land throughout Peru and it was estimated that religious, both male and female, comprised some 10 per cent. of the population of Lima. 'La Encarnación', the largest convent in the viceregal city, housed hundreds of nuns as well as their large retinues of servants and slaves. A seventeenth-century traveller complained that the city had become a huge convent of both sexes, and in 1620 King Philip III observed with annoyance that convents in Lima covered more ground than all public buildings put together. The king added that monasteries held such large areas in Lima and other cities that 'there are but few who do not pay rent to the Church either for their houses or farms'.[3]

If the Church poured much of its wealth into what impressed many observers as nothing more than pomp and display, it also lavished fortunes upon the support of educational and charitable institutions and of missionary endeavours among the Indians. And if the lives of some members of the clergy, including members of the Holy Office, were often openly scandalous and given over to the pursuit of wealth, it is also true that in the late sixteenth and early seventeenth centuries many devout and selfless religious were active in Peru. Four such individuals have been declared saints by the Catholic Church: Rosa of Lima, the patron saint of Peru; Toribio Mogrovejo, an outstanding Archbishop of Lima; Francisco Solano, said to have been able to calm wild beasts and savage Indians by playing his violin; and Martín de Porras, a mulatto of humblest origins often pointed to as an example of the good results of racial fusion.

Officials of Church and State frequently disagreed with each other and among themselves over matters pertaining to the treatment of Indians and of Negro slaves. A number of high-minded and humanitarian clergymen, often supported by scrupulous civilian administrators, sought to protect the Indians and Africans from the exploitation to which other churchmen and civilian settlers wished to subject them. But, by and large, although there were always notable exceptions to the pattern, the humanitarians were overcome by their adversaries. As a result the forced labour of the Indians, who were often slaves in all save name, produced much of the mineral wealth of highland Peru, while imported Africans, who were slaves in law as well as in fact, helped amass the agricultural fortunes of the privileged Spaniards and their descendants who owned the estates of coastal Peru.

The burdens which attached to the Indians of Peru were severe. Every male between the ages of eighteen and fifty had to pay to the crown an annual tribute that ranged from five to eight pesos. Although legally exempt from the impost, in actual practice Indian women were occasionally forced to pay the tribute. Sometimes rendered in silver but more often in money and in produce, the tribute was collected by an official known as the *corregidor de indios* who frequently demanded far more than he was legally entitled to and grossly undervalued the produce which Indians delivered in partial satisfaction of their tax obligations.[4]

Many Indians, moreover, were assigned in trust (*encomienda*) to the Spanish conquerors and their heirs. Initially allowed in many instances to remain in their original settlements, these Indians had to travel once each year to the estate of the Spaniard to whom they had been assigned in order to render a stipulated number of weeks or months of labour. Often they had to travel as much as forty leagues to reach the properties of their *patrones* and as a result were forced to neglect their own lands which frequently were then taken over by Spaniards. Furthermore, the Spanish *encomenderos* – those who had received grants to Indian labour – were notoriously lax in fulfilling their obligations to care for their native workers and to see that they were instructed in the Christian faith.

From the time of the fifth Spanish viceroy, Francisco de Toledo, many of the Indians of Peru were gathered together into towns where they were encouraged to govern themselves according to a mixture of Spanish and Inca political customs, always under the watchful supervision and control of the *corregidor de indios* and the local priest (*cura doctrinero*). In actual practice it soon developed that the main activity of the *corregidor*, in addition to collecting the tribute, was not to facilitate the process of political growth but instead to impress the Indians of his region into a forced labour system known as the *mita*. A system similar to the *mita* had been originated by the Incas. In preconquest times, however, labour performed in the *mita* had served the common good of the Indian confederation. After the conquest, as often as not it served the private interest of a privileged Spanish élite and of an exploitative colonial empire.

According to legal statutes, every *corregidor de indios* was to impress into the *mita* system each year one-seventh of the adult male Indians in his region, sending most of them to labour in the mines. Once at the mines the Indians were required to work one week of every three throughout the year as forced labourers in the *mita* system, receiving a salary of four *reales* per day; the other two weeks they worked as so-called free labourers, receiving the established wage of twelve *reales* per day. The respective rates of four and twelve *reales* remained in effect for over two hundred years, even though inflationary processes drove the cost of living consistently upward. Moreover, in order to earn the wages legally assigned them, Indians had to complete each day virtually impossible assignments. As a result they often had to use their earnings to hire assistants. Because of these and other conditions, many Indians ended their year's *mita* service in debt and were then forced to continue to labour until they had discharged their obligations. Those who escaped this predicament and were allowed to return to their villages after a year's service often found that they were not, as the law provided, exempt for the next six years from renewed conscription. Instead, *corregidores* who were hard-pressed to meet the labour quotas assigned them often reimpressed the Indians at once or after only a very brief period.[5]

If anything the plight of the Peruvian Indians in the eighteenth century was worse than in the century of the conquest. One reason for this was the international warfare in which Spain chronically found itself engaged. Faced with pressing military expenditures, the Crown simply found it too expensive to wage the struggle for justice in dealing with Indians. By the eighteenth century, moreover, the Church had lost the missionary zeal and humanitarian spark that had animated many of its leaders in the conquest and early colonial period.[6] Once interested in the accumulation of wealth at least in part so as to be able to finance important educational, missionary and social projects, churchmen in the late colonial period appeared to be interested in wealth as an end in itself. As a result the once important endeavour of the Church to protect the Indians was partially abandoned.

Still, the story of Spanish treatment of the Indians is by no means one of uninterrupted cruelty and inhumanity. Indians in many communities remained mainly under the control of their own leaders (*caciques* or *curacas*) who were descendants of officials of the Inca period. In 1754 there were over two thousand of these Indian leaders in Peru. They and their children were well educated, and many of them were given important bureaucratic posts in the Spanish administrative system and even granted titles of nobility. Furthermore, when the colonial period came to an end many Indian communities still owned large tracts of lands which guaranteed a reasonable livelihood for the inhabitants.

However much the Indian occasionally benefited from the paternalistic features of the Spanish colonial system, there is little doubt that both he and the *mestizo* (the mixed-blood of Spanish and Indian origins) were generally regarded both by the late Habsburg rulers and by the Bourbon monarchs as only marginal citizens. It is true that during most of the sixteenth century *mestizos* often enjoyed the same privileges as Spaniards, even though men and women with any mixture of Negro blood were already discriminated against. By the end of the century, however, *mestizos* had begun to be regarded as an inferior caste and to suffer various restrictions. They were forbidden to be *encomenderos*, military officers, or notaries, and could not carry arms without special permission. Moreover, unless dispensation was procured, they could not be ordained to the priesthood. More extensive still was the discrimination practised against mixed-bloods with less white blood than the *mestizo* and against those with some percentage of Negro blood.[7]

According to the legal structure of the colonial period, those considered to be in the lower, less-white castes could not dress luxuriously, could not live within the city proper, and could not marry members of a higher caste. They were required to attend stipulated churches where generally, like the Indians, they could not receive the sacrament of the Eucharist unless granted special dispensation. What is more, separate cemeteries were maintained for whites, Indians, mulattoes, and various of the castes so that even in burial the proper racial hierarchy might be observed.

Often the legal restrictions, enforced essentially on the basis of the colour of the skin as a manifestation of blood mixture, were flaunted. It was, in fact, possible to purchase a *carnet de blancos* (white man's identification card) which constituted legal proof that the bearer, regardless of his colour, was white and entitled to the accompanying privileges. Still, even if men of colour bought immunity from the legal restrictions placed upon them, they could not escape from social discrimination. This fact is reflected in one of the more often-repeated sayings of colonial times: 'He may be a minister, a judge, or God, but he's not white.'

If the eighteenth-century Bourbon rulers of the Spanish empire did not concern themselves with the endeavour to improve the treatment of Indians and mixed bloods, they were often zealous in their attempts to introduce political and economic reforms of great significance to those near the top of society. In the interest of greater efficiency they reduced the size of the territory that old institutions had been expected to administer and also introduced many new governmental agencies. Thus, jurisdiction over Quito was assigned to the viceroyalty of New Granada, permanently established in 1739 with Bogotá as its capital, while the viceroyalty of the Río de Plata, created in 1776 with its capital at Buenos Aires, was given control over Upper Peru. In addition, the captaincy general of Chile was granted virtual autonomy from the viceroyalty of Peru. With less territory to supervise, Peruvian viceroys could, it was hoped, become more efficient in their rule.

As a further means of introducing effective governmental machinery the Spanish crown introduced the intendant system to Peru in 1784. The viceroyalty was divided into eight intendancies, each administered by an intendant; and each intendancy was further subdivided into smaller districts under the supervision of sub-delegates. Endowed with fiscal, judicial and military powers and given authority also to supervise certain aspects of police, educational, and ecclesiastical administration, intendants inevitably clashed with longer-established authorities, including viceroys, in jurisdictional disputes.

Of particular significance was the friction that developed between intendants and sub-delegates on the one hand and municipal councils or *cabildos* on the other. Throughout the period of Habsburg rule which lasted until 1700, and indeed until well into the eighteenth century, the *cabildos*, whose membership was made up in large part of creoles or locally-born white men of Spanish ancestry, had enjoyed considerable freedom to govern, or to misgovern, as they saw fit. After 1784 the town councillors found that their freedom of action was greatly curtailed by intendants and sub-delegates who were generally *peninsulares*, that is, Spaniards born in Spain.

Some creole *cabildo* members wanted to return to the days of drifting, inefficiency and fiscal mismanagement that had sometimes characterized municipal government before the reforms decreed by the Bourbons. Others were excited by the possibilities of development revealed by the intendants and sub-delegates who often brought about dramatic material improvement and economic progress on the local level. But they felt that by taking advantage of the new techniques and efficient methods that had been introduced, they themselves could achieve still greater progress and development than the Spanish officials who did not after all have local interests primarily at heart. Whether they wanted simply to return to the easy days of irresponsibility and corruption, or whether they were aroused by a new vision of the possibilities of local development, creole *cabildo* members resented the presence of the intendants and sub-delegates.[8]

During the eighteenth century Bourbon rulers, and especially the enlightened despot Charles III (1759–88), introduced not only political but important economic reforms. The old monopolistic control over trade which had been vested in a few *consulados* came to an end and a period of virtually free trade between Spain and her South American colonies was inaugurated in 1778. However, as was the case with political innovations, the economic reforms failed to please influential creoles in Peru. The members of the Lima *consulado* and their associates resented the loss of prestige and economic power which resulted from the establishment of freer trade. Other men of capital, especially in the 1790's when Spanish involvement in European wars halted commerce between the motherland and colonies, began to demand genuinely free trade and the right to deal commercially with all areas of the world.

After nearly two hundred years during which the political and economic institutions founded shortly after the conquest had remained almost unaltered, Peru and all Spanish America suddenly became subject to the ferment of change and reform. The Bourbon reforms aroused the anger of some arch-conservatives but awakened the desire of progressive creole leaders for more reform. Basically, then, the innovations introduced by the Bourbons served only to intensify the discontent of an educated creole élite whose members had for generations chafed at the unique social, political, and economic privileges which had been reserved for *peninsulares*.

Change and innovation, moreover, were apparent not only in the political and economic fields but in the realm of ideas. The ideas of the Enlightenment, with their emphasis on rationality and scientific investigation, their questioning of previously accepted truth and their accompanying spirit of anti-clericalism, began to produce a ferment not only in the Peruvian viceroyalty but throughout Spanish America. Increasingly, colonial intellectuals began to subject Spanish colonial administration to rational analysis and to find it wanting. As a result they came more and more to demand bold new reforms. By the end of the eighteenth century it was apparent even to many Spanish administrators that the motherland would have to yield to the mounting creole demands for sweeping change or else witness the transformation of what was essentially a movement for reform within the imperial framework into a struggle for independence.

TÚPAC AMARU II THE FIGHTER: JOSÉ BAQUÍJANO THE THINKER

Conditions of life endured by the Indian masses of the sierra towards the end of the eighteenth century have been described by an eminent historian of the Spanish colonial era in the following terms:

Tribute was exacted from those under eighteen years of age and over fifty, contrary to law, and even from the crippled and deformed. The *corregidores* in many places, instead of the statutory seventh, dragged off all the men of the district to the factories or mines, leaving only the women and children behind. Wages were unpaid, hours in the textile factories were incredibly long, and children of six or eight years of age in defiance of the regulations were forced to work in them. There seems also to have grown up a practice of kidnapping Indians, while the system of peonage or debt servitude was already fully developed. It was this oppression which caused the terrible Indian insurrection of Túpac Amaru [II] in 1780.[9]

Túpac Amaru II (the first Túpac Amaru had commanded an Indian uprising suppressed by Viceroy Toledo in 1571), whose real name was José Gabriel Condorcanqui, was an educated *mestizo* landowner of the Cuzco region, a descendant of the Inca nobility, and possessor of the title of Marquis of Oropesa. Goaded by the abuses of Spanish bureaucrats against the native population he seized and had executed in November of 1780 a *corregidor* who had perpetrated notorious outrages against the Indians of the southern sierra region. By this act the *mestizo* rebel precipitated a massive insurrection. Supported by vast Indian hordes, by many of the *mestizos* of the sierra, and in the beginning by a considerable number of creoles, the Túpac Amaru uprising has been described by some as a genuine bid for Peruvian independence and by others as a more limited endeavour to achieve the Indian's social redemption within the colonial framework.[10] Túpac Amaru II proved a vacillating commander and his movement soon got out of hand, turning into a race war in which Indians indiscriminately slaughtered whites and *mestizos*. As a result many early supporters were alienated and Spanish forces were able to suppress the uprising in 1781, punishing its leaders with barbaric cruelty.

The uprising of Indian masses against abuses, their striking out in blind and violent fury against all those remotely associated with the system of exploitation, was not a remarkable or novel occurrence. Túpac Amaru II's movement was but another chapter of Indian violence in the Andes that had erupted periodically since 1536 when the Incas, after having been initially overcome by the conquistadors, arose and vainly sought to expel the European invaders. More surprising than Túpac Amaru's insurrection and in many ways farther reaching in its significance was the response to the event by an influential Lima intellectual.

Born into a well-to-do Lima family in 1751, José Baquíjano y Carillo had embarked for Spain at the age of twenty-two, intent upon perfecting his education. Some time before 1780 he had returned to his native city, bringing with him a notable collection of books and a royal commission as a judge. His library was particularly rich in the works of the French Encyclopedists which were condemned by Spanish officials of Church and state. Despite the restrictions against importing and reading such material, Baquíjano was soon distributing among his friends the works of Voltaire, Rousseau, Fontenelle, Bayle, Montesquieu, Holback, Diderot and others, thus expanding the already considerable knowledge in Lima of the European Enlightenment and its apostles.

Acknowledged as one of Lima's leading intellectuals, Baquíjano was commissioned to deliver in 1781 the principal address of welcome to the recently-arrived Viceroy Agustín Jáuregui (1780–4). Baquíjano's discourse proved to be totally unlike any previously heard by a new viceroy. In the principal part of the address, delivered on 27 August 1781, only some four months after the battle of Checcacuppi in which Túpac Amaru had been defeated, Baquíjano sharply criticized the treatment of the natives, saying that Spanish barbarism had brought hunger, desolation, death and other calamities to the Indians. His passionate description of the horrors from which the natives suffered seemed almost to have been calculated to justify the recent uprising. Sprinkling his discourse with allusions to political theories popularized by the French Encyclopedists, Baquíjano informed the viceroy that it is always prudent for the ruler to remember that the life of each citizen is worthy of respect, and that to destroy men within society is not only evil but undermines the efficiency of the body politic. 'Victories of arms,' declared the orator, 'do not instil fear. They encourage a spirit of revolution which will explode on the first propitious occasion.'[11]

For those who listened to, or soon read, the discourse with care it was evident that far more than treatment of the Indians was being discussed. Baquíjano was using the Indian issue as a pretext for questioning the whole scope of royal power, maintaining that political authority arose from the people (the concept of popular sovereignty) and that the ruler must always govern with the consent of the governed.[12] Here was a challenge to traditional authoritarian precepts that defenders of the established order were not slow in accepting.

REACTION, AND THE DRAWING OF CONSERVATIVE-LIBERAL BATTLE LINES

By 1783 orders had been issued for the authorities to seize and destroy or sequester all copies of Baquíjano's address of welcome to the viceroy. In the same year Baquíjano was thwarted in his efforts to reform the curriculum of the University of San Marcos by placing greater emphasis on modern science and original, empirical research. In a corrupt and hard-fought election for the post of rector, he was defeated by a defender of traditional scholasticism, José Miguel Villalta. As rector, Villalta was able to some extent to protect San Marcos against the currents of reform. In 1785 the new Viceroy Teodoro de Croix (1784-90) threw in his lot with the traditionalists and ordered the seizure and burning of condemned books. Although Baquíjano with his important connections was able to save most of his personal library, he found it necessary to become increasingly circumspect in circulating his books and expressing his ideas. He did, however, together with many Lima intellectuals of like persuasions, continue to be active in one of the capital city's Masonic lodges.

Typical of the conservative reaction to the ideas proclaimed by Baquíjano in 1781 was the position adopted by Juan Domingo González de la Reguera, who in the very year that Viceroy Jáuregui heard the strange address of welcome was installed as Archbishop of Lima. Within a few years, thanks to the primate's efforts, a royal decree was issued forbidding the teaching of Newtonian science and natural law philosophy in the University of San Marcos.

Another clergyman who had been offended by the audacity of Baquíjano was Vicente Amil y Feijóo. Commissioned to preach a sermon on royal authority as ordered by Charles III, who had come to fear general insurrection in Peru after the Túpac Amaru II movement, Father Amil y Feijóo declared:

> Whether the prince uses his power well or badly, this power is always conferred by God, even though the will of the ruler may be most iniquitous. Even if his Government is so tyrannical that he ceases to be a prince and becomes a demon, even so, as St Thomas says, we must maintain fidelity, not allowing ourselves any other recourse than calling upon God, the King of Kings, that He may opportunely help us in our tribulations.[13]

This doctrine, which left the people absolutely defenceless before abuses of power and which did not recognize any other recourse against tyranny than prayer, was the essence of the officially-sanctioned political philosophy in Peru by the mid-1780's.

Despite the official creed, men like Baquíjano, supported by a considerable portion of the creole clergy, continued, although with caution, to expound a 'new philosophy'. Many of the Peruvian-born intellectuals who embraced new philosophical tenets did so in part as a means of freeing themselves from what they regarded as their subjection to and suppression by the *peninsulares*, who had traditionally sought to monopolize the most prestigious and lucrative posts. Beyond this, however, some creoles and even a few *peninsulares* made a disinterested intellectual commitment to a new political, social, and economic ideology that reflected, whether they knew it or not, the concepts of the Enlightenment.

Among the salient features of this new, liberal philosophy of the Enlightenment in Peru was an anti-clerical spirit. It was felt that churchmen, whose proper sphere of knowledge was theology and whose unique function was the attainment of inner perfection and the preservation for others of the revealed truth pertaining to the supernatural means of salvation, should not interfere in temporal affairs. Above all, they should not try to force their authoritarian values upon the educational and political institutions of the temporal world. In part these views reflected the Enlightenment's leaning towards deism, the belief that God having created man left him alone to work out his own destiny free from the interference of providence. If God Himself left man largely alone, then man on earth should be free to work out his destiny without interference from a priestly class. The rise of new attitudes towards the clergy in Peru also reflected the premises of Gallicanism, a doctrine popularized in seventeenth-century France which called for considerable control of the Church by the State and strictly prohibited clerical intervention, especially as directed from Rome, in the temporal affairs of the State.

Because religion involved man's inward values and his individual relationship to God, the spokesmen of the non-official philosophy in Peru asserted that his spiritual life should not be subjected to outwardly-imposed controls and thus condemned the Inquisition, so often used to enforce spiritual precepts through political coercion. Further, since faith was regarded as a gift of God, bestowed on some but not on others, outward coercion should not be directed against those who did not profess a particular religion. Instead, secular authorities should tolerate the free practice of different cults.

In the new philosophy, which like all new intellectual movements was in many ways quite old and embodied some of the perhaps forgotten teachings of the Spanish Jesuit Francisco Suárez (1548-1617), emphasis was placed not so much upon divine positive law as upon natural law, that is the norms of human conduct that allegedly could be discovered by unaided human reason without recourse to revealed truth. A cardinal feature of natural law is its insistence that man is morally entitled to conditions of life that permit him to develop the full potential of his spiritual, intellectual and physical nature.

Subscribing to this line of reasoning, some of the proponents of the new philosophy assumed an academic interest – it was seldom more than that – in the question of race and castes. In their lavishly appointed salons in Lima they noted that natural law was as applicable to Indians, Negroes, and mixed-races as to whites, and demanded the removal of social, economic and political restrictions that prevented non-whites from developing their intellectual and physical potential. Often, these sentiments were expressed by spokesmen of the new philosophy who sought to mask personal grievances against men they considered to be more privileged than

37

they were themselves by assuming an interest in humanity in general.

THE 1785 GENERATION OF LIBERALS, SAN CARLOS, AND THE 'MERCURIO PERUANO'

Ostensibly crushed by the confiscation of Baquíjano's address of welcome to Viceroy Jauregui, by his defeat in the election for the rectorship of San Marcos, by the suppression of the teaching of natural law in the university, and by the book-burning orgy instigated by Viceroy Croix, liberal spokesmen of the new philosophy for a time went underground. If anything, however, they increased their strength. Possibly the key figure in the powerful intellectual underground was Toribio Rodríguez de Mendoza.

Born in the small northern community of Chachapoyas, Rodríguez de Mendoza had studied for a time in the local seminary of Trujillo. In 1766 he had entered the seminary of San Toribio at Lima, then one of the leading educational centres of the viceroyalty. Five years later he had become a charter member of the faculty of theology and philosophy of the Real Convictorio de San Carlos, an institution founded with the assistance of Viceroy Manuel de Amat (1761–76) who had grown concerned over the state of educational facilities in his capital after the expulsion of the Jesuits in 1767. For the remainder of the colonial period San Carlos functioned as the principal *colegio* (the counterpart of a French *lycée*) in Lima, as well as the faculty of humanities of the University of San Marcos. In 1784 Rodríguez de Mendoza, following ordination to the priesthood and six years of parish duty, was named rector of San Carlos by Viceroy Croix. This proved to be one of the conservatively-inclined viceroy's greatest mistakes.

Assuming his duties as rector in 1785, Rodríguez de Mendoza brought with him an avid interest, acquired as a student, in the philosophy of Locke, Condillac, Descartes, and Voltaire. Already determined to accept only those truths which could be confirmed by reason and experience, convinced that the authority of the State originated not in the will of God but, as Rousseau maintained, in a social contract, and that the natural law was ascertainable through human reason alone, Rodríguez de Mendoza embarked upon the thorough revision of the San Carlos curriculum. Realizing the strength of hostile intellectual forces, the rector employed extreme caution which, coupled with the unusual discretion of a generation of San Carlos students, protected him from being unduly molested in his reforming programme.

Rodríguez de Mendoza also profited from the support of influential friends. One of his warmest advocates was Baquíjano, who in spite of official frowns and menacing rumbles from the Inquisition, remained steadfast in his devotion to the new philosophy. An even more important friend was the Jeronymite priest, Diego Cisneros. A leading spirit of the Enlightenment in Spain, Cisneros had on more than one occasion aroused the suspicions of the Holy Office in the peninsula and incurred the lasting enmity of a large group of traditionalist clergymen. Disgusted by what he considered the narrow intellectual atmosphere of Spain, Cisneros came to Lima in the late eighteenth century. Having been well connected in the Spanish court, where he had been the confessor of Princess, and later Queen, María Luisa (the unfaithful wife of Charles IV, King of Spain from 1788 to 1808), Cisneros continued to enjoy powerful backing in Peru and managed to bring with him into his voluntary New-World exile a notable library, made up mainly of the works of the French Encyclopedists. In addition, he soon established a bookstore in Lima specializing in the works of the condemned authors.

One day Rodríguez de Mendoza entered the bookstore of Cisneros, and at once the two priests struck up a friendship. The result was that Rodríguez de Mendoza, who from the very moment of accepting the rectorship of San Carlos had ignored the prohibition against the teaching of natural law, gained access to the reading materials required for the sort of instruction he surreptitiously imparted to his students. Until 1816 when the incredibly sluggish and inept Spanish administration woke up to what was happening at San Carlos, eager students studied condemned theories about popular sovereignty, the natural rights of man, theological relativism and absolute freedom of worship from the pages of condemned books.[14]

For a time, partisans of the new philosophy not only controlled education at San Carlos but profited also from the publication of a periodical in which writers could be fairly free in expressing their opinions. The supporters of Baquíjano's unsuccessful bid in 1783 to become rector of San Marcos had banded together to form the

Sociedad Filarmónica. On 2 January 1791, the successor to this organization, the *Sociedad de Amantes del País* (Society of Lovers of the Country), launched the first edition of the *Mercurio Peruano*. Published originally as a bi-weekly, the *Mercurio Peruano* featured the writings of such men as Baquíjano and Hipólito Unánue.

Generally recognized as the guiding spirit of the *Mercurio*, Unánue was born in Arica, a community in the southern coastal area of the viceroyalty, in 1755. He studied briefly for the priesthood, but, soon realizing that he did not have a genuine vocation, took up the study of medicine, physics, mathematics, anatomy and natural history. Installed in the chair of anatomy at San Marcos in 1787, he followed intellectual developments in Europe with close interest and soon grew convinced that a cultural reawakening in Peru would require the eradication of the influence of scholasticism. A tireless defender of the teachings of Newton, Copernicus and Kepler, Unánue contributed many outstanding scientific articles to the *Mercurio Peruano*, emphasizing the value of empirical methodology and of knowledge based upon scientifically-discovered truth rather than upon the authority of venerated savants and saints. For his studies of the influence of climate on civilization, published in the *Mercurio*, Unánue won world-wide recognition.[15]

With its message of intellectual freedom and rationalism, of the natural rights and essential equality of men, the *Mercurio Peruano* aroused much opposition in Lima. Mainly because it was impossible to obtain sufficient subscriptions to defray the costs of publication – the contributions of Father Cisneros covered most of the final year's operating expenses – the distinguished periodical passed out of existence in 1795. Meanwhile *El Seminario Crítico*, the mouthpiece of the conservative clergy, through which they hoped to refute the liberal ideas printed in the *Mercurio* and founded also in 1791, continued in operation. The intemperate denunciations of Archbishop González de la Reguera against all 'heretical' pronouncements favouring intellectual and spiritual liberty became more frequent and, apparently, more influential. Viceroy Ambrosio O'Higgins (1796–1801) began one of the most thorough and conscientious campaigns yet undertaken to stamp out the importation of condemned books. The cause of the new philosophy seemed once again to be in peril.

1808: THE EMERGENCE OF A NEW GENERATION OF LIBERALS

In the troubled and uncertain beginnings of the nineteenth century, liberal intellectuals received cause for hope with the death in 1805 of their zealous tormentor, Archbishop González de la Reguera. The new primate, Bartolomé María de las Heras, proved to be somewhat more moderate than his predecessor. By 1808, after the French had invaded Spain and attempted to establish Joseph Bonaparte on the throne, Peru's liberal intellectuals enjoyed a freer ambient if only because peninsula-born authorities, apprehensive over events in the motherland and cut off from the usual backing of their monarch, became more circumspect and conciliatory in their administration.

As Spain braced herself to meet the French invasion, José Faustino Sánchez Carrión, a young (b. 1787), country-born graduate of San Carlos, began to attain some prominence in intellectual circles in Lima. In recognition of his rising prestige he was commissioned to present a manifesto to Viceroy José de Abascal (1806–16) on the occasion of the promulgation of the liberal Spanish Constitution of 1812, which had been formulated by the political forces opposing the French invaders. In this document Sánchez Carrión emphasized the need for political liberty and asserted the equality of creoles and *peninsulares*, although he remained silent about the castes and mixed bloods.[16] During the next few years, however, Sánchez Carrión was overshadowed in the expression of liberal ideas by one of his fellow San Carlos graduates, Manuel Lorenzo de Vidaurre. Five years older than Sánchez Carrión and a native of Lima, Vidaurre had been chosen by officials in Peru to represent the viceroyalty in the 1810 Cortes or parliament of Cadiz at which Spaniards, menaced by the French, met as equals with colonial representatives to confront problems of the peninsula and empire.

In Peru Vidaurre had been regarded not only as a man of considerable brilliance, but also as a colossal nuisance – a rather unbalanced egomaniac, possessed of delusions of grandeur which sometimes led him to consider himself 'another Christ'.[17] The *audiencia* in Lima, a combination of supreme court and advisory council to the viceroy, had found the mercurial lawyer's long, bombastic legal presentations too much to bear and had for a time suspended his right to argue before it. His wife also found Vidaurre something of a burden, since after his interminable discourses to her he would frequently upbraid her for being too stupid to understand his brilliant reasoning.

Convinced that he would take Spain by the force of his intellect, Vidaurre prepared in eleven days his *Plan del Perú,* which urged the Cortes to initiate thorough-going reforms and to grant Peru and the other colonies some element of autonomy. Not making quite the hoped-for impression in Spain, Vidaurre was at least sent back to Peru with the commission of judge in the *audiencia* of Cuzco.

Although greeted at the time with relative indifference both in Spain and the viceroyalty by those who heard its contents explained, the *Plan del Perú,* published with extensive additions to the original manuscript in 1823, is important because it gives clear expression to several typical aspects of the liberal, Encyclopedist position as it had evolved in Peru by the time of the generation of 1808 and Spain's grave challenge from the French. In his highly passionate and rhetorical document, Vidaurre called for classical economic liberalism, predicting that from free competition would ensue a relative equality of wealth among all men, advocated political and social liberalism based upon federalism and other United States models, urged education and better treatment of the Indians as a means of hastening their assimilation into society, and demanded the elimination of the Church's temporal power on the grounds that excessive clerical influence was responsible for many of Peru's ills.[18]

MEN OF LIBERAL IDEAS FAIL TO PRODUCE AN INDEPENDENCE MOVEMENT

The liberal intellectual stirrings and verbal bombast in Lima did not contribute directly to an independence movement. In fact, it would be difficult to prove that any revolutionary effort grew directly out of the ferment in Lima which produced so many attacks against the principle of authority in education and politics, against economic restraints, and against abuses of the Indian, and so many affirmations of the natural rights of man and his justification in overthrowing tyrants. Only a tiny minority of the liberal thinkers felt that their purposes could best be achieved through inde-

pendence. The miniscule group of promoters of independence in
Lima was led by José de la Riva Agüero (the great-grandfather of
the historian, José de la Riva Agüero y Osma); but when he was
apprehended and deported in 1810, their radical minority cause
collapsed completely.

From 1812, and even up to 1820, reform to Peru's liberal intellectuals implied not independence, but rather persuading Spain to
make concessions within the colonial framework. This was the
position of Baquíjano who, however fearless in his attempt to
awaken the conscience of Viceroy Jáuregui and in his denunciations of administrative arbitrariness, apparently continued to
oppose independence to the day of his death in a Spanish jail in
1818. Likewise opposed to independence was Rodríguez de
Mendoza, a violator of royal edicts and instructor of a generation
in libertarian concepts; Cisneros, Jeronymite dealer in prohibited
books who died in 1812; and Unánue, the main spirit behind the
avant garde *Mercurio Peruano*, who, until the moment independence was thrust upon Peru, continued to work for reform
within the imperial structure. The wildly liberal Vidaurre continued throughout the 1815–18 period in his *Cartas Americanas*
to urge no more than colonial reform, his plea for respect of
the rights of man being in no way tantamount to a call for
independence.[19]

It is understandable that well-born members of Peruvian society
did not advocate a complete break with Spain. A small, primarily
Limanean aristocracy, whose members had at one time benefited
inordinately from the granting of monopolistic privileges under
royal laws of trade and commerce, longed for a return to the pre-
Bourbon-reform 'good old days'. Other elements saw themselves as
the successful entrepreneurs in a liberalized and vastly expanded
economic activity. They dreamed of favourable new legislation
and of Spanish investment that would encourage new economic
pursuits, make up for the dwindling output of the depleted mines,
and compensate for the turn-of-the-century commercial depression. Whether they wanted the re-imposition of old laws or the
introduction of bold new measures, members of the early nineteenth-century élite were colonial in mentality. They believed that
economic success, which they coveted either out of purely selfish
considerations or out of an incipient sense of nationalism, depended
upon the support of Spain.

Moreover, though a few intellectuals, such as Vidaurre, complained poignantly about Spanish abuses against the Indians and used the natural law arguments for treating the natives as equals, the vast majority of well-to-do and influential citizens entertained doubts and fears about the Indians, accentuated by the Túpac Amaru II uprising, and realized that the natural rights philosophy was a double-edged sword to be used with extreme caution. Natural rights could serve as a basis for claiming greater Peruvian autonomy within the empire and creole equality with *peninsulares*, but to use its philosophical concepts as a justification for independence was obviously foolhardy. When pushed to its natural consequences, the natural rights philosophy could encourage Indians and their sympathizers to demand what most creoles had no desire for: a total social, political, economic upheaval. Aware that they were playing with fire in expounding the privileges of the Enlightenment, discreet creole intellectuals suspected that whether they really wished to or not, they must rely upon Spain and the colonial system to keep them from being burned.

Owing to these considerations among others, Peru's intellectual élite, as one historian has written, suffered from a conflict between head and heart. Those educated at Lima's San Carlos, in particular, had their 'heads filled with Encyclopedist ideas', but their hearts remained 'rooted in the *ancien régime*'.[20] With heart generally prevailing over head, the average creole or *mestizo* intellectual was, as far as independence was concerned, a counter-revolutionary.

The advocates of the new philosophy, by and large, maintained until the last moment their hope for reform within the framework of the colonial system. Only when a variety of unanticipated developments – among them the reactionary obstinacy of Ferdinand VII after his restoration, with the help of British troops, to the Spanish throne in 1814, the later dramatic decline in Spanish military fortune throughout Hispanic America, and finally the arrival of foreign armies of liberation – exercised compelling pressure did they opt, however apprehensively, for independence.

THE MAN OF ACTION, PUMACAHUA, STRIKES FOR INDEPENDENCE

Peru's most significant early nineteenth-century independence movement erupted in the Cuzco area in 1814. It represented the response to a local situation of particularly harsh abuse by inept Spanish administrators and in its origins had little if any direct relationship to the revolutionary philosophy voiced by the liberal savants who seldom left the city of Lima. Angered by plans which had been announced to resume collection of the Indian tribute, suspended by the crown in a conciliatory gesture after Túpac Amaru II's uprising, and by the failure of officials in the sierra to implement the liberal provisions of the 1812 Spanish Constitution calling for individual guarantees and freedom of expression, various men of Cuzco came together in August of 1814 to initiate a serious insurrection. Although at first described simply as an endeavour to win redress of grievances from Ferdinand VII, the movement very quickly came to be regarded both by foes and participants as a genuine bid for independence.

The Angulo brothers of Cuzco, José and Vicente, played a prominent part in precipitating the August uprising, but almost from the outset the *mestizo* Mateo García Pumacahua emerged as its symbol and military leader. Then in his sixties, Pumacahua was a *cacique*, or hereditary chieftain, of a large Indian community, and also a high official in the Spanish colonial system, serving as president of the *audiencia* of Cuzco. One of Pumacahua's friends was Vidaurre, then a judge on the same tribunal. Although he may have inadvertently become implicated in some of the early plottings of the movement, Vidaurre turned quickly against it, professing his undying loyalty to the crown and viciously denouncing Pumacahua as a beast and fiendish barbarian.

Hoping ultimately to join with the remnants of the independence forces which the patriotic government of Buenos Aires sent in 1812 to Upper Peru, Pumacahua at first won a surprising series of military victories. One column of his armies, headed by the priest Ildefonso Muñecas, marched upon La Paz, which it occupied for a short time before being dislodged by royalist troops in early November. Another advanced to, and briefly gained control over, the important Andean communications centre of Huamanga. Meanwhile, Pumacahua and the Angulo brothers, leading the main body of insurgent troops, captured the city of Arequipa, where they found two important recruits for the revolutionary cause.

The young priest Mariano José de Arce, a notable exception at this time among well-born Peruvian intellectuals in his advocacy of independence, welcomed the rebel forces in a state of elation. After attending the solemn high mass of thanksgiving for the success of the insurgents, Arce, although forbidden to do so by the cathedral chapter, mounted the pulpit and pronounced a discourse in which he strongly implied that the cause of the revolution was the cause of God. A short time later he helped to prepare a decree stating that 'the will of the Almighty to protect the revolution is now apparent'.[21] The decree was dated 4 December 1814, 'the first year of Peruvian independence'.

Pumacahua and his army of some five thousand were also joined in Arequipa by the poet Mariano Melgar. Romantic and melancholy in his verses, the artistic merit of which critics still dispute, Melgar wrote with a revolutionary fervour which has caused him to be referred to as Peru's André Chénier. A believer in universal fraternity and liberty, Melgar apparently possessed a genuine, humanitarian love for Peru's Indians and a confidence in the contributions which they could make to his native land. Seeing in the Pumacahua rebellion a movement originating in the Andean soil and supported by the Indians themselves, he gave his unstinting support to the *mestizo cacique*.[22]

An army of five thousand armed mainly with clubs and pitchforks, an enthusiastic young priest, and an eloquent poet were no match for the troops that Viceroy Abascal dispatched to Arequipa. Retreating towards Cuzco, Pumacahua was overtaken and defeated. He was executed on 12 March 1815, and Melgar, not yet twenty-five years of age, the next day. Arce managed somehow to escape, the details are not clear, and later assumed an important rôle in the establishment of republican government in Peru.[23]

Writing on the events of 1814 and 1815, Jorge Basadre has found in Pumacahua the symbol of integral 'Peruvianness':

He stands in contrast to Túpac Amaru ... whose movement was one of collective vengeance, a rebellion against civilization, very just perhaps in its origins and motivation ... but with a regressive orientation. It embodied pure agrarianism and *indigenismo*. On the other hand, there is the integral Peruvianness of Pumacahua, the man with Indian blood who did not alienate himself from the creoles but identified himself with them. ... With close sympathy we can follow his uprising, desire its triumph, and lament its defeat, because the success of Pumacahua would have been the success of the fused Peru, neither separated from the creole as Túpac Amaru nor from the Indian as was the emancipation movement directed by Simón Bolívar.[24]

SAN MARTIN UNDERTAKES THE LIBERATION OF PERU

Between the suppression of Pumacahua's revolution and the arrival of José de San Martín on Peruvian soil in 1820 little happened to advance the cause of independence.[25] As a result it seemed in some ways unlikely that the stern general, born in 1778 in the small missionary outpost of Yapeyú in the viceroyalty of the Río de la Plata, would encounter within the viceroyalty of Peru strong and effective support in his attempt to win its independence.

When he landed in September on the coast near Pisco, some one hundred miles south of Lima, San Martín had behind him an illustrious military record. Since 1812 when he had returned to his native region of the Río de la Plata after extensive military experience in Spain, San Martín had fought triumphantly in northern Argentina and had managed to train his famous Army of the Andes in Mendoza. A rigorous disciplinarian and a master both of strategy and tactics, in 1817 he had led his army across the high Andean ranges into Chile, initiating the most brilliant military campaign ever undertaken in the American hemisphere. Before the end of the following year he had succeeded in liberating Chile from Spanish rule. And now in 1820 it seemed possible that even if San Martín found little support in the Peruvian viceroyalty, the very momentum of his nearly uninterrupted series of military victories might carry him to success in the great objective which he had formulated some six years earlier: the crushing of the Spaniards in Peru, the main centre of their strength, so as to guarantee once and for all the independence of the South American continent.

Only for a very brief period after his landing, however, did events seem to play into the hands of San Martín. The general was aided at first by his well-known political conservatism, resting upon his belief in the need for an ordered, hierarchical society presided over by a monarch. This political philosophy appealed to many members of Peru's upper classes. As these men were coming to see the situation Peru, yielding to the force of circumstances, would soon have to be independent; but it would be ruled by a member of the Spanish royal family and maintain an alliance with Spain. In this way stability could be preserved and Spanish soldiers might still be available as companions in arms should Indians and mixed-bloods attempt a genuine social upheaval.

José Bernardo de Tagle y Portocarrero, the fourth Marquis of Torre Tagle, born in Lima in 1779, was one of several Peruvians who would not have served San Martín loyally had it not been for the general's conservative, monarchical persuasions. The Marquis, a leading figure in viceregal society, had gone to Spain to represent his native Peru in the Cortes that had framed the 1812 Constitution. He had remained in the motherland five years, during which time his disillusionment over the corruption of court life led him to believe that Peru needed greater autonomy, though certainly not total separation, from the Spanish royal family. The landing of San Martín seemed to present the means for obtaining an independence which, though more complete than the Marquis had advocated, would maintain political authority and social stratification through the traditional monarchical form of government.

Pleased, therefore, with the expected consequences of San Martín's landing, Torre Tagle, on 29 December 1820, proclaimed independence in the northern coastal town of Trujillo, of which he was then the Spanish-appointed governor. This act proved to be of indispensable benefit to San Martín who controlled virtually no territory at the time and whose troops were diminishing in number, wracked by disease, and suffering from shortages of supply. Torre Tagle and other men of his class now began not only to provide San Martín with large amounts of money, but to organize well-disciplined militia forces in various provinces.

Sensing that public opinion was turning against them in Lima the Spanish commanders decided by July 1821 that it was necessary to abandon the City of the Kings and to withdraw their forces into the interior where public opinion scarcely existed and damage to military morale and discipline could be repaired. Able to enter Lima without bloodshed, San Martín personally proclaimed independence there on 28 July – he had made an earlier declaration in November 1820 from the balcony of a small house preserved ever since as an historical shrine in the coastal town of Huaura, some forty miles north of Lima. From a convocation of Peruvian notables in Lima, moreover, San Martín accepted the title of Protector, together with virtually dictatorial powers.

The deceptively easy manner in which the initial stage of

independence was simply witnessed, rather than fought for, by Peru's social élite soon produced negative consequences. San Martín, of course, realized that only an ephemeral, tenuous victory had been won with the occupation of Lima and the declaration of independence, and that the fruits of victory could be guaranteed only by an arduous and protracted struggle. But how could he convince Limanean society of this? The average Peruvian was only human in concluding that independence had been won by little more than a mental commitment on his part while a business-as-usual atmosphere had continued to prevail. If independence had been achieved in this manner, why could it not be preserved in the same way?

The élite of Lima did not take the continuing Spanish threat seriously and tried to ignore the orders of San Martín. Soon they divided into two main intellectual camps. On the one hand were those who, like the Marquis of Torre Tagle, equated independence with continuing conservatism and monarchy. On the other hand, many of the voluble propagandists, who since the youthful days of Baquíjano had campaigned for the introduction of liberal, more democratic usages within the colonial structure, felt that there was no need to abandon the desire for liberal institutions now that independence had been declared. To them the conservative inclinations of San Martín seemed to present a definite menace; and so they plotted to rid themselves of the would-be liberator of Peru.

The issue came to a head when, acting upon their monarchical convictions, San Martín and Bernardo Monteagudo, the La Plata-born intellectual who was the general's most highly regarded cabinet member and political adviser, called a secret meeting of notables in December 1821. After a short discussion those in attendance signed a document calling for the establishment of monarchy in Peru and commissioned an agent to go to Europe in search of a suitable prince to occupy the Peruvian throne. Among those signing the monarchical pact was Hipólito Unánue, that renowned scientist and distinguished journalist who had helped to infuse the *Mercurio Peruano* with the spirit of the Enlightenment. Not wishing to appear too high-handed, Monteagudo, who was directing conservative political manoeuvres at this time, sought to create the illusion of more widespread support for his and San Martín's aspirations for a monarchy. In January 1822 he founded the *Sociedad Patriótica*, a group of Peru's intellectual leaders whose forty members were personally selected by Monteagudo. The main purpose of the group was to discuss the major problems then confronting Peru and to agree upon a suitable form of government. Although careful to arrange for what he believed to be a majority of monarchists in the *Sociedad*, Monteagudo did admit to membership some of the country's liberal republican spokesmen. He expected that, after a 'free and open' discussion of issues during which some pleas for republicanism would be made, the *Sociedad* would decide upon monarchical government, thus giving a semblance of popular approval for the course of action which had already been secretly determined.

During the 1 March sessions of the *Sociedad* one of Monteagudo's closest collaborators, the Guayaquil-born priest Francisco Javier Moreno, argued the monarchist cause, asserting that Peru lacked the degree of culture and education necessary for the functioning of democracy and that the land was too vast and populated by too heterogeneous a collection of groups to permit the establishment of liberal institutions.[26] To the considerable annoyance of the monarchists, Manuel Pérez de Tudela, author of the Peruvian 'Act of Independence', who had learned his liberal lessons well at San Carlos under the tutelage of Rodríguez de Mendoza, won an ovation from the gallery for his reply to Father Moreno in which he defended republican principles. Already it was becoming clear that however questionable their contributions to independence had been, the representatives of the new philosophy in Peru would play a major rôle in determining what form of government the new country would have.

Working behind the scenes, as was always his wont, to defend republican values in the *Sociedad Patriótica* was the priest, Francisco Javier de Luna Pizarro. Born in Arequipa in 1780 and educated there in the seminary of San Jerónimo, Luna Pizarro had fallen under the influence of the 'Enlightenment' as propounded by a Spaniard, Pedro José Chávez de la Rosa, a former rector of the seminary who in 1792 had been elevated to the post of Bishop of Arequipa. In 1809 he accompanied the ailing bishop upon a visit to Spain, where he was inspired by the manner in which Spaniards of all social classes rallied to resist the efforts of Napoleon to establish Joseph Bonaparte on the throne. Returning to Peru with his faith in popular sovereignty enhanced by his brief experiences in Spain,[27] Luna Pizarro turned his attention to the United States, following with avid interest what seemed to be its spectacular success in applying liberal political formulae. By 1822 he was satisfied with the universal applicability of democratic institutions and believed it easily possible to make Peru a replica of the United States. An astute political manipulator and tactician 'who combined Jesuitical shrewdness with the guile of Machiavelli',[28] and 'who in every way save in his wearing a cassock seemed unlike a priest',[29] Luna Pizarro preferred to dominate by working through others. While not speaking out himself against monarchy in the *Sociedad*, he played a key part in organizing and strengthening opposition to it.

More direct in his attacks against political authoritarianism was Sánchez Carrión, perhaps the most brilliant and zealous defender of republican liberalism to emerge from the classrooms of San Carlos. Since 1810, along with Vidaurre, one of the most outspoken proponents of the new philosophical tenets, Sánchez Carrión in March 1822 issued the first of his two famous letters under the pseudonym of *El Solitario de Sayán* (The Hermit of Sayán). A distinguished Peruvian writer has said of these letters:

In the history of ideas in Peru, few documents have produced such immediate effects. Published in the press, these passionate and demagogic letters, together with the defence of liberal ideas made by Pérez de Tudela and the priest Mariano José de Arce in the *Sociedad Patriótica*, were ultimately responsible for the defeat of San Martín's monarchical plan.[30]

Meanwhile, as the political debates and intrigue continued and as his frustrations mounted, San Martín concluded that Peruvians could not be relied upon to complete the formidable task still before them. Leaving the Marquis of Torre Tagle in the exercise of executive powers, San Martín embarked for the northern port of Guayaquil to confer with Simón Bolívar in the hope of inducing the Liberator of the North to join with him in crushing Spain's might in Peru. Bolívar's star then appeared to be at its zenith, for the thirty-nine-year-old creole from Caracas, after extensive study and travel in Europe, had been instrumental in achieving the independence of Colombia in 1819, of Venezuela in 1821, and of the future Ecuador in 1822.

The meeting between the two generals in July 1822 proved to be a fiasco, although historians seem unlikely ever to agree which of the two participants was to blame for the consequences. Probably an unavoidable clash of personalities contributed to the interview's failure. The reserved, taciturn, self-effacing, almost shy creole from Yapeyú could not have been expected to respond favourably to the flamboyant, vain, self-centred, demagogic creole from Caracas. Greater knowledge of Bolívar might have revealed to San Martín that egotism and a flair for demagoguery and histrionics were qualities that coexisted with genius, a sense of reality, ability to sacrifice, and a sincere, exalted patriotism.

Less important perhaps than this clash of personalities in preventing the two generals from reaching accord and mutual trust was the disagreement occasioned by San Martín's monarchical and Bolívar's republican persuasions. Also, San Martín hoped that Quito (the future Ecuador) would be joined to Peru, while Bolívar had decided that together with Venezuela and Colombia it must form an integral part of an envisioned Gran Colombia.

Disillusioned by his encounter with the Liberator of the North, San Martín sensed that only if he withdrew from the scene and left affairs entirely to the direction of Bolívar would the volatile Venezuelan commit his own energies and the manpower of his Venezuelan, Colombian, Ecuadoran and foreign-recruited troops to the task of crushing Spanish might in Peru. The situation that he discovered upon his return to Lima confirmed his conviction that his presence could contribute little to the final campaigns of liberation. In his absence a conspiracy, organized by Luna Pizarro, had succeeded in deposing and exiling Monteagudo, thus dealing a mortal blow to the hopes for establishing a monarchy. If this was not a clear enough indication that Lima had lost sympathy and respect for its liberator, there was the additional fact that the city was a hotbed of jealousy and revolutionary plots directed against the provisional executive, Torre Tagle, the Peruvian whom San Martín most trusted and with whom he felt the deepest sympathy. On 20 September 1822, a congress summoned by San Martín held its first session, and to it the Protector resigned his powers and announced his withdrawal from Peru.

Abnegation is the word most frequently used in connection with San Martín's departure. It is the wrong word. Abnegation implies sacrifice and renunciation of power or goods that one holds or can reasonably expect to acquire. Very little remained for him to sacrifice or renounce when San Martín left Peru. He himself was clearly aware that all save some of the outer vestiges of authority had already been lost beyond recall. His departure revealed a profound ability to comprehend reality, a virtue which is certainly as rare and laudable as abnegation.[31]

After San Martín's withdrawal, the newly-convened congress delegated the executive power to a triumvirate called the *junta gobernadora* (governing junta). The three men chosen lacked dynamism and assertiveness and gave no indication that they would be any more successful than the departed Protector in waging war against the royalist forces. In addition, their efforts to provide effective leadership were to a great extent undermined, as San Martín's had been, by the quarrels and intrigues among Peru's intellectual and social leaders over political ideology.

THE LIBERAL CONSTITUTION OF 1823 AND CONTINUING POLITICAL INTRIGUES

The debates initiated in the *Sociedad Patriótica*, which had helped to precipitate the collapse of the monarchist cause, also raised many additional issues which remained to be resolved after the departure of San Martín. The discussions of the *Sociedad* had generally reflected the respective positions of Peruvian conservatism and liberalism as already established and as they would endure for the coming generation and beyond. Defending authority, conservatives evinced little optimism over the perfectability of human nature; they desired the dominance of the executive, whether a monarch or not, over the legislative branch of government; they favoured a strongly centralized political structure; and they did not fear the direct participation of the Church and the military, regarded as institutions generally apt to be 'on the right side' in politics. The liberal spokesmen in the debates of the *Sociedad*, trusting in the innate goodness of man, were optimistic about the perfectability of mankind and wanted to impose virtually no restraints upon the freedom of the individual; they favoured the supremacy of the legislature over the executive, a wide degree of decentralization and local autonomy; and, regarding with disfavour the past performance of many ecclesiastical and military leaders, they wanted to keep the Church and the armed forces out of politics.

With the disappearance of the *Sociedad Patriótica* after the exile of Monteagudo these issues were confronted by the congress which San Martín had summoned late in September 1822. Invested with the power to frame a constitution, this congress was composed of ninety-two delegates, of whom twenty-eight were lawyers; twenty-six, priests; and eight, medical doctors. The remaining members were men of widely varying professions, even including merchants, who in Lima had never been quite the social outcasts they tended to be elsewhere in Hispanic America.

Liberal republicans enjoyed a pronounced majority in the joint constituent assembly and congress. Even the clerical delegates, of whom Rodríguez de Mendoza, Arce, and Luna Pizarro were typical, were under the influence of Gallicanism and thus disinclined to seek political power for the Church and prepared to accept State dominance over it. Moreover, most of the priests favoured freedom of worship, although the overall majority of the congress voted to include in the constitution an article prohibiting the practice of any faith in Peru save Catholicism.

The constitution itself was ready for promulgation in November 1823. Owing to the prevailing political disorder and warfare, both civil and that directed against the Spaniards, it was placed in operation, however, only for a brief period in 1827. With the exception of its religious exclusivism, the charter was notable for the clear and classic principles of individualistic liberalism which it embodied. Affirming that the state could not pass laws that circumscribed individual prerogatives, it tacitly recognized the right of the people to rebel against governments that had become unjust by their attempts to impose undue restrictions. The most powerful institution which it provided for governing Peru was the congress, which completely dominated the executive. Chosen by congress, the president was unable to initiate or to veto legislation; he was simply to be the faithful executor of the legislative will. The federalist aspirations of the liberals, however, suffered a setback in the 1823 charter. In spite of the eloquent defence of federalism by Sánchez Carrión, who based his arguments on the success of the system in the United States, the constituent assembly decided in favour of a centralized political structure.[32]

Not unfairly, the 1823 constitution has been described as an unrealistic and artificial instrument, without antecedents and with no roots in tradition.[33] Conceived in a spirit of wild enthusiasm for liberty, its assumptions included an unlimited faith in human nature and the conviction that progress would necessarily result from the complete removal of all restraints on human action, save those of fundamental morality. Understandably, these hopeful assumptions collided with 'the reality of ignorance that prevailed in the country'. The constitution was bound to prove futile, especially in a period characterized by the disappearance 'of the norms of discipline and social restraint, the absence of an experienced ruling class', and a continuing state of war which awakened 'all the baser appetites' and destroyed the 'civic spirit which is necessary to give stability to a republic'. So wrote Manuel Vicente Villarán, one of Peru's greatest constitutional authorities, on the centennial of the 1823 constitution.[34] Few have cared to quarrel seriously with his appraisal.

Even as liberal idealogues spun their theories of the perfect state, ambitious militarists ignored congressional deliberations and edicts and sought in one way or another to gain political power. All the time that intellectuals endeavoured to frame an ideal state safeguarded by a utopian constitution and that self-seeking caudillos tried to capture control over it, the Peruvian state had not in reality come into being. Spaniards still controlled a vast part of its territory threatening at any moment to obliterate the factious patriots. When Simón Bolívar finally arrived on the scene in September 1823, he did not find many selfless, dedicated, and politically realistic Peruvians to assist him in wresting their native land from Spanish control. Fortunately, however, he found enough.

3

Caudillismo, Good and Bad, 1823–45

THE AGE OF 'CAUDILLISMO' BEGINS

FEBRUARY 1823 marked the inception of Peru's age of *caudillismo*, of political bosses and personal rivalry, of revolution and counter-revolution led by military chieftains whose motives were often as complex as the political situations they created. The militarists who tried their hands at government were sometimes moved by lofty concepts of patriotism. At other times, they were concerned only with personal gain. Occasionally they achieved at least short-term stability, although overall continuity was conspicuously lacking in the political rule which they provided for Peru in its first two decades of independence. Historians have generally stressed the failures and foibles of the caudillos. The accomplishments, both fortuitous and planned, as well as the skills, dedication and idealism of many of the caudillos have most often been ignored.

San Martín had scarcely departed from Peru when a voluble group of military officials began to demand that the constituent congress depose the governing junta of three and confer dictatorial powers on José de la Riva Agüero. One of the few Peruvians who had urged the cause of independence since 1810, Riva Agüero, who had returned to Peru after an exile imposed by royalist officials and had risen to the rank of colonel in the patriot armies, was regarded by the military as a man who could wage war against the Spaniards more effectively than the rather listless junta. In February 1823 congress bowed to the pressures exerted upon it and recognized Riva Agüero as Peru's chief executive. Thus occurred the first military coup against established government in republican Peru. A principal leader of the February coup was Juan Bautista

Eléspuru, a thirty-six-year-old officer from Tacna whose chronic plottings were to contribute much to the confusion and chaos of the age of caudillos.[1]

Riva Agüero proved to be one of those figures in history who while possessing integrity and ability somehow manage to attract misfortune and misunderstanding and pass from the scene with an undeservedly compromised reputation. His adversity began when the Spaniards were able temporarily to recapture Lima in June 1823, forcing the new president and his congress to flee to Callao. There he engaged with the legislature in a heated dispute over a trivial matter. As a consequence, only a portion of the congressmen accompanied the president when, shortly, he abandoned Callao and proceeded northwards to Trujillo where he had a large following of loyal supporters. The other deputies remained in Callao where within a few days of Riva Agüero's departure they were able to welcome the Venezuelan General Antonio José de Sucre to Peruvian soil.

The arrival of the twenty-eight-year-old Sucre marked the beginning of active collaboration in the Peruvian emancipation struggle of the newly-independent republics of northern South America. Sucre, the ablest of Simón Bolívar's lieutenants in whom the Liberator placed unlimited confidence, came to Callao to direct the first phase of Colombian-Venezuelan aid to Peru that Bolívar had agreed to extend after San Martín had withdrawn. Almost from the moment of his landing, Sucre became involved in contention with the recently-departed Riva Agüero, who was attempting to exercise presidential powers from his Trujillo headquarters. Sucre believed Riva Agüero to represent a divisive factor, and soon began plotting to strip him of power. For this he has often been condemned by Peruvian writers who have considered Riva Agüero the defender of the republic's independence against the ambitious schemes of Colombian and Venezuelan generals.

The Sucre-Riva Agüero rivalry was intensified when Spanish forces withdrew from Lima in July. Upon entering that city Sucre proclaimed the Marquis of Torre Tagle, the same man to whom at an earlier time San Martín had entrusted executive powers, president of Peru. Congress, or rather that part of it not loyal to Riva Agüero and holding sessions in Trujillo, approved this appointment.

As he continued his feud with Riva Agüero, General Sucre did all in his power to induce the congressional body in Lima to invite Bolívar to come personally to the area to preside over the final drive against the approximately fifteen thousand battle-tested royalist troops remaining in Peru. For a time Sucre was unsuccessful in his efforts. Many Peruvian officers insisted that they were capable of defeating the Spaniards, while certain congressmen, among them Sánchez Carrión, the *Solitario de Sayán*, asserted that if he came to Peru Bolívar would destroy its independence by joining it to a vast confederation over which he would rule in more arbitrary fashion than had the Spanish Crown.

As political chaos continued unabated, however, Sánchez Carrión and many who had originally thought as he did came gradually to suspect that Bolívar might be Peru's last hope for the establishment of the stability necessary to wage effective warfare. Accordingly, Sánchez Carrión agreed to serve as one of two delegates, appointed by congress, to proceed to Guayaquil to request the Liberator to undertake the task of adding Peru to the list of countries whose independence he had achieved. The other delegate was José Joaquín Olmedo, a Guayaquil poet who in the sessions of the *Sociedad Patriótica* had helped the *Solitario de Sayán* to defeat the monarchical schemes of Monteagudo.

In Guayaquil the penetrating brown eyes and charismatic personality of Bolívar exercised their magic. Sánchez Carrión and Olmedo were won completely by the Liberator. Until his premature death in 1825, Sánchez Carrión was to be one of the most loyal and valuable assistants whom Bolívar found in all Peru. And to the Liberator Olmedo would later dedicate some of the finest lyric poetry that the emancipation period produced in Spanish America.[2]

BOLÍVAR SUCCEEDS IN LIBERATING PERU

Arriving in Callao on 1 September, Bolívar faced a most unpromising situation. There were still two patriot governments contending as much with each other as with the royalist troops which were apparently more powerful than ever. In Lima Torre Tagle and the congressional elements loyal to him invested Bolívar with absolute command over the armed forces and soon conferred dictatorial political powers upon him as well. In Trujillo, however, Riva Agüero still claimed to be the legitimate president.

Aware of the necessity of coming to an understanding with Bolívar, Riva Agüero dispatched his friend Antonio Gutiérrez de La Fuente to Lima. A veteran campaigner from the department of Tarapacá, the twenty-five-year-old La Fuente, who had joined the patriot forces at Huaura in 1821, had issued several proclamations professing his undying devotion to the would-be president in Trujillo. Once in Lima, however, La Fuente's loyalty to Riva Agüero was apparently undermined. Returning to Trujillo, in fact, he overthrew Riva Agüero on the night of 25 November, and subsequently sent him into exile.[3]

With the political situation somewhat clarified by this event, Bolívar, early in 1824, felt ready to begin his campaign against the Spaniards in the interior. Departing from Lima, he went to Trujillo where he added to his forces the troops previously commanded by Riva Agüero and awaited reinforcements from Ecuador and Colombia. In Trujillo on 15 March the Liberator named Sánchez Carrión his minister general, incorporating in this one man all ministerial functions. Veritable dynamos of energy, Bolívar and his minister gave their personal attention to even the most minute details in preparing the patriot forces for the coming offensive. Men were drilled on a gruelling schedule, and factories, most of them newly founded, operated around the clock to produce munitions. Furniture and even Church pews were dismantled so that nails could be recovered and melted down for use in the manufacture of war supplies.

In April Bolívar left Trujillo and proceeded on a south-eastern route into the interior Andean region. In the sierra he was joined by the troops that Sucre had been training elsewhere in the interior, by a large infantry unit directed by General José de la Mar, an able leader from Cuenca, Ecuador, who had been a member of the short-lived three-man governing junta, and by the well-disciplined Army of the South which under the command of Generals Andrés Santa Cruz of La Paz and Agustín Gamarra of Cuzco had fought the Spaniards to a standstill in Upper Peru, soon to be constituted the independent republic of Bolivia.

As he put the final touches to his military preparations in Huamachuco, a small sierra village which had been the birthplace of Sánchez Carrión, Bolívar still faced odds that seemed insuperable. The royalists outnumbered by almost seven thousand men his own army of approximately nine thousand, the largest element of which was Colombian. Moreover, Bolívar's troops were torn by dissension. In the Army of the South, for example, the Peruvian-born Agustín Gamarra had developed a strong enmity towards Andrés Santa Cruz from Upper Peru. This had come about during the Upper Peru campaign when Santa Cruz had ordered Gamarra to countermarch just as the Peruvian general was on the verge of closing with the Spanish forces in a battle which he thought would destroy them.

Notwithstanding dissension and other obstacles, the Andean campaign directed by Bolívar and Sucre was a brilliant success. The Spanish armies were engaged first on the plains of Junín, and there, in a bitter cavalry engagement which lasted only forty-five minutes, the fate of Peru's emancipation campaign was largely decided. The Spaniards were defeated and their ranks decimated. Now only the most obstinate defender of lost causes could fail to recognize the inevitable extinction of Spanish rule in Peru.

After the battle of Junín Bolívar returned to the coast and entered Lima triumphantly on 7 December 1824. Spanish forces which had temporarily recaptured the capital after his departure for the Andean campaign had now retreated to Callao. There, in the castle of Real Felipe, they endured a two-year siege, not surrendering until their forces had been reduced from six thousand to 376.

The defence of Callao was a vain act of Spanish heroism. Long before it ended Spain's cause had been totally lost as the result of a second patriot victory in the sierra. On 9 December, only two days after Bolívar had arrived in the capital city, Sucre manifested his military genius more clearly than ever before as he led the patriot soldiers to a conclusive victory over the main forces of the Spanish army at Ayacucho, an important colonial centre of trade high in the Andes roughly half-way between Lima and Cuzco. Except for mopping up operations, the Ayacucho success completed Peru's quest for independence. Among the men serving under Sucre in the great victory were several Peruvians destined to become, though in some instances very briefly, presidents of their country: Agustín Gamarra of Cuzco (b. 1788); Miguel San Román of Puno (b. 1802); Manuel Ignacio Vivanco (b. 1806), Felipe Santiago Salaverry (b. 1805), and Juan Crisóstomo Torrico (b. 1808), all of Lima.

THE LIBERATOR FAILS IN GOVERNING PERU

At the beginning of 1825 few could have predicted the unsuccessful outcome of the Liberator's attempt to govern Peru, for the situation seemed ideal for him. Congress, appearing to be delighted with the general's conduct, decided to suspend its sessions for a year, thus assuring to Bolívar the continued use of his absolute powers during that time. Determining to rule with the assistance of a council of government, Bolívar wisely selected as its members three of the most able men then in Peru: General La Mar, Sánchez Carrión, and Hipólito Unánue.[4] Acting in collaboration with the council, Bolívar created the first Peruvian Supreme Court, naming Manuel Lorenzo de Vidaurre as its president. At this time the fickle and bombastic liberal idealogue was one of Bolívar's staunchest partisans in all Peru.

Shortly afterwards Bolívar was faced with the loss of the man who had become perhaps his most highly regarded counsellor and friend. In mid-1825 Sánchez Carrión, perennially in bad health, was in the country for a brief period of repose. On 2 June, after returning from a horseback ride, he lay down to rest and within a few moments was dead. The autopsy indicated that death had resulted from a disease of the heart and arteries. The rumour-mongers, although totally without evidence, claimed that Sánchez Carórin had been poisoned on the orders of Bolívar.

That Bolívar had been so promptly maligned after the death of Sánchez Carrión was a good indication that, with the Spanish threat at last removed, Peruvians were beginning to entertain serious reservations about their foreign-born Liberator. This was confirmed early in 1826 when congress reconvened. Liberal members, claiming to be the defenders of Peruvian independence against Bolívar's attempt to force the republic into a vast political confederation and posing also as the champions of individual liberties against authoritarian schemes of government, objected strenuously to the plans the Liberator had formulated for the country's future.

Convinced that no abiding stability would come to the republics whose independence he had won unless rivalries and border disputes could be prevented from erupting into armed clashes between countries, Bolívar proposed a confederation of Peru,

Upper Peru (Bolivia), and Gran Colombia (Ecuador, Colombia and Venezuela). To govern the hoped-for confederation, he emphasized the need for strong political authority, but authority which would be employed 'in making men good'. If anything, Bolívar had too much confidence in the possibility of using force to produce civic virtue. 'If there is a just violence,' he once observed, 'it is that which is employed in making men good, and consequently happy'.[5]

Although persuaded that monarchy was not a feasible form of government for the newly-liberated republics, Bolívar was certain that the times were not yet propitious for the introduction of genuinely democratic political practices. He hoped, therefore, to provide a political mechanism that was a compromise between a republic and a monarchy, liberty and tutelage, democracy and hierarchy. The Bolivarian ideas on the proper form of government were embodied in the constitution which he prepared and which Peruvians, under considerable duress, accepted in December 1826.[6] The Liberator hoped that this constitution would become the instrument through which he, as a lifetime executive, would govern a confederation of Peru, Bolivia and Gran Colombia. One of the most notable features of this ideal political charter was the provision for a house of censors whose lifetime members would exercise ultimate moral authority in the confederation. They were to review laws passed by the congress and to resolve disputes between the legislative and executive branches of government. In the censors, a body of veritable philosopher-princes, Bolívar hoped to create an institution capable of commanding the kind of reverence that in colonial times had enabled the crown to resolve disputes between subordinate centres of power.

The authoritarian features of the Bolivarian constitution aroused the anger of an influential group of Peruvian idealogues headed by the priest Francisco Javier de Luna Pizarro. These men were steadfast in the belief that man should not be reformed through authority exercised from above, but rather be given a vast scope of individual liberty enabling him to pursue his natural inclinations towards good.

It did not take Bolívar long to recognize Luna Pizarro as his main opponent. By the end of 1826, in fact, it was clear to most observers that Luna Pizarro was trying to use the congress, in which he served as one of Arequipa's delegates, as the means to force Bolívar's withdrawal. Angered by these proceedings, the Liberator for a time thought of using military force to purge congress of Luna Pizarro and his partisans.[7]

With creditable realism, however, Bolívar soon abandoned this scheme and accepted the impossibility of enforcing his will on the Peruvians. Despite the eloquent petitions of some of the leading military officers and influential civilians assuring him that Peru would fall into chaos without his presence, the Liberator realized that the opposition against him was rising and decided to leave the republic. Not only the opposition in Peru but the deteriorating situation in Colombia dictated this decision. Bolívar's main interest lay in the North, and he understood that unless he returned there at once he could not hope to dominate the situation. Appointing Santa Cruz, the general from Upper Peru, now become Bolivia, president of the council of government and commander in chief of the national army and navy, the Liberator left for Bogotá. Theoretically, he was still the lifetime president of Peru who would shortly return. But the liberal group in Peru knew better. Probably in his heart Bolívar also knew better.

Factors other than the opposition of liberally-inclined intellectuals contributed to Bolívar's failure as Peru's chief executive. His approval of the creation of Bolivia as a separate republic within an envisioned confederation irritated many Peruvians who felt they were being deprived of territory that was rightly theirs.[8] Moreover, Bolívar was a foreigner who had a low regard for Peruvians in general and tended to surround himself with other foreigners as advisers. A rising desire among Peruvians for self-government clashed with Bolívar's attempt to rule through a bureaucracy whose senior members were mainly Colombians and Venezuelans and also with his dream of an Hispanic-American confederation. In the 1820's the upholders of a self-interested regionalism, sometimes united with the spokesmen of a genuine patriotism and an incipient nationalism, had to have their day. Peruvian generals had to have the chance to show how well they could govern when liberated from the interference of foreign officers. Peruvian liberal intellectuals had to have the opportunity to demonstrate that they could overnight introduce the joys of democratic institutions. However exalted his vision and sound his long-range political judgement, Bolívar did not have a chance in Peru.

It is scarcely surprising that in the years that have passed since his departure Bolívar has often been judged unfavourably by Peruvian writers. One of them at least has appraised the Liberator with impartial fairness: 'He could have been a monarch, but he refused. He could have been simply a perpetual dictator, but he preferred the constitutional way. ... He could have maintained himself through force and dishonest elections, but he chose the way of moderation and frankness.'[9]

THE BACKGROUND OF THE AGE OF CAUDILLOS AND A GLANCE AHEAD

The men who succeeded Bolívar in attempting to govern Peru faced formidable problems. Although the struggle for independence, lasting only from 1820 to 1824, had not been so protracted as in other areas of Spanish America, it had brought about considerable destruction. The port of Callao lay mainly in ruins and many agricultural estates both of coastal and highland Peru had been ravaged by foraging armies. While the rivalry between creoles and *peninsulares* had not been so intense as in other areas of the Spanish-American empire, in part because native-born Peruvians had always been allowed access to some of the highest commercial posts, nonetheless the climate of opinion after the attainment of independence was such as to induce many *peninsulares* to depart from the region. As a result a trained bureaucratic corps largely disappeared.

High ecclesiastical posts, which had generally been reserved to *peninsulares*, fell vacant during the wars of independence and often remained so for years to come as Rome and the governments of Spain and Peru engaged in a three-cornered debate as to who had the right to make new appointments to empty benefices. Not until the late 1830's was a semblance of normality restored to ecclesiastical organization, with the Peruvian government winning the right to present nominations for most benefices. Meanwhile, however, the institution which throughout colonial times had exercised such an important spiritual as well as an economic, social and political influence remained weak, disorganized and relatively impotent. Even with the question of patronage resolved, moreover, the Church was handicapped by a scarcity of vocations which made it difficult to find qualified native-born priests to appoint to important posts.[10] As the nineteenth century wore on, Spanish missionary priests began to arrive once more in Peru and many of them gained high ecclesiastical offices. Often the Spanish ecclesiastical immigrants were arch conservatives and impeded the Church from adjusting itself to conditions in a republic that was at least fitfully and sporadically struggling to join the main stream of nineteenth-century development.

A period of commercial isolation had begun for Peru in the late stages of imperial rule when east-coast ports of South America, enjoying obvious geographic advantages in European intercourse, had been opened to trade. This isolation continued until the late 1840's when, with a modicum of political stability having for the moment been established, Peru began to enter into significant commercial relations with foreign countries, especially England and France. The opening of Peru to foreign trade, however, produced mixed results. Because economic liberalism was unchallenged at the time by Peruvian statesmen, no thought was entertained of affording tariff protection to native industries. As a result many small-scale industrial establishments that had flourished since the late eighteenth century were forced out of existence by foreign competition.

Commerce did, however, provide governments with revenue, for throughout the nineteenth century export-import taxes were the main source of treasury income. When the first Peruvian budget was formulated and approved in the mid-1840's, it showed that a substantial proportion of government revenue was derived from export taxes on Peruvian agricultural commodities produced principally along the coast in approximately thirty river valleys. The main products of these estates included olives, sugar cane, grapes, cotton, alfalfa and grains of all kinds. Peruvian agriculture, and with it the country's treasury, benefited not only from the new access to foreign markets but from the fact that earthquakes, which had several times destroyed soil fertility during the last century of colonial rule, were relatively infrequent in the nineteenth century.

For some time after the attainment of independence the owners of coastal estates continued to depend upon Negro slavery as the principal source of labour. Although San Martín in 1821 had declared the abolition of slavery, the reform measure had never been implemented and by 1835 the slave trade, temporarily suspended, had been re-established. However, in 1849 the British succeeded in cutting off Peru's supply of Africans and five years later the emancipation of all the country's slaves was proclaimed. This time the abolition decree was enforced and Peru's coastal estate owners had to look for a new labour supply. They succeeded in luring some Indians from the sierra to work as *enganchados* (literally, hooked ones), or virtual slaves. Principally, though, they resorted to importation of Chinese bonded labourers.[11]

During the period of the Bourbon reforms heavy new investment and the introduction of more scientific extractive and refining methods had temporarily produced a resurgence in mining productivity. But by the end of the eighteenth century renewed neglect of the mining industry was apparent and output was declining. Mining remained an insignificant sector of the Peruvian economy until the late nineteenth century when new capital, much of it foreign in origin, became available for investment and when railroad construction facilitated the transportation of ore to refining centres or to coastal ports. With the revival of mining activity the labour shortage, caused in part by the ending of the Chinese coolie trade in 1874, became more acute and coastal estate owners competed desperately with mining company managers to secure Indian *enganchados*.

Living conditions for many of the Indians inhabiting the sierra communities declined appreciably after the attainment of Peruvian independence. Contributing to the plight of the Indians was the fact that the traditional tribute of colonial times was continued after independence although its name was changed to *contribución de indígenas*. San Martín had decreed the suppression of the caste tax but had been no more successful in implementing this reform than in securing the freedom of the slaves. In 1854 another chief executive, Ramón Castilla, abolished the *contribución* as a legal impost; but in some parts of the sierra it continued to be collected for many years thereafter.

Suffering from the burdens of the caste tax and numerous other unfavourable conditions, many Indians of the sierra communities chose to become virtual serfs on coastal estates in the early years after independence and later in the century sought employment in the mines. Other Indians migrated to cities in search of employment as *mestizo* artisans. Once Indians left their traditional habitat, abandoned their customary form of dress, and learned to speak a little Spanish they were considered to be *mestizos* and as such were no longer subject to the *contribución de indígenas*. Owing to nineteenth-century migration the Indian population of many areas in the sierra declined perceptibly while the *mestizos* of Peru increased notably in number.

Protected at least occasionally throughout the colonial period by Church and State, Indian communities after independence were subjected to the systematic assault of white and *mestizo* landowners. Sometimes the despoilment of Indian communal lands resulted from sheer greed and selfishness; at other times it was the product of high-minded but misguided idealism. Inspired by the liberal concepts of the nineteenth century, administrators of Peru, beginning with Bolívar, decided that the Indians in order to be truly free and become active participants in a modern society must be given outright ownership over their property and separated, whether they wished to be or not, from their allegedly archaic customs of communal ownership and communal labour. Consequently the property of many Indian communities was subdivided and assigned in fee simple ownership to families to which land, in keeping with Inca traditions, had previously been allotted only in usufruct. Totally uninitiated into the individualistic world of unregulated competition, Indians soon lost their land to creoles and *mestizos* of the sierra and also to opportunistic adventurers from the coast. As a result many native communities disappeared, the concentration of land in the hands of a few private owners became more pronounced, and Indians who had for generations and even centuries enjoyed the use of their own property became the serfs of a new landed aristocracy whose wealth and political influence grew apace.

After this pattern of despoilment of Indian communities had been in effect some one hundred years, well-intentioned coastal intellectuals finally decided that the old communal practices should be preserved and that Indians should no longer be asked to adapt themselves to the competitive system of individual landownership. By that time, however, Indians had in large numbers become accustomed to thinking in terms of the private ownership of land; they had gradually abandoned the concept both of communal use of property and of communal labour and had become individualistic rather than 'communistic' in their attitudes. Thus, the attempts of some would-be reformers to aid the Indians in the twentieth century would occasionally be as far removed from a sense of reality as were the endeavours of nineteenth-century liberals to prepare the natives for assimilation.[12]

As the age of caudillos began, Peru was a country with a rudimentary economy which in certain sectors during the ensuing years would be characterized by retrogression rather than progress. It was a country in which the Church, although in an obvious state of decline, would demand more privileges and advantages than when it had been an internally strong and robust institution. Peru was also a land of two classes, of social stratification and hierarchy. And, because of, rather than in spite of, the influence which nineteenth-century liberalism exercised on many intellectuals, stratification and exploitation of the lower mass by the tiny group at the apex of the social pyramid were quickly intensified.

The attempt undertaken by some leaders during the age of the caudillos to force the masses who had been largely inert in a paternalistic system to become individuals overnight and to compete with others on a basis of liberty and equality only left the masses standing naked and impotent before those who had learned to take advantage of the opportunities provided by rampant individualism. Constitutions, at least until the instrument of 1839, were modelled after those of countries where there was an ethnically homogeneous population and where an industrial revolution and the rise of a bourgeois class had rendered their liberal provisions meaningful. In racially divided, pre-industrial, pre-bourgeoisie Peru the constitutional provisions of advanced nation states were a mockery of reality. At the same time they were an invitation to a form of social and economic exploitation more heartless than the colonial period had known.

Colonial society, because it was an organic creation, because it was frankly, overtly and naturally hierarchical in structure, and because it was based upon recognition and acceptance of these realities, was not only stable but was often characterized by genuine paternalism and a resulting element of social solidarity. In caudillo-ruled Peru an attempt was made by men of announced liberal persuasions to impose a new and incompatible political form upon the traditional social structure whose reality they ignored. Even though the liberal caudillos were often enlightened, they were enlightened only in regard to foreign political concepts and alien political forms; they understood little of the reality of Peru.

Caudillos of conservative persuasion were equally unrealistic. They insisted upon a political form which was strictly a reflection of the past and which made not even minimal concessions to the ideology that had been in vogue ever since the 'Age of the Enlightenment' and which had produced among a majority of educated men an insistence upon a political structure that would be representative and relatively open and democratic at least for those who were at or close to the top in society. Because conservative as well as liberal caudillos, together with their civilian advisers and mentors, chose to ignore rather than to come to terms with Peruvian reality they did not succeed in introducing political stability or encouraging the development of a viable social system.

Only in the 1840's with the rise of Ramón Castilla, a man who was free from doctrinaire intellectual commitments and who understood the reality of Peru in part because he had risen from the masses, did Peru take the first faltering steps towards achieving, at least for an ephemeral moment, the sort of stability that rests upon a matching of social and political systems that are compatible with each other and at the same time in consonance with the prevailing intellectual spirit of the era. Not even the great and prescient Bolívar had understood how to proceed towards this end, and by departing when he did he spared himself the agony of prolonging his failure in Peru.

THE CAUDILLOS BATTLE FOR SUPREMACY, 1827–34

Barely had Bolívar departed when, on 4 January 1827, General La Fuente, the prefect of Arequipa who some three years earlier had hustled Riva Agüero into exile, wrote to José María de Pando, whom the Liberator had left in Lima as minister of government:

> Arequipa and I have received and sworn to the [lifetime, Bolivarian] constitution with the greatest satisfaction, and we are filled with gentle gratitude to the Liberator, our lifetime President, and with those tender emotions which great and beneficial accomplishments can elicit from the human heart. I profess to be Argus in regard to the fulfilment of this national constitution and never will I tolerate the slightest infraction of its letter, not even of a comma. With it I take new nourishment to begin to work for the nation.[13]

Shortly after the self-styled Argus had composed this touching pronouncement, the Colombian troops left in Peru by the

Liberator rebelled. The *coup*, instigated by Peruvian liberals and Bolívar's Colombian enemies, was described as being in the interests of social regeneration. Its leaders, quickly gaining the upper hand over their opponents, decreed the end of the lifetime constitution and on 26 January turned power over to Peru's liberal *políticos*. General La Fuente on 8 February wrote to the new government in Lima: 'I am persuaded that a beneficent star presides over the destinies of Peru, since a change to this new type of government is sanctioned by the natural flow of events; the rights of truth ultimately come to prevail over mistakes of the moment.'[14]

General Santa Cruz, the talented man from La Paz descended on his father's side from Spanish and on his mother's from the Inca nobility and thirty-five years of age in 1827, was not so given to the rapid changing of sides as was La Fuente. On this occasion, however, he recognized the inevitability of the reaction against Bolívar in Peru. Instead of trying to suppress it, the man to whom Bolívar had entrusted provisional executive powers when leaving the country joined in the reaction, hoping to control and moderate it. With consummate skill Santa Cruz arranged for the withdrawal of Colombian troops from Peru and on 4 June convened a new congress.

In this assembly the liberals enjoyed undisputed control. Thus, within a period of four years they had succeeded in discrediting and routing both the monarchists and the advocates of authoritarian government. Luna Pizarro as head of the liberals was in many ways the most powerful man in Peru. Still, in Santa Cruz he recognized a serious rival. As a military commander and an inflexible disciplinarian, and above all as a strong-willed leader who would not stand for congressional domination, Santa Cruz stood in opposition to the political ideals of Luna Pizarro, for whom good government required parliamentary supremacy over the executive. Therefore the priest from Arequipa decided that the general from La Paz had to go.

Not unnaturally, Santa Cruz hoped that the congress he had convened in June would elect him to a full term as president of Peru. He was admired by several influential liberals, including Vidaurre, and might have gained the general support of this group and won the election had it not been for Luna Pizarro. That adept manipulator, while feigning support for Santa Cruz, arranged matters so that congress would elect a weak executive, one who could be controlled by the legislature. Thus it was that the fifty-year-old Ecuadoran General José de la Mar triumphed over Santa Cruz. This was an unfortunate development, for however well-intentioned and honest he was, La Mar lacked sufficient force of character to impose order and stability on the troubled land.[15]

Having placed their man in office, the liberal coterie of Luna Pizarro decided that the president needed a somewhat more realistic constitution than the 1823 charter if he were to succeed in governing Peru. As a result congress hastily prepared and promulgated the constitution of 1828 which corrected some of the more notable weaknesses of the earlier instrument. In the new constitution there was some attempt to provide for a legitimate division of powers. Although congress still emerged as the most powerful agency of government, the rôle of the president was enhanced. Some of the prerogatives granted him were, in fact, similar to those assigned by the United States constitution. The constitution of 1828 suggests, indeed, that its framers were intimately familiar with the work of the founding fathers at Philadelphia and anxious to transfer many of the ideas of these men to Peru's political milieu.

While they were framing a new constitution, the liberal congressional leaders also began to manoeuvre La Mar towards a declaration of war against Colombia. Peru's liberal warmongers were aided and abetted in their schemes by their political counterparts in Colombia. It was hoped that a Peruvian victory over Bolívar's Gran Colombian forces would discredit the Liberator and allow the liberals to gain power in Colombia and at the same time strengthen their position in Peru.

As the congressional majority consciously pursued a policy that could only lead to war with Colombia, Agustín Gamarra, the general who had come to dislike Santa Cruz during the Upper Peru campaign against the Spaniards, who had served at Ayacucho, and who was now in command of his country's armed forces in the south, decided on his own, without authorization from the government in Lima, to invade Bolivia. From a Peruvian point of view, this move was eminently practical. Antonio José de Sucre, the president of the recently-created republic of Bolivia, was one of the few men who had remained steadfastly loyal to Bolívar. If Peru hoped to undertake a successful war on a northern front against

Bolívar's Gran Colombia, then the southern front must be rendered safe by removing Sucre from power. Gamarra's invasion of Bolivia encouraged dissident elements in La Paz to become more bold in their plotting against Sucre and, when some of his Colombian forces turned against him, the loyal friend of Bolívar was ousted from the presidency.

His purpose accomplished with unexpected ease and mainly through the actions of others, Gamarra marched to Arequipa late in 1828 where he conferred with the prefect, the notoriously unreliable General La Fuente. The two were soon joined by Santa Cruz who was passing through Arequipa on the way to his native Bolivia where he hoped to seize control in the aftermath of Sucre's deposal. In Arequipa Gamarra, La Fuente and Santa Cruz agreed that President La Mar was too weak a man to govern Peru. Therefore Gamarra, about to proceed north to aid La Mar in the now-declared war against Colombia, would seek the opportunity to overthrow the president. La Fuente would meanwhile march to Lima and overthrow the vice-president La Mar had left in charge when he headed northward to fight the Colombians. Once these plots had been carried out, and once Santa Cruz had succeeded in becoming president of Bolivia, a confederation of Peru and Bolivia, with Santa Cruz presiding over it, would be proclaimed.

Unaware of the plot, La Mar joyfully received the reinforcements of Gamarra's Army of the South and proceeded into Gran Colombian territory where he was defeated, although by no means decisively,[16] at the battle of Portete de Tarqui in February 1829. The victorious Colombian troops were commanded by General Sucre.

Believing that La Mar had been sufficiently discredited by the loss of the opening battle, Gamarra felt the moment was propitious to carry out the plot against his president and commander in chief. He dispatched Juan Bautista Eléspura, the man who had led the 1823 *coup* in favour of Riva Agüero, to Lima, supposedly to enlist new recruits but actually to arrange with La Fuente the immediate overthrow of the constitutional vice-president. On 4 June 1829, Eléspuru and La Fuente made their move, easily deposing vice-president Manuel Salazar. Three days later in the north Gamarra took La Mar by surprise, made him a prisoner, and sent him into exile in Central America where he died the following year.

The war between Peru and Colombia thus produced the opposite effects from those intended by the liberals. The defeat of La Mar facilitated the successful *coup* of Gamarra, who stood for authoritarian rule and presidential dominance over congress.[17] Sucre's victory, moreover, strengthened the hand of Bolívar and aided his temporary suppression of Colombia's liberals.

In its sessions in Lima on 31 August the Peruvian congress, although still controlled by liberals, bowed to necessity, naming Gamarra provisional president and La Fuente vice-president. The following December electoral colleges confirmed this decision and Gamarra and La Fuente began their constitutional terms of office. A peace treaty quickly arranged with Colombia proved popular as public opinion in both contending republics had been opposed to the war. Shortly after, Luna Pizarro and some of his friends were exiled. Delighted by the uncontested power that now was theirs, Gamarra and La Fuente flaunted the 1828 constitution and also ignored their agreement to declare the confederation with Bolivia under the leadership of Santa Cruz. This led Santa Cruz, who had now gained the Bolivian presidency, to entertain uncharitable thoughts about Peru's president and vice-president and to seek means to bring about their downfall.

To forestall his rival in the neighbouring republic, Gamarra decided the time had once again come to wage war against Bolivia. At the last minute, with the Peruvian armies poised on the Bolivian boundary, Chilean diplomacy succeeded in averting warfare. In August 1831 the two countries that had come to the brink of war signed a treaty of peace and amity that was ratified the following November.

Returning to Lima and aware that his term of office would end in December 1833, Gamarra, barred by the constitution from seeking immediate re-election, began to think about a successor. He, or perhaps his insanely ambitious and domineering wife Francisca Zubiaga de Gamarra, known as *La Mariscala* (the Lady Marshall),[18] decided that Pedro Pablo Bermúdez, a military officer from Tarma, was the most suitable man to succeed to the presidency – probably because he seemed willing to take orders from Gamarra. By this time, however, Luna Pizarro had returned from his short exile and had renewed his intrigues, trying to induce congress to elect as president a man whom it could dominate. He soon won a number of delegates to his way of thinking, persuading them to support the candidacy of General Luis José de

Orbegoso.[19] Like La Mar before him, Orbegoso was a general who had fought creditably in the wars of independence and might be acceptable therefore to the military caudillos. Handsome and personable, Orbegoso was known for his way with women. Despite a façade of arrogance, he was basically meek in temperament. Thus he seemed the perfect figurehead through whom Luna Pizarro and his liberal partisans might govern. In spite of mild pressure exercised by Gamarra in favour of Bermúdez, congress elected Orbegoso to the presidency.

Apparently Gamarra and Bermúdez were at first willing to accept this setback. In good faith they allowed the thirty-seven-year-old Orbegoso to assume office. Gamarra's ambitious wife, however, was not ready to accept defeat. Surrounding herself with some of the more outspoken advocates of political conservatism and executive authoritarianism, La Mariscala worked to persuade her husband to impose Bermúdez by force. Unfortunately, both Gamarra and Bermúdez soon decided to act in accordance with her plans and succeeded in overthrowing Orbegoso.

Many military leaders, including Eléspuru and two who had served at Ayacucho, Miguel San Román and Juan Torrico, supported the Bermúdez coup. The cause of constitutionalism and of Orbegoso, however, also had its military backers. From Arequipa Domingo Nieto expressed his indignation over the *coup*: 'With my lance I will avenge this outrage. . . . Let us perish before becoming slaves.' Nieto was a military man whose proclamations were sincere and always supported by action. Born in the coastal region near Ilo in 1803 Nieto, because of his abiding respect for the constitution and insistence upon the dominance of institutions rather than of personalities, came to be known as the 'Quijote of the Law'.[20] Throughout his life he opposed the militarism of hypocrisy and greed. To him the barracks represented the source of strength to constitutional government, not the spawning ground of plots and revolutions.

In Arequipa many shared Nieto's indignation. To a surprising degree the populace arose in defence of the constitutionally elected Orbegoso, thereby initiating Peruvian *civilismo* (civilianism), a movement aimed at subordinating military to civilian leaders in political affairs. In Lima, also, there occurred the first genuinely popular, mass-supported revolutionary movement of the republican period. Disgusted by the dreary spectacle of yet another military *coup*, the Limeños declared in favour of Orbegoso and drove Bermúdez from the city. Even the socially prominent women of Lima now assumed an interest in politics, by and large supporting the handsome Orbegoso as a means of ending the power of *La Mariscala* whose haughtiness had offended many.[21]

Despite widespread opposition, Bermúdez continued for some time to hold the upper hand because of the preponderance of military support which he enjoyed. In the south his troops, commanded by San Román, defeated the constitutionalist forces led by Nieto at the battle of Cangallo, 5 April 1834. In this battle San Román demonstrated excessive pessimism and discretion, qualities that were soon to become his military trademark. Believing that Nieto was about to defeat his forces, he fled precipitously from the field of battle. A short time later the absent general's troops were reinforced and routed Nieto's army. Having fled too far, San Román did not learn of these happy events in time to rejoin his troops for their triumphant entry into Arequipa.

Notwithstanding a temporary military setback, the reaction against Bermúdez that had begun in Arequipa and Lima spread to Callao and other parts of Peru.[22] Facing for the first time a powerful popular opposition, military leaders began to waver in their loyalty to Bermúdez. Even some of the master-minds of the Bermúdez *coup*, among them the general and future president of Peru José Rufino Echenique,[23] began to foresee the eventual failure of their scheme. Deciding to make his move before it was too late to recoup his reputation, Echenique on 23 April delivered his forces to Orbegoso. Meantime, in Arequipa, many of the soldiers who had triumphed at Cangallo deserted to the Nieto forces. As a result of these events, Orbegoso was able to reacquire his presidential powers. Bermúdez and other military caudillos, among them Gamarra and San Román, were sent into exile and forbidden under pain of death ever to return to Peru. Luna Pizarro and the liberals again had their man in power. And once more their hand-picked president would prove too weak to control a complex and difficult situation.

THE CONSTITUTION OF 1834 AND THE LIBERAL–CONSERVATIVE IDEOLOGICAL DEBATE

With Orbegoso back in power, Peru's liberals had their third opportunity to provide the country with a constitution. Reflecting the spirit engendered by the bitter struggles that had just come to an end, the constitution of 1834 was most notable for its anti-military provisions. Its framers seemed to subscribe to the judge-ment of Vidaurre who wrote that military men were not competent to exercise political power and that civilians should assume control over the appointment of officers as a means of obtaining supremacy over the military and eventually forcing it completely out of politics.[24] Accordingly, the new constitution gave to congress the power to designate the size and composition of the armed forces. A supreme council of war was created, its members elected by congress, as a further means of establishing civilian control over the military. The constitution also stipulated that no additional com-missions to officer rank would be given except as vacancies occurred and that promotions were to be based solely upon distinguished service on the field of battle.

The 1834 constitution, in many ways similar to the 1828 instrument, continued the division of powers and the bicameral legislature, as well as the council of state which assisted and at the same time supervised and restricted the president when congress was not in session. Luna Pizarro, a dominant figure for the last time in a Peruvian constituent assembly and perhaps sobered by the fact that he had suffered three exiles since 1823, exhibited a consider-able degree of moderation. His arguments that chaos was likely to arise from allowing the indigent and ignorant masses to vote and from permitting an exaggerated form of federalism proved con-clusive.[25] Citizens lacking adequate means of support were disfranchised by the 1834 instrument and a fairly centralistic political structure was established.

The 1834 assembly was the last liberal-dominated body to produce and implement a constitution in the nineteenth century – the constitutions written by the 1856 and 1867 liberal assemblies had only momentary application owing to political *coups*. The liberals were by the 1830's, despite their temporary political success in bringing Orbegoso to the presidency, in a state of decline. True, their ranks had been strengthened for a time by Francisco de Paula González Vigil, perhaps the most outstanding liberal thinker and political idealist that Peru has produced.[26] In defending political liberty in 1832 Vigil, a forty-year-old priest from Tacña, had accused Gamarra of shamelessly violating the spirit of most of

Peru's laws and especially of its constitution. In his denunciation of Gamarra, Vigil uttered the memorable words which ever since have been the hallowed motto of Peruvians concerned with civic virtue: 'Debo acusar: acuso (I should accuse; I do accuse).' Thereafter, however, Vigil along with many fellow liberals increasingly concerned himself with religious issues and Church-State relations rather than with strictly political considerations. Because of this change in his interests, apparent especially in the late 1830's and throughout the 1840's, Vigil began to drive more people out of Peruvian liberalism than he attracted to it.

In spite of the fact that he was a priest, Vigil developed a virulent anticlericalism and sought to eliminate every vestige of the Church's temporal power. In the name of the equality of all citizens he insisted that ecclesiastical privileges and immunities be abolished, and in the name of liberty he demanded nearly complete freedom from the teaching authority traditionally claimed by churchmen in matters both mundane and sacred. Vigil's convictions led him ultimately to challenge the authority of popes. Going even further than Peru's early Gallican-influenced clergymen, such as Rodríguez de Mendoza, Vigil wanted the Church in Peru to be locally controlled and free from what he considered the meddling of the Roman *Curia*. He maintained that papal supremacy and the centralistic authority exercised by the *Curia* were innovations that violated the spirit and practices of pristine Christianity. He claimed also that the Church's wealth and temporal power were in conflict with the early and unadulterated nature of Christianity.

Many of the formerly liberal clergy felt that Vigil went to dangerous extremes and came increasingly to fear that the ideas of equality and liberty that once they had so confidently expounded might redound to the serious disadvantage of the Church. The passing years, moreover, tended to disillusion men like Luna Pizarro and Mariano José de Arce about the possibility of transforming Peru overnight into a replica of the United States. They and many other clergymen came increasingly to believe that the political chaos they had witnessed since 1821 was the result of a moral decline in Peru that could only be rectified by strengthening, not diminishing, the temporal influence of the Church.[27] Disheartened by continuing chaos, concerned over the increasing intemperance of anticlerical attacks, the clergy who had defended the cause of liberalism at the dawn of independence turned their attention away from pure politics and political theorization and, led by Luna Pizarro himself, devoted their remaining energies to defending the allegedly threatened Church and the Catholic faith. The withdrawal of Luna Pizarro from the political lists, just at the moment that he was developing into a mature statesman, was a serious loss to Peruvian politics; at the same time it was a great boon to the Church to which by the late 1830's he lent all his services.

With the republic's first generation of liberals wracked by a significant internal cleavage, the restoration of their cause to its one-time prominence awaited the rise to maturity and political prestige of a new group of optimistic idealists. Meanwhile, the conservative intellectuals staged a remarkable political come-back.

Perhaps the main driving force in conservatism's new rise was provided by José María de Pando. Born in Lima in 1787, he had returned to his native city in 1823 after a long and distinguished diplomatic career in Spain. A warm supporter of Bolívar and the lifetime constitution, he had briefly served as the Liberator's minister of government. Apparently believing that the ignorance of the masses could never be dispelled by education, Pando preached the need for a perpetual aristocracy made up of the few men of wisdom. Aristocracy, he said, 'is not so much an institution as an imperious necessity of people'.[28] To him the ideal state was one in which a strong army enforced the laws passed by the aristocracy of wisdom. Liberty, he asserted, could not exist without force, and the exercise of force within the body politic was the proper province of a permanent army. 'The best governors,' he added, 'have always been military men'.[29]

In 1832 and 1833 Pando spread his ideas in his bi-weekly paper *La Verdad*. He also presided over frequent functions in his home at which members of the social aristocracy exchanged ideas on how to create a sound Peruvian government. Among those most consistent in attending these gatherings was Felipe Pardo y Aliaga. Born into an aristocratic Lima family in 1806, Pardo had gone with his parents to Spain upon Peru's declaration of independence. Although he returned to his native land in 1827, he continued to prefer many features of the colonial past to the malfunctioning institutions and 'levelling tendencies' of the republic. Convinced of the need for enlightened despotism Pardo, whose brilliance as a dramatist, poet, and essayist made him a formidable propagandist, desired a strong government that would be responsive to the counsels of an intellectual élite.[30] Like Pando, his frequent host, Pardo condemned the individualism championed by liberals, persuaded that 'the individual is very small indeed compared with the whole of society, above all in those cases where there is conflict between the part and the whole'.[31]

Another frequent visitor to the salon of José María de Pando was the great orator from Arequipa, Andrés Martínez. Like most of those who gathered with Pando, Martínez believed that reform had to be introduced from above, through the instrumentality of authority. Martínez had been particularly influential in shaping the political theories of Gamarra. The Arequipa conservative may well have been responsible for Gamarra's avowal during his term as constitutional president that he would ignore the liberal clergy and lawyers 'who can only write pretty theories which cannot be applied'.[32]

Martínez and others who frequented the salon of Pando exercised even greater influence over Manuel Ignacio Vivanco, a highly-cultured military officer who had fought at Ayacucho. Won by the arguments of the Pando coterie, Vivanco abandoned some of his early egalitarian convictions and accepted the need, at least during a transition period, for rule by the cultural élite, for a political structure directed by a dictator.

The impulsive, handsome, dashing, sometimes generous but often cruel military leader Felipe Santiago Salaverry was also influenced by the conservative philosophy of Pando, Pardo, and Martínez. Born in Lima in 1805 and, like Vivanco, a veteran of Ayacucho, Salaverry was committed to achieving reform through heavy-handed, authoritarian rule, with the executive dominating the legislature.[33]

THE FALL OF ORBEGOSO AND THE PERU–BOLIVIA CONFEDERATION, 1835–9

In February 1835 Salaverry sought to put his ideas into practice and managed to overthrow the liberal-supported Orbegoso administration. But he and his conservative advisers were destined to be thwarted in their plans for implementing authoritarian government. The young caudillo president was threatened by the continuing opposition of Orbegoso, driven from Lima but still in command of a powerful army. Worse still for his cause, Salaverry soon became a mere pawn in the renewed struggle between Gamarra and Santa Cruz.

After his disastrous attempt to impose Bermúdez by force of arms, Gamarra had gone into exile in Bolivia where his old nemesis, Santa Cruz, had been ruling wisely and efficiently since 1829.[34] With ample reason the two generals did not trust each other. Under the circumstances, however, each felt he could best serve his purposes by effecting a reconciliation and agreeing to a joint plan of action. As finally agreed to, the Gamarra–Santa Cruz plan called for Gamarra to seize Cuzco and from there pronounce against Orbegoso and in favour of a Peru–Bolivia confederation to be presided over by Santa Cruz.

Gamarra did indeed succeed in taking Cuzco. Meanwhile, however, the Salaverry uprising in February 1835 had driven the Constitutional President, Orbegoso, from Lima. Salaverry regarded himself as the rightful president of Peru and had no intention of joining his country in a confederation with Bolivia. Gamarra now had to decide whether to recognize Salaverry, whom he had actually encouraged while in exile in Bolivia to oust Orbegoso, as president of an independent Peru or to honour his commitment to Santa Cruz. At this juncture Santa Cruz moved to spare Gamarra the difficult task of making a decision. He abandoned Gamarra and entered into an alliance with Orbegoso, promising him and his liberal supporters assistance in gaining vengeance against both Gamarra and Salaverry. Santa Cruz, who had an innate respect for legalism and constitutionalism, although he did not always allow this fact to dictate his decisions, preferred working through Orbegoso who, after all, did have the strongest legal claims on the Peruvian presidency. In return for his co-operation Santa Cruz wished Orbegoso and his liberal partisans to accept a confederation, made up of the state of northern Peru with its capital in Lima, the state of southern Peru with its capital in Arequipa or Cuzco, and the state of Bolivia with its capital in La Paz. Santa Cruz would exercise an overall hegemony in the three states, each of which was to have its own president, vice-president and congress.

Faced with this development Gamarra, still in Cuzco, conferred feverishly with Salaverry's emissary Felipe Pardo, and agreed to recognize Salaverry as legitimate president of Peru and to join with him in combatting the Orbegoso–Santa Cruz alliance. The invading troops of Santa Cruz, however, carried all before them in southern Peru and in mid-1835 annexed that region to the confederation. Defeated at the hands of the Santa Cruz forces, Gamarra fled to Lima where Salaverry still exercised a precarious control. Deciding that his supposed ally was not altogether trustworthy, Salaverry exiled Gamarra who eventually found his way to Chile. Salaverry then marched southward to do battle with Santa Cruz. In February 1836 he was crushingly defeated, captured, and along with his principal officers summarily executed by the confederation armies.

Prior to this bloodletting, Felipe Pardo had arrived in Santiago, Chile, as minister plenipotentiary of the Salaverry government. After the execution of the man he had recognized as president, Pardo was joined by other members of the conservative, anti-Orbegoso group, among them Vivanco and Martínez. It was not difficult for these accomplished and cultivated Peruvians to convince the main power in Chilean politics, Diego Portales, who like them was a firm believer in authoritarian government, that Peru must be delivered from the horrors of the liberal-dominated confederation. Not only political ideology but, more important, considerations of *realpolitik* inclined Portales to send an army against Santa Cruz. The confederation of Bolivia and Peru threatened to upset the balance of power in southern South America and represented to Portales a potential menace to the security of Chile. The actions of Santa Cruz soon confirmed the worst fears of Portales. The confederation leader helped Ramón Freyre, a leading figure in Chilean liberalism and the avowed foe of Portales, to prepare on Peruvian soil for an expedition intended to overthrow conservative, constitutional government in Chile. Nothing came of the expedition, but the mere fact that it had been organized revealed to Portales what he could expect from Santa Cruz.[35]

Assured by Pardo, Vivanco and Martínez that a small force could easily gain possession of Arequipa and cause that city to declare *en masse* against the confederation, probably thereby dooming the Santa Cruz venture, Portales entrusted a weak army to the Chilean Admiral Manuel Blanco Enclada and instructed him to invade southern Peru. This proved to be a serious mistake for Arequipa was actually a centre of confederation strength. The city's liberal élite, among them the fascinating schemer and chronic plotter Father Juan Gualberto Valdivia,[36] who was slower than most priests in abandoning liberalism, favoured confederation as a means of crushing such traditional adversaries as Gamarra, Pardo, Vivanco and Martínez. Even some of Arequipa's conservatives supported the confederation, believing that its decentralized political structure would allow them to escape from the detested control that Lima's bureaucracy had always sought to impose upon the southern city.

Blanco Encalada's expedition was overwhelmed in southern Peru by the Santa Cruz forces. Despite this initial setback and despite the fact that the unpopularity of the war in Chile had helped to provoke the assassination of Portales near Valparaíso, in the middle of 1837, the Chilean government determined to continue its efforts against the confederation. A more imposing force was quickly organized and placed under the command of the Chilean General Manuel Bulnes. Many Peruvian militarists, among them Gamarra and La Fuente, held high positions in the Bulnes expeditionary force, the vanguard of which succeeded in entering Lima in August 1838.

The main confrontation between the confederation forces and their Chilean–Peruvian opponents occurred at Yungay, nestled in the magnificent Andes north of Lima, on 20 January 1839. For a time it seemed that Santa Cruz would be the victor in the engagement. The cavalry charge against him, directed by Ramón Castilla, emerging as one of Peru's most talented officers, was broken. In discouragement, General Bulnes ordered the horsemen to retire, planning to withdraw his entire army northward to Piura. Castilla had begun to carry out his commander's orders when he observed that the new deployment of the Santa Cruz troops presented an opportunity to renew the attack. In an ensuing charge, Castilla's men changed the tide of battle. At the day's end, with his forces crushed, Santa Cruz was fortunate to escape from the field. The Bolivian general, who eventually made his way into exile in Ecuador, was forty-seven years of age when his dreams of confederation were shattered on the field of Yungay.[37]

Juan Bautista Eléspuru, fighting on the side of Bulnes and Gamarra, was mortally wounded at Yungay. Fighting with the Santa Cruz forces, Pedro Pablo Bermúdez, whom Gamarra had once tried to manoeuvre into the presidency and who had returned from the exile imposed by Orbegoso in 1834 to enlist under the confederation banners, was seriously wounded and captured. He never again played a prominent rôle in politics. A few of the old caudillos were disappearing from the scene. But there were still more than enough to maintain Peruvian politics in its usual turbulence for at least the next six years.

GAMARRA'S SECOND TERM, 1839–41, AND A FINAL ATTEMPT
AT CONFEDERATION

After the battle of Yungay an electoral college chose Gamarra as constitutional president for a four-year term. One of his first and best-considered acts in his new term was to appoint Castilla, the hero of Yungay, as minister of the treasury. Among many other activities, Castilla entered into an agreement with William Wheelwright, agent for the steamship firm known as The English Company. As a result, a steamship service was established along the Peruvian coast in 1840. When the first ship on this run, the *Peru*, appeared off the coast of Chilca, the fumes billowing from it greatly alarmed a local official who dispatched boats to put out the fire and could not understand why his offer of help was rejected. In the report he prepared the next day he noted that the strange ship had disappeared over the horizon, enveloped in smoke, and had doubtlessly been 'totally destroyed'.[38]

A brief period of political stability at the beginning of Gamarra's term was ended by the unreliable men with whom the president had to deal in southern Peru. San Román, the general known for his undue haste in withdrawing from the field of battle, became the prefect of Puno after the battle of Yungay, and was soon planning to enhance his political power. In the Arequipa area at this time Juan Crisóstomo Torrico, a veteran of Ayacucho and a notorious plotter, and the rather high-minded conspirator, Vivanco, formulated revolutionary schemes. All the while Arequipa's liberals, headed by Father Juan Gualberto Valdivia, were seething over the frustration of their hopes of a confederation and the triumph of the hated, authoritarian Gamarra. Many conservatives were also discontented, regarding Gamarra as the symbol of Lima-controlled centralism. Complicating the situation still further, agents of Santa Cruz were circulating in southern Peru, anxiously seeking an understanding with anyone through whom they could gain vengeance against Gamarra.

Quite wisely Gamarra called Torrico to Lima, where he could maintain closer surveillance over him. But Vivanco, tremendously popular in Arequipa and convinced that only he could provide the enlightened authoritarian rule needed to regenerate Peru, decided to rebel against Gamarra. Could Vivanco count on San Róman, the leading power not only in Puno but in Cuzco as well? In a curious letter San Román assured Vivanco the answer was yes, adding: 'I will know how to comply with my commitments despite all dangers, since I glory in possessing strength of character and have given ample proof of my integrity'.[39] Thinking that San Román was safely in the fold, Vivanco pronounced against Gamarra at the beginning of 1841. Thus, 'The Regenerator', as Vivanco called himself, was poised to do battle with 'The Restorer', the title by which Gamarra had come to be known.

Within a matter of weeks, San Román, feeling he was being slighted by Vivanco, declared in favour of the legitimate Gamarra government. In a ringing proclamation, plagiarized from one of Santa Cruz's denunciations of Salaverry in 1835, San Román described Vivanco as a perverse young man educated in a career of crime, inspired always to new offences because of the impunity he had enjoyed in committing earlier ones.

San Román had made his switch in time, and was accepted as a true ally by Gamarra's minister of the treasury who had been dispatched to suppress the Vivanco uprising. Defeated in his initial campaigns, Castilla by his superior tactics slowly overcame the Vivanco armies, finally driving 'The Regenerator' into exile in Bolivia.

The flight of Vivanco provided Gamarra with only a momentary lull. In June 1841 a revolution in Bolivia unseated the constitutional president. The successful insurgents called upon Santa Cruz to return from his Ecuadoran exile and assume the presidency. Asserting that Peru was once again in danger from Santa Cruz, the Council of State authorized Gamarra to wage war against Bolivia. Nothing could have pleased the president more. At last the moment seemed propitious for him to attempt the deed that had always enticed him: the establishment of a centralized Peru–Bolivia confederation under his authoritarian rule. Optimistic and eager for the fray, Gamarra proceeded towards the Bolivian boundary.

By the time he arrived the supposed threat to Peru had evaporated, for Santa Cruz had been turned back in his attempt to re-enter Bolivia and the briefly successful revolution proclaiming his presidency suffocated. But Gamarra was not in a mood to curtail his ambitions. As the new president of Bolivia, José Ballivián and Gamarra tried mutually to deceive one another in a fascinating duel of double dealing, the Peruvian army swept into Bolivia. The main battle took place at Ingavi on 18 November 1841. There, owing mainly to the fact that San Román followed his usual custom of fleeing while the battle was still in progress, the Peruvians were defeated. Not only this, their leader, Gamarra, was killed on the field of battle. The war came officially to an end in June of the following year when the two contending nations signed a treaty of peace.

With the death of Gamarra and the subsequent re-establishment of peace, all serious attempts to establish a Peru–Bolivia confederanation came to an end. Both to Santa Cruz and to Gamarra, confederation had represented far more than a means of serving personal ambition, although ambition undoubtedly was to some degree a motivating factor. The two generals, well aware of the historic tradition of the Inca empire and of the viceregal period, were profoundly convinced that the union of Peru and Upper Peru was the most natural disposition to make, one that would be mutually advantageous to the two regions. Certainly the convictions of Santa Cruz and Gamarra seemed to rest upon a solid and logical foundation. Frequently, however, what is logical cannot be achieved in the world of practical reality.

Perhaps the establishment of a union had been remotely possible in 1828. At that time Chile, torn by anarchy and civil strife, was in no position to frustrate such an endeavour. Strengthened and united in the early 1830's under the genius of Diego Portales, Chile might have accepted a previously-established confederation had it already achieved some element of operational success. By 1836, however, a powerful, unified Chile, led by men who were hypersensitive to possible threats to the country's security, would certainly not tolerate any clumsy efforts aimed at the initiation of a Peru–Bolivia confederation.

Moreover, if a majority of Bolivian leaders in 1828 might possibly have accepted union with Peru, by the mid-1830's their frame of mind had changed. Accustomed to the enjoyment of the prerogatives of self-government, probably self-misgovernment is the more accurate term, they were not prepared to suffer the curtailment of their powers and ambitions, both selfish and patriotic, that union with Peru would have implied. In 1836, opposition to the confederation was considerably stronger in Bolivia than in Peru.

Still, the dream of union was so logical that if Santa Cruz and Gamarra had not attempted to realize it other caudillos surely would have tried to do so. The sad fate of failure in the attempt to achieve confederation fell to these two men simply because they were the outstanding leaders in their respective countries. Intelligent, well-educated, refined and extremely able men, they were destroyed not only by their ambitions but by their high-minded and, as they conceived it, patriotic and statesmanlike ideal of union.

If upon his death in 1841 Gamarra did not leave behind as his principal monument the cherished confederation, the monument he did leave was by no means insignificant. The constitution of 1839, framed in Huancayo under the direct influence of Gamarra, was to be in effect for twelve years (1839–42, 1845–54), thus establishing a new record of longevity for the country's political charters.

Framed by men of political and business experience rather than by theoreticians, the 1839 constitution was the first in Peru to stress order over liberty. It provided for a strong executive with a six-year term of office. The powers of the bicameral congress were somewhat curtailed in comparison with earlier instruments, and those of the Council of State, consisting of fifteen men chosen by congress either from within or outside its membership, expanded. An important advisory body to the president, the council could bestow extraordinary powers upon him.

The constitution provided that only literate male citizens of twenty-five years of age or more could vote (illiterate Indians and *mestizos* could, it was stipulated, continue to vote until 1844), deputies had to be thirty years of age, and senators forty. A considerable income was a necessary requirement for serving as a senator or deputy, and the waiving of this requirement for professors, a feature of early constitutions, was not included in the 1839 instrument, which has led Jorge Basadre to observe that 'income was becoming more important than learning'.[40]

The most unfortunate feature of the constitution, it is often suggested, was the creation of an excessively centralized political structure. By suppressing the municipalities and making no attempt to provide for even a semblance of regional autonomy, it fixed upon Peru an iron-bound centralism which was beneficial to Lima but disastrous to the economic and political life of the rest of the country.

THE STRUGGLE OF THE CAUDILLOS CONTINUES, 1842-5

In the funeral sermon which he delivered in the cathedral of Lima upon the death of Gamarra, the prominent conservative clerical leader Bartolomé Herrera paid high praise to the unfortunate president. By the sacrifice of his life at Ingavi, Gamarra was described as having appeased the Almighty, Who would now preside more benevolently over the course of Peruvian history. Unfortunately, Herrera's prediction was not borne out in the years immediately after the death of Gamarra, a period in which the powers that shaped the course of events seemed anything but benevolent.

After a series of incredibly complex insurrections and insurrections within insurrections, in the course of which Torrico was one of several men to serve briefly as president, Vivanco succeeded in seizing power early in 1843. Again assuming the title of 'The Regenerator', he enjoyed for a time undisputed control over Peruvian politics. His already vast popularity in Arequipa increased still more when he appointed a cabinet whose members chiefly represented the interests of that region. For a time also a solid majority in Lima became enthusiastic over the regeneration which they were told was about to be wrought in Peru. Vivanco's host of admirers also included some who simply enjoyed the general's eccentricities. On his military campaigns, for example, 'The Regenerator', whom some accused of effeminacy, liked to don a long scarlet cloak, an ermine cape, and a cocked hat with an immense plume of feathers.[41]

More than a military leader, Vivanco was a well-read man of ideas, who always carried in his baggage a much-used collection of Spanish classical authors. Basadre has said of him: 'Reading his proclamations with the prior conviction that I would encounter in them empty and exaggerated rhetoric, I was surprised to discover a systematic unity of thought'.[42] The essence of Vivanco's political ideas, influenced only in part by his conservative friends, was the belief that Peru needed radical reforms which could be achieved solely through authoritarian government. Among the reforms he had in mind were the protection of the Indians; the encouragement of industry; the curtailment of military privileges and immunities and the formulation of a professional, apolitical army; and the expansion of education so as ultimately to make possible universal suffrage. This was all for the future, however, and Vivanco made no attempt to hide the fact that so long as he was in power he would rule as a dictator, with the support of the armed forces. He did not apologize for the fact that he appointed his own council of state, failed to convene congress, issued laws strictly on his own, and in general ignored the constitution.

In the final analysis it was lack of moderation that caused Vivanco's downfall. The desire for at least the outer trappings of democratic procedures had become too strongly implanted in a large sector of the Peruvian intelligentsia to be ignored with impunity. Had Vivanco made certain concessions, he might have been more successful. The longer in office, however, the more he resorted to arbitrary actions and used the firing squad to rid himself of men whose loyalty was suspect. Moreover, he was an inefficient dictator, and the salaries and pensions of government employees frequently remained unpaid. The inevitable reaction against him began early in 1844, centring in southern Peru, and was directed primarily by Domingo Nieto, 'The Quijote of the Law', and Ramón Castilla. Calling their armies the constitutionalist forces, Nieto and Castilla demanded obedience to the 1839 constitution. When Vivanco left the capital to try to suppress the constitutionalists, Domingo Elías, a wealthy landowner who professed politically liberal ideas, arose in Lima and pronounced against the dictator. Although Vivanco's chief collaborator, the conservative intellectual and military leader José Rufino Echenique, remained loyal to the dictator, he was unable to overcome Elías. Thus Vivanco's partisans suffered the loss of Lima.

Domingo Nieto died in Cuzco in February 1844 at the age of forty-one. But his collaborator, Ramón Castilla, skilfully directed the constitutionalist forces to victory. At the battle of Carmen Alto, 22 July 1844, Vivanco was defeated and fled directly into exile. In April of the following year Castilla was elected president of Peru. The caudillos would continue to add a good measure of colour and confusion to the history of Peru. With the election of Castilla, however, their ability to plunge all Peru into chaos in their quest for power was for a time seriously curtailed. One man rather than a broad assortment of rival leaders dominated the next epoch in Peruvian history.

THE PERUVIAN CAUDILLOS: AN APPRAISAL

The military chieftains who sought political power in the first generation after Peru's independence were a fascinating combination of rogues and heroes. As often as not, the same man was both rogue and hero. In Domingo Nieto, however, there was almost nothing of the rogue. A Peruvian historian noted for his harsh judgements against militarism has described Nieto as a man who because of his heroic abnegation and disinterested patriotism provided absolution for the officer-politicians of the period.[43] Without attempting a final assessment of every caudillo who appeared between 1823 and 1845, it is possible to note that there was more hero than rogue in Riva Agüero, La Mar, Gamarra and Santa Cruz, and perhaps in Vivanco and Echenique. Undoubtedly, there was more rogue than hero in Eléspuru, Torrico, La Fuente, and San Román, at least in his early years. On the basis of this sampling of caudillos, there emerges a balance that is not such a bad one for human beings.

If Peru had not made dramatic progress in economic development or political organization by 1845 the fault cannot be attributed exclusively or even primarily to the military caudillos. A greater share of blame must go to the civilian aristocrats who considered themselves too well-bred to soil their hands by direct participation in politics, but who often conspired and plotted revolutions behind the scenes to bring to power some favourably disposed military leader. The bad judgement and lack of realism on the part of many civilian intellectuals also compounded the political evils of the period, as did their attempts to enlist military men in fanatically conceived ideological crusades.

In his funeral oration before the tomb of Manuel Ignacio Vivanco in 1873, the great Peruvian statesman Nicolás de Piérola rendered the following homage: '... his public life may abound in errors, misfortunes, and sorrows, but never in direct guilt.' If the word infrequently is substituted for never, this becomes a fitting epitaph for the military caudillos as a group. In their often inept way these men presided over a necessary period of discovery in the years immediately after independence. Among the facts they discovered were: constitutional monarchy was not an acceptable political structure for Peru; the radical schemes of democracy advocated by many liberals were thoroughly out of touch with the circumstances of the time and could not constitute a workable base for political organization; the political structure had to be made more open, at least for men who were educated and socially prominent, than it had been in colonial times; the union of Peru either with Gran Colombia or Bolivia was a utopian dream that could not be realized. These were discoveries that had to be made before Peru could begin to provide for its future development upon a foundation of political realism. Perhaps the essential facts of life for the young republic could have been discovered in no other way than through the caudillos' often chaotic methods of trial and error.

Many of Peru's caudillos, representing the force of militarism, did not disgrace themselves in the early republican period; many of them served their country with greater distinction than its civilian leaders. This may be one reason why militarism has survived as a strong and widely-respected tradition in Peru.

The Age of Castilla, 1845–67

CASTILLA'S FIRST TERM, 1845–51: THE POSITIVE ASPECTS

RAMON CASTILLA, the legal and constitutional president who governed Peru longer than any other nineteenth-century chief executive, was born of lower middle-class parents in Tarapacá, now a part of Chile, in 1799. His early studies, undertaken in Chile, were interrupted by the independence movement. Young Ramón wasted no time in enlisting in the royalist forces. Captured by the patriots, he was sent as a prisoner to Buenos Aires. Managing to escape, he proceeded to Rio de Janeiro and from there made his way across Brazil's vast territory, including the difficult Mata Grosso area, traversed the Andes, and eventually arrived in Lima where he presented himself for renewed service with the royalist troops. Shortly after the declaration of Peruvian independence Castilla changed sides, and was active in forming the cavalry that played a distinguished rôle in the battles of Junín and Ayacucho. Later in the 1820's he served as sub-prefect first of Tarapacá and then of Tacna. Accused of plotting against Gamarra, he was briefly imprisoned but managed to escape to Chile in 1832. The following year he returned and shortly thereafter lent his services to the constitutionally-elected President Orbegoso in suppressing the Gamarra-Bermúdez *coup*. Breaking with Orbegoso when that president declared for Santa Cruz's Peru–Bolivia confederation, Castilla escaped to Chile, was reconciled there with Gamarra, and gained renown, especially at Yungay, for his rôle in the campaign that defeated the confederation armies. Subsequently serving as President Gamarra's minister of treasury, Castilla helped to initiate a steamship service to Peruvian ports and led the troops that crushed Vivanco's Arequipa-centred revolution in 1840. The next year he joined with Gamarra in the ill-fated invasion of Bolivia. Captured by the enemy, Castilla spent a considerable time in Bolivian jails before returning to his native country to join with Nieto in organizing the constitutionalist forces which ousted 'Regenerator' Vivanco from the executive office he had seized through a military *coup*.[1]

Assuming the presidency in 1845 at the age of forty-six, the thin-faced, tight-lipped, rather low-browed Castilla had as his most striking physical attribute his dark, lively, penetrating eyes 'which radiated confidence and security'.[2] Castilla was Indian on his mother's side, Spanish and Italian on his father's. As a mixed-blood, he has often been pointed to as a symbol of the racial fusion upon which the emergence of a Peruvian nation depends,[3] while the success of his administration has generally been referred to as an important factor in winning acceptance for the *mestizo* in even the highest circles.

As he revealed in many of his state messages, the new president was obsessed with the purpose of establishing order and harmony in Peru. This required, in his estimation, the maintenance of a strong army which could impose upon the citizenry the 'submission which constituted authorities deserve'. In the existence of a formidable standing army Castilla, unlike Peru's liberals, saw no necessary threat to constitutional government. To the contrary, he affirmed: 'Our military forces are not the instrument of tyranny or the enemies of society. . . . Imbued with a sense of the importance of their noble destiny, they are the conservers of the public tranquillity, the custodians of external and internal peace, and the loyal defenders of the constitution and the laws'.[4]

At the time of his inauguration Castilla was in desperate need of an effective military organization if he hoped to maintain internal order. The coastal area of Peru, especially the region between Lima and Trujillo, was infested by a tumultuous group of bandits, the *bandoleros*, resembling guerrilla warriors more than mere highwaymen. Made up largely of escaped slaves, as well as free Negroes, zambos, mulattoes, and occasionally Indians, the *bandoleros* were controlled by formidable chieftains who in addition to their rural pillagers maintained well-organized spy groups in urban centres. To travel even the short distance between Lima and Callao had become a most dangerous undertaking because of *bandolero* activities.[5] Castilla did not succeed during his lifetime in totally suppressing the *bandoleros*. But he did manage greatly to increase the safety of travel and transportation of merchandise, and to impress upon the countless brigands the power that the law can possess when a strong president concerns himself with enforcing it.

Castilla was convinced that presidential power must rest upon the law and its rigorous application. In his inaugural address on 20 April 1845 he had stated: 'Power in my hands will be the power of the law.' Yet Castilla, sometimes called the 'Soldier of the Law',[6] also understood that in his cherished task of bringing order and harmony to Peru he would have to depend upon more than a strong army and the stern enforcement of the law. Apparently he regarded it as absolutely essential that the executive be sensitive to the wants and desires of a broad cross-section of the people and create at least the impression that these wants and desires were important determinants of national policy. In this regard Castilla benefited enormously from his skill in mixing with his people. Probably he enjoyed participating in the parades, the festivals, the processions, the imposing religious ceremonies that were so important to the average citizen. Mingling with the masses on these occasions, Castilla gave the impression of 'sharing in the palpitations of his people, of knowing their desires and aspirations'.[7] Without his talent for winning popularity at the grass-root level, Castilla would not have been so successful in making the masses of Peru at least a little more law-abiding.

Castilla mixed equally freely with an amazingly varied group of highly placed, influential persons. He called on liberals and conservatives, friends and opponents alike, to aid him in the service of his country, concerning himself primarily with the talents rather than with the philosophies of men. To a remarkable degree he practised the policy which he proclaimed in an 1845 address: 'The state in selecting men to serve it does not pay any attention to their opinions'.[8]

His gifts in the field of public relations did not, of course, guarantee Castilla immunity against the plots of Peru's chronic political conspirators. Still, especially in his first term, he exhibited an uncanny ability to ferret out plots and crush them before they could produce serious consequences. It may be that one of his biographers is correct in asserting that Castilla's secret of success 'lay in the fact that he had been formed in revolution and under-stood the tricks and devices of the revolutionary caudillos'.[9] Once detected in their work, plotters were generally dealt with quite leniently. Castilla never sent a political foe before the firing squad. Instead the more dangerous enemies were exiled, usually for only a short time, after which they were allowed to return under the terms of a generous amnesty. While troublemakers were in exile, moreover, Castilla remained solicitous of their well-being. If he learned that political exiles lacked funds, he always ordered Peru's foreign legations to attend to their needs. It was humanity and compassion, not just strict enforcement of the law, that enabled Castilla to fulfil his purpose of bringing political order to Peru.

Castilla also introduced a measure of economic order into the national budget and the public services. On 21 October 1845, he sent to congress the first national budget ever prepared in Peruvian history. Formulated by his extremely able minister of the treasury Manuel del Río, this document caused consternation in congress, most of whose members had no idea of what a national budget was. A general accounting bureau was established in 1848. Within the bureau a council of general statistics was organized to direct the acquisition of accurate information on such subjects as demography, agriculture, mining, industry, commerce and all the material resources of the country. Under Castilla, moreover, public servants were paid promptly, and a pension plan for them was introduced, providing for retirement at the age of seventy. Peru also became the first Latin American country in which a railway was built. Running from Lima to Callao, it was opened on 5 April 1851. In addition, roads, churches, aqueducts and bridges were constructed; gas-light, water, and sanitation facilities helped to modernize Lima; commercial steam vessels were acquired; the army was strengthened and provided with up-to-date equipment; and the military school at Bellavista was reopened. Castilla further saw to it that Peru's navy was strengthened so as to make it the most formidable in Latin America and that naval officers received grants for study in Europe.

During Castilla's first term education was encouraged and supported as never before. In Lima a normal school and the School of Arts and Crafts were initiated with state funds. The latter, Castilla hoped, would serve as a model for similar schools that would be established in every departmental capital. For the first time the awarding of government scholarships for primary, secondary and higher education was regulated. The legitimate children of fathers who had served the cause of independence and those of poor and needy families were given priority.

In international affairs the accomplishments of the first Castilla administration were also impressive. With the assistance of his first minister of foreign relations, José Gregorio Paz Soldán, one of Arequipa's most prominent citizens, Castilla reorganized the entire diplomatic corps and raised it to a higher level of efficiency and integrity. Peru sent well-qualified diplomatic representatives to England, France, Spain and the Holy See, and, taking advantage of its mounting prestige in rivalling Chile as the best organized and most powerful of Latin America's Pacific coast countries, assumed a rôle of leadership in a movement aimed at reviving the old Bolivarian dream of Hispanic–American unity.

The immediate occasion for Peru's interest in continental unity arose over the activities of Venezuelan-born Juan José Flores. Either the actual president or the behind-the-scenes power in Ecuador ever since its liberation which he helped to achieve in 1821, Flores was finally overthrown and driven from that country in 1845. With the backing of the Queen-Regent, María Cristina, of Spain, Flores proceeded to Ireland where he attempted to raise a force with which to turn the tables on his enemies in Ecuador. Apparently as the price for Spanish support he had promised María Cristina to establish one of her sons on an Ecuadoran throne. Here was an overt threat against the continuing independence of Spanish America, for if the Flores venture succeeded in Ecuador, Spain might attempt to reacquire hegemony over several of the former colonies.

At the same time that he was worried about the situation in Ecuador, Castilla grew increasingly concerned by the expansionist tendencies of the United States, manifested in its war against Mexico. He was convinced that in their desire to protect a sister nation against schemes of renewed Spanish imperialism, the South American nations could not turn to the United States. Rather, the southern republics should think of unification and joint defence to guard themselves both against Spain and the United States. Like the original Bolivarian model, then, the continentalism of Castilla excluded the United States, resting on the assumption that there was more apt to be rivalry than concert of interests between South America and the powerful northern republic.[10]

Castilla and Paz Soldán worked successfully to induce the British Government to prevent the sailing of the Flores expedition from Ireland and arranged for a meeting in Lima of an American Congress in 1847. Attended by delegates of the host country and of Chile, Bolivia, Colombia and Ecuador, the congress sought to guarantee the independence and territorial integrity of the participating republics, to mould them into an alliance capable of repelling foreign invasions, and to codify a uniform body of American international law that eventually would become applicable to all of Hispanic America. Castilla expressed in unequivocal terms the Americanist concepts that lay behind the 1847 congress. His words marked the beginning of a twenty-year period in which his country provided leadership in working towards Hispanic–American confederation and co-operation:

It is not possible for the Peruvian Government to maintain itself as an indifferent spectator without uniting its votes and efforts to those of all the people of America, so as to sustain the common independence and identity of principles and institutions. ... Peru considers as its own any threat which is made against the people of the American continent, regarding as a violation of natural justice and the laws of men whatever is done, by whomever it might be, with the object of intervening in the internal affairs of a free people of South America and attempting to impose laws upon them, to change their institutions, or to make them adopt another form of government, distinct from that which they themselves have chosen, according to their own convenience and circumstances.[11]

Although little came of the treaty of confederation signed at the 1847 congress in Lima, the events of that year indicated that Peruvians were developing a sense of satisfaction over their accomplishments and believed that the domestic progress made possible by political order equipped their country to play a rôle in international affairs.

CASTILLA'S FIRST TERM: THE NEGATIVE ASPECTS

Some of the internal reforms and the glitter of material well-being that appeared to justify Peru's sally into foreign relations were the fortuitous gifts of providence rather than the results of the economic skills of Castilla. [12] In 1840 when serving as minister of the treasury Castilla had negotiated with English capitalists the first contract for the exploitation and exportation to Europe of guano, the bird-droppings which in the mid-nineteenth century came into demand as a high-grade fertilizer in nearly all parts of the world. Virtually unused in Peru since the time of the Incas, guano had accumulated along the country's coast and offshore islands in deposits many feet deep. Gathering and sacking the stuff proved to be a messy business. The ammonia fumes produced by the droppings sometimes shrivelled the skin about the eyes of the labourers and even caused blindness. The stench was so foul that, it is reported, when the first guano shipment arrived in Southampton the entire town took to the hills. Despite the difficulties of marketing it, however, the high price commanded by Peru's rediscovered guano brought to the country its greatest wealth since the sixteenth-century discoveries of silver mines.

Beginning in 1840 a system was devised whereby exclusive rights to sell guano to designated regions of the world were granted to consignees (*consignatorios*), which were generally powerful London and Paris corporations. The Peruvian government originally entered into these arrangements because, driven by desperate need for the immediate acquisition of large sums of money, it required as consignees firms that were in a position to advance ample loans which would be repaid by subsequent guano shipments. Seeking prompt delivery of the borrowed capital under any terms, Peruvian officials undervalued guano in the repayment commitments, and accepted exorbitant interest and commission rates. As a result the consignees generally paid considerably less for the guano delivered to them than the optimum price obtainable on the open market. Furthermore, a considerable part of the profits that should have accrued to the Peruvian government on guano sales never reached the national coffers. Instead these funds remained in far-off countries to meet vastly-inflated claims on loans that had been extended to Peru since the 1820's.

With the income from advances on guano shipments covering national expenditures, Castilla did little to develop a balanced revenue system. Guano earnings for the most part went to defray the ordinary costs of administration and to finance various services which, however laudable in themselves, rested on an economic windfall rather than on a self-sustaining economy. Under Castilla, the greater the windfall gains became, the less self-sustaining the economy grew.

Early in his first term, it is true, Castilla spoke out in favour of direct government exploitation of at least some guano-deposit areas as a means of regulating the industry. He recommended further that part of the guano revenue be channelled into special, government-planned development projects.[13] And he reacted with approval when the minister of the treasury, del Río, suggested that congress should each year determine the number of tons of guano to be sold, and that the State should then contract the stipulated amount to the highest bidder. None of these ideas, however, was pursued. The established and questionable methods had already become too well entrenched.

It may well be that subsequent critics of the Castilla economic policies have judged his administration in terms of twentieth-century standards, ignoring the possibility that at the time Peruvians lacked the knowledge and the techniques to manage their economy differently. However that may be, the fact remains that by 1849 Peru's economy was largely at the mercy of Antony Gibbs & Sons of London, with exclusive rights to sell guano during that year in all of Europe save France, and the Montané Company of Paris which had the franchise for France. In 1850 Castilla did begin to assign guano rights to certain Peruvian consignees, in return for the usual advances. But this did not result in any additional government revenue; nor did it lead to productive investments by the Peruvian consignees in their own country. Entirely free to do as they chose with their income from guano sales and loans to the government, the native consignees devoted their profits mainly to conspicuous consumption. All the while the undirected Peruvian economy remained largely stagnant, insufficient economic activities were opened to the 'incipient middle class, and its members could only find a livelihood by joining the alarmingly expanding bureaucracy'.[14]

THE ECHENIQUE ADMINISTRATION, 1851–4

The principal but by no means the only contenders in the 1851 presidential elections to choose Castilla's successor were the two men who had once co-operated closely with each other in the conservative fold: José Rufino Echenique, President of the Council of State and, as such, Castilla's vice-president, and the 'Regenerator', Manuel Ignacio Vivanco, who had been granted amnesty in 1848 and allowed to return from exile. Vivanco did all in his power to vilify his former close associate and political ally. Open warfare between the partisans of the two contenders was narrowly averted, and the elections were marked by a good deal of scandal. The success of Echenique, who was proclaimed by congress to be the new president on 31 March, was mainly attributable to the open support which Castilla had extended to him.

Echenique has been accurately described as

... a man of good heart and intentions, possessing high intelligence, who in private life would have been an excellent citizen and father of a family. But neither by natural inclinations nor by talent was he a statesman. Timid and lacking confidence, he isolated himself within a narrow little circle, and knew of nothing that transpired outside of it. . . . Having made up his mind on the basis of restricted advice he was obstinate, insisting upon following his opinion even when all events manifested his error; and thus he marched to certain doom.[15]

Showing particularly poor judgement in the choice of his immediate advisers, Echenique placed the arch-rogue, Juan Crisóstomo Torrico, in the all-important post of minister of war. The cause of dismay to most Peruvians of integrity, Torrico's appointment was particularly abhorrent to Castilla. The ex-president had never made any attempt to hide his contempt for this unscrupulous caudillo who in 1849 had plotted unsuccessfully to overthrow Castilla's government and as a result had been briefly exiled. Subsequent developments made it all the clearer to Castilla that he would have no influence in the régime of the man he had helped to raise to the presidency and soon he was living as a solitary, and dangerously resentful, political outcast in Chorillos, a suburb of Lima.

Compounding his error of appointing Torrico to an important ministerial post, Echenique selected as one of his closest private counsellors the inflexibly stubborn and reactionary churchman Bartolomé Herrera (1808–64). Contemptuous of the masses and concerned only with the 'aristocracy of intelligence', Herrera really desired to convert Peru into a theocracy. The people could never question or censure the acts of duly-constituted governments, he taught, unless the rulers acted in a manner contrary to the teachings of sacred religion as interpreted by ecclesiastics, so that in the final analysis the clergy decided whether the people could assert themselves or must bear in resignation even the most repressive and totalitarian régimes. During the 1840's when he had served as its rector Herrera had converted the Colegio de San Carlos, which under the influence of Toribio Rodríguez de Mendoza had once spread the ideas of the Enlightenment, into the intellectual bastion of extreme conservatism.[16] Now he had, as an impressionable student, the president of the republic.

Echenique was slow to perceive the errors and scandals to which the doctrinaire inflexibility of some of his associates and the vindictiveness and dishonesty of others were driving his administration. Although honest in intentions, he was at his gullible worst in directing his country's economic policies. Castilla had already made the decision that the internal debt of the State, incurred since the time of independence, should be recognized and paid in full. During his first term some five million *soles* of public indebtedness had accordingly been recognized,[17] and he had estimated that another six million would be adequate to complete repayment in full.

However justifiable and laudable in its origins under Castilla, the consolidation of the internal debt as administered by Echenique gave rise to some of the most monumental graft and peculation that Peru had experienced. By the beginning of the third year of the Echenique administration the government had recognized an internal indebtedness of twenty million *soles*. The simple declaration of witnesses before public functionaries was considered by the régime as adequate to establish the validity of pecuniary claims lodged by citizens against the government. Unprincipled speculators enjoyed a field day, and it is probable that in just one of the manipulations involved in the consolidation the minister of war, Torrico, and a few of his closer friends made a profit of some four million *soles*. Trusting his small group of advisers who assured him that the consolidation was honestly managed, Echenique had no idea of the intensity of the mounting popular reaction against the abuses which were so widely rumoured.

One economic blunder seemed inevitably to lead to another. Echenique had to contract a large loan in Europe, at 6 per cent. interest, in order to service the wildly-inflated internal debt. Desperately in need of ever-mounting sums of money, he relied even more than had Castilla on advances from the guano consignees, extending to them terms so generous as to redound to the serious disadvantage of the national treasury. In addition to receiving high interest and commission terms, the average consignee during the Echenique administration could command on the open market a price of close to nine pounds sterling for each ton of guano. Yet consignees paid to the Peruvian government only two to three pounds sterling for each ton delivered to them from Peru.[18]

Incensed by the magnitude of the consolidation and related scandals Fernando Casós (1828–82), a promising writer and political theorist who had at first been a staunch Echenique supporter, broke with the administration and published convincing proofs of gross financial irregularity. Shortly thereafter Domingo Elías (1805–67), a wealthy owner of vast estates around Ica who had helped to overthrow Vivanco in 1844, emerged as an even more influential critic of the president.

Elías, in 1841, had invested some of his fortune in establishing in Lima the Colegio de Nuestra Señora de Guadalupe. For the next two decades and more Guadalupe served as the principal intellectual breeding ground of a new generation of liberal statesmen, counteracting the cult of conservatism nourished by Herrera at the Colegio de San Carlos. Undoubtedly the liberalism taught in Guadalupe exceeded that of its founder, Elías, who opposed Echenique not so much on account of his political conservatism as because of his ruinous economic policies. Possibly also Elías, who had aspired to the presidency in 1851, resented the man who had attained the post.

In a celebrated series of *Cartas políticas* published late in 1852 in *El Comercio*, Elías accused the Echenique administration of assuming through the consolidation a debt so vast that not even the guano reserves of Peru would be adequate to provide for its amortization. He further asserted that nearly all of the debts recently recognized were fraudulent, based on false documents and forged signatures of San Martín, Monteagudo, Bolívar and subsequent administrators.[19] When Echenique tried to defend himself in the press, Elías levelled an even stronger series of charges, including the accusation that Torrico was one of the principal beneficiaries of graft. After this exchange in the press, Echenique, goaded by self-seeking advisers who assured him that unrest in Peru reflected the seditious actions of a handful of plotters rather than any widespread dissatisfaction, resorted increasingly to newspaper censorship and heavy-handed, even terrorist, repression. Elías, having failed to change the course of events by his writings, rose in open rebellion, and though defeated by Torrico in January 1854, started a movement which spread rapidly and which Echenique soon found himself powerless to extinguish.

The ever-restless city of Arequipa, smarting under centralistic despotism and blaming Echenique for weakness in handling an economic dispute with Bolivia,[20] went into rebellion. Castilla surreptitiously departed from his Chorillos home, boarded a Chilean ship, and sailed down the coast to Atico from where he made his way to Arequipa, placing himself by mid-February at the head of the insurgent forces. San Román, who had just returned from an exile imposed by Echenique, joined the Arequipa movement which soon received significant reinforcements from Puno and Cuzco. By the time the dilatory General Torrico arrived on the scene it was too late to suppress the revolution. Soundly defeated by Castilla, he withdrew from the Arequipa region.

Torrico was not the only general who arrived too late at Arequipa. Vivanco, who had been exiled as a result of his conspiracies against Echenique, hastened to his old Arequipa stomping grounds once the fighting began, hoping to oust Echenique and once again seize the presidency. By the time he arrived, however, he found Castilla firmly in control of the situation. Perceiving that if Echenique fell it would be Castilla who became president, Vivanco decided he might best serve his own interests by at least temporarily siding with the legal executive. Betraying Castilla, with whom he had ostensibly reached an understanding, Vivanco withdrew to Islay and placed his troops at the disposition of the Echenique government. Perhaps he could justify this action on the grounds that he and Echenique were, after all, both conservatives. With the old conservative–liberal feud about to flare anew, and with an increasing number of liberal intellectuals flocking to the Castilla camp in Arequipa, there did seem to be a need for all true-hearted conservatives to band together.

With his forces steadily augmented by the arrival of liberal partisans, Castilla prepared for the final struggle with Echenique. Before the battle began he was joined also by a talented military leader of uncertain political persuasion, Mariano Ignacio Prado, later destined to serve his country twice as president. Exiled by Echenique and on a ship bound for Chile, Prado had jumped overboard at Arica and swum to freedom. By late 1854 he had made his way to Castilla's headquarters. Both he and San Román, who this time remained on the field of battle until the issue had been decided, lent valuable assistance to Castilla the following 5 January at La Palma, about a league and a half from Lima. There the Echenique armies, again under the command of Torrico, were routed. Torrico sought asylum in the United States legation in Lima, from whence he issued dramatic accusations of corruption against Echenique. He had neglected to switch sides in time, however, and had to undergo a European exile which lasted until 1861. The unfortunate Echenique, whose downfall had been brought about because of inability to defend himself against his friends, escaped to Panama and later made his way to the United States before eventually returning to Peru.

Prior to the victory of La Palma Castilla, in July 1854, issued a decree abolishing Indian tribute, and another providing for the immediate emancipation of all slaves with just compensation to be paid by the State to their former owners. In part these decrees represented a response to the liberal philosophy of the advisers with whom Castilla had surrounded himself. The emancipation decree in particular was the culmination of a long campaign conducted by such liberals as the historian Santiago Távara,[21] and joined by the newspaper *El Comercio*, which in 1853 had run in serial form a translation of Harriet Beecher Stowe's *Uncle Tom's Cabin*. But liberal idealism may not have been exclusively responsible for Castilla's actions. The 1854 decrees were good for the business of making revolution.[22] Indians and Negroes were expected to, and to some extent did, show their gratitude by enlisting in the Castilla forces. Whatever their motives, the decrees won for the victor at La Palma the title of Liberator. Since that time this title has belonged in Peru not to San Martín or Bolívar, but to Castilla.

CASTILLA'S SECOND TERM, 1855–62: THE CONSERVATIVE-
LIBERAL DISPUTE RESOLVED BY COMPROMISE

In February 1855 delegates to a new constituent assembly were chosen, for the first time in Peruvian history, by direct suffrage. There was little, however, that was free or democratic about the elections. All who had sided with Echenique were disfranchised and, in addition, often subjected to harsh reprisals by the curiously vindictive liberal advisers who had become influential with Castilla. Elected principally by men who had participated in driving Echenique from power, among them the newly-emancipated Negroes who had voted as instructed by liberal political bosses, the deputies to the 1855 assembly were in their majority members of Peru's second generation of liberals. In some important respects they differed from their intellectual counterparts of the first generation after independence.

Responsible for the constitutions of 1823, 1828 and 1834, Peru's first-generation liberals had declined in power when many of their number, including their early leaders among the clergy, had grown apprehensive about liberalism's mounting anticlericalism. The new-generation liberals were not intimidated by anticlericalism. They made it, indeed, the essence of their programme. Standing for political and economic individualism, democracy and equality, liberals saw in the Catholic Church a powerful institution which by virtue of its own internal organization, and also of the temporal influence which it exercised, appeared to be in opposition to all these ends. Liberals felt that they could not succeed in their hopes of rebuilding the political and economic order until the enormously powerful Church was made internally more democratic and liberal and until all the artificial advantages which it enjoyed in its dealings with laymen and temporal institutions were removed.

With some exceptions, the second-generation liberals were highly romantic, wanting freedom of competition and unfettered political and economic individualism because they believed in the essential goodness and equality of men. They are not to be confused with the late nineteenth-century liberals who, under the influence of positivism and Social Darwinism, desired unregulated competition precisely because they believed in the inequality of men and wanted to establish conditions which would lead to the elimination of the unfit by the fit.

Among the prominent second-generation liberals who joined in the move to overthrow Echenique because they hoped thereafter to impose their own ideological approach upon Castilla was José Gálvez (1819–66). A native of Cajamarca, Gálvez was the epitome of Peru's revived liberalism. Attracted by every measure of radical reform, very much under the influence of the French thinker and writer, Benjamin Constant, Gálvez was inflexible and dogmatic in his attitudes, violent and aggressive in his declarations. Unmistakably, however, the remarkable powers of his mind and his forceful personality endowed him with the qualities of leadership.

Owing to his importance and success as an educator, Gálvez had at hand a talented supporting cast for the major rôle he was about to play in Peruvian politics. He and his brother Pedro (1822–78), who, as Castilla's secretary, had countersigned the decree of July 1854 ending Indian tribute,[23] had exercised a dominant influence over instruction at Guadalupe. As a result the school founded by Elías in 1841 had turned out class after class of confirmed liberals, committed to anticlericalism, democracy, equality, popular sovereignty and individualism.[24] Among the products of this liberal education, who were now ready to help the Gálvez brothers as they attempted to bend Castilla to their will, were the fiery champion of political liberalism Ignacio Escudero (1820–66),[25] who contended that the rehabilitation of the people would begin only when they were allowed completely to govern themselves, and the idealistic defender of classical economic liberalism, José Simeón Tejeda (1826–73),[26] who asserted that free enterprise was the means of achieving an egalitarian Utopia.

Opposing the second-generation liberals were, of course, the conservatives, very little different from their intellectual predecessors except for their attitude towards the Church. Just as the new liberals made anticlericalism their cardinal tenet, so the conservatives of the 1850's, led by Bartolomé Herrera, were more zealously and unanimously committed than their counterparts of an earlier time to defending the traditional position of the Church. Arguing that the one true faith had to be protected and promulgated by a special class which, because of its divine mission, deserved unique privileges and immunities, asserting that free competition of religious beliefs was tantamount to treating truth and error as equals, Herrera and his followers insisted that ecclesiastical as well as temporal institutions would court disaster by departing from a stratified, hierarchical and authoritarian organization. Whereas liberals wanted the Church, even in its internal structure, to reflect the politico-economic ideals which they championed, Herrera and the conservatives wanted temporal society to reflect what for them was the ideal organization of the ecclesiastical institution. As opposed to the liberals who felt that their model society would be endangered so long as the Catholic Church deviated from the temporal patterns they desired, Herrera and his partisans believed that the Church would be in jeopardy until society was so framed as to resemble the hierarchical ecclesiastical organization. To conservatives the fundamental facts of life that must guide both Church and State were the baseness and worthlessness of the vast majority of men, save in their capacity for supernatural salvation, and the necessity for the many to submit to discipline and to accept the truth as interpreted by the few men upon whom providence had placed the mantle of leadership.

Subsequent developments established that both liberals and conservatives were at least partially mistaken in their assumptions. It was not altogether true that the political and economic milieu could be liberalized only if the Catholic Church was also thoroughly liberalized in its internal organization. Nor was it altogether true that the Church's position as an ecclesiastical institution rooted in authority and discipline could be maintained only by forcing the political structure into a similar mould. Ramón Castilla was able to prove this by a brilliantly-administered programme that rested upon a considerable degree of liberal-conservative give and take. Castilla stumbled upon this solution through a pragmatic process of trial and error, at first allowing the liberal majority in the constituent assembly to make the mistakes from which he later profited in devising a workable compromise between Peru's antagonistic ideological camps.

After prolonged discussion,[27] the assembly in 1856 produced a new constitution that incorporated many of the most cherished projects of the Gálvez brothers, Ignacio Escudero, José Simeón Tejeda, and their fellow liberals. The State collection of Church tithes was prohibited, and ecclesiastical and military *fueros*, providing private law courts for ecclesiastics and soldiers involved in civil and criminal cases, were abolished. After heated debate, however, the liberals were defeated in their attempt to separate Church and State and to establish freedom of worship.

On the political front, the liberal victory was almost complete. Departmental juntas were re-established as a means, so it was hoped, of ending centralism and of allowing all parts of Peru truly to enjoy the privilege of self government. The powers of the president were curtailed and it was stipulated that his cabinet members, over whom congress exercised the powers of censure and removal, were to be co-directors with him of national policy. The scope of extraordinary powers traditionally extended to presidents in time of emergency was sharply limited and the conferring of these powers was made subject at all times to congressional approval. The 1856 constitution further weakened the presidency by vesting in congress control over military promotions, although Escudero's plea in the assembly that permanent armies be prohibited and the executive office denied to soldiers was rejected.

In swearing to the new constitution Castilla forthrightly expressed disapproval of many of its features, especially the under-mining of presidential control over the armed forces. Through Juan M. del Mar, his able minister of government, he gave the warning that reforms should always be considered not only in the light of their ends, but in terms of whether the times were propitious for their introduction. Fully to implement the con-stitution, he declared, would lead to public disturbances, and he urged the modification of many of its articles.[28]

The assembly ignored Castilla's admonitions and the predicted disturbances were not long in developing. On 31 October 1856, Arequipa rose in revolt against both Castilla and the new con-stitution, justifying the move on the grounds that religion was under attack. Returning from one of his many exiles in Chile, Vivanco assumed direction of the insurrection and attracted to it many prominent men, among them Ricardo Palma, soon to be recognized as Peru's leading literary figure, and Miguel Grau, destined to become the country's greatest naval hero.

Not only in Arequipa, but in the northern coastal city of Trujillo and elsewhere Peruvians took up the struggle against Castilla and the liberal constitution with which he had protestingly been saddled. After many of Peru's naval officers pronounced against the legal government, giving Vivanco control of the sea, he moved a large number of men to Trujillo where he personally took command, expecting to undertake a march against Lima. Much to Vivanco's amazement, Castilla soon appeared in the environs of Trujillo, having accomplished the incredible by trans-porting his men on a barely seaworthy ship, the only craft available to the government after the naval mutiny. Vivanco, avoiding con-tact with Castilla, rushed his men aboard his well-equipped fleet and sailed to Callao, from where he hoped to take Lima. After a bloody engagement in which he failed to gain possession of Callao, Vivanco continued far down the coast, landed his troops, and marched them back to Arequipa. The dogged pursuer Castilla soon arrived, and after an eight-month siege Arequipa surrendered to him on 6 March 1858. Vivanco returned to exile in Chile.

Although drowned in the blood of hundreds of the city's youth, Arequipa's revolution, in large part a conservative protest against the liberal 1856 constitution, achieved its purpose. Even while Castilla was trying to close with Vivanco a subordinate of his in Lima, acting probably without direct orders from but in accordance with the general wishes of the president, forcibly disbanded the assembly which had framed the liberal constitution and which had continued thereafter to sit as a national legislature. Convinced even before the Arequipa uprising of the need to find a constitutional middle ground between liberalism and conservatism, Castilla, after defeating Vivanco, apparently resolved that the next Peruvian constitution should be framed by men of moderation willing to accept suggestions from the president. To get his way Castilla had to exile numerous opponents, silence critical newspapers, and illegally dissolve a recalcitrant congress that had met in 1858. In the following year his electoral manipulations secured for him a manageable assembly which framed the practical and workable constitution of 1860.

Like the ill-fated constitution of 1856, the new constitution prohibited State collection of tithes and suppressed ecclesiastical and military *fueros*. These, however, were the only important concessions made to the liberals. Full control over the armed forces was restored to the president and in general his powers were so expanded as to provide once again for executive dominance over the legislature. Perhaps liberals derived a grain of satisfaction from the article that reduced the presidential term from six to four years and proscribed, as had earlier constitutions, immediate re-election. Municipal councils were provided for, but departmental juntas were eliminated, and so Peru returned to centralized rule.

Essentially, the Constitution of 1860 satisfied the conservatives. True, the temporal power of the Church had apparently been diminished. But the new constitution demonstrated that this diminution did not of itself preclude authoritarian, centralized political rule. Moreover, Castilla soon took actions which proved that in actual practice the ending of State collection of tithes could be to the economic interests of the Church. Deprived of its traditional source of income, the Church was now given an annual direct government subsidy which exceeded the amount previously realized from tithes.

On the surface, the liberals appeared to have sustained a serious defeat, and their anger was such that in 1860 they joined in two vain attempts, conceived in the Masonic lodges of Lima, against Castilla's life. Refusing to abandon his usual equanimity, Castilla did not deliver the captured liberal plotters to the firing squads. Instead, a few ringleaders, among them José Gálvez and Ricardo Palma, were for a time sent into exile. After that liberal discontent subsided, at least temporarily.

Although by no means satisfied with the new constitution, liberals could at least regard with satisfaction and with hope for the future the fact that certain traditional privileges of the Church had at last been modified. They were also encouraged by the increasing attentiveness of Castilla to State-supported education, regarding this as the ultimate means of undermining the Church's historical control over intellectual life. Accordingly many liberals decided to trust in the future and await the gradual introduction of reforms.

CASTILLA'S SECOND TERM: THE CONTINUATION OF POSITIVE ACCOMPLISHMENTS

The relative tranquillity that Castilla achieved by mitigating liberal–conservative antagonism enabled him to make notable contributions to his country between 1860 and the end of his second term in October 1862. His approach to the problems of education was particularly noteworthy and progressive. Explaining his educational purposes in 1860, Castilla stated:

The Government desires the propagation and the rapid advance of all facets of knowledge. It wants useful knowledge and the study of sciences to be vastly extended ... it wants practical schools of arts and crafts; it wants universities to emerge from the inertia and prostration and complete uselessness in which they now find themselves; it hopes that instead of spreading illusions and fantasies and words without meaning they will begin to assume a real and active existence, and come to be worthy and respected centres for the teaching of scientific doctrines, conforming to the ideas and spirit of progress of modern times.[29]

Although not all of Castilla's dreams were realized during his era of power, or for that matter within the next hundred years, progress was made. Most notably the University of San Marcos, despite the opposition of its faculty and its administrators, underwent an extensive reform in the hope of transforming it into a modern centre of learning.[30]

As in his first term, so in his second, Castilla showed a passionate concern for military preparedness. Insistent upon obtaining modern equipment for the army, he also advised that whenever Chile bought one ship for its navy, Peru should purchase two. Undoubtedly his difficulties in defeating Vivanco after that tireless revolutionist won control of the navy in 1857 impressed upon Castilla the importance of seapower in providing for national security.

Even before he managed to secure domestic tranquillity in the final two and a half years of his second term, Castilla had exhibited the interest in foreign affairs that had characterized his first régime. Continental unity remained an important goal of his foreign policy, all the more so when he became seriously alarmed by the incursions of Tennessee-born William Walker into Nicaragua. After a military campaign in which he commanded a motley following of Yankee adventurers and gained the backing of local liberals, Walker had in 1856 seized the Nicaraguan presidency. Walker's actions had no official support, but Castilla shared the misapprehension of many Latin American statesmen that the Tennesseean was carrying out the policies of the Washington government and that his expedition heralded a new era of United States expansion that would ultimately threaten South America. Consequently the Castilla government eagerly accepted a Chilean invitation to participate in an American Congress in Santiago in 1856. Out of the meeting, attended also by Ecuador, Bolivia, Paraguay, Nicaragua, Honduras and Mexico, emerged the Continental Treaty which pledged joint action in resisting foreign attacks against the independence and sovereignty of the signatory powers.[31]

Even more clearly than in his first term, Castilla recognized continental unity as the principal means whereby Hispanic America might protect itself against the economic imperialism of the United States and other foreign powers. In a statement in 1860 which would have been timely even a century later Castilla stated:

'The relative weakness of the South American republics, divided and isolated among themselves, is in the judgement of this government the deplorable cause of the fact that on many occasions we have been treated with grave lack of respect, as if for the great international potentates there did not exist a common law of nations.' Only through unity, he thought, would the South American republics achieve sufficient power to require all foreign investors to abide by the laws of the country in which their investments were made and to refrain from appealing to their home governments for special protection.[32]

In the second term Castilla was again troubled by occurrences in Ecuador. A complex situation, made worse by an Ecuadoran government grant to foreign creditors of land claimed by Peru, led, in October 1859, to the landing in Guayaquil of Peruvian forces under the command of the president himself. The expedition produced no lasting results. A boundary treaty signed by Castilla and certain conciliatory Ecuadoran representatives was highly favourable to Peru, but could have been enforced against an angered Ecuadoran populace only by an extensive Peruvian military campaign, a course of action which Castilla spurned. Discouraged by the prevailing political chaos which necessitated his dealing not with one but with two rival Ecuadoran governments and feeling that his presence was required in Lima to keep the precarious situation there from deteriorating, Castilla departed from Guayaquil. He noted that the honour of Peru had not yet been satisfied, but added: 'The honour of Peru, which is also mine, ought never to be augmented by taking advantage of the internal conflicts of a sister people. . . .'[33] Although Castilla's attitude was magnanimous and further showed his desire to end rivalry and to prepare the way for unity and co-operation among the South American republics, it has frequently been condemned by chauvinistic Peruvian writers. They have blamed Castilla for not seizing the opportunity to wrest from Ecuador a great slice of territory, including Guayaquil.

CASTILLA'S SECOND TERM: THE NEGATIVE ASPECTS

Despite the many brilliant successes of the second administration, Castilla's conduct of economic affairs proved to be careless and often lacking in foresight. The results were all the more disastrous because the Peruvian economy in the mid-1850's faced challenges and crises far more severe than those of the previous decade. The consequences of the 1854 emancipation, by which more than twenty thousand slaves were freed overnight, were far reaching. The stipulation that former owners would be compensated with bonds worth three hundred *soles* for each liberated Negro placed a heavy burden on the treasury – even though ultimately the owners received only some 40 per cent. of the compensation promised them. The sudden abolition, moreover, produced serious difficulties within the private sector of the economy. With the masses of freed slaves refusing to work, agricultural production declined alarmingly in the second half of the 1850's, and the price of farm products in some instances increased three- and four-fold.

Even on humanitarian grounds the emancipation decree was of questionable value, for it did not actually end slavery. In the desire to obtain substitutes for the liberated Negroes, coastal landowners began the large-scale importation of Chinese under a system of bondage which meant that once in Peru their status was essentially that of slaves. Widely publicized abuses and scandals led to the enactment in 1856 of a law suspending the traffic in Asian labourers. In 1862, however, Castilla, bowing to the pressure of landowners, rescinded this law and by 1875 some eighty thousand Chinese embonded workers had been brought to Peru.[34] Thus Castilla, the Liberator, sanctioned a policy which resulted in the virtual enslavement of Asians whose number vastly exceeded that of the Africans he had freed.

The suppression of the Indian tribute, which previously had produced at least 10 per cent. of the annual national revenue, placed an additional strain on the country's finances and produced some unfortunate social and political results. When required to pay the tribute, Indians had raised crops in order to meet their obligations and had thus, to some extent, participated in the national economy. Relieved of the tribute, they frequently produced only enough for bare subsistence and came to be increasingly isolated from the economic and also the political life of the coast.

In still another way the suppression of Indian tribute had adverse effects. Previously Peruvian departmental governments, especially in the sierra where the large concentrations of native population were found, had relied upon Indian tribute, only a portion of which went to the national treasury, for the revenue with which to meet necessary annual expenditures. These governments now found themselves dependent upon the largesse of the central bureaucracy in Lima. Most frequently money was doled out from Lima not to aid the development of the provinces, but to entrench in power supporters of the political machine that was at the moment in control of the capital. The reduction of the provinces to mendicancy produced a type of centralism that actually still further separated the various parts of the country rather than binding them together. The longer this centralism, which was based on the exploitation of the many parts of Peru, especially the sierra, by the capital remained in effect, the more intense became the regional animosities that it generated.

Burdening his government with obligations to former slave owners as well as with the expensive responsibility of supporting the Church now that the State no longer collected tithes; pursuing a military preparedness programme that resulted in a four-fold increase in armed forces expenditures between 1852 and 1858; and incurring new fiscal demands from the provinces, Castilla at the same time had deprived the treasury of its customary income from Indian tribute. He might still have met the immediate economic needs of the country by resorting to a broad programme of taxation aimed at capturing some of the internal capital that was available. This policy was urged on him by some of the nation's best economic minds.[35] The president rejected such advice, which appeared to menace the programme of complete economic *laissez-faire* adopted originally in his previous administration, and decided instead to meet the day-by-day needs of the government through larger advances from the guano consignees. Thus, as the internal economy deteriorated, the foreign debt mounted rapidly and Peru's main source of collateral, the guano deposits, was depleted at an accelerating pace. Nor were the abuses accompanying the Echenique administration's consolidation of the internal debt curtailed. Virtually all the fraudulent claims recognized by Echenique were honoured by Castilla.[36]

Accurately predicting a future economic crisis for his country, José Casimiro Ulloa writing in an 1860 edition of the influential *Revista de Lima* noted that in 1845 Peruvian exports and imports had been in balance. From 1859, the value of imports was four times that of exports, and the balance of payments deficit was met by resorting to larger advances on guano consignments. 'Guano exports of the present proportions', warned Ulloa, 'can continue only for some fifteen years. Then will come the crisis, if in the meantime Peru has not vastly diversified its economy and augmented its production and export of goods other than guano'.[38] A later writer has described Peru's economic situation during the second Castilla régime in the following terms:

> Guano and the form of wealth it produces has contributed only to the affluence of a speculator class, and to the corruption and laziness of the majority of the citizens and, as a consequence, to the paralysis of industries. Because of the false guano prosperity, Peruvians have failed to develop the capitalist mentality that leads to the founding of industries and the generation of wealth. . . . As of 1862 when Castilla stepped down from power, the guano of Peru had served only to sustain the servants of the nation. The wealth it produced actually discouraged people from seeking riches in agriculture and manufacturing.[38]

CONSOLIDATION OF CASTILLA'S POLITICAL SUCCESS, ENTRENCHMENT OF HIS ECONOMIC FAILURE, 1862–7

With his term of office about to come to an end, Castilla manipulated the presidential elections so that San Román, the former caudillo then serving as minister of war, would follow him in office. Juan Antonio Pezet, a well-intentioned but rather colourless moderate, was elected first vice-president and as such was in line to succeed to the presidency should it for any reason become vacant.

Although he owed his election to Castilla, San Román surrounded himself with the enemies of his predecessor in office, among them Vivanco. Besides the conservative Vivanco, his main advisers included a number of anti-Castilla liberals. No one could discern a political orientation in the new administration beyond hostility to Castilla.

Early in 1863, with uncertainty at its height, San Román fell gravely ill. Castilla now put aside the rancour he had come to feel against San Román since his inauguration and called upon the ailing president, paternally advising him to prepare for eternity. San Román did so, resigning his membership in one of Lima's Masonic lodges and receiving the last rites from the Catholic Church from which he had long been separated. The end came for the old marshal on 3 April. In his brief presidency he had at least shown respect for republican institutions, spurning, for example,

Vivanco's advice to exile Castilla. He died, 'if not the object of popular love, at least quite widely respected'.[39] Pézet, who was on a European mission, returned to be sworn in as president. Almost at once the new executive found himself embroiled in serious difficulties with Spain. Some Basque settlers brought to Peru in 1860 to work on a large coastal agricultural estate had quickly begun to bicker over the terms of their contract. The disagreement led to an armed clash in August 1863 between the Basques on the one hand and some of the agents of the estate's management and many native Peruvian labourers as well on the other. Two of the immigrants were killed. Spain promptly lodged with the Peruvian government a strongly-worded protest containing a demand for apologies and a large indemnity payment. On 14 April 1864, claiming that Peru was not showing a sufficiently conciliatory and contrite attitude, she ordered a naval expedition already in the area, supposedly on a scientific mission, to seize the Chincha Islands, some one hundred miles offshore south of Callao. The occupation was a challenge not only to Peru's sovereignty over its territory but to its economy, for the islands were one of the richest guano areas of the republic. Moreover, rumours began to circulate in various American capitals that Spain's occupation of the islands was the first step in an effort to re-acquire political control over all of Peru and perhaps other South American republics as well.

Impressed, perhaps, by adverse reaction from the United States and the nearly solid front which South America assumed against its actions, Spain in January 1865 signed the Vivanco–Pareja Treaty. Although achieving what was most vitally important to Peru, Spain's withdrawal from the islands, the treaty contained stipulations which were considered by many to be an affront to national honour, particularly the acknowledgement that Spain was the aggrieved party and should receive an indemnification of three million pesos for expenses incurred in the occupation of the islands. Certain critics even went so far as to make the accusation that Vivanco, who, together with the Spanish Admiral, José Manuel Pareja, had prepared the treaty, was at heart a monarchist and had manipulated a supine surrender to the motherland as a preliminary step in establishing a Spanish prince on a Peruvian throne.[40]

Among the most outspoken in condemning the handling of the Spanish issue was ex-president Castilla, at the time senator for

Callao, who alleged that the Pézet administration was insensitive to obligations of national honour. Accurately gauging the extent of popular resentment against the Vivanco–Pareja Treaty, Castilla planned to lead a revolution against the Pézet regime. In early February, however, a heated exchange with Pézet in the national palace resulted in Castilla's arrest and exile without even the chance to bid farewell to his wife. His revolutionary plans were at once taken up by others and on 28 February 1865, Arequipa rebelled. By the following November the leader of the Arequipa insurrection, Mariano Ignacio Prado,[41] who some ten years earlier had helped Castilla to overthrow Echenique, was in Lima serving as *de facto* dictator. Pézet had been exiled and the Vivanco–Pareja Treaty disavowed.

When officials in Madrid revealed that they would not drop the matter without making a show of force against Peru and its ally Chile, the Prado régime in January 1866 declared war on Spain. A strong Spanish squadron blockaded the Chilean–Peruvian coast and bombarded the defenceless Chilean harbour of Valparaíso. On 2 May, however, Peru's forces heroically beat back a Spanish attack on Callao and one week later Spain lifted the blockade. Finally in August 1869 Spain and Peru signed a treaty of peace and amity. Peru thereby at long last obtained Spanish recognition of its independence.

Shortly after the Peruvian victory Castilla was able to return from exile. His enforced absence had been costly to the country, depriving the popular uprising against Pézet of its natural leader and placing it instead in the far less capable hands of Prado. Lacking firm convictions and strong principles, Prado by the time he became *de facto* dictator had allowed Peru's well-organized, extreme liberal factions to capture virtual control over the movement he ostensibly headed. Once the business with Spain had been settled, the liberals, having easily arranged for the election of a majority of their partisans to the constituent assembly which convened in February 1867, proceeded, as they had in 1856, to fashion an injudicious and unpopular constitution. José Gálvez was dead – he had died a hero's death in the defence of Callao on 2 May which he had brilliantly directed as minister of war – but the 1867 assembly was dominated by equally intransigent liberals anxious to impose their views, regardless of the cost, on the entire country.

The constitution produced by the 1867 assembly continued the proscription against government collection of tithes and the suppression of ecclesiastical *fueros*. It struck a new blow against the Church by forbidding the holding of land in mortmain. By only three votes the delegates failed to incorporate into the charter the long-time liberal objective of religious toleration, but they advanced farther than any previous group of lawmakers in divesting the Church of its educational influence. The constitution which they approved provided for a more exaggerated form of parliamentary government than the short-lived 1856 instrument, stripping the executive of many traditional prerogatives. The liberals of 1867 showed the customary concern for decentralization by re-establishing departmental juntas and endowing them with broader powers than ever before. They also struck a blow against the power of the army by an article that permitted enlisted soldiers and sailors to declare, under defined deliberative procedures, that orders given by their superiors were contrary to the spirit of the constitution or civil laws and accordingly not to be obeyed.[42]

As the liberal constitution makers went about their business, Manuel Pardo, the son of the conservative *pensador* Felipe Pardo and soon to become president of Peru, struggled hard to guide the Prado administration towards some positive accomplishments. As minister of the treasury, Pardo sought to remedy the mistakes of Castilla's economic policy by establishing a balanced revenue system that would liberate the government from its disastrous dependence on guano advances. In the revenue programme devised by Pardo a 3 per cent. *ad valorem* duty was placed on exports, a new stamp tax was levied, and an excise tax on the consumption of alcohol was introduced. Moreover, a semi-graduated personal contribution won legislative approval and inheritance imposts were decreed. Enlightened measures were also enacted to reduce national expenditures. Unfortunately these well-conceived innovations came to nothing because the constituent assembly insisted upon trying to destroy the admirable political compromise that Castilla had forged. The actions of the assembly gave rise to a revolution whose leaders, upon overthrowing the Prado administration, would indiscriminately rescind not only its unsound political programme but also the wise economic policies that it had backed.

In March 1867 insurrections broke out in Ayacucho and Huancavelica and signs of impending trouble became unmistakable in Trujillo, Cerro de Pasco and Tacna. Peruvians in general had been incensed by the reforms which the 1867 constitution makers tried to enforce upon them, reforms which President Prado admitted were not popular.[43] Ramón Castilla, who had withdrawn from Lima to his native Tarapacá because of the initial coolness towards him of the Prado administration, followed the new developments with keen interest. Sensing that the old soldier-president was on the verge of placing himself at the head of the burgeoning revolutionary movement, Prado ordered that Castilla be arrested and brought to Callao. But the captain of the ship on which Castilla was placed, persuaded by the pleas of his distinguished prisoner, decided not to comply with orders and took the ex-president to Valparaíso. From Chile Castilla returned to southern Peru, landing on 15 May, and proclaimed his leadership of a revolution that had as its ends the overthrow of Prado and the return to the Constitution of 1860.

Throughout his career Castilla had been amazingly successful in winning both moderate liberals and conservatives to his cause, even when extremist elements in the two groups opposed him. Because of this rare skill, he had been able to prevent the division of Peruvian politicians into intractable liberal and conservative associations. Even at the end his talent did not fail him, for as he prepared for the struggle with Prado he was supported by moderates from both of the main ideological camps. Thus the country was spared the bloodbath that might have resulted from a confrontation between only liberals on one side and conservatives on the other.

If Castilla's political skill did not desert him in 1867, his physical strength did, and, as the sixty-eight-year-old general forced himself on and on across the deserts of southern Peru in the direction of Lima he felt the end approaching. Close to Tiviliche and still on his horse, Castilla is said to have gasped: 'My God, one more month of life, and I will achieve the well-being of my country; no, only a few more days . . . I cannot go on . . . be brave . . ., yes, forward . . . the nation . . . impossible.'[45] Helped from his mount, the old soldier died within a few moments. It was shortly after dawn on the bright, clear morning of 30 May.

The body of the fallen warrior was taken to Arica and after a simple funeral buried there. In rapid succession, then, the cities of Chiclayo, Puno, Cuzco and above all Arequipa, took up the cause of the revolution. After a protracted but vain attempt to capture Arequipa, Prado returned to a Lima that had grown increasingly hostile and, early in 1868, resigned from the presidency. Quickly occupying the capital, the successful revolutionists declared the constitution of 1860 to be once more in effect. The body of that constitution's father was brought from Arica and after a fittingly splendid ceremony interred in Lima on 20 July.

The masterful political compromise between liberalism and conservatism that Ramón Castilla had achieved, and that had been threatened by the 1867 constitution, endured because the old soldier had been willing to take up his sword in its defence. True, the insatiable greed of a future generation of politicians and the demoralization accompanying the defeat administered by Chile in a devastating war (1879–83) would destroy much of the political harmony that Castilla had brought to his country. This sad development in no way makes less remarkable the fact that between 1845 and 1867 Castilla succeeded in taming the two wild forces, liberalism and conservatism, that otherwise might have torn Peru asunder, as they did so many other Hispanic American republics.

But the Peru which Castilla had saved from political disaster was at the time of his death courting economic ruin. That Peru in 1867 was in many ways no better off than it had been at the end of the first age of caudillismo in 1845 must partially be traced to the fact that, so far as Peru's economic life was concerned, Castilla was never able to discover the secret for effecting a compromise between liberalism and conservatism, between liberty and unrestricted initiative on one hand, and supervision and control on the other. In his economic policies Castilla was a pure liberal in the nineteenth-century meaning of the word.

Perhaps the best balanced appraisal of the *mestizo* from Tarapacá who for over twenty years helped shape his country's destinies was made by Bartolomé Herrera. 'Enjoy happy soldier,' said the high priest of conservatism, 'the reputation which fortune has bestowed upon you. The merit acquired is yours. The errors into which your government and the congresses have fallen belong to the epoch and are the patrimony of humanity'.[45]

The age of dominance by one man had come to an end in 1867. For the next decade Peruvian history would be essentially a tale of two men: Nicolás de Piérola and Manuel Pardo.

5

Caudillismo and Statesmanship in Peacetime and War, 1869–83

BALTA AND PIÉROLA AND AN ERA OF ECONOMIC FOLLY,
1868–71

WITH the revolution against the liberal constitution of 1867 having swept all before it, and with Mariano Ignacio Prado having fled from the capital, General Pedro Diez Canseco, an honest soldier-politician from Arequipa and the brother of Castilla's widow, became provisional executive. Under his supervision presidential elections were shortly held, with José Balta as the victor. A soldier of humble origins noted for his spartan habits, Balta had led from Chiclayo the opposition in northern Peru against Prado and the liberal constitution. Inclined towards the conservative approach to politics, he had been a loyal friend of Echenique, defending that president until the last minute against Castilla in 1855. In his successful presidential bid of 1868 he was supported by self-styled defenders of order and authority and by agents of the guano consignees who felt mistakenly that the unsophisticated soldier would not do anything to interfere with their economic privileges.[1]

Inaugurated in August 1868, Balta began an administration that has been highly praised by some historians and scornfully denounced by others. At least there is unanimous accord that Balta was colourful and, in fact, often quite bizarre in his actions. On one occasion a journalist made the president wildly angry by writing that it was necessary to 'put a brake on the government'. To Balta a brake meant the bit that is placed in the mouths of beasts to halt and direct them, so he ordered the offending writer brought into his presence, whereupon soldiers placed a horse bit in the man's mouth. Another time he forced a journalist to chew and swallow in his presence an anti-government editorial that had been published in a Lima newspaper.[2]

A man of strong, sometimes uncontrollable passions, Balta was sufficiently wise to recognize many of his limitations. Doubting his own ability to direct Peru's economy, he exercised particular care in selecting his ministers of the treasury. The first man he called to this post was Francisco García Calderón, a hard-working and impeccably honest lawyer and a well-informed intellectual. Although convinced that Peru must escape from its financial dependence on the guano consignees, García Calderón was unable to hit upon an alternative to this system for gathering revenue and shortly was removed from his post by a congressional vote of censure. Following the advice of his friend Echenique, recently returned to the country, and of his secretary, Ricardo Palma, Balta then decided to entrust the ministry of the treasury to a rapidly rising young businessman and political journalist, Nicolás de Piérola.[3]

Born on 5 January 1839, in Arequipa, Piérola came from a distinguished and extremely devout family. His father, educated in Spain, had held various colonial administrative offices and though a staunch opponent of independence had subsequently continued his promising career in Peru and served as a deputy to the constituent congress of 1827. The mother of Nicolás came from a well-to-do and socially prominent creole family. Young Nicolás' education was the best available at the time in Peru. He began his studies in Arequipa and when he was fourteen entered the seminary of San Toribio in Lima. His father assured the rector that the boy had a fervent desire to become a priest.

When his parents both died in 1857, Nicolás left the seminary and shortly afterwards obtained an ecclesiastical dispensation to marry his cousin, Doña Jesús de Iturbide. The marriage, although yielding many children, was not a happy one. Rather cold and withdrawn, Doña Jesús became more and more a religious fanatic, while Don Nicolás turned for compassion, understanding and physical satisfaction to the French wife of a Spanish artist and photographer who had settled in Lima.[4]

After his wedding Piérola at first dedicated himself to commerce; but the small, elegant, fastidious, nervous and quick-moving young man needed additional outlets for his energy. Conservative in his political ideology, a supporter of Vivanco in his 1857 revolution against Castilla, Piérola founded in 1864 the newspaper *El Tiempo* as the instrument for propagating his political doctrine. Defending President Pézet in the pages of *El Tiempo* against a rising tide of liberal criticism, he had even praised the Vivanco–Pareja Treaty, urging Peru on a course of conciliation and pacifism in its dispute with Spain. On Pézet's fall, Piérola for a time abandoned his newspaper activities and was devoting his attention to business and commercial undertakings when called in 1869 to the ministry of the treasury on the recommendation of Palma and Echenique.

The political and economic philosophy which Piérola had formulated by the time he accepted a cabinet post was a curious combination of traditional conservatism and liberalism. In politics, Piérola believed in authoritarian, centralized rule. Convinced of the infallibility of his own ideas, he had little tolerance for contrary views. Devout in his religious beliefs throughout his life, he was almost as convinced as Bartolomé Herrera that Catholicism was the one means for bringing unity and cohesion to the heterogeneous Peruvian population. Nationalism to him was really synonymous with Catholicism. Accordingly, the Church should, he felt, be guaranteed an especially favoured position by the State.

In his economic policies Piérola's most notable quality was his unbounded, wild optimism about the wealth and resources of Peru. Impressed with the guano and the newly-discovered nitrate and copper resources of his country,[5] he became obsessed with a vision of overnight, painless and easy, material development. He chose as the formula for achieving this goal the contracting of huge foreign loans which would be guaranteed by the unlimited natural resources of Peru.

There was much that was colonial and traditionally Latin Catholic in Piérola's economic thought. Wealth to him depended on providential windfalls, not upon the slow and laborious accumulation of capital based on individual sacrifice, savings and reinvestment. He spurned the 'Protestant Ethic' with its insistence upon the exercise of natural virtue (frugality, sobriety, responsibility, uninterrupted hard toil, avoidance of conspicuous consumption) as the means of achieving wealth. Affluence to him seemed to depend more upon supernatural factors. Providence had obviously lavished magnificent resources upon Peru. All that its citizens had to do was to sit back, relax, and enjoy the lives of cultivated eighteenth-century gentlemen while foreign capital and foreign technological expertise produced from its resources a modern, progressive, materially advanced country. There was no need to instil in Peruvians themselves, through a long and arduous educational process, a respect for economic virtues and a mastery of practical knowledge.

In his fatally easy approach to economics, Piérola did at least advocate the establishment of a more effective revenue system to provide for the ordinary costs of government. Revenue was to be obtained primarily from property, customs and excise taxes. Other than sending its agents to collect taxes, however, the government in Piérola's opinion should refrain absolutely from any intervention in the national economy, leaving private capitalists and entrepreneurs completely unregulated in all their operations. More extreme in his classical economic liberalism than even Castilla, the naïve Piérola of 1869 in many ways resembled the romantic liberals of the José Simeón Tejeda school who sincerely believed that the unregulated structure of pure economic individualism would usher in an ideal human existence.

When the thirty-year-old Piérola assumed the duties of minister of the treasury in January 1869, the budgetary deficit approved for the coming year amounted to seventeen million *soles*. Piérola determined to enter at once into a bold economic arrangement which in theory would provide funds to cover the deficit, make possible additional investment in railroad and other public works projects, and allow the treasury to escape from its dependence on the guano consignees. In preparing his plans Piérola was closely advised by Luis Benjamín Cisneros,[6] at the time consul in Le Havre and later Peru's poet-laureate, and his brother Luciano Benjamín Cisneros,[7] a distinguished lawyer who had as one of his clients the French firm of Dreyfus and Company. The guiding spirit of the concern, Auguste Dreyfus, had arrived in Lima about the time Piérola became minister of the treasury, intent upon finding lucrative commercial opportunities for his French corporation. His ambitions, as it turned out, were more than fulfilled, for he found both fortune and love in Peru. By the time he died in France in 1879 he had accumulated a fortune of some seventy-five million francs and had been twice married to Peruvian ladies.

The complex, multi-faceted plans of Piérola, the Cisneros

brothers, and Dreyfus culminated in August 1869 in the signing of one of the most controversial documents in the economic history of Peru, the Dreyfus contract. This agreement provided that the Peruvian government would cease its dealings with the consignees to whom guano had previously been sold and deliver two million tons instead to the Dreyfus firm. The price of sixty *soles* per ton, which Dreyfus and Company agreed to pay for most of the guano delivered to it, was more favourable to Peru than that previously received from foreign consignees. The French corporation also agreed to advance at once 2,400,000 *soles* to the Peruvian government, to make monthly advances of 700,000 *soles* for one year, and to assume the obligations of servicing Peru's foreign debt. So long as the contract was in effect, Dreyfus and Company would have an exclusive franchise on the sale of guano in Europe and would also serve as the financial agents of Peru in France.

The defenders of the contract argued that it liberated Peru from the great variety of commitments with numerous consignees which had made it impossible to predict from year to year just how much the treasury could expect to receive from guano sales. Now, with a steady and predictable source of income assured, realistic economic planning leading to a balanced national budget would be possible. A group of Peruvian capitalists, however, headed by Manuel Pardo, objected strenuously to the contract and unsuccessfully challenged its validity before the supreme court. They argued that a situation more favourable to the overall economic development of the country would result from the sale of virtually all Peruvian guano to a corporation of native consignees which they proposed to form. Before the defeat of their campaign against the Dreyfus contract Pardo and his Peruvian capitalist friends conducted a skilful and well-publicized campaign which drew the attention of informed Peruvians away from political and philosophical issues, focusing it on the economic dispute. Angered by the opposition to his plans, which he considered a personal affront, Piérola developed an unrelenting animosity against Pardo.

With the Dreyfus contract a *fait accompli* and the treasury saved from bankruptcy, Piérola showed little concern over putting into operation the other announced features of his economic programme. He failed to implement the plans to curtail government expenditures which he had outlined to congress. He failed also to institute the balanced tax programme about which he had talked.

Convinced that in Dreyfus and Company he had struck an inexhaustible well of capital, Piérola contracted for huge new loans with the French firm. While the original contract was defensible, the new loan agreements were not, for they resulted in an unrealistically large debt for Peru as well as ruinous interest and commission rates.

In July 1871 the ebullient Piérola, after one of many personal clashes with the effervescent Balta – in one such dispute the president had attacked the minister of the treasury with a chair – resigned his cabinet post. Thereafter the hapless Balta proceeded with ever more reckless abandon in incurring new debts from the French firm. By the end of his term in 1872 he had saddled Peru with a foreign debt of some forty-nine million pounds sterling, approximately ten times the amount it had been when he assumed office.[8]

In fact, Balta was more a victim than a cause of the economic excesses of the period. He had the misfortune to be president at a time when Peru first entered a period of obsession with material progress. The profits of guano, of nitrates and copper, of utility companies, commercial concerns, and mushrooming banking enterprises had created a class of new wealth, located almost exclusively along the coast. The rapid rise to affluence had imbued the new rich with an unbounded confidence in a still brighter economic future. The spirit of the times was one of audacity and prodigality.[9] It is scarcely to be wondered at that the untutored Balta allowed himself to be swept along by the infectious spirit of easy and inevitable progress that had captured the far more sophisticated and better-educated Piérola.

Balta in particular came to believe that by criss-crossing Peru with railroads, the full economic potentialities of so richly-endowed a country could be readily realized, while at the same time anarchy and revolutionary activity would be stamped out. He was assured by many advisers that railways had been the main if not the sole cause of the incredible advance in United States economic activity immediately after the Civil War. Thus it seemed apparent to Balta that Peru should begin at once to take the steps that would soon enable it to rival the material accomplishments of the Great Republic of the North.

One of the most convincing advocates of railways as an all-purpose panacea was the North American Henry Meiggs,[10] some of whose business ventures had involved him in difficulties with the law in his native country. Shifting his operations to Chile, Meiggs had accumulated a considerable fortune by carrying out in that republic some of the most remarkable feats of railroad-building ever witnessed in Latin America and also by exhibiting a disregard for personal and business ethics that distinguished him even in highly competitive company. Turning his attention to Peru, in 1867 he supported the publication by Simón Camacho of a thick volume proposing the construction of a railroad system which, given the country's sparse population and lack of immediate possibility for heavy commercial transportation, was judged in certain circles to be preposterous. Meiggs, however, had a way of convincing doubters and in 1869, even before Balta became president, he signed, together with provisional executive Diez Canseco, a contract to build a railroad from Mollendo at the coast to Arequipa. This was only the beginning of Meiggs' projects, for he had come to Peru at the right time. In Balta and Piérola he found men willing to seek a realization overnight of the most ambitious ventures through the use of the money that Dreyfus and Company stood ready to lend.

In rapid succession the Balta government signed contracts with Meiggs to build railways from Arequipa to Puno, from Puno to Cuzco, and from the main seaport of Callao across the towering Andes to La Oroya, the heartland of the rich ore deposits of central Peru. Irrigation projects were neglected, education was neglected, sanitation facilities, industrial and manufacturing development were forgotten, concern with mining expansion was abandoned, and the collection of tax revenue was ignored as Peru poured all its energies and borrowed money, and committed the sum total of its dwindling guano reserves to the building of railroads which, although virtually unique in the triumph of engineering skill over obstacles of land transportation, could not possibly be profitably operated in the foreseeable future. Peru had begun a precipitous advance towards bankruptcy. Before the day of economic reckoning came, however, Peruvians were distracted by one of the most singular political campaigns in the entire history of the republic.

THE 1871–2 CAMPAIGN AND THE BIRTH OF 'CIVILISMO'

There was something new on the Peruvian political scene when the presidential campaign got under way in 1871. For the first time an organized, cohesive party with a consistent and also practical political philosophy and a broad programme of action stood ready to seek the presidency of its candidate. The party bore the name *Civilista* ('Civilianist' as opposed to militarist) and its candidate, named in April 1871 although Balta's term did not end until August of the following year, was Manuel Pardo.

The son of conservative statesman and writer Felipe Pardo, Manuel was born in Lima on 9 August 1834. His earliest years were spent in Chile, where his father was sometimes a political exile, sometimes the diplomatic representative of his government. The Pardo family returned to Lima in 1848, with the father serving briefly as Castilla's minister of foreign relations. Manuel was placed in the Guadalupe school, but, when his father objected to the liberalism of its instruction, was transferred to San Carlos where the conservative ideas of Bartolomé Herrera prevailed. In 1850 the Pardo family went to Europe, and Manuel studied both in Spain, at the University of Barcelona, and in Paris, where he was influenced by economic theories of state participation in and control over the economy. Returning to Peru in 1853, he soon began to establish a reputation both as a businessman and as a writer. In some of his most widely-read articles of this period he analyzed problems in the province of Jauja, complaining that most coastal Peruvians knew nothing about the sierra and worse still held all *serranos* in disdain. Pleading for a broadly-based Peruvian nationalism, he outlined plans for bringing about co-operation between coast and sierra.[11]

Interrupting his business and literary activities, Pardo became minister of the treasury for the dictator, Mariano Ignacio Prado, in 1866. In this post he concerned himself primarily with trying to create a permanent source of income which would liberate the administration from depending for its ordinary expenses on guano resources 'which are not eternal and whose exploitation would have been disrupted already if providence had not favoured Peru in the battle with Spain'.[12] Pardo's reforms were, of course, undone by the revolution that led to Balta's assumption of presidential power. The young man returned, however, to public life when the Society of Public Beneficence of Lima (*Sociedad de Beneficencia Pública de Lima*) elected him its president in 1868. By his spectacular success in revitalizing the Beneficence Society Pardo incurred the enmity of many clergymen. As a civilian-controlled, semi-official charitable organization, the Society was regarded by the Church as a serious rival in a field in which it had once held a virtual monopoly.[13]

In 1869 a hundred-member Junta of Notables, appointed by Balta, chose Pardo as mayor (*alcalde*) of Lima. Under his energetic administration of the capital city, streets were paved, the water supply and sanitation facilities were improved, better gas-light service was provided, and controls were placed on the prices of essential commodities. Pardo also levied municipal taxes on the well-to-do for the support of Lima's public schools.

Through his widely-acclaimed activities as president of the Beneficence Society and as mayor, Pardo won the devotion of Lima's masses. In addition, because of his family background, his education, his business success and his wealth, and also his marriage to one of Peru's richest ladies, Pardo had an assured place among the aristocracy. In a way, then, he was a living symbol of what he constantly advocated as Peru's way to greatness, that is, contact and co-operation among all social classes.[14] Moreover, because he was a born aristocrat but a self-made millionaire, his life and career presented a classic example of a new social phenomenon in Peru: the mutual assimilation of a traditional, well-born class and a rising group of the new rich.

Instrumental in its founding and almost automatically chosen as its first candidate, Pardo, 'the most reform-minded man of the élite . . ., and the most prudent of the innovators',[15] made of the *Civilista* Party a reflection of his own experience and political philosophy. In many ways the political amalgamation of an old aristocracy and a newly emerging capitalist class,[16] the *Civilista* Party espoused a significant part of the traditional liberal programme: it favoured decentralization and state support of education and opposed military and clerical intervention in politics. In shaping the programme of the new party, however, Pardo, who admired administrators more than philosophers and preferred to concern himself with the 'practical republic' rather than with theoretical Utopias, 'eliminated all of the abstract features of early liberalism . . .';[17] he gave 'scientific form and substance to the nebulous thought of the earlier liberals who had included such men as Sánchez Carrión, Luna Pizarro, José Gálvez. . . .'[18] Under his direction the *Civilista* Party was an instrument designed to achieve tangible progress on all fronts by avoiding old doctrinaire pitfalls and by placing political control not in the hands of a dictator, as Vivanco had been, or in those of an authoritarian, personalistic military manipulator 'such as Castilla, but rather in those of an open, Jeffersonian, natural aristocracy, an oligarchy of talent that enjoyed genuine popular support. In this Peru took a step, however imperfect, towards the evolution of republican government'.[19]

Pardo's carefully thought-out, fully-developed programme of government was in many fundamental respects opposed to the still inchoate and vaguely felt goals of Piérola. Although true to his conservative background, and also simply revealing his practical bent, in favouring firm rule by a relatively small group of talented men, Pardo did not attach to formal religion the same importance that most political conservatives did. In this respect he differed markedly from the ex-seminarian Piérola. Pardo hoped that a new mystique of progress, rather than traditional religious beliefs, would bind all social classes and geographic sectors together and thus facilitate Peru's evolution into a nation. To Pardo, many of the value judgements associated with Catholicism as customarily practised in Peru seemed to be impediments to the sort of progress he envisioned.

Progress, as Pardo saw it, depended not upon windfalls and the largesse of providence in endowing a country with resources. Rather, it depended upon the development of the natural virtue and skills of the entire populace. Unlike Piérola, Pardo was pessimistic about the short-term economic future of Peru. To the *Civilista* leader the veneer of wealth produced by guano, nitrates, and copper undermined the Peruvian character and delayed the day when the population would seriously go to work to develop a sound, self-sustaining, diversified economy. Over the long-term economic future of his country he was guardedly optimistic. Once Peruvians had passed through several generations of a practical educational system accessible to all, they would acquire, he believed, the capitalist skills and virtues, the incentives, the technological expertise, and the habits of using wealth to generate more wealth that would lead to balanced and genuine material development.

Piérola had spoken glibly about the feasibility of an instantaneous economic revolution, but Prado stressed the slow 'revolution in the hearts and minds of people' that could only come about gradually.[20] Pardo reasoned that while the country was preparing the way for the full development of its material potentialities, basically by training its human resources, it had to live within its means and sustain various measures of austerity. Certain pleasures and spectacular projects had to be postponed until the country could truly afford them. Forethought, planning, and discipline had to replace headless profligacy. Rather than hoping for a windfall tomorrow that would make it possible to pay for today's extravagance, frugality had to be practised today to make possible the extravagance of tomorrow.

In the Pardo programme as advanced by the *Civilista* Party there was an element of economic nationalism, something totally lacking in Piérola's economic blueprints. Pardo was by no means totally opposed to luring foreign capital to Peru. He simply felt that excessive reliance upon foreign loans and investments would cause Peruvians to become permanently inferior in economic matters. The *Civilista* programme differed also from Piérola's in urging an end to unchecked economic individualism and emphasizing the need for overall government economic planning and supervision. *Civilistas* even urged a mixed system, with the government participating directly with private entrepreneurs in developing certain sectors of the economy.

While Piérola had become almost as obsessed with military preparedness as Castilla had been, Pardo saw little need for armed might. To him a national guard that could be quickly mobilized was a more effective means of guaranteeing internal stability than a large standing army. An occasionally-mustered national guard, he also felt, would be presented with fewer temptations and opportunities to intervene in politics and could be more effectively controlled by civilian administrators than a permanent army. When it came to protecting Peruvian interests against threats from abroad he was willing to rely on a small, but thoroughly professional army. Above all else, as the means of defending Peruvian security, Pardo hoped to enter into alliances and treaties with sister republics. In the means through which they chose to protect national interests in foreign relations, Pardo and the *Civilistas* were to be guilty of one of their few radical departures from a sense of practical reality.

When elections to select the members of an electoral college were held in October 1871, Pardo won a spectacular triumph over the two rivals who had challenged him. Alarmed at the prospect of of a civilian president who was committed to reducing the permanent army, Balta and some of his military cronies decided at this late stage to put forward a new candidate, Antonio Arenas. A distinguished civilian statesman, Arenas was considered by conservative elements to be preferable to Pardo because of his favourable attitudes towards the military and the Church. Among those who extended unstinting support to him was Nicolás de Piérola, who thereby widened the already broad gulf between himself and Manuel Pardo. But despite the support of Piérola and others, the Balta administration was not able to manipulate a victory for Arenas in the electoral college. Instead, that body in May 1872 decided in favour of Pardo.

At this point Balta, influenced by his secretary, Ricardo Palma and the trusted Yankee entrepreneur, Henry Meiggs, among others, appears to have made a reluctant but firm decision not to prevent Pardo's inauguration in August. Dismayed by Balta's attitude, his Minister of War, General Tomás Gutiérrez and his brothers Marceliano and Silvestre, and various other military officials hatched a plot to depose the president and block Pardo's assumption of power. The conspirators struck on 22 July, arresting Balta, confining him to prison, and declaring Tomás Gutiérrez provisional president. Pardo hastily fled from Lima, boarded a fishing boat and headed out to sea, shortly encountering the warship *Huáscar* under the command of a widely-respected naval officer, Miguel Grau. Following a conference with Pardo, Grau organized a powerful naval opposition movement against the Gutiérrez coup.

Meantime in Lima an aroused people had also taken up arms against the crude attempt to prevent their favourite candidate from becoming president. With the streets of Lima a battleground, word reached the national palace that the populace of Callao had also risen. Silvestre Gutiérrez rushed to the railway station, hoping to proceed to the port to calm the situation. At the station, however, he was killed by rioting mobs. One of the worst orgies of violence that Peru was ever to experience was underway.

In rapid succession José Balta was shot down in cold blood in his prison cell by some of the soldiers entrusted to guard him, and Tomás Gutiérrez, trying to escape from a capital city that had arisen *en masse* against him, was apprehended by the mobs. Not content with killing him on the spot, Gutiérrez's captors proceeded to mutilate the corpse. After the heart had been cut out, the naked body was hung from one of the Cathedral towers overlooking the Plaza de Armas. From the other tower was suspended the naked corpse of Silvestre. The rioters then decapitated the two corpses and, when the headless bodies fell to the ground, burned them in a huge urn, all the while adding a bit of cannibalism to the grisly rites they were performing. Soon another body was thrown into the urn, that of Marceliano Gutiérerez who had been apprehended and executed some distance outside of Lima.

To some writers these events of 27 July represented the defence by the people of the inviolability of free suffrage, of popular sovereignty against despotism. Less romantic observers have regarded the July violence as simply the work of a criminal mob. Jorge Basadre is doubtlessly correct in attributing the grim events of that July day to the sense of outrage produced by the murder of Balta, mistakenly assumed to have been directly ordered by the Gutiérrez brothers, and above all to the presence in Lima of an undesirable transient population attracted by the Andean railroad project. 'This element converted itself into a senseless, heedless mob, led on by base passions and not by any exalted ideas'.[21]

The immediate effect of the ill-fated attempt of Gutiérrez to seize power was to justify in the popular mind all Pardo's campaign of criticism of military intervention in politics. The mere name *Civilista* was enough to arouse the enthusiasm of the masses in 1872 after the manner in which militarism had been disgraced by the Gutiérrez brothers and their cohorts. More than ever Pardo was the hero of the hour, and an exuberant but this time happy and peaceful mob joined with the aristocracy in the huge procession that accompanied the *Civilista* leader to the national palace immediately upon his return to Lima.

THE PARDO ADMINISTRATION, 1872–6

Commanding a widespread and even frenzied popular support not enjoyed by any previous executive, Pardo was inaugurated in a metropolis that on the surface seemed as gay, bustling and affluent as at any time in its history. Many of the happy scenes typical of a carefree Lima at play during this period have been captured by the great artist of Indian and Negro origins, Pancho Fierro (1803–79).

His water-colour paintings of processions, of well-dressed, prominent creoles, of military officers at dances, of Negro and creole religious brotherhoods, of soldiers in parades, and of bullfights in the famed Plaza de Acho suggest a pleasure-seeking and pleasure-finding existence.[22] Soon, however, the people of Lima were to feel the pinch of the worst depression that the republic of Peru had suffered, and Pardo was to find his initial popularity barely adequate to enable him to weather the economic storm.

Presenting his first message to congress in September 1872, Pardo stated flatly that the economy was in ruins.[23] Because the budget was alarmingly unbalanced it would be necessary to limit expenditures and to introduce many new taxes. Pardo insisted that Peru's financial troubles could not be solved through additional loans. The country, he maintained, had already over-extended its credit, and must begin conscientiously to pay off existing debts while scrupulously avoiding new ones. The following April he painted a still less encouraging picture of the economy. He explained to congress that all profits from guano sales had to go to meet payments on the foreign debt and that no income from this source was available to defray internal expenses. The treasury lacked funds to continue the public works already begun or even to meet the salaries of a bureaucracy which had grown unjustifiably large during the previous administration. Twenty thousand labourers were unemployed, Pardo concluded, and the number was likely to grow. By the next year, 1874, the fiscal situation was worse still, and the government was forced to resort to the issue of paper money inadequately backed by metallic reserves. The nightmare of an unstable, rapidly depreciating currency had begun and Peru would not awaken from it until the end of the century.

The Dreyfus contract expired in 1874 and Peru was free to seek other arrangements for disposal of its guano. However, the price of this fertilizer was declining and its reserves were nearly depleted. To make the situation worse, guano was competing in the international market with nitrates, a newly-popular source of fertilizer which was just beginning to be exploited in Peru. In 1875 the government nationalized a large part of the country's nitrate resources, hoping to control sales so as to minimize the disadvantage of guano-nitrate competition. Pardo also hoped that through nationalization the nitrate industry could be so controlled as to provide a regular and predictable source of income, one third of which would be used to finance the costs of internal administration, with the remainder going to service the foreign debt so that the country might improve its credit. Given the prevailing circumstances, however, with the economic crisis worsening not only in Peru but in other parts of the world as well, the hopes that Pardo placed in the reorganized nitrate industry were impossible of realization. All that he had to show for the nationalization decree were added government obligations for indemnity payments that promptly fell in arrears.[24]

Despite the government's fiscal problems, private individuals still encountered excellent economic opportunities in the country. Some of the three thousand European immigrants who came to Peru during the Pardo régime, among them English and Frenchmen, Germans and Italians, founded successful fishing and small commercial firms, although the government's intention that the new arrivals should come to constitute a small and independent yeoman farmer class was not fulfilled. At the same time that the government's economic distresses multiplied, the business operations of an Irishman, W. R. Grace, expanded dramatically. Launching his Peruvian career in 1850 in a British–Peruvian commercial establishment, Grace had soon become a director of the firm. After marrying Lillian Gilchrist, the daughter of a Yankee merchant-marine captain, he had gone to the United States, leaving his younger brother Michael in charge of Peruvian operations. In 1862 he established an export-import company in New York. By the end of the 1860's the company had obtained its first ship, the *Lily Grace*, and was also expanding its sphere of activities in Peru. W. R. Grace and Company in 1871 acquired its first industrial plant in that country, the Vitarte textile mill situated in the foothills a few miles east of Lima. Within the next ten years the Grace interests came into possession of vast sugar estates and established Peru's first large-scale sugar refining plants.

However much various private concerns prospered during the period, the government remained on the verge of bankruptcy. One set of statistics suffices to attest to the seriousness of the situation In 1869 guano sales amounted to over four million pounds sterling, and service on the foreign debt came to one million pounds. In 1875 guano sales earned only 2·6 million while service on the foreign debt had climbed to 2·57 million pounds.[25] In view of the adverse economic conditions which he inherited and which plagued him throughout his term, Pardo's contribution to the reform and expansion of educational facilities is all the more remarkable.

A Peruvian writer has stated: 'If Bolívar gave us political independence and Castilla racial liberty, and if Balta established freedom of enterprise, it is Pardo who liberated the people from ignorance'.[26] Certainly it was the intention of Pardo to perform this essential task of liberation. He was as vitally concerned with education as Argentina's famous 'Schoolmaster President', Domingo Faustino Sarmiento, who governed at about the same time (1868-74). If Pardo was somewhat less successful than Sarmiento, it was owing to his government's lack of funds and also to the attitude of the Catholic Church, a far more powerful institution in Peru than in Argentina.

Pardo's great ambition was to establish a system of state-supported and controlled primary education that ultimately would be both free and universal. Through primary education Pardo felt that each Peruvian citizen could learn to develop and to protect his own human dignity and at the same time to contribute far more effectively towards the material and cultural development of the country. So long as the populace remained illiterate, the president insisted, Peru could never hope to emerge from its backwardness.

The national congress did not give to Pardo the power he sought to establish centralized government control over the primary educational system. As a result of this congressional setback to the president public primary schools fell mainly under the control of municipalities, many of whose officials did not share Pardo's interest in education. However, Pardo accomplished other notable items in his educational programme. Because of his interest in preparing the Indian for assimilation into Peruvian society, he ordered the founding of Peru's first workshop school. Located in the sierra community of Ayacucho, its purpose was to teach Indians industrial skills. Eight annual government scholarships were provided for the school.[27] Pardo further decreed that all Indians must study the *Gramática y diccionario español-quechua* of José de Anchorena as a means of learning Spanish. A thousand copies of the work were printed at government expense and distributed among the natives of the sierra as an initial step in Pardo's endeavour to prepare them for citizenship.[28]

Pardo also turned his attention to higher education. Under his urging the faculty of political and administrative sciences was established in San Marcos, its purpose being to impart higher education of a more practical, utilitarian nature than that provided by the faculty of letters. Pardo's stimulus led in addition to the founding of a normal school for women in Lima and of two normal schools, one for men, the other for women, in each of three provincial cities: Cajamarca, Junin and Cuzco. The president had the further satisfaction of witnessing the opening in Lima of schools of applied agriculture, of arts and crafts, and of civil and mining engineering.

For a variety of reasons many churchmen opposed Pardo's educational reforms. Even though the president insisted on including religion and ecclesiastical history in the primary school curriculum, clergymen in general felt that the overall educational purpose desired by Pardo was too practical and not sufficiently attentive to spiritual values. In particular they objected to the periodical *El Educador Popular*, regarded by Pardo as an essential element in his educational programme. Printed in New York under the direction of José Arnaldo Márquez (1830–1906), a much-travelled statesman, poet, a translator of Shakespeare, and the inventor of a linotype machine, *El Educador Popular* began to circulate in Peru in mid-1873. Intended as a teaching aid for primary and secondary teachers, the periodical included complete courses in a variety of subjects, educational pictures, moral stories for children, hints on sanitation and household management, and useful information on a wide selection of other topics. Charging that *El Educador* did not place sufficient emphasis on religion, that it ignored the soul of the child and stressed 'unimportant, superfluous education', clergymen denounced the periodical from the pulpit and urged the faithful to seize and destroy all copies of it.[29]

In addition to not wishing to see their monopoly over instruction jeopardized, many Peruvian ecclesiastics questioned the usefulness of mass education, regarding it in the liberal nineteenth century as more likely to corrupt than to uplift the soul of the child. They further objected that the members of the Polish, German, French and United States teaching missions which Pardo brought to Peru to help to improve educational standards, although almost all were Catholic, were in general excessively liberal in their views and inclined to base their instruction on scientific knowledge rather than on the wisdom of St Thomas.[30] In addition churchmen, especially missionaries, were alarmed by Pardo's plans to assimilate the Indian. They felt that the aborigine's spiritual purity could best be protected by his remaining isolated from contact with the urban civilization of the coast and by his continuing to converse in native dialects rather than in Spanish.

As well as giving offence to clergymen, many of whom were friends of Piérola and used religion as a mask in launching politically-inspired attacks against the government, Pardo had difficulty with the military. Choosing to rely on an armed citizenry organized in a national guard, Pardo reduced the standing army to 2,500 men, thereby driving into at least temporary unemployment some 75 per cent. of those previously enlisted in the military service. Pardo also offended naval officials when, pleading lack of funds, he broke a contract with an English shipyard for the purchase of two warships. The two vessels, already under construction, were subsequently acquired by Chile.

Numerous influential Peruvians, soldiers as well as civilians, were understandably disgruntled by Pardo's attempts to economize on military preparedness. This seemed especially rash since Pardo's nitrate nationalization decree had offended powerful Chilean capitalists who had gained control over a good deal of the industry in what was then southern Peru. Pardo apparently assumed that the likelihood of signing an alliance with Argentina, hostile to Chile at the time because of a boundary dispute, together with an offensive-defensive treaty which had been secretly signed with Bolivia in 1873 and had quickly come to be rather widely known, gave Peru all the protection it required against the possibility of Chilean military retaliation. Critics of the government's military and foreign policies claimed that Argentina as a potential and Bolivia as an actual ally were untrustworthy, and they recalled with approval Castilla's admonition that when Chile bought one naval ship Peru should purchase two.

By the middle of his term, Pardo had alienated the clergy and the army, two groups that had long since proved their skill in revolutionary plotting. On 22 August 1874, he was given a good indication of the dangers inherent in this situation. On that day Captain Juan Boza, who had been released from the army as a result of Pardo's retrenchment programme, took a shot, happily poorly aimed, at the president as he was leaving the national palace.

As Boza was firing, his fellow conspirators shouted 'Long live religion, death to Pardo'.[31] Nor was this all. Pardo had to face military uprisings in Huancayo, Canta, Ayacucho, Arequipa and other parts of the country. The old conspirator, Vivanco, led his final attempt at revolution. After Pardo crushed his insurrection, Vivanco went into exile in Chile where shortly afterwards he died. The main spirit behind the military uprisings, however, had not been the old army caudillo, Vivanco. It had been the young civilian caudillo, Piérola.

Already hostile to Pardo for a variety of reasons, some no more exalted than personal ambition, others the result of conflicting economic, political and religious ideas, Piérola began in October 1872 to fret over what he considered a grievous insult to his honour. *Civilista* deputies had introduced charges against all sixteen ex-ministers of the Balta regime, accusing them of responsibility for Peru's economic plight. The main target of the parliamentary attack was Balta's one-time minister of the treasury, Piérola. The senate eventually absolved the ex-ministers, but only after a series of intemperate speeches and calumnies had aroused the passions both of *Civilistas* and *Pierolistas*. After this incident Piérola had gone to Chile to enlist aid in the revolution he had resolved to lead against Pardo. To Chilean capitalists he promised more advantageous concessions in the nitrate and other industries than they could expect from Pardo. At the same time he entered into communication with many discontented military officers in Peru, urging them to insurrection. The skilful hand of Piérola was behind most of the barrack uprisings that plagued the Pardo administration.

The affronted ex-minister also tried his fortune in directing the revolution himself. Leaving Chile he led an uprising against Pardo in southern Peru. However, the masses did not arise as he had anticipated to proclaim him their providential leader. Pardo placed himself at the head of the government troops and crushed the insurrection. Piérola returned to his exile in Chile where he promptly resumed his plotting, as well as an affair with his French lady-love who happened then to be in Chile.

Because of the uninterrupted turmoil which had marred his administration and also the well-known fact that Piérola was continuing his attempts to incite revolution, Pardo became convinced that only a military man could hope to maintain order during the next presidential term. Thus a civilian President, Pardo, used his influence to persuade his *Civilista* Party to choose as its candidate for the 1876 elections General Mariano Ignacio Prado. So far as Pardo was concerned Prado was, as military men went, not without merit. The two men had worked well together when Pardo had served during Prado's dictatorship as minister of the treasury beginning in 1866.

Prado, as the *Civilista* candidate, was opposed by Admiral Lizardo Montero. In the elections, marred by violence, the General, supported by the outgoing administration, easily prevailed over the Admiral. In a revealing commentary on political conditions of the time, a Lima newspaper expressed the opinion that Prado had won because his partisans were armed with modern Winchester carbines, whereas Montero's supporters were equipped only with revolvers.[32]

THE PRADO ADMINISTRATION AND THE OUTBREAK OF THE WAR OF THE PACIFIC, 1876–9

Prado assumed his presidential duties in August 1876, governing a population that, according to a recently-completed census, had risen to 2,699,106. Many of these Peruvians, already plagued by their country's internal crisis, watched helplessly as further political and economic deterioration added to their distresses and uncertainty. Political troubles began almost at once with a quarrel between the new president and the *Civilista* majority in congress. As the dispute grew bitter the friends of the executive, hoping to intimidate the legislature, organized a 'spontaneous mass meeting' at which speakers hurled insults against the congress and even demanded the death of ex-president Pardo. The mob responded more enthusiastically to the demagoguery than the organizers of the meeting had anticipated and, out of hand, proceeded to the house of Pardo and began to storm it. Informed of the ugly turn of events President Prado arose from a sick bed and dashed to Pardo's house where he succeeded in calming the rioters. Had the president arrived ten minutes later, the ex-president might have been assassinated.

Naturally resentful over these events, *Civilista* congressmen unleashed a tirade of criticism against Prado and brought about the fall of his cabinet. The loss of support from the *Civilistas*, his original allies, did not gain Prado the backing of Piérola's partisans.

The harassed president was, in fact, more and more blatantly denounced by the *Pierolistas*, who took the line that only their absent leader could save Peru. In October Piérola once again set out from Chile, trying to stir up a revolution in southern Peru. Prado easily suppressed the insurrection. The next May, however, some friends of Piérola seized the warship *Huáscar* in Callao and sailed to the south to join him. A group of army officials simultaneously proclaimed Piérola to be the rightful president of Peru.

The suppression of this revolution presented Prado with grave difficulties. One problem was that the other naval ships in Callao were in such a state of disrepair that it was a week before they could be made ready to put to sea in pursuit of the *Huáscar*.[33] Eventually the president did manage to restore order, but at this point the *Civilistas* launched an armed attack in Lima against the administration. It, too, was suppressed and ex-president Pardo, blamed for complicity, fled to Chile.

The situation improved slightly when in February 1878 Piérola, abandoning for the moment his plots and schemes, left Chile and went to Europe. The following September Pardo returned to Peru, having been elected senator for Junín. Reconciled with the president, Pardo warned him of the imminent danger of a Chilean attack against Peru. In the senate Pardo also warned his countrymen to desist from their financial follies. In one of his most brilliant addresses he explained much of his economic beliefs:

> We suffer from an infirmity, the horror of taxes. This is a grave sickness. . . . Gentlemen, taxation is not bad in itself . . . taxes are a symbol of work, of productive labour. . . . The lack of taxes is far from being something that is good. . . . One of the greatest evils that can overtake a society is to live off providential resources. . . . When during a long period of time an individual's or a society's aspirations are satisfied by favours, or by luck, or by providence, the habits of work, the capacity for effort, for sacrifice, the will to set oneself against obstacles, are all lost . . . that which remains is only ambition, while the legitimate means to satisfy it disappear.[34]

Very few heeded either Pardo's warning about an attack from Chile or his advice that Peruvians should assume the burdens of taxation and by hard work restore some balance to the economy. Rather than seriously concerning themselves over the plight of their country, Piérola's supporters exhausted their energies in a campaign of vile vituperation against Pardo. Setting the tone of this campaign Pedro José Calderón in the 2 September 1878 edition of the pro-clerical, *Pierolista* organ *La Patria*, had addressed himself to Pardo and written: 'I will kill you in the end, but I will do it when no honourable mouth can fail to cheer your assassination.'

The following 16 November, only one day after he had completed delivery of the notable address pleading for economic responsibility, Pardo was shot and mortally wounded as he entered the senate chamber. The assassin was Melchor Montoya, a sergeant who blamed the ex-president's military policies for blocking his promotion to officer rank. Giving the lie at the moment of death to the many clergymen who had delighted in calling him an impious heretic, Pardo gasped out, 'A confessor . . . I pardon all, even my assassin'. A priest rushed to hear his confession and a moment later Pardo expired. He was only forty-four years of age.

The tragic death of the man who was as great a statesman as Peru has produced sealed the political doom of the country for years to come. *Civilistas* blamed Piérola for being, at least indirectly, responsible for the assassination. Only the flimsiest circumstantial evidence linked the wily caudillo to the crime and responsible historians of the twentieth century have not discovered any material that suggests Piérola was the intellectual author of the deed. Nevertheless, *Civilistas* continued to nourish suspicions about Piérola and certainly they never forgave his followers for the assassination. The *Pierolistas*, on the other hand, never pardoned the *Civilistas* for the charges of assassination recklessly hurled against their leader, nor for the fact that after Pardo's death the wife of Piérola was for a time imprisoned in a senseless act of vindictiveness. The assassination of Manuel Pardo inflicted on Peru a wound which intellectual and political figures even after the passing of generations would not allow entirely to heal.

Under the administration of the luckless President Prado, Peru's economic débâcle continued to match its political deterioration. Payment on the foreign debt had temporarily to be suspended in 1876 and a new guano arrangement entered into with the London firm of Raphael and Sons provided only a temporary fiscal respite.[35] After 1877 the Prado régime came to rely almost exclusively on unbacked paper money. By the beginning of 1879, government expenses were going up and income was decreasing.

This, then, was the desperate situation when word came that Chilean forces had begun hostilities against Bolivia.

Chile's legal justification for initiating warfare lay in the fact that the Bolivian President, Hilarión Daza, had, in violation of treaty agreements, raised taxes on nitrate exports. Most of Bolivia's nitrate industry was at the time in the hands of Chilean investors and they justifiably refused to pay the increased imposts. The Daza government thereupon ordered the seizure of the largest Chilean-controlled nitrate operation on Bolivian soil, located at Antofagasta. Chile dispatched an amphibious force to occupy Antofagasta and the War on the Pacific had begun.

If Peru chose to honour its 'secret' alliance of 1873 with Bolivia, then automatically it would become involved in the war. Immediately a strong pacifist element in Lima began to advocate that the treaty be ignored and that Peru avoid war at all costs because of her lack of preparedness. The influential newspaper *El Comercio* urged Peruvian neutrality and *La Tribuna* even recommended the signing of a pact with Chile.

Responding to the pacifist sentiments in his country and also personally hoping to prevent war, President Prado sent the historian and diplomat, José Antonio Lavalle, to Santiago as the head of a mission which was to try to find a formula for maintaining peace. These efforts failed because the Peruvian negotiators became convinced that if they did not come to Bolivia's aid that unreliable country might quickly reach terms with Chile and actually join with it in despoiling Peru of its Tarapacá nitrate lands. At the last minute, then, Peru failed to disavow its treaty with Bolivia. As a consequence Chile declared war on Peru on 3 April 1879.

The fundamental cause of the War of the Pacific was the mounting power and prestige, the economic and political stability of Chile on the one hand and the weakness, the political and economic deterioration of Bolivia and Peru on the other. Both Bolivia and Peru had valuable nitrate lands which they seemed unable to utilize effectively because of internal disorder. Circumstances seem to have destined Chile to despoil its inept sister republics.

INTRIGUE AND PRONOUNCEMENTS BEHIND THE LINES:
HEROISM AND DEFEAT ON THE FRONT, 1879–81

Reluctantly involved in war, President Prado at once dispatched

José Arnaldo Márquez on an all-important mission to Argentina. If that republic could be drawn into hostilities against its traditional enemy Chile, then the prospects of Bolivia and Peru might be bright after all. By the time Márquez arrived in Buenos Aires, however, it was already too late for him to achieve his purpose. When in the early 1870's war with Chile over boundary disputes had seemed highly likely, Argentina had desired an alliance with Peru. Although Pardo had responded favourably to the idea, his and the succeeding Prado régimes had pursued the matter with vacillation and ineptness and thus no treaty had been signed. By the time the War of the Pacific began Argentina and Chile were well on the way towards resolving the most serious of their boundary questions and the Buenos Aires government no longer had to assume troublesome commitments with Peru in order to serve its national interests.[36]

Peru's diplomatic rebuff, combined with the financial mismanagement that had begun at the time of Castilla's government, the loss of naval power under Pardo, and the political turmoil occasioned by the *Civilista–Pierolista* feuds, made a Chilean victory inevitable. Awareness of the overwhelming odds in its favour undoubtedly influenced the Santiago government's decision to declare war. For a time, however, some remarkable feats of military valour challenged the inexorable flow of events and provided Peruvians with more than a glimmer of hope.[37]

At first it was Miguel Grau of Piura, a friend of the late Manuel Pardo and the leader of the naval opposition to the 1872 Gutiérrez coup, who kept Peruvian hopes alive. Although Peru's most modern warship, the *Independencia*, was lost in the first important naval engagement of the war, the battle of Iquique on 21 May 1879, Grau saved his ship, the *Huáscar*. During the next four and a half months he became the scourge of the Chilean navy, performing prodigies that prevented the enemy from obtaining the effective control of the sea that its superior naval power should have guaranteed from the outset. Ranging up and down the coast of Chile, capturing cargo ships, destroying port facilities, bombarding Antofagasta, he managed with what seemed diabolical cunning to escape the always pursuing Chilean warships.

Briefly interrupting his operations in early June, Grau returned to Callao to pick up supplies and overhaul his ships. On 6 July, taking farewell of his family with the presentiment that he would never see them again, he once more set to sea. Four days later he surprised the Chilean blockaders of Iquique, captured one of their ships, and then miraculously escaped when the enemy rushed additional war vessels to the area. He captured a frigate at Antofagasta and wrought havoc in the ports of Chañaral and Caldera. He captured the transport ship *Rimac* and again bombarded Antofagasta, silencing its powerful shore batteries. Next he attacked the ports of Huásco, Coquimbo and Tongoy. Then on the morning of 8 October the Chilean fleet finally caught up with him off the point of Angamos, some forty miles north of Antofagasta. It was one ship against five and the battle lasted less than two hours. The command tower of the *Huáscar* was hit and the body of Grau was blown to pieces. A moment later the second-in-command, Elías Aguirre, was killed. The carnage of officers and men continued and when the command finally fell on Lieutenant Pedro Garezón he gave the order to open the valves. Just as it was being boarded by the Chileans the *Huáscar* sank. 'Purification by blood, expiation by suffering,' one of Peru's finest historians has written, 'are the rules in the secular as well as in the religious realm . . . by his blood Grau offered a sacrifice for all the follies and weaknesses of Peru'.[38]

The death of Grau meant that Peru had lost its power upon the seas and therefore the war with Chile. Once again, however, heroic action this time on land, delayed the moment of reckoning. On 27 November Peruvian forces inflicted a stunning defeat on the Chileans at Tarapacá. By the end of the day the Chileans had not only been routed, but had fled some five miles before the shoeless Peruvian soldiers. In the engagement Andrés A. Cácares and Francisco Bolognesi emerged as new Peruvian heroes. Their exploits and their sacrifices would soon rival those of Grau. Still, their actions at Tarapacá had produced only a sterile victory. The Peruvian troops could not live from the land in the desert region and their ammunition was virtually exhausted. Their government, lacking seapower, was in no position to send supplies or reinforcements. The Chileans, on the other hand, were well supplied and able to renew the campaign at once. Peruvian commanders were compelled to order their forces to fall back upon Tacna and Arica.

Shortly before the battle of Tarapacá President Prado had left his troops in southern Peru and returned to Lima. There he found a disturbing situation. Congress had refused to vote taxes to support the war effort, determining instead to rely on printing new paper money. The populace was discouraged over the death of Grau, comprehending what Chile's control of the sea implied. Piérola, who had now returned to Lima, and other prominent citizens, reluctant to bury old political grudges and perhaps also convinced that Prado lacked the capacity and resolution to direct a successful war effort, refused to serve as cabinet officials. Shaken by conditions in the capital, Prado sailed for Europe on 18 December 1879. The president was well acquainted in European financial circles and perhaps sincerely convinced that only he could succeed, through on-the-spot negotiations, in obtaining the large foreign loans and new ships which might yet snatch victory from defeat. Prado had not anticipated the consequences of his departure. Suspicious that their president had fled the country in cowardice, the majority of the population of Lima supported an uprising on 21 December which proclaimed Piérola president of Peru. Installed two days later in the national palace, Piérola promptly declared Prado a traitor to his country. When Prado arrived in Europe he did not have the prestige of the presidency and banking circles were unwilling to deal with him. Prado did not, in fact, try very hard to obtain aid for his country. Furious at Piérola who had refused to co-operate with him in Peru even in the midst of war, he decided to do nothing in Europe that might benefit even indirectly the new revolutionary president.

By the time Piérola arrogated to himself control of the government and of the war effort, Peru had already lost control over much of its nitrate lands. It had also lost, for all practical purposes, the assistance of Bolivia whose President, Daza, had, after a few disastrous military engagements, decided to spend the remainder of the war in Europe. As the Chilean troops continued to advance, Piérola devoted more time to composing dramatic pronouncements predicting spectacular victories than to attending to the needs of his army in the south. Although Andrés Cáceres, a hero of the battle of Tarapacá, and Lizardo Montero, the admiral who had run against Prado in 1876, exhibited commendable valour and tactical skill, Peruvian troops were defeated at Tacna on 6 May 1880. For a moment the Peruvians had seemed close to winning the battle, but the needed reinforcement failed to arrive. When he realized that defeat was certain, Colonel Francisco Bolognesi called on his men to fight to the last cartridge. Setting the example himself, Bolognesi fired the last bullet from his pistol after being sent reeling to the ground by his mortal wounds. Peru had acquired another martyr hero and sustained a further military setback. The Chileans, unimpressed by Piérola's continued outpouring of ringing pronouncements, pushed on relentlessly. On 7 June they administered a crushing defeat on a vastly out-numbered Peruvian force at Arica.

Taking advantage of their control of the sea, the Chileans now prepared an amphibious operation and on 20 November landed a large force at Pisco which immediately took up the cry of 'On to Lima!' Piérola set up the capital's first line of defence at San Juan, adjoining Chorillos in the environs of Lima. He stretched his troops out along the coast where they were needlessly subjected to a merciless bombardment from the Chilean navy. It was the usual story when the Chileans attacked the line on 13 January 1881. New heroes like Guillermo Billinghurst, who had previously demonstrated his skill at political plotting in the interests of his friend Piérola, and Miguel Iglesias, who was ultimately destined to arrange peace terms with Chile, joined the veteran Andrés Cáceres in a display of inspiring valour; but the artillery, commanded by inexperienced officers, was ineffective, and the troops, equipped with rifles of two different calibres, frequently had the wrong ammunition. Chilean reinforcements were pressed into battle at the right moment, while those of Peru were not properly utilized. Once again the Peruvians retreated. That night the victorious Chilean troops rioted, burning, sacking and looting Chorillos where many members of the Peruvian aristocracy maintained summer seaside estates. The following night the invaders pillaged and burned Barranco. Between them and Lima itself there now remained only an improvised Peruvian line at Miraflores.

On 15 January the Miraflores defenders, made up mainly of untrained civilians, were overcome in a bloody slaughter. Piérola displayed great courage, passing time and again up and down the battle lines exposing himself to enemy fire. 'But he never gave an effective order or had an idea. Six thousand well-armed reinforcements never entered the fray because no one gave the order. Piérola succeeded only in demonstrating that it takes more than putting on a military uniform and Prussian boots to become a general'.[39] Among the many Peruvians who fought heroically at Miraflores and died in a vain endeavour was a son of Castilla, another of Vivanco, and another, the first-born, of Iglesias.[40] Immediately after the defeat at Miraflores, Piérola withdrew into the interior. The Chileans occupied Lima on 17 January, subjecting the city to a reign of terror. When they finally withdrew in 1884, much of the city was in shambles, including the national library with only 738 books remaining of the fifty-eight thousand volumes it had boasted when the occupation began.

A DIVIDED PERU SEEKS PEACE WITH CHILE, 1881-3

From the headquarters he established at Ayacucho Piérola at first refused to admit defeat. He named Andrés Cáceres, who had been wounded in the battle of Miraflores and had been hidden for a time in Lima by the Jesuit fathers, commander of the central interior region. Lizardo Montero was appointed commander of the north, with headquarters in Cajamarca.

Meantime in Lima an assembly of notables had come together and, deciding to ignore the claims of Piérola, named Francisco García Calderón as president. With the consent of the Chilean forces of occupation, García Calderón, who had been Balta's first minister of the treasury, was installed in temporary presidential quarters at Magdalena, a suburb of Lima. A short time later in the same month of March a congress was assembled in near-by Chorillos. Made up mainly of *Civilistas* who supported García Calderón, it declared null and void all acts and decrees of the Piérola dictatorship.

From Lima Ricardo Palma smuggled a series of letters to his friend Piérola in Ayacucho. He complained that García Calderón spent all of his time courting the daughter of the Chilean who had been his country's counsel in Arica for twenty-four years. And he railed against the conduct of his fellow Limeños:

In our indolent and lazy Lima not a straw is moving. It seems that we begin to accustom ourselves to the permanent occupation of the Chileans, as already some four or five natives of Lima have entered into marriage with them. Here the people are resigned to their ignominy, and no one wishes to emerge from it. . . . It is not munitions and arms that we lack, it is patriotism, virility and virtue.[41]

Limeños were not really so shameful in their conduct as Palma implied. What most annoyed Palma was that the majority of men

147

who supported García Calderón were *Civilistas*. For this offence the staunch young *Pierolista*, who stood at the threshold of a brilliant literary career, could not forgive them. Nor was it true that the president devoted himself to his romance, which culminated shortly in matrimony, to the exclusion of matters of state. He bravely and resolutely sought to withstand Chilean demands for territorial cession as the price for ending the war. For a time it even seemed that García Calderón might succeed in this, for he had the backing of the United States Secretary of State, James G. Blaine, and of his envoy to Peru, Stephen A. Hurlbut.

Blaine hoped to obtain nitrate concessions for United States capitalists in the southern Peruvian territory that Chile desired to annex as the spoils of war. But he hid this economic interest in the peace terms between Peru and Chile and proclaimed the high-sounding principle that in the American Hemisphere transfer of territory based on force should not be tolerated. Blaine's plans for obtaining Peruvian nitrate concessions rested, of course, on Peru's retaining its southern lands, and thus García Calderón was encouraged to hope that the United States would not permit Chile to despoil his country of territory. As a result the *Civilista*-supported president maintained such a firm attitude in his dealings with the Chileans that in November 1881 he was arrested by the army of occupation authorities and sent to Santiago where he and his family suffered grave privations.

The protection by the United States which the unfortunate García Calderón had been led to expect never materialized. When Blaine was replaced by Frederick T. Frelinghuysen as Secretary of State after the assassination of President James Garfield the United States lost interest in the whole affair and abandoned Peru to its fate. Thus Blaine's policies produced only needless delay in arranging peace terms, the prolonging of the Chilean occupation, and the imprisonment of García Calderón.[42] That aggrieved individual never forgave the United States for its War-of-the-Pacific diplomacy,[43] nor did his sons, Francisco and Ventura García Calderón Rey, who would in the next generation become two of Peru's most eminent intellectuals and writers.

The luck of Piérola in Ayacucho ran out at about the same time as that of García Calderón in Lima. The chronically restive Arequipa had already pronounced against him. Then, when the Chileans arrested García Calderón, Lizandro Montero, supposed to be Piérola's agent in the north, pronounced against the Ayacucho government, proclaiming himself president. Shortly afterwards Montero went to Arequipa and took charge of its several thousand troops. When Cáceres, in charge of the guerrilla army (*montoneros*) of central Peru also declared against him, Piérola gave up. In a resolution issued in Tarma on 28 November he renounced all claims to the presidency, complaining that the treachery of Montero and Cáceres had crushed his hopes just when 'with new supplies already accumulated and in co-operation with our ally Bolivia, we were about to undertake the final plan of operations against the enemy'.[44]

Cáceres in the central sierra won a series of astounding but relatively small-scale military victories and entertained wild delusions about weakening the Chilean forces to the point that peace could ultimately be attained without loss of territory. Montero in Arequipa, totally out of touch with the true facts of the situation, still believed that the United States would save Peru from territorial despoilment and was determined that hostilities must meanwhile be continued. But Miguel Iglesias, a former minister of war for Piérola and a hero of the battle of San Juan, realized that Peru must bow to reality and sign a treaty with Chile based upon loss of territory. Otherwise the task of reconstruction would only be unnecessarily delayed and Chile might in the interim increase its demands. A congress of the northern departments convoked by Iglesias in Cajamarca proclaimed him president of Peru, despite the objections voiced in the central and southern interior by Cáceres and Montero.

His somewhat tenuous claims on the presidency recognized by Chile, Iglesias proceeded to Ancón, a small seaside community a short distance north of Lima, to fulfil his grim mission of statesmanship. After considerable negotiation, and after rejecting out of hand the first set of demands presented by the enemy, Iglesias, on 23 October 1883, signed the Treaty of Ancón, ending hostilities between Peru and Chile. The treaty provided that Chile would obtain outright the southern desert region of Tarapacá with its important nitrate centre of Iquique. Chile would also occupy and administer Tacna and Arica for ten years, after which a plebiscite would be held to determine the final disposition of the two areas.

At the time the treaty was signed three men claimed to be president of Peru: Iglesias, Cáceres and Montero. Early in the following year Montero abandoned his claims and fled from Arequipa. In June 1884 Cáceres at last accepted the validity of the Treaty of Ancón, but prepared to challenge Iglesias for the presidency. Once both of the leading Peruvian soldier-statesmen with claims on the presidency had recognized Chile's acquisition of the nitrate territory for which the war had been undertaken, the occupation was no longer deemed necessary and in August the troops were ordered to return home.

Peru emerged from the unsuccessful war with a greater respect for its military personnel and institutions. It was the general conviction that the war had been lost behind the lines, not on the fighting front. Peru's soldiers and sailors had distinguished themselves by their heroism in combat. The war produced a number of military heroes, but not one civilian political leader emerged who commanded widespread respect. The conflict with Chile vindicated Castilla's policies of lavish spending on the armed forces, throwing into disrepute the *Civilista* programme of military retrenchment. Betrayed once by lack of preparedness and more sensitive than before to the dangers inherent in unresolved boundary questions with Brazil, Colombia and Ecuador, Peruvians determined henceforth to spare no expense in maintaining a powerful military machine.

In a way, Peru's defeat did not have quite the disastrous long-term consequences that might have been anticipated. Instead, events were to demonstrate that providential wealth was often the curse rather than the blessing of nineteenth-century Latin American republics. Chile, once in possession of the coveted Peruvian and Bolivian nitrate territories was to a certain degree overcome by the vices of the conquered republics. Peru, on the other hand, was purged of much of its economic madness. Only for a comparatively short span of ten years or so after the war's end did Peruvians behave as if they had not learned a lesson. Then, the responsible economic policies that Manuel Pardo had advocated were placed in operation.

The Aftermath of War: The Wasted and the Fruitful Years, 1884–99

A NEW AGE OF MILITARY 'CAUDILLISMO', 1884–95

WHEN he signed the Treaty of Ancón Miguel Iglesias expected that his efforts to spare Peru further suffering in a lost cause would be rewarded with popular gratitude. He felt that his act of statesmanship at Ancón gave him the right to the Peruvian presidency. It took him almost two years to understand that most people could not admire the man who had made himself the symbol of the admission of defeat.

Iglesias tried sincerely to rule in an enlightened manner. Remembering that one of the first acts of San Martín after Peru's declaration of independence had been to establish a national library, he decided that the government should at once concern itself with the restoration of the ruined library, even though the administration had no funds to provide for the acquisition of books. Through his minister of education he requested Ricardo Palma to take charge of the task. Palma asked, 'Do you propose that I become a begging librarian?' and was told he would be expected to 'ask alms for the benefit of his nation'.[1] He resolutely accepted the assignment and proved to be such an assiduous and successful beggar of books and documents that within ten years the national library was as rich in its holdings as at the outset of the War of the Pacific.

Iglesias was able to initiate the restoration of the library, but he did not discover the secret of how to rebuild Peru's political institutions. Faced with criticism of many of his actions by persons who felt that reconstruction could be accomplished overnight and unable to win friends through the judicious use of money because of the depleted state of the national treasury, Iglesias resorted increasingly to repressive measures to silence the opposition. As resentment mounted against the president's heavy-handed rule, Limeños looked to Andrés A. Cáceres, the indomitable young guerrilla leader of the interior, as the man of providence who would lead them towards a better tomorrow. A native of Ayacucho who had rendered valuable services both to Castilla and Pardo in maintaining order and suppressing revolutions, Cáceres was the only hero of the War of the Pacific who had won battles more consistently than he had lost them. Proclaimed by his soldiers and friends in the sierra as the rightful ruler of Peru in 1882, he had never recognized the claims of Iglesias to the presidency. In 1884 his partisans in Lima organized the Constitutionalist Party. Its platform was simple: the restoration of the 1860 constitution, mostly ignored by Iglesias, and the elevation of Cáceres to the presidency.

During the same year in which the Constitutionalist Party was founded the followers of the absent Piérola came together in Lima and established the Democratic Party. And, in the same politically eventful year, the *Civilistas*, out of power since their leader, García Calderón, had been deposed by the Chilean occupation forces, began to regroup under the direction of Aurelio Denegri, a man who had accumulated a fortune in commercial and mining activities prior to the War of the Pacific. Although disagreeing acrimoniously on many issues, the resurgent *Civilistas* and the new Democratic and Constitutionalist Parties found accord in the conviction that Iglesias must be deposed from the presidency.

The man in the best immediate position to act upon this conviction was Cáceres. On 27 August 1884, guerrilla warriors under his direction launched an assault against Lima and almost fought their way into the national palace. The tenacious defence of Iglesias succeeded at the last moment in hurling back the attackers. In December 1885, however, when the Cáceres forces returned to the outskirts of the capital city, large numbers of Limeños joined them. At last realizing the full degree to which he lacked popular support, Iglesias decided to avoid further bloodshed, renounced his claims on the presidency, and departed from Peru.

Civilistas now joined with Constitutionalists in giving enthusiastic support to Cáceres. In impressive numbers they flocked to the polls in March 1886 when Cáceres ran unopposed for the presidential office. Piérola's partisans in the Democratic Party, unwilling to join their votes with those of the hated *Civilistas* and aware that the time had not yet come when they could hope to elevate their own caudillo to power, boycotted the polls. Despite this Cáceres received one of the largest votes yet to have been cast for a Peruvian presidential candidate. On 3 July 1886, he was inaugurated at the age of thirty-three and amidst some of the most enthusiastic displays of public approval that had been seen since Manuel Pardo took office in 1872.

As *Civilistas* and Constitutionalists celebrated their victory, the Democrats glumly settled down to a period of waiting. Not for a moment, however, were they inactive. At once they set to work to bring about a rupture between *Civilistas* and Constitutionalists and to undermine the popularity of Cáceres. Returning to the country, Piérola assumed the editorship of the newspaper, *El País*, through which he began to wage a propaganda campaign against the new president.

Trying to ignore the attacks of *El País*, Cáceres dedicated himself to the economic rehabilitation of his country. The most immediate problem facing him was that a group of bondholders, with their headquarters in London, were demanding resumption of service on the foreign debt. The bonds which they held, issued during the late 1860's and in the 1870's, had a face value of between forty and fifty million pounds, an indebtedness which Peru was totally unable to amortize. Late in 1886 Michael A. Grace came to Peru as the representative of the London bondholders and began a series of lengthy conferences with Cáceres and his ministry of treasury officials. By May of the following year a preliminary agreement was reached: Peru would satisfy its obligations to the bondholders, thus cancelling most of its foreign debt, by ceding to them control over its railroads for a period of sixty-six years; in addition, she would deliver to the bondholders all of the guano, up to the amount of three million tons per year, that was not required for domestic use; and the government would make thirty-three annual payments of eighty thousand pounds sterling to the bondholders. On their part the bondholders agreed to invest in the Peruvian railroads, for the purposes of the repair and extension of various lines, and to advance new loans to the government not to exceed six million pounds.

While this arrangement, known as the Grace Contract, cannot

be regarded as an act of charity towards Peru on the part of foreign capitalists, it probably was as good a settlement as the Cáceres government could have obtained under the circumstances. Through the contract Peru at least reacquired a foreign credit standing and provided also for the rehabilitation and continuation of its railroads which, by the end of the war, had either been destroyed by the invaders or else allowed to fall into a dreadful state of disrepair. Moreover, since the Peruvian government ultimately decided that it needed almost all of its guano for domestic agriculture, the bondholders obtained relatively little of the valuable fertilizer.

However justifiable it appeared to be on many grounds, the Grace Contract was bitterly opposed by many of Peru's leading political and intellectual figures. President Cáceres had to convene four extraordinary sessions of congress and, finally, to get rid of recalcitrant senators and deputies, replacing them with docile individuals selected by carefully-manipulated special elections, before he could win legislative ratification for the Grace Contract. Not until October 1889 did the contract finally enter into effect.

Once Peru had approved the contract, the bondholders in London formed the Peruvian Corporation, Ltd, as the organization through which they would carry out their part of the arrangement. Controlling not only the railroads of Peru – the control was eventually extended beyond the stipulated sixty-six year period – but exercising for some time a considerable control also over the country's entire range of fiscal activities, the Peruvian Corporation became the favourite target of those who saw inevitable chicanery and villainy in the operations of foreign capitalists. Critics of the Peruvian Corporation often fail to note that the London firm in its early years generally fulfilled its obligations and began at once to extend Peru's railroad lines to important mining centres. By 1893 the Central Railroad, beginning at Callao, had been pushed on to La Oroya, the heartland of an area fantastically rich in a broad variety of ores. Had it not been for expanding railroad services the development during the 'silver era', which is considered to have begun in 1886, would have been retarded significantly. As it was, the silver produced between 1886 and 1895 reached a value of nearly thirty-three million dollars and made an indispensable contribution to the initial stages of economic reconstruction which occurred during the rule of Cáceres.[2]

With the question of the foreign debt resolved and with an unexpected silver boom in full progress, Cáceres and his economic advisers turned their attention to the domestic economy. After levying imposts on tobacco and alcohol,[3] they acted to curtail the wildly-inflated paper currency which had been popular with the landowners who sold their agricultural products abroad for stable currencies and were able to convert their francs, pounds and dollars into steadily-mounting numbers of *soles*. The government called in the paper money then circulating, exchanging it for a new and somewhat more adequately backed currency. The conversion rate of old to new money was regarded by many to be so unfavourable that they simply used the paper bills in their possession to stoke huge bonfires on the streets of Lima.[4]

Although well-advised and reasonably successful in his economic policies, Cáceres was unable to find the right touch for dealing with political issues. The *rapport* between the executive and legislature which had existed at the beginning of his term soon disappeared and congress became more and more concerned with finding petty pretexts for overthrowing ministries rather than with seeking solutions to internal problems. As early as 1888 congressional and other political leaders also began their preparation for the presidential elections, still two years away. By 1890 discussion of the presidential succession had become bitter, producing what Piérola had been impatiently waiting for and working towards: a split between *Civilistas* and Constitutionalists. The *Civilistas* had decided that one of their most distinguished members, Francisco Rosas, a civilian who had served as a minister under Manuel Pardo and had attacked the Piérola dictatorship while defending the cause of García Calderón during the War of the Pacific, should become president. The Constitutionalists, responsive to the wishes of Cáceres, maintained that the country should continue to be ruled by a military man and nominated Colonel Remigio Morales Bermúdez as their candidate.

In the campaign of 1890 Piérola did all in his power to aggravate the break between *Civilistas* and Constitutionalists. At the same time he engaged in vitriolic propaganda against his *Civilista* antagonist of long standing, Francisco Rosas. Piérola and his partisans even hired thugs to break up the political meetings of Rosas and his enthusiasts. Because of the campaign of violence to which he resorted, Piérola was arrested and imprisoned by the

Cáceres government on 5 April. Eight days later elections were held and to the surprise of no one, Colonel Morales, with the backing of the army and the administration, was declared the winner. Thus did Cáceres reward a man who had rendered brave and loyal service to him during the guerrilla campaign of the War of the Pacific. At the same time, however, the outgoing president drove from the Constitutionalist Party the vast majority of its civilian leaders and imposed upon the country one of the most completely military régimes which it had ever endured.

Assuming power on 29 July 1890, Morales proved to be reluctant to make decisions. He tried to run the country according to the written instructions sent by Cáceres from Paris where he had gone on a diplomatic mission. With revolutionary activity intensifying and with the general political situation deteriorating steadily, Cáceres returned to the country in May 1892 and began to set the stage for his re-election to the presidency. Elections were still two years off, but Cáceres wanted to leave nothing to chance. At once the *Civilistas* organized to oppose the Cáceres candidacy, selecting as their standard bearer Mariano Nicolás Valcárcel, a prominent political and social figure who had created a considerable sensation by his much-publicized defection from the Constitutionalist Party.[5] In their campaign, *Civilistas* attacked Cáceres as a symbol of discredited and purely selfish militarism.

Early in 1894 the Constitutionalists, desperately seeking some semblance of popular support for the Cáceres candidacy, attempted to reach an agreement with Piérola, who had escaped spectacularly from jail and after a brief stay in Guayaquil had set up his headquarters in Valparaíso. Piérola coldly rejected the Constitutionalist overtures. The political situation grew more strained and confused when President Morales died on the first of April. According to constitutional provisions he should have been succeeded by the first vice-president, Pedro Alejandrino Solar. Military officers, however, lacked confidence in Solar who was suspected of harbouring pro-*Civilista* sentiments. Hence a military *coup* displaced Solar and elevated the second vice-president, Justiniano Borgoño, to the presidency. As Borgoño, like Morales before him, was little more than the obedient servant of Cáceres, it appeared that nothing could prevent the re-election of the one-time military idol who lately had begun to show mammoth feet of clay. To make more certain still of the electoral outcome, the Constitutionalists began to imprison *Civilista* leaders.

More fortunate than some of his political companions, the *Civilista* candidate, Valcárcel, managed to escape from Callao on board a German ship, and accompanied by the deposed Solar, made his way to Chile. There, on the soil of the republic that had recently humiliated them, Peruvians took the most important step of the post-war years towards the political reconstruction of their country. Valcárcel met the Democratic chieftain, Piérola, and reached with him an agreement for mutual co-operation. For the moment at least the feud that had divided Peru since the time of Balta, that had contributed to the chaos of the 1870's, to the loss of the War of the Pacific, and to the political instability that followed the Treaty of Ancón, came to an end. In Peru the electoral sham was performed and the re-elected Cáceres was duly installed in office. In Chile, however, Valcárcel and Piérola were supremely confident that the accord at last achieved between Peru's two largest and most popular parties would result in the speedy termination of their country's reversion to military *caudillismo.*

Piérola in October was at Iquique, a part of Chilean territory since the Treaty of Ancón. Deciding to sail northwards some five hundred miles and to land on Peruvian soil near Pisco, he procured a twenty-one-foot boat built only to navigate in ports and never intended to sail on the high seas. The old and dilapidated craft was equipped with two oars, a mast, and a Latin sail. Looking at the vessel one day along with his trusted friend, Guillermo Billinghurst, who had fought heroically at San Juan, Piérola inquired: 'Would you embark in this boat?' 'Not I,' replied Billinghurst, 'but I am not in charge of the regeneration of Peru.'[6] The man who did believe himself providentially called to that mission unhesitatingly embarked and with a crew of four men made his way to the selected spot on the Peruvian coast. After landing, he at once went a short distance inland to Chincha, one of many centres then under the control of guerrilla fighters or *montoneros* who had gone into open rebellion against Cáceres and thereby touched off what proved to be one of the most widely-supported political revolutions in Peruvian history. At Chincha Piérola carefully laid his plans for an assault against Lima to the north, incessantly spreading false rumours about the movement of his forces so as to confuse the government, while his ranks were daily swelled by new recruits who included not only many of the socially prominent youth of Lima but numerous artisans and labourers as well.

By the morning of 17 March 1895, Piérola and his reinforced *montoneros*, aided by a thick fog, had fought their way into the centre of Lima. As the thousands of loyal troops still commanded by Cáceres launched a series of furious counter-attacks, Piérola standing in the doorway of the Augustinian Church was advised by his son and a close associate to withdraw from the city. 'I will not budge from here,' replied Piérola, 'for it is here that the revolution triumphs or ends.' Inspired by the example of their leader, the *montoneros* fought on and in two days held the capital firmly in their power. Between two and three thousand bodies lay on the streets of Lima. An additional eight thousand men had died in the provinces in the course of the fighting that had preceded the final assault upon Lima.[7]

Guaranteed a safe-conduct out of the country, Cáceres left the national palace, walking through blood-splattered but now quiet streets that nine years earlier had been filled with a deliriously happy populace hailing the election of the legendary guerrilla leader as their president. Had he withdrawn from politics at the end of his first term in 1890, he would have continued to be revered by his countrymen. But Cáceres had been unable to adjust himself to changing times. Ever impressed with the example of virtue, self-sacrifice and patriotism which he and his followers of the sierra had set while so many civilian politicians were conducting themselves shamefully, he had remained stubbornly convinced that only the soldiers who had rescued the country's dignity during the War of the Pacific deserved the privilege of governing it in peacetime. And if there was some justification for this attitude in 1886, there no longer was in the 1890's. By then a distinguished group of civilians had emerged from the classrooms of San Marcos and had begun to establish for themselves a prominent place in public life. With greater realism and dedication to practical knowledge than any generation of intellectuals since independence, these young men had set themselves to the study of the problems of their country and to the formulation of solutions. When he broke with the *Civilistas* in 1890 and surrounded himself almost exclusively with military advisers, Cáceres had cut himself off from the promising, educated and sincerely patriotic civilians who were busily laying plans for propelling Peru towards a better future.

Cáceres in the 1890's still thought that military virtue, resting essentially on a foundation of authority, discipline, courage and occasional stubbornness, was adequate to solve the ills of Peru. The civilian intellectuals of the 1890's thought otherwise. That is why they joined with the *montoneros* to bring about the fall of Cáceres and why they turned out *en masse* to vote for Piérola, running unopposed, in July 1895. In Piérola they hoped, although not with total confidence, in view of some of his past actions, to find a man who would be responsive to new currents of thought, and would co-operate with them in the reconstruction of Peru.

'NEOPOSITIVISTS' LAY THE INTELLECTUAL FOUNDATION FOR PERU'S RECONSTRUCTION

Beginning in the 1870's with the rise of *Civilismo*, the positivism associated with the French intellectual Auguste Comte had won many disciples in Peru. Obsessed with material progress and convinced that a small group of men representing an intellectual élite could by scientific and empirical investigation discover and then apply the laws that would lead to dramatic development and the generation of national wealth, the positivists had rejected the traditional teachings and values of the Catholic Church which stressed other-worldliness and resignation on earth to a difficult and even cruel physical ambient. Influenced also by the Social Darwinism that became so popular in the United States after the Civil War, Peru's positivists had frequently preached the need for a ruthless and unregulated economic struggle out of which the fit would survive, while the unfit would be eliminated. The majority of Peruvian positivists were further convinced that the Indians represented the country's unfit element and looked forward to the day when this group, which they alleged to be racially inferior and a drag on the nation's development, would disappear.[8]

In the late 1880's and in the 1890's a new intellectual influence appeared which should probably be referred to as 'neopositivism'. Its typical representatives were concerned with benefiting and uplifting rather than suppressing and eliminating the Indians. In part their concern with the native can be traced to the belief becoming rapidly prevalent after the War of the Pacific that the long-standing neglect and exploitation of the Indian had been in the final analysis responsible for Peru's defeat. If the Indian had been educated and assimilated into Peruvian life, he would have been able to contribute effectively towards the war effort and Peru would have been the victor. If an assimilated, educated Indian with some dignity and status in society could have helped to win the war for Peru, it followed that, properly initiated into Peruvian society, he could also contribute towards the peacetime development and prosperity of the country.

Spurning in another important respect the influence of Social Darwinism, neopositivists accepted the need for government planning and intervention in the economic order. The old notion was abandoned that a successful capitalistic class would, while serving its own interests and increasing its fortunes, at the same time contribute to the economic development of the country as a whole. Neopositivists in general maintained that the government must regulate and supervise the affluent groups so that at least some of the wealth generated by private Peruvian capitalism would go towards financing state-planned projects that would directly benefit a wide cross-section of social classes.

The spirit of neopositivism became apparent at San Marcos almost immediately after the War of the Pacific. A new group of practically-minded teachers and students, distrustful of old-guard politicians and bureaucrats but hopeful about what the people, whether high or lowly born, might under proper direction be able to contribute towards national rehabilitation, turned their attention to the Peruvian present and away from the exotic theories of philosophers of bygone ages. Regarding science rather than scholasticism as the key to knowledge, they were outraged when the Iglesias government in May 1884 promulgated a New Regulation of Instruction that gave preference to scholastic philosophy and neglected the history of Peruvian civilization as well as scientific studies. The San Marcos faculty of letters, led by its dean, the Spanish-born Sebastián Lorente, objected strenuously. But Lorente died the next November, and not until 1895 was the objectionable decree rescinded.[9]

Carlos Lissón (1823–91), who introduced the study of sociology in Peru, succeeded Lorente as dean of the faculty of letters. Reverting to the economic ideas of Manuel Pardo and at the same time anticipating one of the themes that would be most emphasized by Peru's neopositivists, Lissón urged Peruvians to acquire habits of hard work and extolled the values generally associated with the Protestant Ethic. Foreign investment and loans, he argued, could not be regarded as the solution of Peru's economic problems. Fearing the exploitation which he felt was inevitably connected with foreign capital, he repeatedly insisted that the only way for his country to progress was by the efforts of Peruvians themselves. 'The country', he wrote, 'requires practical men who realize that miracles cannot be wrought overnight, who are patient, and who appreciate that the prerequisite for progress is hard work and that only gradually will improvement be wrought'.[10]

Lissón's views on the need for government regulation of the economy influenced many of his students who were shortly to become the leaders of neopositivism, destined to reign as the dominant intellectual force in Peru until the early twentieth century and to retain great influence until the end of World War I. It was the government, Lissón argued, that must furnish leadership in the task of regeneration, mainly by stimulating and controlling to some degree both education and economic activities.[11] Lissón was also one of the first to sound the note of optimism about the Peruvian Indian, a note that was repeated by so many intellectual leaders of the 1890's. The laziness, inertia, and drunkenness commonly ascribed to the Indians were not the result of racial inferiority, Lissón maintained, but rather of the 'narrow, limited world in which they have been forced to live'. The Indians, he argued, had retained the spirit of work. Therefore Peruvians could erect upon the foundation of the native population 'the solid building of the future'.[12]

One of the most distinguished of Peru's neopositivists who studied at San Marcos and was influenced by Lissón was Javier Prado (1871-1921), son of the former president of the country, Mariano Ignacio Prado. At the age of twenty Javier completed his impressive doctoral dissertation on the evolution of the idea of philosophy in history and immediately thereafter won in public competition the chair of modern philosophy at the university, thus embarking upon a career as one of Peru's most highly regarded teachers and statesmen.

Although Prado like most of the neopositivists went even beyond the nineteenth-century liberals in making a blanket attack on all vestiges of the Spanish past, he did not feel that the faults which Peruvians had allegedly inherited from this era would prevent future progress. 'I do not belong to the number of sceptics and pessimists who think that there is no solution for the problems of Peru. I firmly believe that our problems have a solution, provided the great work of national reform is undertaken with energy.'[13] In spite of the troubled times Prado was 'contagiously optimistic about his country's future',[14] and felt that education was the key to Peru's coming greatness. Education, as he saw it, would have to impart to all Peruvians a sense of social solidarity, civic virtue, and technological, scientific knowledge that would enable them to contribute effectively to their country's material development. Beyond this, it had to awaken in the individual the desire for greater material well-being. Material ambitions would not only cause the properly-educated man to employ his technical skills with zeal, but would also instil in him a higher degree of civic and personal morality:

It is necessary ... to educate, and to educate through labour, through industry, which is the greatest medium of moralization. There is nothing which will better elevate the character of man today, nothing which will make him interest himself more effectively in the future of his country, than to educate him to be practical and prudent and to desire to acquire wealth by means of his personal efforts.[15]

Prado reflected the prevailing judgement of the young intellectuals of his day in asserting that the unreasoning masses must be guided for many years by an élite of wisdom. Only when the masses had through education acquired traits of morality and virtue, only when they had become patriotic and hardworking, could democracy be expected to function. In his appraisal of the Peruvian Indian, however, Prado departed from the general consensus of Peru's neopositivists of the 1890's, pointing to the 'pernicious influence which had been exercised in Peru by the crossing of the blood of inferior races with that of white settlers'. Flexible enough to abandon his racial prejudices before his death and to acknowledge that Indians were not inferior, as a young man he regarded massive European immigration as essential for the establishment of a modern and progressive Peruvian state. 'It is necessary,' he wrote, 'to modify the influence of race, to renew our blood and our inheritance by crossing with other races which will supply new and beneficial elements.'[16]

Three years after the signing of the Treaty of Ancón, Mariano

H. Cornejo (1873–1942), who was in 1896 to occupy the first chair of sociology at San Marcos, completed his dissertation for the bachelor's degree. The work dealt with the topic of unlimited progress and revealed that Cornejo was just as optimistic about the future as Javier Prado.[17] Cornejo, however, emphasized that progress was not inevitable. It depended upon direction by leaders perceptive enough to discover the sociological laws which governed it. Thus, argued Cornejo, superior, initiated, scientific spirits should provide political leadership. He also believed that excessive inbreeding weakened the intelligence of an aristocracy. Hence, society's directing classes should constantly admit new blood, and a 'hierarchy of favouritism should at all times give place to one of capacity, for this is the true meaning of social equality'.[18] Under these conditions, progress could be achieved, but only at a gradual pace, and Cornejo ridiculed the long-held conviction of most nineteenth-century liberals that revolution could in a day change the nature of society. 'By their excessive haste, extremist liberals only evoke a reaction which sooner or later destroys all the reforms they have introduced.'[19]

Like Lissón and Prado, Cornejo emphasized the necessity for widespread public education. Influenced by the United States sociologist, Lester Frank Ward, he believed that apparent divergences in intelligence among people were the result more of differences of education than of native intellectual endowment. Universal education appealed to Cornejo as the best means for minimizing the intellectual inequalities which gave rise to social, economic and political injustices. Certainly not all could be trained to the point where they could assume responsibility in interpreting the laws of society and providing political direction, but they could at least acquire sufficient knowledge to enable them to make a respectable living and to protect their essential dignity and rights. Education, directed, controlled, and subsidized by the state, should be concerned in most instances with imparting technical skills to the student and should be accessible even to the most humble classes and regardless of sex.[20]

Extolling the advantages of social solidarity, Cornejo urged Peru's fortunate classes to take more thought for the Indian and to work resolutely to uplift the native and bring him into society. In advocating this approach Cornejo denied that race was the determining factor in history:

Race is only one of the social factors so that even if it remains invariable, it can be tempered by others ... race is a synthesis of qualities in evolution and is modified slowly but constantly; ... colour is one of the most superficial characteristics, so that even if it is conserved it is possible and even probable that there will be cerebral modifications completely independent of colour. ... Time will gradually substitute for the biological concept of rival races, of antagonistic social classes and professions, the reality of the utilitarian concept of the co-operation of people.[21]

Joaquín Capelo (1852–1928) was another intellectual with a wide range of interests who helped to infuse San Marcos with a new spirit in the late nineteenth century. A professor of mathematical science as well as a highly respected sociologist and engineer, Capelo was obsessed with the need to unite the various parts of Peru by means of a vast road-building programme. He was not interested in the lavish railroad schemes of the Balta and Meiggs days, but rather in more modest, even unpaved, but still functional roads of the type the country could better afford to build in its rudimentary state of development. An enthusiastic member of the Democratic Party, in 1900 he began a long career as senator for the Andean department of Junín. Like Manuel Pardo who had also had a vital interest in the problems of Junín, Capelo was concerned for the Indians of the area and worked as steadfastly as any man of his time towards preparing the way for assimilation of the native into Peruvian society. He also did all in his power to protect the mining workers of Junín against what he considered to be the exploitative conditions imposed by the foreign capitalists who largely controlled the extractive industries.

A reformer who wanted to avoid revolution, Capelo devoted much thought to the problem of whether Peru's regeneration should begin at the top and be imposed by a small group, or should originate at the bottom in the masses themselves. France in 1789, said Capelo, tried to achieve reform through the individual action of the people below, whereas late nineteenth-century Japan relied upon the impetus furnished by a strong, central government. Which was the proper path for Peru? Capelo decided that a mixture of the two methods might be devised, but that primary importance should always be attached to the improvement of the individual through his own actions.[22] The government could take steps to provide more propitious circumstances in which the masses might begin the task of self improvement. Capelo urged, for example, government action to force landowners to treat their peons more humanely.[23] However, after the government had established somewhat more equitable relations between capital and labour, it would be for the individual worker to procure his own advancement. If unable to improve his lot once minimum conditions of justice had been established, then the worker simply showed his lack of virtue and application, and deserved no further solicitude from the government.

Although a deeply religious man, Capelo criticized the Catholic Church in Peru for its characteristic attitudes and value judgements. He felt that the Church should transform its traditional outlook and become a positive force in the quest for Peruvian regeneration by preaching self-confidence, love of labour and hatred of laziness and prodigality. In short, the Church should begin to concern itself as much with natural as with supernatural virtue and acquire some of the values that had characterized Protestantism in such economically developed countries as England and the United States.[24]

At the age of twenty-one Manuel Vicente Villarán (1873–1958) completed his doctoral dissertation writing on the topic of civil and political liberty. Two years later in 1896 he joined Prado, Cornejo, and Capelo on the San Marcos faculty, teaching courses in natural law and the philosophy of law. Villarán quickly became one of the most popular and effective professors. Unlike some of his colleagues he conscientiously prepared his lectures, met his classes at the assigned hour, and devoted much time outside the lecture hall to his students. A practising lawyer as well as a professor, Villarán also embarked at an early age on a career in politics. Along with fellow-professor, Javier Prado, he rose to a position of great influence in the *Civilista* Party.

In his class work and in his political discourses and publications, Villarán emphasized that the interests of society as a whole placed definite limitations on the rights of property ownership.[25] His social consciousness led him also to insist on universal, government-supported primary education:

Do you think that the gains won in contemporary times by labouring classes in their relations with capital have been the result of the pious sentiments and spontaneous generosity of the powerful classes? Certainly not. These splendid triumphs are won by the working classes;

they are the fruit of money and of instruction among the masses. . . .
Only if given education will the lower classes be able to protect themselves and contribute to, because they are sharing in, the increase of national wealth. Unless the lower classes are educated, any increase in wealth that is achieved in the country will go to the exclusive benefit of the already rich and directing classes, and thereby serve only to create greater social tension.[26]

Not only did primary education facilities have to be expanded, but the character of instruction had to be vastly changed. Like so many of the neopositivists, Villarán insisted that unless Peruvian education began to stress practical knowledge the republic would increasingly become the economic colony of those foreign nations in which citizens were encouraged to acquire scientific knowledge and technological expertise.[27]

Far from being a defender merely of utilitarian, material values, Villarán was interested in economic progress because he considered it an essential prerequisite for the development of a country's intellectual and cultural capacity. Schools should promote material advances so that ultimately the broader diffusion of culture would be possible. 'Each rich nation,' asserted Villarán, 'when its wealth is not the opulence of the few aquired through the misery of the many, is an instructed and cultured nation. Wealth educates, in that the force to create and to conserve it develops the spirit for higher and nobler pursuits.'[28]

Reflecting the majority trend among the neopositivists, Villarán challenged the prevailing view of Peruvian upper classes that the Indians were racially inferior. Convinced that the future of his country lay in the development of its own population resources Villarán stated that Peruvians rendered a disservice to their country by preaching the need to replace the Indian with European immigrants. 'The adverse prejudice against the Indians,' he observed, 'reaches the extreme of considering them a race without ability, a degenerate race. It is essential to combat this prejudice because in truth it can be said without exaggeration that everything has degenerated in Peru except the Indian.' The Indian was still, according to Villarán, healthy and strong. 'The acts of genius and labour which raised the monuments of the Inca civilization can be repeated today and made greater still by the help of modern arts, sciences and education.' The habits of labour acquired by the aborigines through the centuries when Inca civilization was gradually mastering the environment, he confidently affirmed, were still conserved in their fullest vigour by Peru's contemporary Indian population.[29]

One of Villarán's closest friends was another San Marcos professor and active *Civilista* politician, José Matías Manzanilla (1870–1947). Beginning his teaching career at the university in 1895, Manzanilla initially offered courses in economic policy and economic legislation. In his economics courses and later as an eloquent congressional deputy he helped to found a powerful Peruvian movement whose objective was the enactment of social legislation. As a practising lawyer Manzanilla delighted in contributing his services free of charge to the poor, frequently helping them to press their claims against large corporations, especially those that were foreign-controlled. Like many of his fellow neo-positivists something of an economic nationalist, Manzanilla refused, despite frequent opportunities, to become the lawyer of the foreign corporations operating in Peru. Moreover, he urged his students not to argue the cases of the huge mining, industrial and commercial firms in disputes with labour.[30]

Whereas Joaquín Capelo had been primarily concerned with the efforts of individuals to develop their potentialities and had merely made a few vague pronouncements that government should impose certain basic conditions of justice, Manzanilla devoted much of his life to the specific formulation of social legislation. Whereas Villarán emphasized that only an educated lower class could win through its own endeavours conditions of security and material comfort, Manzanilla felt that government should meet the labouring masses half-way by providing social legislation even before it had been demanded by an aroused proletariat. In this way social solidarity could be preserved and destructive class warfare avoided. Summarizing these views, the famous lawyer of the poor stated:

> The State would fail in its duties to care for the conservation and development of the moral and material conditions of human existence if it . . . did not give an impulse to industry, communications and credit facilities, if it abandoned the woman and the child to their own resources, if it contemplated with indifference the unsanitary life in the workshops, excessive hours of work, unfair contracts between management and labour, deplorable conditions of worker housing, if in short, it did not concern itself with the origin and effects of industrial malaise. . . .

When in the name of liberty the State abstains, the strong each day become stronger, and the weak more miserable.[31]

Lissón, Prado, Cornejo, Capelo, Villarán and Manzanilla constitute only a half dozen of the many prominent figures in education and government who introduced new political, economic and social values in late nineteenth-century Peru. A few spokesmen of traditionally conservative Catholic values might rail against the excessive rationalism and materialism of the new intellectual milieu, but their voices were scarcely heeded. For the time being neopositivism had become the dominant intellectual force in Peru.

Had its spokesmen been vindictive and militant, neopositivism might have rekindled the old religious polemic and the Church-State debate which Castilla had extinguished. Fortunately, however, the neopositivists, while not generally regarding the Catholic Church as destined to play a major rôle in the regeneration of Peru, refrained, out of respect for the recognized religious fervour of the people, from directly attacking the traditional faith. Some of them were even convinced that in time they could persuade the Church to accept many of their values and to join with them in working to fashion a modern and progressive Peru.

The most important contribution of the neopositivists was their refutation of the popular notions of racial determinism and their insistence – against which Javier Prado raised only a minority and an ephemeral dissent – that Peru's future depended upon the assimilation of its Indians. The greatest shortcoming of the neopositivists was that nearly all of them demonstrated a disdain for the Peruvian past. While optimistic about the future, they could find nothing worthy of respect in Peru's historical development up to the late nineteenth century. Turning their backs contemptuously upon the traditions and experiences of their country, they looked abroad, borrowing from the foreign thinkers then in vogue, to find patterns that might bring about Peru's future development. While they tried to instil in Peruvians a sense of nationalism and pride in what could some day be accomplished, they insisted that the past be regarded with shame.

THE PIÉROLA ADMINISTRATION, 1895–99

Elected in July and installed as constitutional president in September 1895, Piérola was no longer the impetuous, irresponsibly ambitious *politico* of earlier years. Able now to doubt a little his own infallibility, willing to turn to others for advice, and having come to accept many ideas which he had previously found abhorrent, Piérola had developed into a mature statesman. During his four-year term the interaction between the force of a charismatic leader and the intellectual currents generated by neopositivism produced significant results. Had Piérola not been operating against the intellectual background which the neopositivists had created, he could not have become the effective instrument of Peruvian rehabilitation. In fact, without the prior existence of the ideas of neopositivism, Piérola probably could not have even formulated his programme of government. But, had it not been for the administrative genius displayed by Piérola as president and his magnetic appeal to Peruvians of all classes, the new ideas could never have been channelled into a systematic effort for national transformation.[32]

In Peruvian literature Nicolás de Piérola has aptly come to be identified by the title of the 'democratic caudillo'. Personable and dashing, possessing a sense of histrionics, always something of a *poseur*, the small, slightly-built, elegant and refined Piérola who wore high and uncomfortable boots to remind him at all times to maintain his impressive, erect posture – his detractors accused him of wearing a corset – was definitely a caudillo. Aristocratic at heart, he was convinced that providence had imposed upon society a perpetual class structure that could never be swept away by 'inevitable laws' of social evolution. Yet the caudillo possessed democratic proclivities. He hoped to keep the aristocracy as open as possible. He also demonstrated democratic leanings by his faith in the capacity of his people, including the Indians. He genuinely aspired to provide the masses with an opportunity to perfect their abilities. By 1895 Piérola had finally come to believe that the wealth of a nation was dependent upon the development in each generation of the virtue and capitalist skills of the people.

While the material attainments of one age could obviously be passed on to the next, Piérola was convinced that the virtue by which each age generated its wealth died with it. Since each generation had to begin anew to wage its own struggle for virtue, human nature did not improve by any inevitable straight line of evolutionary development. Piérola also believed in a certain providentially-imposed immutability of human nature that placed definite restrictions on what people could accomplish on earth, and so did not hopefully look forward to a future Utopia. Nor did he disdainfully dismiss the past. Many aspects of the Peruvian past, in his view, were worthy of admiration as well as emulation. Unlike the neopositivists Piérola voiced a nationalism that had continuity, a nationalism based upon love of Peru in all of its periods of historical development and not just upon a lukewarm acceptance of the present and an infatuation with the future. The new president called upon Peruvians to improve themselves and their country not just because of a belief in future progress, but because of pride in the past and the desire to match in the present the occasional grandeur of distant times. Even as Castilla in his age formulated a compromise between conservatism and liberalism that welded together much of what was best in the two systems, so Piérola united many of Peru's traditional values with the new and progressive ideas of neopositivism.

Piérola's accomplishment in this respect is demonstrated in his attitudes towards religion. Contrary to the neopositivist spirit he did not worry about the so-called superstitions of his people, or fret unduly over the occasional loss of a few days' productive labour owing to religious holidays. While he hoped that Peruvians would acquire capitalist virtues and achieve material success, he realized that many would inevitably fail. Those who fell economically by the wayside, however, were not to be disparaged, for they still possessed the God-given dignity in which all human beings shared. However poor, then, the Peruvian citizens could still have self respect and demand the respect of society. Piérola's approach provided a status of dignity for all Peruvians, whereas the neopositivists, by implying the need to regard at least with suspicion all who did not achieve reasonable material success once they had been given minimal opportunities to do so, introduced a set of values which in their ultimate effect tended to attach a stigma to the poor.

Described as a mystical, idealistic Catholic who was at the same time a scientific revolutionist,[33] Piérola believed that a blending could be achieved between the religious beliefs and practices of the past and the new values upon which material progress seemed to depend. By combining his religious beliefs with the new cult of materialism, utilitarianism, and economic progress, by fashioning a workable programme that depended upon the two streams of influence, Piérola was able to proceed far towards proving that the past and the future need not be incompatible.

Shortly after his inauguration Piérola proceeded to act in accordance with the belief, expressed by so many intellectuals, that the government should intervene in economic and social matters. Abandoning the economic liberalism he had professed when serving as minister of the treasury for President Balta, he created a ministry of development (*ministerio de fomento*), appointing Eduardo López de Romaña as its head. The new ministry undertook and actually completed many public works projects, including roads, railroads and buildings. The Piérola administration also established the national society of industries (*sociedad nacional de industrias*), intended to co-ordinate, to plan and to facilitate through the co-operation of the government and private enterprises the advance of Peruvian industry.[34] Stimulated by the encouragement of the government, and aided by the initial steps which Piérola took to return the country to the gold standard and thus provide it with a more stable currency,[35] industrial concerns made rapid advances. Peru's age of industrialization, in fact, truly began during the Piérola régime. The new industrial bourgeoisie which appeared 'would soon begin to demand from the mine- and land-owning aristocracy a share in the control of national policies'.[36]

By imposing a number of excise and export-import taxes, by replacing the old procedure of auctioning off tax-collecting privileges to private firms with the systematic government collection of imposts, and by insisting upon rigorous adherence to carefully planned budgets Piérola re-established fiscal stability. Government income increased from seven million pounds in 1895 to twelve million in 1899. Service on the internal debt, in suspension when Piérola came to power, was restored in 1896 and in addition the country's foreign credit rating was improved. Owing largely to the stable economic conditions established by Piérola, the whole tempo of business activity accelerated rapidly. During his administration the combined value of Peruvian exports and imports rose from 2·46 to 4·9 million pounds.[37] It is little wonder that a leading Peruvian economic historian has written that the period of Piérola's administration 'marks Peru's entry into the modern capitalistic world'.[38]

One of several new excise taxes established by the reform-minded president was a special impost on salt. Revenue from this source was channelled exclusively into a fund to support Peru's efforts to reacquire Tacna and Arica, if possible by means of a financial award to Chile. The plebiscite to determine the final disposition of these areas had not been held in 1893, despite the provisions of the Treaty of Ancón. Peru had insisted that only natives of Tacna and Arica be allowed to vote, while Chile maintained that all residents should do so. When the two countries were unable to resolve their disagreement, the plebiscite was cancelled. In 1898 a renewal of the Argentina–Chilean boundary dispute led Piérola to hope that Chile might be induced to settle the Tacna-Arica matter. He dispatched his close friend, Guillermo Billinghurst, to Santiago to attempt to wrest a favourable settlement from the Chilean government. Billinghurst owned valuable nitrate holdings in the Iquique area which had been annexed definitively by Chile as part of its War of the Pacific spoils. Living after the war in Iquique and travelling often to Santiago to protect his interests, Billinghurst had made friends with many highly-placed Chilean officials and thus seemed ideally suited to carry out his mission.

Aided by the fact that Peru was able to promise a large settlement because of its salt-tax income, and taking advantage of Chilean apprehension over the dispute with Argentina, Billinghurst negotiated in Santiago the Billinghurst–La Torre Protocol. Favourable to Peru in that it permitted only natives of Tacna–Arica to vote in the still-pending plebiscite, the protocol was ultimately rejected by the Chilean congress after the boundary dispute with Argentina had been amicably settled.[39] With the unused Tacna-Arica special fund continuing to grow, but to no purpose, Piérola with some bitterness described in his principal message to congress in 1899 how all of his efforts to reacquire the coveted areas had been frustrated.

At the same time that he was bringing order to the economy and attempting to reacquire national territory, Piérola also turned his attention to political affairs:

So long as elections have only the character of a farce, the public peace will continue to be nothing more than a transitory period of rest between bloody combats; law and authority will neither be worthy of respect nor respected; not even the slightest possibility will exist that the republic can enter upon the paths that lead to its well-being.[40]

Moonlight on the ocean at La Herradura in the environs of Lima

View of the Lima Country Club

The Plaza de Armas, Arequipa

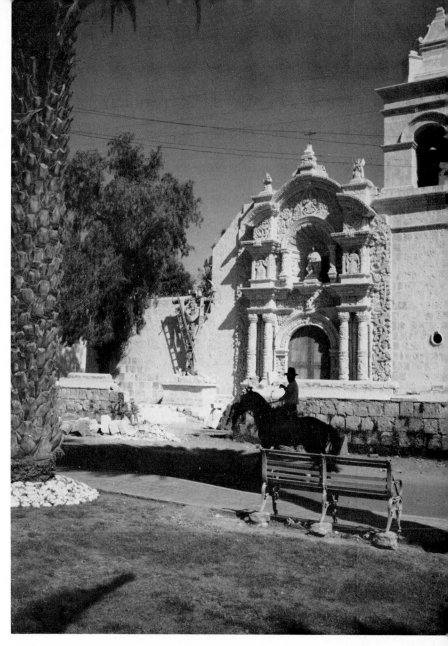

The Church in Yanahuara on the outskirts of Arequipa

Huacachino; a spa located close to Ica

An Indian family in front of their house in the Cuzco area

(*opposite*) The recently rebuilt San Cristobal Church in Cuzco

Street scene in Puno; vendors at the Plaza de Armas

The sugar-refining plant on a prosperous estate near Chiclayo

(*opposite*) Houses of Indian rural labourers near Cuzco

The Franciscan Church, Cajamarca

The Peruvian declaration of independence in Lima, 28 July 1821, with
José de San Martin in the centre, arm outstretched

(*opposite*) The ruins of Machu Picchu with Mt Huayna Picchu rising in
the background

(*above left*) Ramon Castilla, President of
Peru 1845–51, 1854–62

(*above*) Manuel Pardo, President of Peru
1872–6

Nicolas de Pierola, the 'Democratic
Caudillo', President of Peru 1895–9

Augusto B. Leguia, President of Peru 1908–12, and dictator during the *oncenio*, 1919–30

(*below left*) Luis M. Sanchez Cerro, President of Peru 1931–3

(*below*) Oscar R. Benavides, President of Peru 1933–9

Manuel Prado y Ugarteche,
President of Peru 1939–45,
1956–62

Fernando Belaúnde Terry,
President of Peru since 1963

Quickly taking advantage of the actual opportunity to improve the political processes of his country, Piérola in 1896 secured the enactment of a law that eliminated the electoral colleges and provided for direct suffrage. To supervise all elections and resolve disputes that might arise, the new law created a nine-man National Electoral Junta (*Junta Electoral Nacional*). Each house of congress appointed two members of the junta, choosing one from majority and one from minority representatives; four members were named by the judiciary, and one by the executive. The electoral reforms did not create an ideal ituation, in part because they did not provide for the secret ballot. Thus landowners and industrialists were able to herd their peons and labourers to the polls and insist that they vote as instructed. Further, Piérola himself undermined the prestige of the Electoral Junta when he ignored one of its decisions in 1899. Still, the national electoral process did improve to the point of 'becoming at least as good as in any other Latin American republic'.[41]

On the level of local politics, the reforms of Piérola were in some ways more effective. The central government relinquished its control over local appointments, and re-instituted municipal elections. With justifiable pride the president noted in an address in 1897 that he had returned to the municipalities the rights of self rule of which they had been deprived by the military administration of 1892.

On the issue of militarism, which once again was arousing heated discussion because of the inefficiency with which Cáceres and his officer friends had directed affairs, Piérola proceeded with somewhat more discretion than had Manuel Pardo. Far from advocating replacing the permanent army by a civilian militia, Piérola declared that the man who thought the need for standing armies would disappear was 'a foolish Utopianist, an idle dreamer, a being who did not realize that this world is but a brief and imperfect transition, not the mansion of eternal happiness'.[42] At the same time the president hoped to remove the army from politics, to provide its officers with sound scientific and technical knowledge, and to instil in them a sense of professional pride. To create this pride it was necessary, he felt, to establish respected military schools and to provide security in the form of adequate salaries and pensions. Piérola also hoped to utilize the officer class, once its members had obtained through education a technological proficiency, in carrying out government-sponsored engineering projects, such as the building of roads, that would lead to the overall betterment of the country. In addition he wished to put a stop to the practice of filling the ranks of the army by kidnapping Indians from the sierra and to introduce a law of obligatory military service that would require men of all social classes to serve at least briefly in the military forces.

To all of these goals Piérola turned his attention. The military school of Chorillos was re-organized and obtained the services of Peru's leading intellectuals, many of them civilians. Before long it came to be regarded as one of the finest technical as well as liberal arts schools in the country. Besides courses on strategy, tactics, warfare, armament and engineering, the faculty of the military school taught history, geography and even some of the elements of sociology and economics. Young officers were encouraged to think in terms of what they could contribute to their country in peacetime and in war through their profession, not by sallies into politics. A French military mission brought to Peru in 1898 contributed significantly to establishing in the commissioned and non-commissioned officers a sense of pride in military professionalism. In the same year that the French mission arrived, a new law of compulsory military service was passed. It imposed the obligation of short-term military service on all male citizens between the ages of nineteen and fifty. Unfortunately, after Piérola's term came to an end, the law was not enforced with adequate vigour and the army reverted to the practice of kidnapping Indians.[43]

From the time of Piérola, irresponsible military caudillismo declined dramatically. Henceforth the army intervened in politics with decreasing frequency. When its men did leave the barracks to become political arbiters, they generally did so only after having been prevailed upon by civilian politicians to 'save the country'.

Concerned with educating not only the armed forces but the people in general Piérola took steps, albeit somewhat slowly because of his desire to avoid large budget deficits, to establish a public system of primary instruction. He was just as insistent as Manuel Pardo had been upon an emphasis on practical knowledge and the empirical approach in all of Peru's schools. Unfortunately the men in charge of implementing the president's educational programme 'were products of the old school of verbalism and decorativism and thus they brought about no fundamental change in the orientation of instruction'.[44]

As the time for the 1899 electoral campaign approached, many of Piérola's partisans quite understandably approached him with the suggestion that he should alter the constitution in order to permit his immediate re-election. Those who urged this course of action held up approvingly the example of the Mexican strong man, Porfirio Díaz, who had ruled his country since 1876. The 'democratic caudillo' wisely replied that although Díaz was leading Mexico towards impressive material development he was not contributing to the establishment of permanent institutions. Therefore when Díaz fell from power, chaos was likely to ensue. This was the weakness, stated Piérola, of all prolonged, personalistic administrations.

While refusing to change the constitution to permit immediate re-election, the president was not at all adverse to using his vast popularity and influence – even though it meant flaunting a decision of the Electoral Junta – to secure the election in 1899 of his hand-picked successor, Eduardo López de Romaña, the man who had served as Peru's first minister of development. Probably Piérola looked forward to succeeding his friend four years later in the presidency, as the constitution permitted re-election after an intervening term.

At the end of his administration Piérola was presented with a medal at a lavish banquet attended by leaders of all political groups. One of those who spoke on this occasion was Francisco García Calderón, the old *Civilista* leader and now the rector of San Marcos, who had been a short-term president and the bitter political rival of Piérola during the War of the Pacific. In concluding his discourse García Calderón effectively expressed the feelings of most of those in attendance. Turning towards Piérola he stated: 'In the name of all, I say to you that we are satisfied with your work and that you have fulfilled your duties.'[45]

GONZÁLEZ PRADA AND THE PHOENIX CONCEPT OF RECONSTRUCTION

One person not satisfied with Piérola's conduct of affairs or, for that matter, with anything else about Peru was Manuel González Prada (1848–1918). Born into an aristocratic Lima family of pure

Spanish antecedents and educated for a short time in the San Toribio Seminary, González Prada, although rejecting many of the neopositivist tenets, had emerged as an important figure among the group of intellectuals who after the War of the Pacific sought to regenerate the national spirit and strength. Becoming president of the *Círculo Literario* in Lima in 1887, Prada utilized its membership – essentially composed of artists, writers and critics – as the nucleus for a new political party, the *Unión Nacional*, which he organized in 1891. The *Unión* never attracted many members or attained real influence, and Prada abandoned it in 1902.[46]

The world in general seemed bad to Prada. He once wrote that the most worthy work which God could perform would be to destroy the universe because what the Almighty had created was bad, very bad indeed.[47] Actually, Prada could not even look forward to God's destruction of the universe, because he did not believe in God, except on rare occasions. 'There are days', he is reputed to have said, 'when I believe, and days when I do not believe. Most of the time I do not believe.'

Bad as was the world in general, Peru seemed particularly bad to Prada. Largely to blame was the legacy which Peruvians had received from the Spanish colonial past. Prada regarded Spaniards as the most depraved people to have appeared on earth and could not find one worthwhile accomplishment they had made during the centuries they had governed Peru. Not only was the entire colonial period without a single redeeming feature, but in the nineteenth century there was not one Peruvian who was truly honourable.[48] With the exception of the independence movement and the activities of 2 May, 1867, when they had defeated the Spaniards at Callao, Peruvians had never spilled a single drop of blood for an ideal or made a revolution for a principle; they had only fought because of greed, avarice and personality clashes.[49] Peru was a sick organism: 'everywhere you press it pus comes out.'[50] According to Prada, Peru had nothing at all to be proud of: 'Peruvians could not even look at one another without blushing in shame.'[51]

Never had there been such a wholesale condemnation of Peru and Peruvians. Bartolomé Herrera had attacked the liberals and blamed them for the decline of virtue; José Gálvez had flailed the conservatives and attributed a national deterioration to them; 'but Prada indicted an entire country.'[52] Still, Prada most definitely looked forward to a better day and for a time regarded himself as about the only man who understood the secret of national regeneration. To him it seemed that Peru could by destroying all vestiges of the depraved past rise to a worthy status. Peru, like the Phoenix, had to emerge from its own ashes. Not only the dead of Peru, but those who had grown old, Prada regarded as worthless. He found no place for them in the task of regenerating Peru. 'Old people to the grave,' he said in one of his best-remembered pronouncements, 'the youth to work.'[53]

In 1891, the very year in which he founded the *Unión Nacional*, Prada went to Europe. He returned to Peru only in 1898, strongly influenced by European socialism, and began to speak of the need for intellectuals to join with workers in leading a revolution which would exterminate the parasitical capitalists of the Peruvian coast. In his socialist stage Prada appeared to relish the prospect of violence:

Better to shed the blood of a bad man than that of a good animal . . . the hands which liberate us from tyranny are worthy of being grasped by honourable men. . . . Of course the assassin who kills in the name of justice will still be punished in today's world. But today's men of vengeance will be the Christs of tomorrow. . . . If anyone should desire our opinion on strikes we would reply to him, all strikes should be general and armed: general to combat and kill on all sides the capitalist world and oblige it to surrender; armed to impede the interference of authority in the struggle where its only proper rôle is that of a witness. . . . Capitalism never cedes voluntarily a single iota of its so-called acquired rights. When it cedes it is not by force of reason but in virtue of force of arms. Therefore there is no better means to obtain justice than to appeal to the armed strike and to sabotage.[54]

Perhaps because he wished to enhance the possibility that an armed people could impose its will, Prada recommended the suppression of standing armies. Far more extreme in his opposition to the military than ever Manuel Prado and nascent *Civilismo* had been, Prada regarded professional soldiers as no better than policemen, about whom he wrote: '. . . anyone can be a man, no matter how he earns a living, except the police agent. Dedicate yourself to the lowest and dirtiest labour, be a garbage collector, a chimney sweep, a swineherd . . . even doing all of this you will appear cleaner than the person installed on a corner with his khaki uniform, his white hat and his club of the law.'[55]

The virulent anticlericalism and the atheism which Prada preached arose in part from his faith in science as a substitute for religion. Catholicism and science, thundered Prada in a pronouncement by no means original at the time, could not exist side by side:

> Science proclaims health, happiness and life as its goals, while religion glorifies sickness, suffering and death. . . . How is it possible to glorify death, the final brutal triumph of anonymous forces over intelligence and the will of the individual! . . . Would society be better off without belief or without knowledge? . . . Clearly without belief; for without belief it will still establish a satisfactory natural morality, but without knowledge, which proceeds from science, it would revert to the stone age. . . . Catholicism is the mountain of sand, science the stream of water which grain by grain wears away the mountain.[56]

A shy, sensitive individual who, despite his bombast and the aggressiveness of the 'canine literary school of howling and barking'[57] which he introduced, seemed to suffer from an inferiority complex, Prada experienced a mounting frustration as the majority of Limeños paid scant heed to his revolutionary urgings. Rebuffed by the literate populace of the capital city, Prada turned to a mass of people who could not rebuff him because they never even knew that he was addressing them, the Indians of the sierra. From the late 1890's Prada, although he did not bother to visit the sierra,[58] began to write and talk as if only the Indians could save Peru.[59]

The more Prada eulogized the Indians and urged them to resort to violence to redeem themselves and their country, the more he heaped scorn on the whites of Peru:

> We do not believe very much in profound differences of race. . . . But we recognize that the social life of the white has created in him many fictitious necessities which oblige him to proceed as if a savage and a cat. . . . The desire for profit, the fever for gold, convert the pale man into the implacable instrument of blood and fire. The Asiatic affirms that the white man does not have a heart. We do not know what the Africans say on the matter. . . . Probably they would say that the white man combines in himself all three colours, having a white skin, a yellow heart, and a black soul.[60]

Coming dangerously close at times to a racism that denied virtue to the white 'race', Prada applied something of the same treatment to the *mestizo*: 'Nothing compares with the glacial greed of the mixed bloods that leads them to play a game with human flesh.

Very little does the suffering and the death of their fellow human beings matter to them when it results in a few pennies profit.'[61]

Prada, of course, was not the first Peruvian to discover the Indian problem. Nor did he make as valuable suggestions about the possible solution of it as did many of his contemporaries. Piérola and the neopositivists, as well-intentioned as Prada and frequently better-informed about the Indians, believed that a prerequisite to their elevation was the transformation of coastal Peru. They planned and worked successfully towards creating a more viable coastal economy so that the wealth thereby generated could in part be used to initiate the necessarily expensive programme of education, agrarian modernization, and road construction that could lead to the assimilation of the Indian. All the while Prada was urging the immediate violence of the Indian and the bloody destruction of the productive coastal economy.

Ultimately abandoning faith in socialism because of the governmental oppression which he felt it must lead to, Prada decided that only the totally unfettered and unchecked individual could, through his own efforts, develop his innately good qualities. Embracing a Rousseau-like belief in the virtue of the 'noble savage' before his corruption by institutions, Prada began to preach the destruction of all restraining influences on man. He became, in short, an anarchist. 'The anarchist ideal,' wrote an approving Prada, 'can be summarized in two lines: unlimited liberty and the greatest well-being of the individual, together with abolition of the State and of private property.'[62]

In his late stage as an anarchist Prada abandoned the cry for immediate revolution. The development of an anarchistic consciousness even among the people of Peru most favourably disposed towards it, the Indians, would be a long-term project which could not greatly be advanced by outside stimuli. Anarchism would create a new Christianity without Christ, stated Prada; and then in one of his rare touches of realism he added: 'If in twenty centuries it has not been possible to Christianize the world, how many centuries will it take to Anarchize it?'[63] Before he settled back into resigned patience, however, Prada had established a programme which every future Peruvian iconoclast who believed in the phoenix approach to national regeneration could enthusiastically embrace. He had tried to set the sierra against the coast, the Indian against the white and the *cholo*, the poor against the rich, the free-thinker and atheist against the believer, the young against the old, the civilian against the soldier, and the citizen against the policeman.[64]

Prada, who had begun by disliking Piérola at the time when the two had been students in the San Toribio Seminary, ended, understandably, by hating the man. Piérola was the living refutation of most of what Prada wrote and spoke. Piérola searched for and found much that was worthwhile in the past and used it as a foundation for his constructive ideas on the present. He attracted men of integrity to public life; he united social classes and enlisted the army in the task of Peruvian reconstruction. Without having to resort to exotic socialistic ideas, he established an administration that was honest and firm, yet tolerant of dissenters; and he went far towards establishing the basis for a self-sustaining national economy. Instead of encouraging disunion he effectively exhorted Peruvians to seek a consensus on issues over which they had previously fought. Piérola proved, in short, that in order to regenerate Peru it was not necessary first to reduce it to ashes.

7

Beginnings of Modernization in One of the
Perus, 1899–1919

FORCES OF MODERNIZATION CONFRONT BARRIERS TO CHANGE

IF history were logical and rational, it has been written, Nicolás
de Piérola would have again become president of Peru in the early
twentieth century.[1] Piérola was not re-elected, but in other ways
the history of Peru appeared to be quite logical in the twenty
years after his notable presidential term. There were no drastic
deviations from the policies advanced by the democratic caudillo
and the institutions introduced by him appeared to grow stronger.
Continuity in political development seemed at last to have been
achieved. Administrations were most of the time cautiously progressive and inclined to respect the personal liberties of citizens
and the laws of the land, at least in coastal Peru. A short-term
President, Manuel Candamo, with his equanimity and circumspection, and José Pardo, son of Manuel and twice president in the
post-Piérola years, with his restraint and probity, his respect for
the ways of legality, and his interest in gradual change, were sym-
bols of the time. Ruling between the two terms of Pardo, the
ebullient Augusto B. Leguía and the visionary, impatient
Guillermo Billinghurst, neither of whom suffered gladly the
restraints imposed by the constitution and legal codes, did not
seem to belong to the period. Bored by institutionalism and in-
fatuated by the rapid development that the wealth of Peru seemed
to make possible, they were a throwback to the era of José Balta
when heedless activists had controlled the country.

It is surprising that the prosperity actually enjoyed by the
country did not turn the heads of more Peruvian statesmen.

Between 1900 and 1914 Peru experienced one of its most dramatic periods of economic development.[2] Exports of mineral products, especially copper, as well as of cotton, sugar, wool and hides increased rapidly. For the 1905–15 period the value of trade and commerce was on an average 475 per cent. higher than between 1900 and 1904. After 1907 exports consistently exceeded imports, greatly encouraging Peruvian economists who at the time were convinced that a favourable balance of trade was virtually all that was needed to assure national prosperity.

At the beginning of the twentieth century Peru was also in the early stages of a fairly rapid population increase. Between the censuses of 1876 and 1940, the number of inhabitants rose from 2·7 to 7 million. Rural labourers in mounting numbers entered the cities and as early as 1903 Lima had a population of nearly 140,000. The growing population and the demographic shift from country to city provided Peru with an abundant supply of cheap, unskilled labour, greatly facilitating the rise of factories along the coast.[3]

Expanding population and increasing economic opportunities produced an impact on politics. Towards the end of the nineteenth century the *Civilista* leader, Mariano Nicolás Valcárcel, had observed that all the members of any political party in Peru could fit into one railroad car.[4] By 1900, however, approximately 110,000 voters, many of them with definite party affiliations, were inscribed in the electoral registry and the number climbed steadily if not spectacularly in the ensuing few years.

Although close to 90 per cent. of the population was illiterate and therefore disfranchised, the urban middle groups, which were at least partially educated, claimed in ascending numbers the right of participating in politics. Membership in traditional professional groups, especially the bureaucracy, was expanding significantly. There began to appear an ample number of small merchants, in many instances the descendants of Spanish and Italian immigrants. There was also an increasing number of small-scale manufacturers of consumer goods, and the ranks of skilled or semi-skilled workers employed by foreign and locally controlled mining, industrial and services firms were growing. These people found their way into the traditional political parties. During the first decade of the twentieth century membership in the *Civilista* Party included professional groups both of Lima and the provinces, urban property holders, industrialists and business heads, rural landowners, bureaucrats of the central and departmental governments, and the social leaders of the coastal cities. The Democratic Party had as its members many talented lawyers, a few merchants, a good number of large-scale rural landowners, and a generous sprinkling of skilled and semi-skilled labourers. If the Democratic Party had the broadest base of popular support, the Constitutionalist Party enjoyed the least. With the exception of a few civilian politicians of note, Constitutionalists were mainly active or retired military officers.

Prosperity and expanding opportunities for upward social mobility enjoyed by new sectors of the population did not bring a halt to the quest for reform initiated principally by the neo-positivists in the lean years following the Treaty of Ancón. In the years between 1899 and 1919 an impressive number of Peruvian intellectuals turned their attention to social problems and devised reform programmes that were often quite sweeping. Elvira García y García (1862–1951) inaugurated a feminist movement that elicited widespread support[5] and also won powerful backing in her pleas for the expansion of primary school facilities.[6] For the first time numerous studies were published dealing not only with the general economic and social problems of the country,[7] but with such specific topics as public health and sanitation, prostitution, infant mortality,[8] workers' housing,[9] and even agrarian reform.[10] In addition a notable body of legislation aimed at protecting urban labour was approved by congress and some of the provisions of the enlightened social laws were actually enforced by administrations impressed by the need to deal paternalistically with a growing city proletariat so as to avoid class warfare. The story was different in regard to the Indian labourer of the sierra. Although intellectuals more and more spoke and wrote of the need to protect, uplift and assimilate the Indian,[11] little was done to aid the native.

The period from the end of Piérola's term to the conclusion of World War I has been described as one of parliamentary *caquicuismo* or 'bossism', and bureaucratic Caesarism.[12] The owners of large sierra estates, unchecked *caciques* of their kingdoms, focused their attention on national politics around the turn of the century and easily arranged to have themselves elected to congress. Once installed therein these landowners, referred to in Peru as *gamonales*, were content to become the bureaucratic puppets of the executive

Caesar. Dependent upon the support of these congressmen, the president was not inclined to restrain their powers as absolute *caciques* in the sierra. Thus assured of the tolerant forbearance of the executive, the *gamonales* continued to impose feudal conditions on their labourers and, utilizing semi-legal methods of chicanery as well as force, expanded their rural holdings at the expense of Indian communities.

However much some leaders of the *Civilista* Party, which shortly after the end of Piérola's administration became the dominant political group, were committed to the modernization of coastal Peru, they retreated before the obstacles that confronted them in the sierra and tended to forget about the region. Meantime, other *Civilista* leaders began to display boredom with modernization and reform whether in the sierra or on the coast. The outstanding intellectual spokesman for men of this type was Alejandro O. Deustua (1849–1945).

Beginning his teaching career at San Marcos as a member of the department of philosophy, Deustua came by the turn of the century to wield considerable intellectual influence through his popular courses on subjective philosophy and aesthetics. Reacting against the rationalism and utilitarian materialism of positivism, Deustua worked out a complex and highly eclectic philosophy of aesthetics that stressed the importance of intuition and above all the complete liberty of the will. Categorizing the activities of the human mind according to a hierarchical scale of values, Deustua taught that the pursuit of scientific knowledge and the use of science in the quest of utilitarian objectives represented the lowest form of intellectual occupation. On a higher plane was the endeavour to understand the 'moral ideal'. Higher still was the quest for the 'ideal image of God', while the highest of all human undertakings was 'the free activity that creates the fine arts, in which there is realized the greatest of all values, that is, the pure, the absolute, the most unattenuated human liberty'.[13]

Outside of those studying in the faculty of letters at San Marcos, very few Peruvians concerned themselves with mastering the complex, idealistic philosophy concocted by Deustua. Many, however, embraced wholeheartedly the social, political and economic implications which Deustua derived from his philosophy and which he tirelessly propagated not only in the classroom, but in newspapers and periodicals and in his several widely-read books.

If the early positivists had wanted to ignore the plight of the masses in order to bring about material progress through elimination of the unfit, Deustua wanted to ignore the lower classes so as to bring about the higher cultural and artistic development of the élite. Only a small handful of select souls, in Deustua's view, possessed the spiritual and intellectual capacity to succeed in the most exalted of all human enterprise, cultural and artistic creation resulting from the energy of the totally liberated will. According to him, it was with the small élite possessing the potentialities for sublime creativity that society should almost exclusively concern itself. The newly-generated wealth of Peru should be used for the advantage of the handful of Peruvians capable of pursuing the highest calling in life, not squandered on the masses who, if indulged, would lower the level of human activity because of their inability to appreciate any save material values. Above all, it was a waste of time and money to attempt to uplift the Indian, because the native was by nature incapable of being more than a machine for the production of material commodities.

In Deustua's opinion the number of primary and secondary schools should be curtailed rather than expanded, as the neo-positivists and especially Manuel Vicente Villarán had advocated. The more universal education was the more inevitably it would be concerned with imparting only utilitarian knowledge pertaining to the production of tangible wealth. Widespread popular education aroused the materialistic appetites of the masses and made them less content with the lowly place they were destined to occupy in the properly ordered society because of their lack of capacity to free their wills from temporal influences and become artistically creative. In the ideal educational structure, attention should be focused on the university. It was only the university which could be properly concerned with the highest goal of education, the preparation of a small directing class dedicated to liberating itself from the grubby world of material reality through artistic creativity. Deustua argued against the establishment of additional universities, insisting that one institution of higher learning in Lima and attended by a minuscule student body was sufficient to serve the true needs of Peru.[14]

Deustua was personally persuaded that higher education must seriously concern itself with instilling in the directing élite, made up of the hereditary classes of privilege, a sense of paternalistic responsibility to provide the lower classes with at least a modicum of that which the masses were capable of appreciating, that is, material comfort. However, many who most enthusiastically accepted Deustua's teachings ignored the attitude of *noblesse oblige* which he preached. They adhered to what they understood of the Deustua philosophy simply because they saw in it the justification for their own bloated wealth and their heartless exploitation of the masses. All they had to do in order to quiet their consciences and to satisfy themselves that they belonged to the élite whose creativity was its justification for existence was to read an occasional book and sometimes write and pay for the publication of one of their own.

Deustua's followers never gained control over the *Civilista* Party. But they did impede the advance of progressive elements within it. Moreover, the element of reaction introduced into *Civilismo* by a minority hiding behind the mask of philosophical idealism served by the 1920's as the justification for a new group of iconoclastic, phoenix-style reformers who argued that all virtue and progressive thought had disappeared within the most important traditional party and that the entire political structure had to be destroyed before the genuine quest for national regeneration could begin.

THE RULE OF LÓPEZ DE ROMAÑA AND CANDAMO: THE DECLINE OF THE DEMOCRATS AND RESURGENCE OF 'CIVILISMO', 1899–1904

The 1899 elections of Eduardo López de Romaña, arranged by Piérola with the support of both Democrats and *Civilistas*, quickly touched off an abortive revolutionary uprising, led by Guillermo Billinghurst and Augusto Durand. Although in the past a close personal friend of Piérola, Billinghurst could not forget old political prejudices and insisted that his party should not continue to co-operate with the *Civilistas*. He felt further that he was entitled to the presidency because of the past support and economic backing he had extended at critical times to Piérola and the Democratic Party. Durand, a fiery politician born in Juánuco in 1871, had fought with Piérola in the 1895 revolution against Cáceres, but had subsequently been alienated by what he considered the excessive clericalism of the democratic caudillo. 'The last of the truly romantic figures of Peruvian politics,'[15] noted for his dramatic escapes from the jails which he frequently occupied because of his political activities, Durand never had to look far to discover provocation for revolution. In addition to rebelling against López de Romaña, Durand, whose San Marcos thesis was appropriately enough entitled *The Right of Rebellion* (*El derecho de rebelión*), had earlier arisen against both Cáceres and Piérola, and in the future would do so against presidents Candamo, Leguía and Billinghurst, and against a provisional executive, Oscar R. Benavides. Billinghurst and Durand in 1899 sought the support of Cáceres, still in exile in Buenos Aires, for their insurrection. The hero of the War of the Pacific replied with a plea that Peruvians of all political persuasions should support López de Romaña as the constitutional president. Shortly thereafter the revolutionary movement collapsed.

Fifty-two years of age when he assumed office on 8 September, López de Romaña was the first engineer to serve as a Peruvian president. A native of Arequipa, the new president had received his higher education at King's College, London, and had pursued his engineering profession both in England and Brazil before becoming his country's first minister of development during the Piérola administration. A self-effacing, cultured man who wrote comments in Greek and Latin in many of his books, López de Romaña was the soul of integrity. Obsessed with frugality, he scrupulously supervised the preparation and implementation of the national budget, accumulating a substantial treasury surplus by the time he left office. During his régime Peru adopted the gold standard – Piérola had begun the use of the gold standard in all government transactions – and from then until the late World War I period the *sol* retained its stability, being valued at approximately one half a United States dollar ($0·486). Peruvian politics, however, exhibited a mounting trend towards instability.

In Lima's bitterly-contested election for municipal officials held on 1 December 1900, Democrats and *Civilistas* supported separate lists. Piérola himself was one of the councillor candidates and the assumption among his partisans was that the former president would be named mayor (*alcalde*) by his fellow city officials following a Democratic sweep. As it turned out, the *Civilistas* gained the electoral majority. Denied not only the expected office of mayor, but also failing to win a councillor's post in the Democratic defeat, the frustrated Piérola vowed to retire from politics, accusing President López de Romaña of having been partial to the *Civilistas* during the campaign.

Although Limeños were denied the services of the ex-president, they did obtain in 1901 perhaps the best mayor their city had had since Manuel Pardo. In that year Federico Elguera began his eight-year tenure in the mayor's office. With the collaboration of the revered Inspector of Hygiene and university professor Juan Bautista Agnoli, Elguera introduced modern sanitation facilities in Lima. Under his direction streets were paved, sidewalks built, markets opened and free public baths initiated. In addition electrified streetcar lines were introduced, while various plazas were either constructed or restored, and a model working-class district was built in the suburbs of Lima. The civic-minded mayor also supervised the construction of a modern race track and of an imposing municipal theatre (today the Teatro Segura). 'Elguera interrupted forever,' wrote a sympathetic observer, 'the profound sleep of ignorance and routine to which the city had been consigned by its inhabitants. The new Lima ... had its inception under the energetic hand and the intellectual foresight of Federico Elguera.'[16]

As Lima's local government found a new impetus, mounting problems beset the national administration. After experiencing a series of cabinet crises, López de Romaña tried to effect a reconciliation with Piérola, asking him to become prime minister. Still blaming his defeat in the Lima elections on a lack of executive support, Piérola spurned the request. Thereafter the president began to favour *Civilistas* over Democrats in filling cabinet positions. He also formed a fast friendship with Manuel Candamo, the man who had emerged as *Civilismo*'s most influential leader. While some Democrats felt that the president was justified in this policy, others accused him of treason to the party. The split within the ranks of the Democrats was widened in 1902 when Billinghurst, living in Chile since his ill-fated revolution against López de Romaña, returned to Peru. His intense hatred of the *Civilistas* in no way diminished by the passing years, Billinghurst employed such intemperate terms in accusing his old political adversaries of cowardice during the War of the Pacific that it is reported Piérola was moved to comment: 'My dear Guillermo, how is it that you hope to govern Peru if you cannot govern your emotions.'[17]

Harshly denounced by the branch of the Democrats that looked to Billinghurst as the hope for the future, and increasingly snubbed by those who still followed the lead of Piérola, López de Romaña's problems mounted with the definitive rupture that occurred between both branches of the Democrats and their former allies, the *Civilistas*. The two parties quarrelled bitterly in selecting the candidates for the one-third of the congressional seats that were up for election in 1901. Following that, Democrats and *Civilistas* abandoned all attempts at co-operation in formulating congressional lists. Faced now with the utter impossibility of maintaining even a semblance of the alliance that had been formed in 1895, the harassed president cast off his remaining ties with the Democrats and ruled exclusively with the *Civilistas*. He found a new ally in 1902 when Andrés Cáceres returned to the country following his seven-year exile, determined, come what may, to prevent the re-election of his old enemy, Piérola. Before long an agreement was celebrated between *Civilistas* and Constitutionalists, with both parties pledged to support the régime and policies of López de Romaña in the hope of obtaining his support for the presidential candidate they would jointly present in 1903. There thus began a long-enduring collaboration between the *Civilistas*, who had come into being largely to thwart the political activities of the military, and the Constitutionalists, made up predominantly of military officers.

The last half of the López de Romaña administration was further complicated by the appearance of the Liberal Party. Ignoring the advice of some of the elder fathers of Peruvian liberalism to avoid the use of a name so intimately associated with anticlericalism, 'because Peruvian men were dominated by the pious women (*beatas*) who in turn were dominated by the priests from the confessional',[18] a group of young men among whom Augusto Durand was by far the most colourful leader launched the Liberal Party in 1901. The new party enjoyed considerable support from the professional classes and the new urban middle sectors, and also attracted recruits from the landowning *caciques* of the sierra, as well as from the former members of the *Unión Nacional* that began to languish when González Prada withdrew from it in 1902. In addition to expounding an anticlericalism that was considerably attenuated from the José Gálvez and González Prada variety, the Liberal Party attacked the alleged electoral manipulations begun by Piérola and continued by López de Romaña, called for absolute honesty of elections and inviolability of the constitution, provincial autonomy, greater congressional power accompanied by the curtailment of executive prerogatives, and liberty of industry rather than the economic intervention which both Democrats and *Civilistas* were said to favour.

Not having been in existence long enough to acquire significant strength, the Liberal Party took little part in the presidential elections of 1903. Maintaining that none of the major parties deserved their support, Liberals backed a weak candidate whom they realized had no chance of success and watched sullenly as President López de Romaña and his *Civilista* and Constitutionalist partisans endorsed the presidential bid of Manuel Candamo. Finding it impossible at the moment to heal the breach within his Democratic Party, Piérola decided to await more propitious circumstances in the future and meantime to stand by his 1900 declaration of withdrawal from politics. He therefore gave tacit approval to the campaign of the *Civilista* leader, Candamo, who happened to be a close personal friend, and persuaded many fellow Democrats to follow a similar course. Probably the former president hoped that his actions would win the gratitude of *Civilistas*, inducing them to resume their collaboration with the Democrats and ultimately to support his candidacy in 1907.

The sixty-year-old Candamo was inaugurated on 8 September 1903. A pronounced liberal and follower of José Gálvez in his youth, Candamo had entered the *Civilista* Party at the moment of its founding by Manuel Pardo. Subsequently he had served as mayor of Lima. During the War of the Pacific he was captured by enemy troops and sent as a prisoner to Chile. In 1886 he entered the senate and began his major political task of rebuilding his party. A figure of moderation by the time he came to the presidency and noted for his profound respect for the law, Candamo stated shortly before assuming the executive powers that great men were not needed to govern the republic, but rather 'just and honest men'. 'My ambition will be fulfilled,' he added, 'if upon leaving office my conscience tells me and the citizens recognize that I have been just and honest in discharging the functions which the nation has conferred on me.'[19]

Unhappily for Peru the talented, modest, and tolerant Candamo, who in the early days of his presidency went a long way towards re-establishing a basis of co-operation with the Democrats, was already in the final stages of a fatal sickness when he took office. Acting on the advice of his physician he travelled to Arequipa in early April to avail himself of the medicinal springs in the area. Treatment and rest were to no purpose, and the president died on 7 May. New presidential elections were at once scheduled for August.

In attempting to select a candidate, the *Civilistas* revealed serious internal dissension. One faction of the party, a predominantly youthful group in which such intellectuals as Javier Prado, Manuel Vicente Villarán and José Matías Manzanilla were active, wished to defend and to advance the progressive, reform spirit in which Manuel Pardo had founded *Civilismo*. Their preferred candidate for the 1904 elections was the forty-year-old José Pardo, son of Peru's first full-term civilian president. Another and generally older element wished to convert the party into a defender of the *status quo*. *Civilistas* of this type, acknowledging Deustua as their intellectual prophet, hoped to nominate an elderly party hack named Isaac Alzamora as the candidate. In the 'battle of the generations' within *Civilismo* the so-called Young Turks won out and Pardo was proclaimed the party's candidate. Of incalculable help to the young generation in gaining the victory were the shrewd manipulations of Augusto B. Leguía, a promising business and political leader who like Pardo had held a cabinet post in the Candamo administration.

Piérola's plans had gone awry. His friend Candamo had died before being able to consummate the hoped-for reconciliation between Democrats and *Civilistas*. Realizing that if he was to become president again he would have to wage his campaign without *Civilista* support, Piérola began to search for new political allies. He found them, curiously enough, in the Liberal Party. Although founding their party largely to combat the 'reactionary clericalism' that the democratic caudillo was said to stand for, the Liberals, unable to reach an understanding with the *Civilista* – Constitutionalist alliance, decided that their only chance to acquire political patronage lay in co-operating with the Democrats to oust the incumbents.

The campaign of 1904 was spirited and by no means free from violence. A new Lima daily, *La Prensa*,[20] founded in 1903, supported Piérola, while *El Comercio* favoured Pardo. The rival editorials were lively, but not as lively as the street harangues of

Piérola who accused the *Civilistas* of lacking honesty and respect for Peruvian institutions, and of trying to impose upon the country a tax system that would impoverish the masses while enriching the élite. But sensing that the rather haphazard Democratic–Liberal campaign could not successfully challenge the smooth and well-organized effort of the *Civilista*–Constitutionalist coalition, Piérola withdrew from the contest five days before the scheduled elections. He justified this move on the grounds that the electoral tribunal would not permit an honest counting of returns. Unopposed at the last minute, Pardo received approximately 100,000 votes and assumed his presidential duties in September 1904.

THE 'CIVILISTAS' IN POWER, 1904–12

José Pardo, who had begun to play a conspicuous rôle in Peruvian politics only during the 1900 Lima municipal elections, had previously won respect as an expert defender of Peru's boundary claims in disputes with Ecuador and Bolivia and also as a San Marcos professor of diplomatic law and international treaties. The new president wasted little time before he began to fulfil the hopes which the young reformist wing of *Civilismo* had placed in him. 'Dynamic and progressive within his conservatism,'[21] Pardo quickened the tempo of economic development that had begun during the Piérola administration, improved the organization and efficiency of the treasury, acted in statesmanlike manner to resolve some of Peru's international disputes, and, most important of all, encouraged the advance of education and co-operated with the drive towards enactment of social legislation.

As dedicated to widespread popular education as his father had been, José Pardo enjoyed the advantage over the first *Civilista* president in that the economic prosperity of Peru enabled him to proceed further towards the realization of his dreams. In his four-year term the portion of the national budget allotted to the ministry of justice and instruction rose from 9·63 to 17·2 per cent. of the government's expenditures, 'one of the most dramatic increases in educational spending which Peru has ever experienced.'[22] Among the fruits of Pardo's generous support of education was the building during his administration of more than two thousand primary schools. This made possible an increase of from 85,000 to 156,000 primary students between 1904 and 1908.[23] The

President also encouraged the establishment of the school of arts and crafts in Lima which later came to be known as the José Pardo National Polytechnical School, founded the Peruvian Academy of History, and provided new quarters for the San Fernando School of Medicine.

As a San Marcos professor Pardo had become acquainted with the social legislation which his colleague, José Matías Manzanilla, had been advocating in his various classes. Early in his administration Pardo named Manzanilla, at the time a promising *Civilista* deputy, head of a committee to prepare a series of labour laws. Having already devoted long hours to the matter, Manzanilla was able quickly to prepare ten legislative proposals calling among other things for sanitary and safe working conditions, regulations of child and woman labour, employer's liability and compensation for all workers injured in industrial accidents, guarantees of the right of workers to organize and strike, specific contracts to govern employer-employee relations, and obligatory rest periods and reduction of work hours with the ultimate aim being nation-wide adoption of the eight-hour day.[24] Manzanilla's proposed social legislation was enthusiastically supported by one of his closest friends and colleagues in the chamber of deputies, Luis Miró Quesada, a crusading journalist for the newspaper *El Comercio* which his family owned.[25]

Owing to the resolute opposition of conservative congressmen, the Manzanilla proposals, generally supported by President Pardo, failed for some years to gain legislative approval. Not until 1911, in fact, was the first of the bills introduced by Manzanilla, that establishing employer's liability in industrial accidents, proclaimed the law of the land.

In economic administration, renovation proceeded more rapidly during the Pardo régime. Under the supervision of the minister of the treasury, Augusto B. Leguía, the collection and disbursement of the national revenue was placed upon a more efficient basis. At the same time several state agencies were created to bring about the more systematic handling of the revenue and also to encourage the wider exploitation of national resources. Leguía was the guiding spirit behind the founding in 1906 of the Peruvian Steamship Company (*Compañía Peruana de Vapores*) and the building of a dike at Callao. The optimistic treasury minister also presented plans for railroad expansion that in their ambition rivalled the schemes of Henry Meiggs. While the Pardo régime did not come close to realization of the full scope of the Leguía railway plans, the Andean community of Sicuani was at least linked by rail to Cuzco and the Central Railroad was extended northward from La Oroya to Cerro de Pasco and southward to Huancayo.

The expansion of railroad facilities was in large part responsible for the interest that North American capitalists began to assume in the copper resources at Cerro de Pasco. In 1901 and 1902 mining experts A. W. McCune and James B. Haggin, backed by capitalists who included J. P. Morgan the elder, Phoebe Apperson Hearst, D. C. Mills and James Higgins, took the initial steps to organize a company to exploit the Cerro de Pasco reserves. After gaining the upper hand in a dispute with a Peruvian firm, the North American controlled Cerro de Pasco Copper Corporation acquired nearly six thousand acres of land, laid some eighty-three miles of railroad track in addition to what had already been constructed under government auspices, and established a refining plant eight miles south of the town of Cerro de Pasco. American capital had made its first significant plunge into Peru's extractive industry, helping to initiate the age of copper.[26]

Another new resource which Peru began to exploit during Pardo's first term was rubber. The President gave full support to the legendary native of the vast Amazonian department of Loreto, Julio C. Arana, who as early as 1901 was beginning to be referred to as 'the king of Peru's black gold'.[27] In the region between the Marañón and Amazon Rivers on the south and the Napo and Putumayo to the north, claimed in the early twentieth century by both Colombia and Peru, Arana carved out a tremendous Amazonian empire of nearly 25,000,000 acres which he ruled with a personal army of ten thousand men. Throughout his rubber kingdom Arana dispatched his workers, many of them aborigines, to tap the rubber trees. During the rubber boom, which lasted until approximately 1912 when British plantations in the East Indies began to dominate the market, men from all parts of the world flocked to Arana's kingdom where they lived as often as not according to the law of the knife, the machete and the Winchester rifle.

Because the rubber boom focused attention on the long-smouldering boundary dispute with Colombia, President Pardo undertook diplomatic negotiations to try to settle the matter. Before the end of his term a convention favourable to Peru had been signed. The Colombian congress, however, refused to ratify the instrument, and not until the 1920's were efforts resumed to resolve the issue. Pardo's energetic endeavours to settle boundary disputes with Brazil, Ecuador and Bolivia likewise failed to produce the hoped-for results and Peru thus continued on uneasy terms with its neighbour republics. Probably this is why Pardo, unlike his father, pursued a policy of military preparedness. Military garrisons and schools were improved, and in acquiring up-to-date warships Pardo won for himself the title of father of the modern Peruvian navy.

By the end of 1907 Pardo, with an impressive record of accomplishment behind him, turned his attention to finding among the *Civilistas* a man who could successfully carry out his programme. Understandably, the President hit upon his minister of the treasury, Leguía. Following an unsuccessful revolution on 1 May led by Augusto Durand, which resulted in the imprisonment of many Democrats and Liberals, Leguía remained as the sole candidate in the field. The elections of 25 May 1908, were a mere formality and the following September Leguía was installed in the presidency. Pardo, more popular at the end of his fruitful administration than upon assuming office four years earlier, was determined to give the new executive a free rein in the conduct of affairs and so departed for Europe. He did not return to Peru until 1914.

Born in the northern department of Lambayeque in 1863, Leguía had completed his early education in Valparaíso, Chile, having been sent there because he suffered from a bronchial ailment. In Valparaíso Leguía learned English, which proved of inestimable value in his later business career. Short, slender, wiry, agile in movement and thought, Leguía possessed remarkable resources of energy which he lavished both on business and politics. After the War of the Pacific he became general manager of the Peruvian–Bolivian–Ecuadoran branches of the New York Life Insurance Company. In addition he organized with his brother Carlos a commercial firm which exported hides to the United States and sugar to Chile. Leguía also established his own insurance company (*Compañía de Seguros Sud América*) and, following a trip to London, became manager of the British Sugar Company Limited and also president of the National Bank of Peru.

A shrewd and highly successful businessman, it was only natural that during his first term as president Leguía would make his main contribution in the economic order. Taking advantage of the provision in the Grace Contract permitting Peru to retain all of the guano deemed necessary for domestic use, the new president established the Guano Administrative Company (*Compañía Administradora del Guano*). This firm encouraged the increased use of guano on the agricultural estates of coastal Peru and as a result the entire annual production of the rich fertilizer began to be employed within the country. According to an eminent Peruvian economic historian the marked increase in guano use 'was the most important contribution of Leguía to the development of a capitalist economy . . . with the new stimulus of government, the coastal landowners began to amass their great fortunes, and sugar and cotton became the basic products of the Peruvian economy'.[28]

In political matters, Leguía was decidedly less successful than in the economic ones. The crisis that ultimately led to the frustration of many of his political aspirations began with a Democratic-Liberal uprising in 1909.[29] On 29 May Carlos de Piérola, the brother, and Isaias and Amadeo de Piérola, the sons of the democratic caudillo who may or may not have been personally involved in the plot, launched what was perhaps the most audacious uprising in Peru's political history. Joined by about twenty-five supporters, they stormed the national palace and succeeded in making Leguía their prisoner. With the President in their power, however, the insurgents could not decide what to do with him. Proceeding almost aimlessly down the main street, the *Jirón de la Unión*, with their distinguished prisoner in their midst, the rebels shot their pistols into the air and shouted 'Viva Piérola!' The military attaché of the United States legation came upon the strange procession, spotted Leguía in its midst, and ran to tell his friends that the President had gone berserk and was participating in a pro-Piérola street demonstration. The procession ultimately made its way to the statue of Simón Bolívar before the senate chambers where a small detachment of troops rescued the President. Leguía inquired as to the name of the officer who commanded the loyal troops and the man replied, 'I am Ensign Gómez.' 'Thank you Ensign Gómez,' said the President, 'you are now a captain.'[30]

With the rebellion against him so easily crushed, Leguía grew more arbitrary in his rule, giving many hints that he intended to dissolve the somewhat recalcitrant congress. This led to a split within the *Civilista* Party, which had managed to maintain a fairly solid front ever since the 'battle of the generations' in 1904. While some *Civilistas* were willing to support the President in any and all of his actions, others formed the 'bloc' or 'Independent *Civilista* Group', which sought support from other parties in resisting the presidential ambitions and protecting the prerogatives of congress. When Leguía interfered scandalously in the 1911 congressional elections in order to assure the victory of men completely subservient to the presidential will, the Independent *Civilistas* and the Democrats began seriously to explore the possibility of joining in a united front against the executive. At this point Leguía played into the hands of his foes when, ignoring the popular clamour in favour of amnesty, he insisted that those suspected of involvement in the abortive *coup* of May 1909 remain in jail.[31] The students of San Marcos now made their first significant move into the political arena. Led by the respected young intellectual José de la Riva Agüero y Osma (1885–1944), descendant and namesake of the leader of the independence movement, the university students in September of 1911 demonstrated in support of political amnesty. When Leguía responded by putting Riva Agüero in jail, the Independent *Civilistas* and Democrats joined in demanding the immediate release of the student leader, as well as freedom for the political prisoners who had been languishing in jail since May 1909. Organizing impressive demonstrations, Independent *Civilistas* and Democrats alternately shouted 'Viva Pardo!' and 'Viva Piérola!' It seemed that some *Civilistas* at least were in as close *rapport* with the Democrats as they had been in 1895.

Following a massive student demonstration in which many young men were injured owing to needless police brutality, Leguía capitulated for the moment and signed an order of amnesty. At the same time he began plotting to cancel the 1912 elections and to prolong his stay in office. His dreams of dictatorship were shattered, however, when the Democrat's second-in-command Guillermo Billinghurst returned from Chile, announced his candidacy, and, as the result of a dynamic campaign, built up the most massive and frenzied popular following of any political figure up to that time in Peru's republican history.

THE RESUSCITATION AND DEMISE OF THE DEMOCRATIC PARTY 1912-15

Born in Arica in 1851, Billinghurst was the grandson of an English naval officer who had fought on the side of the independence movement in the Río de la Plata. A millionaire, owing to his own successful nitrate ventures and a generous inheritance from a brother, and a journalist who had helped to found the newspaper *La Industria* in Iquique, Billinghurst was in spite of his lack of university education a man of culture and had one of the best libraries to be found at the time on the Pacific coast of Latin America. Dissatisfied on one occasion with available Spanish versions of Shakespeare, he had made his own translations. Brilliant but erratic, according to some even mentally unbalanced, Billinghurst had already alarmed Piérola by his inability to control his emotions. Piérola, in fact, is reported once to have said that placing presidential powers in Billinghurst's hands would be as foolish as giving a loaded gun to an infant.[32]

Billinghurst has been described as a mixture of 'syndicalist, socialist, anarchist and Jacobean Leftist'.[33] But Jorge Basadre is closer to the truth in asserting that the ideas of the businessman-politician did not even remotely approach socialist or other extremist doctrines. Instead, according to Basadre, Billinghurst was the precursor in Peru of 'enlightened and demagogic capitalism'.[34] An enthusiastic supporter of capitalism, Billinghurst nonetheless repudiated the unregulated economy advocated by liberals because of the abuses it engendered. He feared that if the upper classes did not begin to make greater concessions to labourers, the masses would arise and destroy the capitalist system. Pessimistic about the willingness of Peruvian capitalists to make voluntary concessions in the name of enlightened self-interest, Billinghurst sought by demagogic appeals to arouse the masses as a means of putting pressure upon the directing groups to initiate socio-economic reforms. Thereby capitalism's survival would be assured, with a spirit of social solidarity being substituted for that of the class struggle.

The times were right for the sort of campaign that Billinghurst, who had been a popular mayor of Lima in 1909 and 1910, chose to wage at the end of Leguía's first term. Especially in Lima the rise of industry and the expansion of general business activity had brought into being an urban proletariat that was anxious to assume a more assertive rôle in politics. An organized labour movement had appeared in 1904 and with it had come strikes at the Vitarte textile mills and other factories in the capital city. In 1911 Lima had passed through a period of serious labour unrest and there were thousands of people ready to respond ecstatically to the offers of better housing and working conditions and the promise, which Billinghurst stressed above all others, of a bigger loaf of bread for five cents.

From the moment of his arrival in Lima, Billinghurst won the backing not only of the masses, but of upper-class politicians representing the Independent *Civilista* group as well as the Liberal Party and his own Democratic Party. The candidate's position, however, appeared to be weakened when during the course of the campaign Piérola withdrew his support. Piérola advised the members of his party to boycott all electoral processes until the entire political structure had been thoroughly renovated, and, without bothering to explain what type of renovation he recommended, asserted that Billinghurst was not committed to sweeping political reform.

The introduction of a schism within the party he had founded proved to be Piérola's last significant political act. On 23 June 1913, the disillusioned political veteran died at the age of seventy-four. Although he left it sorely divided, his Democratic Party, or at least a large segment of it, had in the meantime savoured the first fruits of victory since 1895. Co-operating with the Independent *Civilistas*, with many Liberals, and even a smattering of Constitutionalists, the Democrats who chose to ignore the advice of Piérola succeeded in sweeping 'Big Bread' Billinghurst, as he had come to be known, into the presidency.

Assuming his powers on 24 September 1912, the new President displayed from the outset his vaunted energies in attacking government profligacy. Promising to eliminate careless expenditures and to reduce the bureaucracy, he blamed Peru's directing classes for having permitted an annual increase in government spending since 1895 that averaged close to 25 per cent.[35] In order to effect the economies which he claimed were necessary, the President reduced the portion of the budget allotted to the military from 24·75 to 21·6 per cent.[36] The resulting savings were, to a considerable measure, poured into the public health service that was reorganized and placed under the direction of Dr Enrique León García.

At the risk of offending his partisans among the capitalist classes, Billinghurst began to speak out frequently, and perhaps with unnecessary and provocative emotionalism, in favour of an eight-hour day for all Peru's industrial and commercial establishments. For a few worker groups, mainly in Callao, he even went so far as actually to decree the eight-hour day.[37] The President further sought to solidify his support among the urban masses by expanding public education facilities and by acquiring a large section of land near Lima where he proposed to construct through government and private financing a model village of low-cost workers' houses. A labour law which he succeeded in steering through congress in 1913 was advanced for the times but by no means radical, calling for obligatory collective bargaining between management and workers in individual plants.

In addition to the urban lower classes, Billinghurst turned his attention to the rural proletariat, the Indians, and appointed Teodomiro Gutiérrez Cuevas, his personal emissary, to study social conditions in the southern sierra. An army officer who had held minor posts also in the government bureaucracy, Gutiérrez had written a book condemning the abuses perpetrated by landowners against the native race. Late in 1913 several congressional leaders accused Gutiérrez of stirring up Indian uprisings and inciting *bandoleros* to seize rural property from its rightful owners. Billinghurst responded bitterly that selfish landowning interests were fabricating false charges against his administration. He refrained, however, from introducing legislation to benefit the native, perhaps realizing he could never secure its passage in congress.

Within a year after his inauguration, the President was encountering mounting congressional opposition to a wide variety of his policies. Billinghurst responded by encouraging the workers of Lima and Callao to stage demonstrations intended to intimidate the lawmakers. These tactics only stiffened the resolve of congress to resist the impetuous President. Advised at this point by a close friend, the San Marcos sociologist and respected senator, Mariano H. Cornejo, Billinghurst apparently determined to dissolve congress. It was Cornejo's conviction that the political troubles of Peru stemmed from the fact that the legislature was renewed by thirds, which meant that a President carried into office by a landslide could be thwarted by an opposition majority in congress. Believing that the congress should be elected in its entirety at the same time that the President was chosen, Cornejo urged Billinghurst to suppress the legislature then in session and hold elections for its total renewal in 1914.

As it became increasingly clear that Billinghurst was planning an assault against constitutional regularity, opposition to him mounted. Two undistinguished politicians of the right wing of *Civilismo*, Jorge and Manuel Prado, sons of Mariano Ignacio Prado and brothers of the distinguished intellectual and somewhat left-wing *Civilista* Javier Prado, took a leading rôle in convincing the army that it had the duty to preserve constitutional procedures by overthrowing the dangerous Billinghurst. The wily and astute Colonel José Urdanivia Ginés finally was convinced of the need for intervention by the army and with the help of Oscar R. Benavides, Chief of the General Staff and hero of a 1911 clash between Peruvian and Colombian forces in the Putumayo region, organized a military *golpe* against the President.

On the morning of 4 February 1914, a young infantry officer named Luis M. Sánchez Cerro (1890–1933), who knew nothing of the impending move against Billinghurst was awakened by a companion shouting 'Let's get out into the street.' 'Why?' asked the sleepy soldier. 'Because we're going to take the national palace.' Without demanding to know more, Sánchez Cerro, having quickly arisen, replied, 'All right, then, let's go.'[38] With these words he began a career of revolution-making that would soon establish him as a worthy rival of Augusto Durand.

In their first charge against the national palace the revolutionary troops were hurled back by forces loyal to Billinghurst. At this critical juncture it looked as if the President might gain the upper hand. But Sánchez Cerro, demonstrating the reckless courage that typified his entire career, dashed towards one of the doors of the national palace and succeeded in opening it before crumpling to the ground critically wounded by the bullets of the defenders. Through the breach opened by their fallen comrade, the attackers poured into the palace and within a matter of minutes brought an end to the tumultuous Billinghurst administration. The following year the exiled President died in Iquique.

In the final analysis it is likely that Billinghurst was overthrown not, as some have contended,[39] because of his intentions to benefit the lower classes, but because of his personal idiosyncrasies, his lack of restraint, and his inability to brook opposition which led him to assume a messianic complex at a time when Peruvians had begun at last to place some real faith in institutionalism and constitutional development. During the second term of José Pardo (1915–19) Peruvians would calmly accept a body of social legislation exceeding in scope anything proposed by Billinghurst. It was Billinghurst and his methods, rather than his programme, that Peruvians in an impressive cross-section of class and professional groups ultimately came to regard as abhorrent.

With the overthrow of Billinghurst a new type of militarism had appeared. In the nineteenth century the military had on their own initiative stepped into politics in part to fill a vacuum created by the withdrawal of civilian leaders in their general apathy towards civic affairs. In 1914 the army returned to politics under the urging and prodding of civilians, when the civilians had been unable to find a solution to problems of their own making. From this time on the so-called military problem in Peruvian politics would in most instances be simply a ramification of a civilian problem.

On the very afternoon of Billinghurst's overthrow, congress met and named a civilian-military junta to wield provisional executive power. Appointed at first as the junta's presiding officer, Oscar R. Benavides was on 15 May, following a bloodless *coup* engineered by the junta and a part of congress, declared provisional President.

During his brief term Benavides faced numerous problems.[40] The outbreak of World War I had produced troublesome economic dislocations. As commerce diminished, government income fell sharply, a serious gold outflow began, and many banks were threatened with failure. Benavides was forced to suspend payment on the foreign debt and to resort to the issue of paper money. The provisional President also had to confront an outbreak of Indian violence in the sierra.[41] Most disturbing of all to him was that essentially he felt out of place in the political milieu into which he had been projected. Desiring to be relieved of his burdens and also to see Peru restored to its ordinary constitutional procedures, Benavides began to urge the holding of an inter-party convention to choose a presidential candidate who could win the support of all political groups.

A convention along the lines suggested by Benavides met in March 1915. Presided over by Andrés Cáceres, who had just returned from a three-year assignment as Peru's Envoy in Germany, the convention was attended by representatives of the Civil, Constitutional and Liberal Parties. The Democratic Party alone among the established and traditional political groupings failed to send delegates. It was at this time disorganized, demoralized, and, in fact, already in its death throes. The overwhelming majority of those participating in the convention temporarily forgot their political and personal differences and in a burst of patriotic enthusiasm nominated José Pardo, recently back from Europe and serving for the moment as rector of San Marcos. Although there were rumours that Benavides would have preferred the convention to choose a military man, he did not interfere in its deliberations or with the ensuing elections. Running unopposed, Pardo received 131,289 votes and in troubled times embarked upon his second term.

THE APPEARANCE OF THE ARIELISTS OR FUTURISTS

A new political party, the National Democratic Party (*Partido Nacional Democrático*), founded in February 1915 by the ex-*Civilista* and leader of the 1911 student demonstrations, José de la Riva Agüero, had not participated in the convention of parties that nominated Pardo. Most of its members, moreover, although mildly favourable to Pardo, boycotted the elections, 'not wishing yet to incur political responsibilities'.[42] National Democrats, drawn largely from an intellectual élite of poets, professors, doctors, journalists, philosophers and lawyers, tended to feel it was beneath their dignity to collaborate with the sordid political parties then in existence. Someday, they believed, the overwhelming majority of right-thinking Peruvians would come round to their point of view, following a lengthy process of education to be carried out in the schools of the country. Until the times had become propitious, the National Democrats decided largely to shun politics. Because of this the brilliant editorial writer of *La Prensa*, Luis Fernán Cisneros, fittingly labelled them the Futurists.

The National Democratic Party was the rather apathetic political action group of a generation of gifted intellectuals, the so-called generation of 1900. Because they were strongly influenced by the Uruguayan *pensador*, José Enrique Rodó (1872–1917), whose best-known book *Ariel* (1900) stressed the need to place spiritual, cultural and aesthetic values above materialistic and utilitarian considerations, the men of the 1900 generation came to be known as Arielists. In their generic capacity as intellectuals, then, they were called Arielists, while specifically as politicians they were designated Futurists. Herein lay something of a paradox, for if in politics they ignored the present because of infatuation with the future, in their intellectual pursuits they often tended to ignore the present because of an obsession with the past.

The basic intellectual convictions of the Arielists consisted of a mixture of a Deustua-like belief in the need for the predominance of intellectual élites, a fascination with traditions of the past that was as strong as Bartolomé Herrera's had been, and a paternalistic zeal for protecting the lower classes, rural and urban, that exceeded Billinghurst's. Arielists were convinced that spiritual development in Peru had suffered because of exclusive concern with material development. They believed that the utilitarian values which positivists and neopositivists had asked Peruvians to adopt inevitably produced mediocrity and destroyed 'that which only the disinterested inspiration of intellectual élites can create, that is, a flourishing, vigorous and rich culture'.[43]

Although they turned their attention to both the Indian and Spanish past to discover the true glories of Peru, the traditions and cultural values that had been cherished before the country had fallen under what they considered the baneful and alien influence of liberalism and positivism, the Arielists were by no means totally mired in the past. In one very important respect they were vitally concerned about the present. They realized that the search of an intellectual élite for the authentic values of the past which could be employed as a foundation for the creation of a new and flourishing culture could be interrupted and even permanently ended if social tensions should become so acute as to result in a levelling revolution. Therefore, in order to safeguard culture, not capitalism which had been the primary concern of Billinghurst, the Arielists tried to awaken the social consciousness of the directing classes and to win from them concessions that would ease the plight of the masses.

José de la Riva Agüero was the outstanding figure of the generation of 1900 and the most eloquent spokesman for many of its typical ideas. A firm believer in rule by the élite, Riva Agüero maintained that the truly liberal party was not one which demanded rule by the middle class, but one which maintained a place of leadership for 'men of the superior classes'.[44] While the neo-positivists had also defended rule by the élite, they had regarded this as a temporary necessity within the present stage of develop-ment that society had attained. In a future state of evolution, the neopositivists had generally predicted, the people as a whole would advance to the point of being able to deal effectively with the complexities of democracy and the need for rule by superior minorities would diminish. In doubting that social evolution would ever basically alter the existing realities of political organiz-ation, Riva Agüero reflected the prevailing judgement of the generation of 1900. The older he and his intellectual companions grew, the more convinced they tended to become that government would always have to remain the province of the few.

Predicting that the pursuit of utilitarian values and the worship of the golden calf would lead to 'the destruction of all social ties, the unchecked influence of ferocious selfishness, the destruction of moral restraint, and violent disorganization', Riva Agüero called on Peruvians to resist the abject surrender to industrialism 'which kills all enthusiasm and degrades all nobility'.[45] Turning to the past to discover the values which his countrymen should guard,[46] Riva Agüero found much to admire not only in Spanish but in Indian traditions, and became a champion of cultural *mestizaje*. The future greatness of the country, he maintained, depended upon a blending of the higher spiritual values bequeathed both by Incas and Span-iards. He was particularly impressed by the paternalistic despotism of the Inca empire and by the level of virtue which the Inca aris-tocracy had been able to maintain.[47] Not only because he believed that unless paternalistically protected the Indians would resort to violence, but also because he felt the natives had definite and positive values to contribute to their country, Riva Agüero ad-vocated the humane treatment and ultimate assimilation of the descendants of the Incas.

Another leading intellectual of the generation of 1900 who believed in the value of Peru's traditions and who inclined sym-pathetically towards the Indians[48] was Víctor Andrés Belaúnde (1883–1966), a member of an old and aristocratic but no longer wealthy Arequipa family. Not until Peru devised paternalistic laws and institutions to protect the natives, affirmed Belaúnde, could it overcome its chronic crises.[49] Maintaining that cultural and ethical values were more important than economic factors in influencing human affairs, Belaúnde liked to point out that although the country was prospering as never before, political stagnation had already set in. The reason, he said, lay in the moral crisis which the directing classes were suffering. Obsessed only with accumulating personal fortunes and developing the material wealth of the nation, they had lost the concern for moral and cultural values, a concern which in earlier times had often been displayed by the country's leaders.[50]

One of Peru's first intellectuals to concern himself with the plight of the growing middle sectors, Belaúnde maintained that immediate social upheaval was more likely to be produced by the suffering and discontent of an incipient middle class than by the poverty of the proletariat. Middle sectors, in his opinion, were being denied adequate income and security because of the selfish interests of the coastal and sierra plutocracy.[51] Convinced that the 'superior men of creative force' whom all societies had to turn to for leadership would in the future come more and more from the middle groups, Belaúnde wanted to provide a basis for co-operation and remove the mounting sources of friction between the entrenched oligarchy and the burgeoning middle sectors.

Because they spent most of their mature years in Europe, Francisco (1883–1953)[52] and Ventura García Calderón Rey (1886–1959),[53] sons of the short-term President at the time of the War of the Pacific who had headed the Magdalena government and vainly sought United States protection of Peru's territorial integrity against Chilean demands, were not as influential in Peru as Riva Agüero and Belaúnde. They did, however, attend San Marcos in the early twentieth century, becoming authentic spokesmen of the values of the generation of 1900.[54] Both agreed that in the Peruvian past the rule of paternal tyrants had been infinitely preferable to that of liberal assemblies, that the most useful constitutions had been those which strengthened the central power against the forces of anarchy, and that for the future Peru should proceed cautiously towards democracy 'by the road of oligarchy'.[55] The two writers also concurred that while a broader cross-section of society could come to share in political responsibility, Peru should never try to depart totally from the traditional rule by an enlightened élite, an élite that should be constantly aware of its duties to care paternalistically for the masses and to create conditions of greater economic democracy by providing adequate educational facilities and encouraging the rise of a class of small property owners.[56]

Like others of their generation, Francisco and Ventura García Calderón saw the future of Peru in *mestizaje,* and advised their countrymen to put aside the unscientific and anti-humanitarian racial prejudices which had produced lamentable consequences. Ventura stated the case with some eloquence:

> We are a *mestizo* people in whom the white, the Indian, and the Negro have entered historically in unequal but constant proportions. My friends, to have Indian or Negro blood in our veins should not be the source of snobbish pride that certain men begin to affect today; nor should it be the object of shame. Let us destroy forever the racial complexes which still exist among us, fomenting hatreds which are the cause of our political quarrels. . . . Let us accept, my friends, the evidence of a country of three races which will be fused some day into only one. . . . Men feel in their hearts that they are the same people when, regardless of race, they have a community of ideas, of interests, of memories and of hopes. This is what makes a nation.[57]

While they looked forward to the assimilation of the Indian, the García Calderón brothers, in a manner that was typical of the generation of 1900, believed that this would be a long, slow, gradual development. Probably they thought it would take longer than did the neopositivists who in the late nineteenth century had turned their attention to the Indian problem. The neopositivists had been concerned with making the Indians a productive part of the Peruvian economy. The men of 1900, with their emphasis on cultural and spiritual values, hoped the Indians could some day come to share in, to appreciate, and even to contribute to a unique Peruvian culture and set of spiritual values.[58] It seemed obvious to them that this would necessitate a longer period of tutelage for the native than would the endeavour simply to provide him with a technical training that would make him an efficient producer.

Although beginning their university careers generally as anti-clericals and lapsed Catholics, many members of the generation of 1900 in later years returned to the Church – the García Calderón brothers who remained agnostics were notable exceptions – and contributed to a marked resurgence of the intellectual influence of Catholicism. Riva Agüero was reunited to the Church only in the

early 1930's, but many of his university companions of the beginning of the century, among them Belaúnde, found their way back
to the traditional faith long before this. Affirming the need to
reanimate the positive values of the past in order to create a
nationalism with continuity, it was not surprising that many of the
Arielists would begin to look with increasing favour on the institution that boasted the most powerful of all ties with the past and
that through the years had been the most consistent defender of
tradition. It was not long before some of the Arielists were beginning to proclaim that the most fundamentally important ingredient
of a genuine Peruvian nationalism was Catholicism. Unless rooted
in Catholicism, they asserted, there could be no national culture or
morality.

In this spirit some of the Arielists under the leadership of Carlos
Arenas y Loayza decided that Peru needed a Catholic University
'to rectify the false judgements on Peru's past, and to instil respect
for and pride in the past grandeur of the country'.[59] With the
French priest Georges Dintilhac as its first rector, the Catholic
University was founded in Lima in 1917. More like a seminary
than a university in its early years, it sought to prepare a new élite
'to conquer the sensual epoch, to banish the dominance of science
in the modern generation, and to overcome its laziness and love
of pleasure,' an élite that would also give precedence to spiritual
over material values and arrest the spread of Marxian-inspired
class violence. Urging the solution of social problems through
charity and the shaping of a social consciousness among the élite,
demands that reflected the new spirit of papal encyclicals, the
founders of the Catholic University regarded themselves as the
only group that understood the meaning of 'true social reform'.[60]

One of the most distinguished groups of intellectuals that Peru
has produced, the men of the generation of 1900 were high minded,
honourable, and dedicated to the well-being of their country. They
alerted Peruvians to the mounting social problems and induced
many leaders of society and business to recognize the need to do
better by Peru's Indians and urban masses. Unfortunately,
however, they were able to make few specific suggestions as to
how unsatisfactory conditions could be remedied. When they
turned away from the past and towards the need for present
reform, they tended to be excessively philosophical, vague
and general. Moreover, they were never able to establish the

sort of *rapport* with the masses that Piérola had known how to achieve.

By their disdainful refusal to co-operate with Pardo in his second term, the Arielists–Futurists robbed of a valuable source of support a man who was just as high minded and well intentioned as they were, but a great deal more practical. Pardo was unfortunate in that the intellectual community of his era offered him neither the backing nor the fecund and workable ideas of renovation that the neopositivists had contributed to the Piérola régime.[61]

THE 'CIVILISTAS' AGAIN IN POWER: THE SECOND JOSÉ PARDO ADMINISTRATION, 1915–19

Beginning his second term in August 1915, Pardo faced difficulties that could easily have plunged the country into strife and chaos had executive powers been in less capable hands. When congress began discussion of a bill to grant non-Catholics the right to practise their religion in Peru, many conservative interests were scandalized, and the President himself was mildly upset. Not allowing personal feelings to interfere with the passage of a bill that obviously had wide popular support, Pardo urged the champions of religious exclusivism to accept defeat with calm resignation. On 11 November 1915, the law of religious toleration was promulgated.

The religious issue might have continued to arouse passions but for the fact that Peruvians were distracted by foreign affairs. From the very outbreak of World War I Mariano H. Cornejo had spearheaded a 'crusade of justice' intended to persuade Peruvians to demand a declaration of war against Germany. At first, however, Pardo insisted upon a policy of neutrality. Many accused him of harbouring pro-German sentiments, but in truth the President, influenced by Andrés Cáceres and other military leaders who thought that Germany was invincible, merely sought to follow a practical and realistic course. In 1917 after the Peruvian ship *Lorton* was sunk off the coast of Spain and Germany refused to satisfy his government's reparation demands, Pardo obtained congressional approval for severance of diplomatic relations with the Central Powers.[62] The President declared at the time that his country could not be indifferent in the world struggle because its citizens ardently desired the predominance in the world of the principles of morality and international justice 'as proclaimed in firm and elevated terms by Woodrow Wilson'.[63]

Pardo's rather tardy commitment to the allied cause was probably due to more than an interest in international morality. The chronic Tacna–Arica dispute had reached another stage of crisis.[64] By placing themselves unequivocally on the side of the United States and praising the wisdom of its President, Peru's statesmen hoped to gain that country's support in their controversy with Chile, which throughout the war clung to a policy of neutrality that was actually quite pro-German.[65]

The Peruvian economy gradually overcame many of the difficulties experienced at the outset of World War I, even though certain sectors remained depressed. Petroleum, copper, sugar and cotton found highly favourable foreign market conditions. Moreover, a new type of cotton developed by Fermín Tanguis, who according to one historian 'made the greatest contribution of any man since independence to the national economy',[66] began to be exported in 1915, helping Peru to fill the vastly augmented orders for the commodity placed by the warring nations of Europe. While merchants and raw produce producers gained immense profits during the war, and while government revenue based largely on export taxes recovered from the Benavides-period decline, rising from twenty-eight to forty million *soles* between the end of 1915 and 1918, urban labourers often found their economic situation deteriorating. Part of the trouble was that dietary staples were becoming scarce and increasingly expensive because many landowners withdrew property from food production and dedicated it solely to raising such lucrative export commodities as cotton and sugar.

With worker discontent on the rise, the Pardo régime supported and obtained passage of several of the social laws originally put forward by Manzanilla in 1904, including legislation that regulated woman and child labour. In many of the country's industries, however, mushrooming as never before because importation of manufactured goods virtually ceased with the war, the enlightened statutes were ignored. Workers responded to this situation in January 1919 with a three-day general strike in the Lima–Callao area. Supported by San Marcos students, the strikers demanded in addition to the implementation of existing legislation the reduction of food prices and the introduction of the eight-hour day. Following the eruption of violence when the army was called out to disperse strikers, Pardo yielded in part to the demands of labour and decreed the eight-hour day for manufacturing and extractive industries.

Many of the worker organizations of the period were moderate in their demands and basically committed to the capitalist system. The Regional Peruvian Labour Federation (*Federación Obrera Regional Peruana*) which came into existence after the January violence and sought, unsuccessfully as it turned out, to establish industry-wide, nation-wide collective bargaining, proclaimed frequently that capital and labour could and must find a basis for amicable accord. On the other hand, anarchist-socialist elements and, increasingly after the Russian Revolution of November 1917, communist sympathizers were also active in Peru's labour movement. By the middle of 1919 a Socialist Party and a Workers' Party appeared in the country, both frankly dedicated to social upheaval and class struggle.

In addition to supporting labour demands, mainly those that were evolutionary but sometimes the revolutionary ones as well, the students of San Marcos began to speak out in favour of sweeping university reform.[67] In this they were strongly influenced by the 1918 Argentine student movement which had as its focal point the University of Córdoba. Alfredo L. Palacios, perhaps the most important leader of the Argentine university reform movement, arrived in Lima near the end of the Pardo régime and gave inspiration as well as practical advice to the San Marcos leaders.

The university students of Peru had much to complain about. The deans of the particular faculties, in the desire to secure indefinite re-election to their posts, appointed only their partisans, however academically unqualified they might be, to professorial positions. As a result the university had become a bastion of bureaucratic Caesarism. Secure in their tenure so long as they did not antagonize the deans, professors prepared their lectures carelessly, failed to keep up with new developments in their fields, and frequently did not bother to meet their classes. Students sought, therefore, the right to censure incompetent professors and to initiate processes leading to their dismissal. Moreover, since the abuses were the result of administrative misconduct as well as of professorial inadequacy, students demanded that along with the faculty and deans they be given some voice in determining the policies of their particular schools and, through a council that would include student representatives from all schools, of the university as a whole. Thus arose the famous plea for co-government (*cogobierno*), a system which however much originally justified by faculty and administrative failures to meet responsibilities was destined, once placed in effect, to lead to lamentable excesses and abuses.

In another phase of their reform programme, students insisted that universities, previously reserved to the privileged few, be vastly enlarged and made accessible to men from all walks of life and social backgrounds. In view of the fact that as late as 1916 the enrolment in Peruvian universities was only 1,791,[68] the students seemed to have ample justification for their demands.

In dealing with the university problem, Pardo for one of the few times in his two presidential terms proceeded with a striking lack of statesmanship. Although many social and political leaders, such as Javier Prado and the distinguished medical doctor Carlos Enrique Paz Soldán,[69] sympathized with the student position, President Pardo simply advised the university youth to respect their teachers 'and maintain discipline, the indispensable foundation for all worthy human organizations.'[70] Rebuffed by the President, university students turned increasingly to political action. Hoping to gain the sympathy of Pardo's foe Augusto B. Leguía and to hasten his return to Peru from his lengthy stay abroad, they declared this man who had no real ties with the university or teaching circles in general, Mentor of the Youth (*Maestro de la Juventud*).[71]

In having to deal with serious labour and student questions, Pardo became the first President of Peru to face some of the modern problems that have beset the republic ever since. Another of Peru's modern problems, the control of foreign-capital operations, was also beginning to come into focus during Pardo's second term. By vastly expanding its holdings after 1914 and acquiring in 1919 the shares of the Backus and Johnson Mining Company, the North American Cerro de Pasco Corporation became a giant in the mining industry and one of the favourite targets for a group of economic nationalists beginning to appear on the political scene. More serious still, so far as economic nationalists were concerned, was the petroleum issue.

The London and Pacific Petroleum Company in 1889 had come

into possession of the oil-rich La Brea-Pariñas region near the northern coastal settlement of Talara. In 1916 Standard Oil of New Jersey entered into negotiations to acquire the concessions of the London firm. Nothing came of these negotiations until 1924, because a dispute was raging at the time as to the exact status of London and Pacific in Peru.

In the late-nineteenth-century inception of its Peruvian operations, London and Pacific had obtained subsoil exploitation rights for ten *pertenencias* of land (a *pertenencia* consists of forty thousand square metres, approximately ten acres). In return for these rights, London and Pacific paid the Peruvian government the modest sum of three hundred *soles* per year. A survey and measuring of the land being used by London and Pacific, carried out by two engineers, Héctor Boza and Alberto Jochamowits, during the Benavides rule in 1914, showed that the company was actually utilizing not the ten, but 41,614 *pertenencias*. The discussion over the issue of back imposts owed the government by the English firm grew extremely heated during the second Pardo administration, with many Peruvian congressional leaders, among them Mariano H. Cornejo, José Matías Manzanilla, and *El Comercio* owner Antonio Miró Quesada, urging that London and Pacific because of its contract violation be driven from the country, with all petroleum deposits to be exploited henceforth only by Peruvian groups. This proposal was rejected, and in 1918 both houses of congress agreed to Pardo's suggestion that the petroleum dispute be submitted for settlement to an international tribunal. Unfortunately, this did not end the matter and the issue of who owned what concession in the La Brea–Pariñas area would create difficulties for many later administrations. Economic nationalists have never forgiven Pardo for not having settled the question once and for all in 1918 by simply cancelling the London and Pacific concessions.[72]

As his troubled term drew towards a close, Pardo sounded out the leaders of the various political parties about holding an inter-party convention similar to the one of 1915 to agree upon a single candidate. When it became apparent that the rival ambitions of a number of political leaders would make it impossible to repeat the 1915 electoral pattern, Pardo, backed by many *Civilistas*, decided to advance the candidacy of Antero Aspíllaga, a member of a distinguished coastal landowning family and long a dabbler in politics. The President thereby committed a serious political blunder. The lacklustre Aspíllaga, however good his intentions and however widely recognized his integrity, was too staunchly conservative to be able to win the confidence of the masses or even of moderately reform-minded political and intellectual leaders.

With Pardo grooming Aspíllaga as his successor, Augusto B. Leguía, living temporarily in Panama after a lengthy residence in London that had begun with his exile by Billinghurst, decided the circumstances were right for him to seek re-election. He could not, he said, stand idly by while a handful of political bosses who did not understand the vast social and economic changes under way tried to saddle the country with a reactionary administration. By February 1919 he was back in Peru, and his campaign won the quick support of many elements within the *Civilista* Party itself as well as the enthusiastic backing of Augusto Durand and the Liberals and Andrés Cáceres and the Constitutionalists. Whether the military officers of the Constitutionalist Party favoured Leguía out of anger because Pardo had reduced the expenditures of the armed forces from 25 to 18 per cent. of the budget, or because they wished to be associated with a movement of sweeping modernization and social reform is a point on which Peruvian historians have long differed.

Claiming that his extended stay in Europe had demonstrated to him the irresistible power of the world-wide movement for social change, Leguía pictured himself to his upper-class supporters as the man who understood how to avoid class revolution by making timely modifications in the capitalist structure. To the lower classes and to the students who had named him their mentor, Leguía held out the vague promises of such drastic reforms that he won even the support of the new Socialist Party.

Pardo refrained from interfering in the outcome of the May elections and Leguía won a resounding victory over Aspíllaga. The victor did not wait to be constitutionally installed. Following the advice of Mariano Cornejo and Augusto Durand, and with the backing of Andrés Cáceres and various elements of the armed forces, Leguía and his henchmen seized the national palace on 4 July and exiled Pardo.

The revolutionists justified their actions by claiming that Pardo and the congress had entered into a last-minute plot to annul the results of the elections and deny Leguía the presidency. No adequate proof of a Pardo conspiracy has ever been advanced. Instead, it has become increasingly clear that Leguía and his supporters decided to resort to force so as to be able to dissolve congress, which contained a majority that was hostile to the successful candidate, and to arrange for the election of a new legislature composed of loyal partisans. Had Leguía forcefully suppressed congress after being constitutionally installed in the presidency he might have seriously alienated public opinion. So he created the pretext for seizing power before the inauguration by spreading the calumny that the President and his congress were devious plotters who deserved to be turned out of office in the name of preserving democratic procedures.

In his prematurely-terminated second term José Pardo had committed blunders, notably in his handling of the student movement and in his backing of the Aspíllaga candidacy. Still, the appraisal of Pardo made by Manuel Vicente Villarán is accurate and just:

> His political methods were those of a civilized man who wished to govern a civilized nation. He did not try to make himself feared or adulated; he did not propose to rule by subjugating, by corrupting, or by fanaticizing. He tolerated with inexhaustible patience the habitual criticisms of certain bad newspapers. . . . His enemies tried to bring him into disrepute by giving him the title of aristocrat. . . . If aristocracy consists in employing the manners of a gentleman, Pardo was an aristocrat. . . . If being an aristocrat consists in having an outstanding education, Pardo was an aristocrat. But, if to disdain productive labour is a sign of aristocracy, Pardo was not an aristocrat. . . . And finally if by aristocrat is understood the rich man who forgets the poor, Pardo was not aristocratic, because his presidential terms were characterized by an interest in extending education to the poor classes and to the underestimated Indians . . ., and by the inauguration in Peru before they were introduced in many American states of modern social laws for the protection of labourers.[73]

Many of the men who wielded political power in Peru after Nicolás de Piérola, and above all others José Pardo, built impressively on the foundation which the democratic caudillo had bequeathed them. If the post-Piérola generation of intellectuals was not as practically constructive as it might have been, at least its vagueness and excessively philosophical bent were employed in the service of achieving class and ethnic-group solidarity. Like Pardo, moreover, the Futurists exhibited the virtue of gentlemanliness, conducting themselves in a civilized manner within a country which hopefully they assumed to be civilized, or at least on the verge of becoming so. In the two decades following the rule of Piérola, political and intellectual leaders presided over an era in which in one Peru, that of the coast, there was much that deserved to be admired and to be utilized and incorporated into the programmes of future directing groups. Unhappily for the nation many of the politicians and intellectuals who rose to prominence after 1919 refused to see anything good in the past, even the immediate past, adopted a González Prada-like phoenix approach to the problems of national development, and proceeding often as rowdy ruffians plunged Peru into such chaotic disunion that not until the early 1960's was the country able to return to the level of consensus, co-operation, co-ordinated progress and institutional development that it had attained by the end of Pardo's second term.

8

The Country is not what it seems to be: The
Oncenio of Leguía, 1919–30

THE 'ONCENIO' AS A PERIOD OF INTENSIFIED DISUNION

'I HAVE come not only to liquidate the old state of affairs,' the newly-inaugurated Leguía is reported to have said, 'but also to detain the advance of communism which, because it is premature among us, would produce dreadful consequences.'[1]

Allowing for a certain element of exaggeration, Leguía was sincere in the first part of this statement. Throughout his eleven-year period of rule (the *oncenio*) he did seem to seek, if not the liquidation, at least the vast modification of the old state of affairs. With genuine patriotic zeal, singleness of purpose, and personal integrity – in which, unfortunately, he did not insist that his sons or colleagues share – he strove to transform Peru into a thoroughly modern, progressive and dynamic capitalist nation. Essentially, he set for himself the task that Billinghurst had hoped to accomplish, to render the country more advantageous for the operation of capitalism. Leguía's formula for achieving this was to encourage the rise of middle sectors and to give just enough in the way of improved living conditions to the lower classes to remove their potentialities as a revolution-making factor. Until the depression of 1929 began to menace the very survival of capitalism in Peru, Leguía appeared in some ways to have been as successful as any president in his country's history in fulfilling the fundamental objectives of his programme.

In raising the issue of communism, Leguía was not totally sincere. His great desire was to rule in Peru through the support of the only socio-economic sectors he understood and admired, having himself come from them, the middle, urban, business-minded sectors. In order to bind the middle groups to him, it was useful to frighten them with the spectre of communism. Thus, Leguía permitted the circulation of communist literature and in general worked to create the impression that there was an immediate Bolshevik threat. This was only one of the many ways in which the President, attempting to forge what he described as the 'New Fatherland' (*Patria Nueva*), seemed more concerned with the Peru that was only apparent and largely the figment of his imagination, than with the real Fatherland.

To many observers the greatest accomplishment of Leguía during the *oncenio* was the fostering of a new, self-conscious and assertive middle sector, as a countervailing force to the aristocracy.[2] Here also, however, appearances only masked reality. What actually occurred was that part of the middle sector, rather than acting as a countervailing power to the traditional aristocracy, joined with it in supporting Leguía, in accepting his concept of personalistic rule, and in feeding his vanity. At the same time other elements of the middle group began to preach an increasingly extremist message of violent and total revolutionary change, seeking not to balance but to eliminate the upper classes. Diverse factors contributed to the making of this new situation of political and social division. One was the collapse of the old-line political parties.

Leguía has been accused by his detractors of destroying the traditional party organizations of Peru.[3] In truth, he only applied the *coup de grace* to organizations that were already moribund. *Civilismo*, torn by internal dissension, was no longer a power to be reckoned with in 1920. The Democratic Party had come virtually to an end with the Piérola–Billinghurst split of 1912. Even under the best of conditions, neither the Constitutionalists nor the Liberals, woefully lacking internal discipline and adequately prepared young leaders, could have survived the deaths in 1923 of their respective caudillos, Andrés Cáceres and Augusto Durand. The real tragedy was that Leguía showed no interest in building a new political party that might have absorbed and provided a basis of continuity for the energies, idealism and talents of the many well-intentioned men who supported him. Choosing to rely only on personalism as his means of government, the wily *politico* from Lambayeque dealt a staggering blow to the political institutionalism that had evolved in Peru between 1895 and 1919.

Suffering the frustration of their own political ambitions because the all-encompassing personalism of Leguía prevented other stars from appearing in the political firmament, some Peruvians, inspired by little more than greed and opportunism, began to urge radical and revolutionary panaceas, heaping calumnies not only upon Leguía but all who supported him. Other, more idealistic men pursued essentially the same line of conduct. Genuinely perturbed and disgusted by the hypocrisy of the *oncenio*, the ever-widening gulf between the apparent and the real Peru, they came to the conclusion that the country could only be saved and transformed into the true Fatherland of the Indians and the urban proletariat by a sweeping series of changes that would eradicate all vestiges of the *oncenio* and also of the allegedly totally depraved past that had spawned it.

Because of the radicalism, the class hatred and the violence preached by a new group of phoenix-style regenerators, the advocates of gradual, moderate and evolutionary change grew apprehensive. In order to stem a movement that appeared to be, and actually often was, needlessly nihilistic and more menacing to the interests of Peru than even the worst features of the *oncenio*, they gave their support to Leguía and accepted all the unfortunate features of his personalistic rule. They had little alternative to this because the dictator would not permit the champions of moderate reform, with their long and fruitful tradition in Peru, to assemble in a true political party.

Leguía's *oncenio* was a watershed in Peruvian history. The neo-positivist and Futurist spokesmen of reform, the men who had urged a gradual, evolutionary approach to regeneration, who were interested in co-operation, consensus, organic development and continuity, who desired class alliances and social solidarity rather than animosity and warfare, gradually ceased to wield a significant influence. If they did not discredit themselves by becoming the sychophantic supporters of Leguía, they were in many instances forced into exile. In their place as the wielders of intellectual influence there appeared a new generation of total revolutionists, anxious to destroy all before starting to rebuild. There developed as a result a gulf between the political realm of Peru, commanded by landed aristocrats, new business groups and tired, frightened, non-assertive men of letters, and the intellectual realm of Peru, controlled more and more by angry young violence-mongers. The rapid widening of this gulf in the 1920's brought to a halt Peru's advance towards becoming a true nation, an integrated body of ethnic, cultural, economic, social and functional interest groups, bound together by some element of consensus in regard to major issues.

THE CONSTITUTION OF 1920, MODEL OF THE PERU THAT NEVER WAS

Following the suppression of congress after his seizure of power, Leguía decreed elections for a new legislature which would also be endowed with faculties to frame a constitution. Promptly upon convening, the new congress, presided over by Mariano H. Cornejo, elected Javier Prado as the head of a constituent committee charged with framing a fundamental charter.

Replacing the durable 1860 instrument, Peru's new constitution was promulgated in January 1920. In line with the political thought of Leguía and Cornejo, it provided for simultaneous election, every five years, of the entire legislature, both upper and lower chambers, and the President of the republic. Much in the pattern of earlier constitutions, it included a long list of individual guarantees which, theoretically, could be suspended only in times of crisis and emergency. More striking than the charter's concern with individual liberties was its attentiveness to the common good of society. The instrument provided that in the interest of society as a whole the government could limit the rights of property. Moreover, the government was empowered to control prices, impose progressive taxes and establish in business operations an equitable balance between capital and labour. Hours of work, it was stipulated, were to be limited by the government and management was to be forced to provide adequate compensation for labourers, as well as safe and sanitary working conditions.[4] The new constitution further committed the State to the construction of hospitals, asylums and clinics which would safeguard and serve all the nation's needy. In the field of public instruction, the constitution declared that the State would provide free primary education for all children, male and female, and vastly expand secondary and higher educational facilities.

Article 58 of the 1920 constitution dealt with the Government's obligations to bring about the rehabilitation of the Indian race by providing for their education and gradual assimilation. It guaranteed that Indians would be protected in the ownership of their communal lands and benefited by a school system that would offer a primary education to each of their children. Javier Prado, having dismissed his youthful racial prejudices against the Indians, spoke eloquently in favour of Article 58 and asserted that Peru's aborigines were a people of great virtue who had been inexcusably treated and deserved at last an adequate opportunity to become participating members of society.[5] When submitted to the vote of the assembly the article was approved 79–0. It was widely hailed as the most important legislative contribution to renovation in Peru's republican history.

The new charter also included promising reforms in the sphere of relations between the central and local governments. Three regional legislative provinces were created, one in the north, one in the centre and one in the south. Each was to have its own legislature, chosen by the registered voters in the respective regions and authorized to pass laws for those regions, subject to presidential approval. The constitution also contained a guarantee of municipal autonomy. However, the friends of Leguía in the assembly introduced another measure stipulating that until order and regular legal procedures had been restored in the Peruvian municipalities, the President could on his own appoint provisional municipal officials. Only after a protracted debate and two tie votes was the measure approved. Its effect was to suppress the municipal autonomy which another section of the constitution guaranteed.[6]

LEGUÍA AND THE REAL PERU: THE ISSUES OF
INDIAN TREATMENT AND DECENTRALIZATION

During the early years of the Leguía administration it became quite fashionable for intellectuals to discuss the Indian and his plight. An increasing number of Peruvian intellectuals turned their attention to Inca history, folk-lore and archaeology. In Lima the Society of the Golden Arrow was formed, the purpose of its members being to study the glories of the Inca past. Many of those who joined in the cult of paying homage to the native were merely adopting a modish pose. One of the most conspicuous *poseurs* was Leguía himself, who liked to be referred to as Viracocha. According to Inca mythology, Viracocha had been a white-skinned, culture-bearing deity. Leguía promised to serve as a new bearer of culture to the Indians and as their guide towards a better life.

The Indians had, especially since 1918, staged a series of bloody uprisings aimed at retrieving land which through violence or legal chicanery had been plundered from their communal holdings by the *gamonales* of the sierra. In the attempt to restore tranquillity in the Andes at the beginning of his term, Leguía, with the collaboration of congress, appointed a commission to investigate some of the rival claims of land ownership. Heading the commission was Erasmo Roca (1893–1963), while one of its most prominent members was José Antonio Encinas (1886–1958).[7] These two men were genuinely concerned with the protection and uplifting of the native race and have come quite properly to be regarded as among the most notable precursors of Peruvian land reform. President Leguía, moreover, created within the ministry of development a section of Indian matters (*sección de asuntos Indígenas*), naming as its chief Hildebrando Castro Pozo (1890–1945), one of the most articulate and sincere defenders of Indian rights that Peru has produced.[8]

The Roca commission established its headquarters in Puno and began an extensive investigation of land-ownership titles. It also prepared and submitted for congressional approval a comprehensive legislative code, intended to implement Article 58 of the constitution which provided for the protection and education of the natives. Greatly alarmed by these developments, the landowners of the sierra expressed their dissatisfaction to Leguía[9] and the President promptly dissolved the Roca commission. Its legislative proposals were never so much as considered in congress. Furthermore, in 1923 Hildebrando Castro Pozo, regarded by then as a dangerous trouble-maker because of his efforts to make of the section of Indian matters a genuine instrument for the service of the native, was sent into exile.

Not able to hope for redress of grievances from the government, the Indians between Puno and Azángaro resorted increasingly to violence. The army was therefore ordered into the sierra and, after a number of Indian massacres, succeeded by the end of 1923 in making the area safe once again for the white and *cholo* landowners.

As with Indian protection, so also with decentralization, the Leguía administration was interested more in appearance than substance. In actual practice the three provincial congresses, ostensibly aimed at providing considerable autonomy for the different regions of Peru, only proliferated the system of bureaucratic Caesarism. Controlling the towns through his appointed municipal officials who actually became permanent bosses, Leguía was able to determine to a large extent the composition of the three provincial congresses and to see to it that their membership was confined to obedient servants.

LEGUÍA AND THE REAL PERU: THE ISSUES OF UNIVERSITY REFORM AND INDIVIDUAL RIGHTS

Leguía, 'Mentor of the Youth', went through the motions in 1920 of rewarding the university youth who had enthusiastically supported his presidential bid. With his backing a university reform law was passed on 30 June which provided for the elimination of incompetent professors and allowed students at San Marcos to share in administration by electing a member of the university council. Actually, however, Leguía used the reform primarily as a means of getting rid of professors who were his political opponents. Their politically safe replacements in most instances did not contribute to an improvement in teaching quality.[10]

Falsely encouraged for a time to think that the new president was truly inclined to allow students a greater voice in university administration and to co-operate with them in efforts to transform education into an instrument of social and economic progress, members of the Federation of Students (*Federación de los Estudiantes*) under the leadership of its President, Víctor Raúl Haya de la Torre (b. 1895), organized the First National Congress of Students, which convened in Cuzco in March 1920. The congress discussed various means of making student participation in university administration more effective, considered carefully the rôle of student strikes, and also debated the means for initiating broad social reforms in the country. The need to educate the Indians and urban labourers was stressed and the majority of participants in the congress agreed with Haya de la Torre that 'one of the greatest national absurdities was for the State to maintain and support a useless priestly class'.[11]

In perhaps its most significant act, the Student Congress approved the creation of popular universities. As conceived by

Haya de la Torre, the popular universities, which were to be named in honour of González Prada, would offer extension work from San Marcos, with students and teachers of that venerable institution giving academic and practical training, including instruction in the organization of labour unions, to artisans and labourers. It was quite apparent, however, that Haya de la Torre and those who assisted him in the actual founding and short-lived operation of the popular universities intended through them to induce the masses to take up the cudgels of the class struggle and initiate revolutionary activity.[12] Leguía's opposition to and suppression of the popular universities in 1924 was understandable given their revolutionary orientation. But his actions towards San Marcos University were inexcusable.

The crisis in the relations between the Government and San Marcos began when Leguía launched a campaign to silence newspapers hostile to his régime. By the end of 1919 the respected dailies *La Prensa* and *El Comercio* had both begun to criticize his administration. When Luis Fernán Cisneros, the most talented and courageous of *La Prensa*'s editorial writers, was put into jail early in 1921, the university students led by Víctor Andrés Belaúnde, one of the most distinguished San Marcos professors and recently returned from a diplomatic mission in Uruguay, demonstrated in protest. Leguía relented and ordered Cisneros' release from jail. Immediately Cisneros published an open letter, stating that although he had been released there were still forty political prisoners on the island of San Lorenzo, 'each of them as innocent as I'. Belaúnde then obtained from Javier Prado, rector of San Marcos, permission to deliver a public lecture at the university dealing with judicial power and democracy. Following the Belaúnde discourse, which was a strong indictment of Leguía for having ignored a decision by the judiciary that the forty prisoners on San Lorenzo should be released, a cavalry detachment brutally dispersed a parade of enthusiastic student marchers bearing Belaúnde and Cisneros on their shoulders. A short time after this both Belaúnde and Cisneros found themselves in exile.

They had ample company. Before the end of 1921 the tyrannical minister of the interior (*ministro de gobierno*), Germán Leguía y Martínez, a cousin of the President who had come to be known as 'the Tiger', had harried out of the country such prominent men as Oscar R. Benavides, Isaias de Piérola, and Jorge Prado. José de la

Riva Agüero on a voluntary basis shortly joined the colony of Peruvian exiles in Europe, which included José Pardo who had under pressure left the country immediately after his overthrow in 1919. Another Leguía critic was silenced in 1921 when death, from natural causes, claimed the rector of San Marcos, Javier Prado.

President Leguía and his minister of interior also sent into exile Antonio Miró Quesada, director of *El Comercio*, and thereafter the oldest of the Peruvian newspapers began consistently to endorse administration policies. The Government then seized *La Prensa* outright and turned it into the official organ of the régime. In 1923 the former director of *La Prensa* and founder of the Liberal Party, Augusto Durand, died under mysterious circumstances while being transferred from jail to a ship on which he was to be sent into exile.

It was not long before the *oncenio* began to devour its own. As a concession to public opinion, and owing to a 'little falling out between cousins',[13] Leguía first imprisoned and then in 1924 exiled his minister of the interior, 'the Tiger'. Germán Leguía's exile resulted in part from his ambition to succeed his cousin in the presidency.

Meanwhile, the San Marcos professors had gone on strike, protesting against the deportation of Belaúnde and Cisneros. For a time all activities were suspended in the university. Then, in 1922, San Marcos reopened under a new rector, Manuel Vicente Villarán. Increasingly, however, it was subjected to government harassment, and the following year a new crisis occurred. When Leguía, a high-order Mason, sponsored a massive religious convocation at which Peru was dedicated to the Sacred Heart of Jesus, Haya de la Torre and many student leaders, moved both by opposition to the Government and hostility to the Church,[14] staged a counter-demonstration at which Haya delivered a characteristically emotional and anticlerical tirade. The counter demonstration was broken up by government forces, an action which Leguía justified on the grounds that the students were showing disrespect for the religious sentiments of the overwhelming majority of the Peruvian populace. Quickly thereafter police forces assaulted San Marcos itself, wounding several students. Haya de la Torre and some thirty other student leaders were arrested and deported. At the same time, twenty-six professors of the University of Trujillo, each of them suspected of anti-Leguía sentiments, were dismissed from their positions.

In protest against the Government suppression, Villarán early in 1924 resigned as head of San Marcos, and for a time the university again suspended operations. It reopened within a short time, however, under the rectorship of José Matías Manzanilla, who by his apparent collaboration with the dictatorial president incurred the hatred of many Peruvian students. Although San Marcos was open again, Leguía in 1927 temporarily closed the University of Cuzco.

In 1928 the President created the National Council of University Education. Mainly political in nature and completely dominated by the Government, the Council was vested with the power to select university rectors and deans and even to appoint professors. It also controlled budgets. In exercise of its prerogatives the Council promptly named Alejandro O. Deustua rector of San Marcos. The old philosopher accepted the appointment, thereby giving another of many indications of his approval of the Leguía administration.

Other Peruvian intellectual figures of prominence also demonstrated their approbation of the régime. Leguía's early advisor, Mariano H. Cornejo, who became an important cabinet member, referred to the President as a man who had realized the difficult task of creating a new Peru: 'You have substituted for the medieval frame of mind,' rhapsodized Cornejo in one of his speeches in praise of Leguía, 'the mentality of work and effort. You have turned an exploited colony and a backward republic into a modern nation.'[15] The country's most celebrated young poet, José Santos Chocano, who had fought with Pancho Villa in the course of the Mexican Revolution, in 1922 published a book in which he frankly defended the policies of the dictatorial Leguía.[16] Democracy, according to the poet, was a farce and a universal failure. Without an organizing dictator of genius to whom ordinary legal restraints should not be applicable, destructive social revolution was inevitable.

Enjoying the backing of some elderly scholars and now and then even of a few young intellectuals, and enthusiastically supported by many leaders of politics and business, Leguía, with most of his troublesome opponents in jail or exile, easily managed to have the constitution amended to permit presidents to serve for two successive terms. Elected to a second five-year term in July 1924, he subsequently had the constitution amended to permit indefinite re-election. In August 1929, running unopposed, he was elected to his third term.

PERU'S APPARENT PROSPERITY DURING THE 'ONCENIO'

With political stability firmly established and with prosperity beginning to result from the rising prices for Peruvian exports, Leguía presided over one of the most remarkable periods of economic expansion and of rapidly-completed building and public works projects that Peru has ever experienced. A favourable balance of trade amounting to an annual average of between three and four million dollars was maintained, and by 1929 the annual total value of combined Peruvian exports and imports had climbed to nearly two hundred million dollars.[17] The *sol* remained stable at approximately thirty-seven cents in comparison with the United States dollar, and two able finance ministers, Fernando Fuchs and Abraham Rodríguez Dulanto, followed efficient methods of fiscal administration.[18]

Lima and near-by communities, such as Chosica, Callao, Miraflores, Barranco, Chorillos and Magdalena, as well as the cities of Arequipa, Mollendo, Pimentel and Cuzco were provided with modern drinking water and sewage facilities. Similar works were under way in Iquitos, Puno, Ayacucho, Pisco and Cañete when Leguía was overthrown in 1930. In Lima, furthermore, twelve new plazas and scores of new public buildings were erected. The face of the capital city was changed more completely than during the early twentieth-century period when Federico Elguera had been such an industrious mayor, more completely, in fact, than it has been at any time since the attainment of Peruvian independence. That Lima came to be known as one of the loveliest of South American capitals was owing largely to the work of transformation carried to completion during the *oncenio*.

Under Leguía's administration over eleven hundred miles of new roads and hundreds of bridges were completed, and more than six hundred miles of railroad track were laid. More than eight hundred new primary schools were also constructed and the enrolment of primary students increased from 176,680 to 318,735 between 1921 and 1929. In addition an attempt was made to protect the health of the youth through the launching of campaigns against various childhood diseases and through the expansion of clinical facilities and nurse-training programmes. Furthermore, a model children's hospital was erected in Lima.

Partly as a result of irrigation projects undertaken on some 100,000 acres in the regions of Cañete, Olmos and Lambayeque, agricultural production almost tripled between 1919 and 1930. Agricultural experimentation stations, moreover, were established in the cities of Lambayeque, Piura and Tumbes. Scientific rice cultivation was introduced in the departments of Cajamarca, Ancash, Junín and Huancavelica, while model sheep and cattle breeding farms were founded in Puno and other cities. The National Agricultural School was installed on the outskirts of Lima in new and splendid quarters built on the old private estate of *La Molina*, which had been purchased by the State. Ever since then *La Molina* has been one of the finest agricultural schools in South America.

All these projects were expensive, but Leguía was able to obtain some of the needed revenue from imposts on the expanding operations in Peru of foreign, especially United States, capitalists. It was during the *oncenio* that United States private investments came to eclipse those of Great Britain. By 1925 the Cerro de Pasco Corporation's investment was conservatively estimated at fifty million dollars. Also, the International Petroleum Company (IPC), a Standard Oil subsidiary, came into possession of the rich oilfields of La Brea-Pariñas. Facilitating the IPC acquisition was a 1921 arbitration award, handed down by an *ad hoc* tribunal established in Paris, confirming the questionable claims of the old London and Pacific Petroleum Company on the vast territory it had begun to exploit in the late nineteenth century, territory which had not been surveyed and measured by Peruvian authorities until 1914 during the provisional presidency of Oscar R. Benavides. With its rights confirmed, London and Pacific disposed of its concessions to the IPC. Ever since 1921 many Peruvians have steadfastly denied the legality of the arbitration award and the subsequent IPC purchase. They contend that the arbitration decision never became legally binding on the country because it was not ratified by the Peruvian congress.

Besides its taxes on foreign trade and investment operations, the Peruvian Government depended for its revenue on loans from abroad and deficit financing manipulations. Between 1918 and 1929, Peru's foreign debt rose from approximately ten to one hundred million dollars.[19] Peru obtained nearly all of its foreign loans from international banking concerns in the United States, thereby increasing its economic ties, to the alarm of many nationalists, with the so-called Colossus of the North.[20] Largely owing to loans from abroad and deficit financing, the Peruvian budget by 1929 called for an expenditure of approximately eighty million dollars, a figure which exceeded income by a considerable margin and represented nearly a four-fold increase over government outlays in 1920.

Without question, some of the Government's expenditures were channelled into productive ventures and contributed to the development of a balanced economy. Still, Dora Mayer de Zulén (1868–1959), a respected intellectual and talented writer who dedicated much of her life to working for social reform and the protection of the Indians, was justified in voicing criticisms. To her, the greater prosperity achieved by Leguía was suspect because it was not based on internal capitalization and improved labour habits and therefore had not contributed towards a self-sustaining economy. Rather, it depended on foreign capital 'lavished upon us because of the imperialistic intentions of the United States'. The credit extended from abroad was depicted as being in the nature of 'champagne loans', because the proceeds often went into non-productive ventures.[21] Dora Mayer de Zulén added with perception:

Leguía with his programmes of material development appealed to the silly, pompous spirit that leads so many Peruvians to think their country can be a great world power. Leguía was like the bartender who gave unlimited alcohol to the alcoholic. He convinced the Peruvians that their country could painlessly become as great as England. The Peruvian society lived for a few years in a dream of *A Thousand and One Nights*.[22]

FOREIGN AFFAIRS AND MOUNTING OPPOSITION TO LEGUÍA'S RULE

In the conduct of foreign affairs Leguía was plagued by two troublesome boundary questions that earlier régimes had failed to resolve. To begin with, there was the dispute with Colombia over the ownership of vast tracts of Amazonian jungle region, a dispute that had generated much heat and produced occasional armed clashes ever since the beginning of the twentieth century when the two countries had begun to compete in carving out rubber-producing kingdoms. Rubber was no longer an important consideration, but national pride compelled the two countries to press the claims that each had established in the days of the 'Black Gold' boom.

In 1922, with the United States playing an important behind-the-scenes rôle in urging the two republics to settle their dispute, Peru and Colombia signed the Salomón–Lozano Treaty. Favourable on the whole to Colombia, the treaty gave to that country possession of a narrow jungle corridor extending south from the Putumayo River to the Amazon and terminating at the small Amazonian port of Leticia. Realizing that the treaty represented a surrender of Peruvian claims, Leguía delayed submitting it to congress for ratification, properly fearful that by backing it he would incur charges of betraying national interests. Finally, late in 1927, bowing in part to pressure applied by the United States on which his administration had come to be so economically dependent, the President sought and obtained ratification of the treaty.

The unfavourable reaction which Leguía had feared did indeed appear. Leguía's defenders argued, probably with considerable justification, that he had been forced by the United States, much against his wishes and better judgement, to support the Salomón–Lozano Treaty. Their explanation was that the United States, anxious to obtain oil concessions in Colombia and realizing the need to make amends to that country for having contributed to its loss of Panama in 1903, decided to oppose Peru's claims in the Amazonian region regardless of the merits of the case.[23] In spite of the efforts of his collaborators to exonerate him, popular resentment against the treaty with Colombia seriously damaged Leguía's position.

The other major boundary question inherited by the Leguía administration concerned the dispute between Peru and Chile, dating back to the 1883 Treaty of Ancón ending the War of the Pacific, over ownership of Tacna and Arica. The plebiscite to provide the final disposition of the two towns and their surrounding area, which the treaty had stipulated should be held in 1893, had been delayed again and again and it did not seem likely that the two countries could ever reach accord on the conditions under which it might be held. In 1919 there had been a distinct possibility that war might erupt between the rival powers over the old and vexatious issue. By the end of 1921, however, moderates both in Peru and Chile succeeded in winning acceptance of a United States offer of good offices to facilitate settlement of the Tacna–Arica problem. Both disputants appointed delegates to argue their respective cases in Washington. The understanding was that if these delegates could not reach an agreement, they should consider submitting the matter to the arbitration of the United States.[24]

Discussion in Washington, beginning in May 1922, soon centred on whether a plebiscite was still a workable means for the settlement of the controversy. When this issue produced an impasse, Peru and Chile formally requested the direct assistance of the United States and by 20 July had accepted the so-called Washington Protocol. According to this instrument Peru and Chile would submit the question of the plebiscite to the arbitration of the President of the United States. In the event that the President decided the plebiscite should be held, he was empowered to lay down the conditions of balloting.

The terms of the arbitration protocol represented a diplomatic triumph for Chile, which had administered both Tacna and Arica ever since 1880 and had succeeded in establishing a much firmer rule and in 'Chileanizing' the regions far more thoroughly than had been the case in 1893 when the plebiscite should have been held. The worst fears of the Peruvians appeared to be realized when on 5 March 1925, President Calvin Coolidge announced his decision that the Tacna–Arica matter should indeed be settled by a plebiscite, to be held under United States supervision.

Peruvians were outraged. Twenty thousand ladies of Lima, led by the widow of Miguel Grau, hero of the War of the Pacific, paraded through the streets in protest against the arbitration decision. Alberto Ulloa, professor of international law at San Marcos, stated that the Coolidge decision simply proved that one could not find morality in the United States White House. Peru, he said, had been blind in expecting justice and impartiality from the powerful republic of the North.[25]

When the two generals sent by the United States to supervise the plebiscite, first John Pershing and after him William Lassiter, made it clear that they would not permit the Chileans to manipulate the vote in Tacna and Arica in accordance with the original hopes of the Santiago government, Peruvian statesmen began to breathe more easily. Their joy was unbounded when in 1926 General Lassiter flatly announced that the plebiscite was unpractical in view of the refusal of Chilean officials to co-operate in providing for a fair vote. Soon Albert Ulloa was talking about the 'useful and valuable' róle of the United States,[26] and the professor of economics at San Marcos, César Antonio Ugarte, stated that all Peru owed a debt of gratitude 'to the spirit of justice and moral grandeur of the people and government of the United States'.[27]

By 1929 a new spirit of moderation had come to prevail both in Lima and Santiago, and the two governments agreed to a compromise solution. Tacna would be returned to Peru, and Chile would retain Arica. Neither the Peruvian nor the Chilean government, however, wished to incur the anger of chauvinistic elements by publicly conceding a willingness to compromise the old dispute. Hence, the Peruvian and Chilean ministries of foreign relations requested that the United States Secretary of State, Frank Kellogg, suggest the settlement that had in actual fact already been agreed upon. In this way both the Lima and Santiago governments could attribute their willingness to accept less than total victory to State Department pressure.[28]

For all his cunning in trying to place the onus for the compromise solution on the United States, Leguía did not escape the censure of Peru's extreme nationalists. Charges that he had betrayed the public interest by yielding to the dictates of Washington and accepting the loss of Arica seriously undermined his popularity in many circles.

By no means all the opposition to Leguía by 1929 could be traced to the allegations that the dictator had failed to make a patriotic defence of the national boundaries. More and more Peruvians were becoming concerned over what Manuel Vicente Villarán had five years earlier pointed out as one of the main dangers inherent in Leguía's style of rule:

The people have been much abused by unfulfilled promises . . ., the result being that a great part of the people turn their backs on all parties and, beguiled by evil and dangerous exotic ideas . . ., begin to abominate all extant political structures and to desire in the quest for the salvation of the proletariat to substitute for suffrage, parliament and the Government itself, strikes, violence, direct battle against the upper classes and anarchy. I want the people to realize the value of suffrage rather than of direct action. Nor is it only the proletariat that is disillusioned and deceived. . . . The brilliant generation that founded the National Democratic Party now marches disillusioned. Behind it has surged a new generation for whose members the leaders and programmes of the existing parties seem futile and unattractive; it finds itself now anxious to enter political life and if given no other opportunity will enter it through violence.[29]

By 1929 Villarán's warning had assumed the appearance of a prophecy well on the way to fulfilment. There had indeed arisen a new generation of intellectual leaders anxious to take advantage of the disillusionment of the proletariat in initiating a struggle to tear down and eradicate the entire existing social, economic and political order.

EXTREMIST VOICES OF 'INDIGENISMO', ANDEANISM AND SOCIALISM

During the *oncenio* the men who preached moderation and patience in confronting the Indian problem, who argued that it would ultimately be solved through *mestizaje* and through the long-term leadership and instruction with which whites and *mestizos* should provide the native, came to be opposed by an increasingly outspoken group of Indiophiles or *Indigenistas*. So far as the *Indigenistas* were concerned, the Indian was ready at once to assume a rôle of full participation and even leadership in Peruvian society. The Indian, so they said, was prepared to accomplish his social, economic and political salvation and to assume his rightful place in society, by means of his own efforts, and should not rely on or accept the tutelage of white and *mestizo* elements. Finally, affirmed many *Indigenistas*, the true destiny of the Indian was not to adapt himself to the civilization of the Europeanized populace, but rather to impose his superior culture and values on Peru's non-Indian sectors.

Antenor Orrego (1892–1960), a philosopher born in Trujillo, was among the many prominent intellectuals who preached the message of *indigenismo* in the 1920's. Influenced by Oswald Spengler, Orrego was convinced that the world of Western Europe and the United States was in the throes of inevitable decline. Predominant in Latin America ever since the conquest, the culture and values of Western Europe had, stated Orrego, begun on all sides to decay. In contrast to the crumbling European world in Latin America, there was a virile and still energetic world, the American, or more properly, the Indian world. Indians, who in their civilization had always been closer to Eastern than to Western attitudes and values, would revitalize Latin America and provide the inspiration for a new *mestizo* civilization. They would do so by peeling off the veneer of European culture that had been super-imposed by the conquistadors.[30]

A more active leader in the *Indigenista* crusade of the 1920's was Luis E. Valcárcel (b. 1891), a gifted writer and student of Indian affairs from pre-conquest to contemporary times. Influenced like Orrego by Spengler and convinced of the decadence and inevitable decline of the West, Valcárcel, at this point of his career, was even more extreme than the Trujillo philosopher in his insistence that only the Indian could redeem and regenerate Peru. While Orrego hoped the Indians in conjunction with *mestizo* and perhaps even white population groups would ultimately achieve in America a synthesis between the ways of East and West, Valcárcel saw the future not in terms of a synthesis, but in the imposition by the Indian of his civilization, pure and uncontaminated, on all Peru and all Latin America, or, as he preferred to call it, Indo–America. 'European culture,' he wrote, 'has never truly affected the Indian. Peru is Indian and will be Indian. ... The only true Peru is Indian Peru.'[31]

Persuaded that the Indian's lowly estate in the Peru of the 1920's was owing exclusively to the economic and social exploitation he had endured since the time of the conquest, Valcárcel felt that the moment this exploitation ceased the Indian would be ready instantaneously to begin his task of bringing about his country's regeneration. As exploitation could in his opinion be terminated only through revolution, Valcárcel frankly advocated the violent elimination of the institutions and even much of the human resources of white and *mestizo* Peru.[32] The Indian violence, the 'Tempest in the Andes', which he observed and wrote about in the 1920's was to Valcárcel the hopeful harbinger of the massive Indian uprising that must soon take place.[33]

To their message of the redemption of Peru through the Indian *Indigenistas* of the 1920's, many of whom had only slight traces of Indian ancestry, generally attached an unrestrained denunciation of coastal Peru. In January 1929 some of them came together in Cuzco to found the periodical *La Sierra* as the instrument for spreading the ideas of a movement known as Andeanism. In the editorial of its first number *La Sierra* described itself as 'the voice of protest in the Andes, of the men who have been relegated to a secondary position. *La Sierra* is an impetuous force of combat'.[34] When Lima's daily *El Comercio* criticized the excessively regionalistic and combative spirit of the new periodical and went on to say that Peru would be better off without its sierra region, *La Sierra* retorted: 'When it comes to deciding if Peru would be more fortunate without the sierra or without the coast, it can be demonstrated that it would be much more fortunate without the coast.'[35]

Certain voices of moderation in the Andean movement urged no more than greater autonomy for the sierra.[36] However, the hope of the movement's more militant spokesmen was that a wave of regeneration, originating in the Andes and led by men of the Andes, especially the Indians, would sweep down and destroy the institutions, the social, economic and political patterns of the coast, and then impose upon the entire country an Andean way of life. Until the Andean movement had succeeded in this goal, the coast was to be regarded as hostile territory.

When the poet César A. Rodríguez was asked in an interview published in *La Sierra* what he thought of the intellectual movement in Lima, he replied: 'I do not even want to hear mentioned the name of Lima, whose existence in its present form I execrate. . . . It is the focal point of the degeneration of our nationality.' Rodríguez then argued that once the Andean way of life had been imposed throughout the entire national territory, Quechua would become the exclusive language, for 'Spanish would always be foreign to the true Peru', and its continuing use would be a symbol of the country's enslavement.[37]

What was the Andean way of life that had to be imposed upon the coast and all Peru in order to redeem and provide for the future greatness of the country? The majority of *Indigenista* spokesmen replied it was socialism. José Carlos Mariátegui (1895–1930), perhaps the most original twentieth-century Peruvian intellectual, declared in 1926 that he was an *Indigenista* because he was a socialist. In Peru, asserted Mariátegui, socialism must inevitably be associated with *indigenismo* and the Andean movement. 'Socialism preaches solidarity with and the redemption of the working classes. Four fifths of Peru's working classes consist of Andean Indians. Therefore, socialism means the redemption of these Indians.'[38]

Like Mariátegui, Hildebrando Castro Pozo, whose services had briefly been enlisted by Leguía at the beginning of the *oncenio*, felt that *indigenismo* and socialism were simply the two sides of the same coin. The harsh, unjust, exploitative capitalism of the coast, maintained Castro Pozo, must be replaced by socialism, and the Indian was the most likely element in Peru to bring about a revolution of such proportions. The Inca empire had been based on a socialistic structure, argued this widely-respected writer, the descendants of the Incas living in the Andes still maintained the customs and values of socialism, and therefore they were uniquely qualified to socialize all Peru.[39] Luis Valcárcel, also then an ardent socialist, praised the 'communistic' nature of land ownership and labour which had prevailed in the Andes for over a thousand years. It was necessary, he said, to restore to all Peru the advanced socialistic organization which the Incas had created and perfected. 'The Indian world must necessarily be the teacher of today's social reforms. The Indians only await the appearance of their Lenin.'[40]

COMMUNISM AND 'APRISMO' ARE NOT WHAT THEY SEEM TO BE IN PERU

In 1923, three years before he had asserted the necessary connection between *indigenismo* and socialism, José Carlos Mariátegui had returned to Peru following a period of travel and study in Europe. While in Italy the frail, chronically ill traveller had, as he explains it, 'acquired a woman and some ideas'.[41] The ideas acquired were strongly Marxist. Back in Peru Mariátegui became active in the popular university movement before its suppression by Leguía. In 1926 he founded the review *Amauta*,[42] in which for a time were published the views of reform-minded intellectuals, whether or not the authors subscribed to Marxian interpretations.[43] Two years later, however, apparently having resolved an intellectual dilemma with the decision at least for the moment that he was an orthodox Marxist–Leninist, Mariátegui moved to transform *Amauta* into more of an instrument of communist propaganda. In 1929 with a number of associates, among them

Eudocio Ravines[44] and Ricardo Martínez de la Torre,[45] he helped to found a party which while it was called Socialist was actually Peru's first Communist Party and which in 1930, after the death of Mariátegui, affiliated itself with the Communist International.

Mariátegui, increasingly in bad health after his return to Peru and forced to undergo the amputation of a leg some months before his death, seemed in many of his views to follow the strict Communist party-line. Capitalism, he confidently predicted, was doomed to an imminent death and there was no possibility of co-operation between the proletariat and the *bourgeoisie*.[46] On the other hand, he deviated from communist orthodoxy in asserting that the mystique needed to inspire Peruvians to undertake the socialist revolution would be provided not by Marxism–Leninism, but rather by pride in the past accomplishments of the Inca empire and the desire of contemporary Indians to duplicate the glorious deeds of their pre-conquest ancestors. Certain that a socialist, classless society had existed in Peru before the arrival of the Spaniards, Mariátegui dreamed of returning the country, in its social organization and institutions, to its Inca origins. For him, Peru's problems could be solved by direct transition from the feudalism then prevailing in the sierra to the communist practices of bygone days. In arriving at communism, Peru would not need to pass through the intermediary stage of industrialization with the attendant formation of urban proletariat and bourgeois groups.[47]

Above all, Peru's quest for socialism, according to Mariátegui, should not be guided by European experiences. The 'heroic creation' of socialism in Peru and all 'Indo–America', should instead be brought about in accordance with the 'reality of Indo–America', with the basically socialistic traditions of its past. 'The most advanced primitive communist organization which history records', stated the gaunt cripple, 'is that of the Incas.'[48] It is not the civilization or the alphabet of the white world which will elevate the Indian's soul, he added: 'It is the mystique, the idea of the socialist revolution,' inhering within, springing from the Inca civilization.[49]

Mariátegui decidedly questioned the materialistic interpretation of history advanced by communism. At heart something of a spiritual mystic and apparently never able totally to discard the deep Catholic faith of his youth, Mariátegui insisted that communist materialism was much less materialistic than commonly thought.[50] He argued, in fact, that communism was essentially a spiritual movement. 'The force of the communist revolutionaries,' he wrote, 'does not lie in their science; it lies in their faith, in their passion, in their will; revolutionary movements embody a mystical, religious, spiritual force.'[51] In seeking converts to communism, Mariátegui often employed arguments that were primarily spiritual in nature:

Historical materialism in no manner interferes with the development of the absolute, free spirit. Material considerations, on the contrary, are the preliminary condition for the emergence of such a spirit. And it is precisely our thought that a society resting upon an ample economic base . . ., where the free workers will be animated by a vivid enthusiasm for production, will give prodigious impulse to art, religion and philosophy, and transport the workers towards new heights. . . . The materialist who professes and religiously serves his faith can be distinguished from the idealist only by a convention of language . . . There is a mysticism in Marxism and those who adhere to it come very close to the spirit of the Christianity of the catacombs.[52]

Concerning the development of Marxist thought Mariátegui boldly proclaimed: 'The true disciples of Marx are not those pedantic professors who can only repeat his words, those incapable of adding to the doctrine but rather limited by it; the real disciples of Marx have been the revolutionaries stained with heresy.'[53]

It was in April 1930 that Mariátegui succumbed to his lingering illness. Had he lived it is possible that he would have produced a significant and lasting schism within the communist movement as it was developing in Latin America. Certain it is that so long as he did live communism in Peru did not slavishly follow Soviet dogma and thus was not what to many observers it seemed to be.

During Leguía's *oncenio* another political movement, seeking its ideological inspiration primarily in Marxism, came into being. This was the *Alianza Popular Revolucionaria Americana* (APRA), founded in Mexico City in May 1924 by Víctor Raúl Haya de la Torre and several other Peruvian intellectuals who had been harried out of their country by the Leguía administration. Because the APRA leaders were generally in exile between 1924 and 1930, most Peruvians were not aware of what the movement initially stood for, although the inquisitive intellectual could gain some idea by reading certain books and especially the 1926–8 editions of *Amauta* in which several articles written by *Apristas* appeared. Understandably ill-informed about its real significance, Peruvians in general tended to err seriously in their early appraisals of *aprismo*. Many assumed it was simply another manifestation of the *indigenista* movement that was gathering momentum at the time. Others judged it to be a new front for international communism, and still others saw in it a democratic reform movement seeking to accomplish its ends without violence. *Aprismo* in its first six years of existence was actually none of these things.

The *Aprista* programme, furthermore, was not very helpful to those seeking to learn about the movement. Couched in general terms and high-sounding rhetoric, it revealed little of *aprismo*'s essence. Adding to the confusion about its nature and purposes was the fact that *aprismo* had not a single programme but rather two programmes. One of these was a maximum programme which *Apristas* hoped would eventually be implemented throughout Latin America or, as they referred to it, Indo–America. It called for action against Yankee imperialism, the political unity of Indo–America, the nationalization of land and industry, the internationalization of the Panama Canal, and the solidarity of all exploited peoples and all oppressed classes, with special reference to the Indians of the New World.

The minimum programme, to apply to Peru alone, although its major points had been clearly developed in the 1920's, was officially formulated at the first national congress of the *Partido Aprista Peruano* in 1931. It stressed the need to end the traditional exploitation of the Peruvian masses by the ruling classes. Although advocating a powerful State to which the individual would be subordinated, *Apristas* in their programme paid lip service to what was described as functional democracy, and by inference guaranteed the rights of opposition parties to organize and compete freely in politics. Specifically the minimum programme declared the intention to protect the basic freedoms of speech, press and assembly, and professed that the State should guarantee to every citizen life, health, education and material and moral well-being. In its economic section the minimum programme urged long-range nationalization, although seizure by the State of those mining firms that were principally controlled by the United States was an immediate goal. Economic policy also called for the State to create new enterprises and institute a planned economy that would bring an end to the exploitation of man by man. While not stating exactly how they hoped to gain control over the state apparatus, the *Apristas* in their official programme implied that they hoped to come to power through peaceful, constitutional means.[54]

For all the importance that has been attached to and all that has been written about them, neither the maximum nor the minimum programmes of the APRA, nor some of the more widely-publicized utterances of its leaders provided the best means for gaining a clear understanding of a movement that was not always what it seemed to be. In many instances, less widely-circulated writings of its leaders afforded a better insight into the nature of early *aprismo*.

Like Mariátegui and the Communists, Haya de la Torre and the *Apristas* stressed in many of their early pronouncements the need to redeem the proletariat classes of Peru, especially the Indians. Even as many of the *Indigenistas* then rising to prominence, *Apristas* often spoke and wrote as if they believed that the only worthwhile and virtuous population element south of the Rio Grande was the Indian.[55] Notwithstanding this, from the very founding of the movement the main endeavour of the APRA was to win the support of the Peruvian middle sectors. *Indigenismo* was professed, in part at least, because it was in style at the time among many intellectuals, a circumstance from which the wily Leguía had also originally sought to derive advantage.

Writing in the mid-1920's on the Peruvian proletariat, by which he meant principally the Indian race, the leader of the *Apristas*, Haya de la Torre, referred to it as a sector 'still in formation: it has no class consciousness. In its great majority it is comprised of rural labourers who are illiterate. It lacks both the class consciousness and the cultural level which have characterized the proletariat of more advanced capitalist countries.' Haya then revealed clearly where his immediate class interests lay:

   . . . there is a middle class, made up of artisans and peasants who own means of production, of mining and industrial workers, small capitalists, landowners and merchants. To this class belong also the intellectual workers, the professionals, the technicians, as well as private and state employees. It is this middle group that is being pushed towards ruination by the process of imperialism. . . . The great foreign firms extract our wealth and then sell it outside of our country. Consequently, there is no opportunity for our middle class. This, then, is the abused class that will lead the revolution.[56]

The emphasis placed by *aprismo* on the plight of middle groups and the need to bring security to their members was nothing new in Peruvian ideology. Víctor Andrés Belaúnde, beginning in 1914, had brilliantly described how the insecurity and impoverishment of Peruvian middle sectors underlay many of the country's fundamental problems. When *aprismo* began ten years later to propagate Belaúnde's thesis as its own, adding a real although often camouflaged ingredient of revolutionary violence in the tradition of the González Prada phoenix approach to regeneration, the picture of middle-group impoverishment was no longer an accurate reflection of the Peruvian reality.

As Peru's economy made advances, real and apparent, under the Leguía régime, the middle sectors gained in number and strength. Not only was their economic status less precarious, they also benefited socially and politically from the many political favours and special economic concessions extended to them by an administration consciously set upon currying their favour. Consequently, the middle sectors did not respond to the APRA cry to lead the proletariat in an anti-capitalist, anti-imperialist revolution that would topple the aristocracy. During the *oncenio* the middle sectors and the traditional upper class had begun to co-operate with each other and both groups seemed to be prospering from the experience.

APRA's preoccupation with Peru's middle sectors explains why Leguía was so harsh and unrelenting a foe of its spokesmen at the same time that he was relatively tolerant of Peruvian Communists who especially after 1928 grouped around Mariátegui. The dictator's hope to continue as the dominant political power in Peru, a position which apparently he wanted to occupy indefinitely, depended to a great degree upon the support of the middle elements. This was the very socio-economic group which the APRA was seeking to proselytize. Leguía therefore rightly regarded the APRA as his most immediate and dangerous enemy, and was careful throughout his rule to keep most of its spokesmen in jail or in exile. Communists, even of the unorthodox variety of Mariátegui, purposely alienated the middle elements, contemptuously dismissing them as the *petit bourgeoisie* and advocating their liquidation. As a result, communism did not loom as an immediate challenge to Leguía's political aspirations.

Aprista ideology definitely departed from communist norms in stressing the importance of the middle sectors in bringing about the socialist revolution. In other respects it was not only similar to, but according to its own spokesmen, more directly in line with Marxian–Leninist analyses than the programme advanced by Mariátegui. By the late 1920's *aprismo* and communism were engaged in a running dispute as to which was the most authentically and uncompromisingly anti-capitalist and anti-imperialist. *Apristas* and Communists alike urged the immediate undertaking of Latin America's second emancipation movement, aimed at throwing off the yoke of United States imperialism.[57] They both agreed that the relations of an economically underdeveloped with a powerful and advanced capitalist country inevitably worked to further impoverish the weaker country; that imperialism fixed upon Peru a system of economic exploitation in which its raw goods were drained off at ever lower prices, and prevented the accumulation of native capital so essential to bring about the solution of national problems; that no social or economic progress could be made until the forces of imperialism had been overthrown and a socialist structure introduced.

Once again, however, *aprismo* was not entirely what it seemed to be. There was an inconsistency in the APRA line towards imperialism. At the same time that he and other *Apristas* called for a concerted effort to end imperialism so as to make possible the introduction of socialism and the attainment of social and economic reforms in Indo-America, Haya de la Torre was revising Marxism–Leninism along the following lines. True, said Haya, imperialism is the last stage of capitalism, but only in the developed, highly capitalized countries. In contrast, the imperialism to which underdeveloped countries are subjected is the first stage of their capitalism. Hence, the weak nations must encourage the imperialist process, for it will create the capitalism which will generate a powerful proletariat together with the middle sectors necessary to lead the downtrodden in a socialist revolution.[58]

Just how Haya de la Torre proposed to co-operate with United States imperialism, which in effect he had identified with Yankee investments, as a means of developing capitalism in Peru and thus hastening the socialist revolution, while at the same time urging the immediate end of imperialism and the liquidation of North American investments, which he so often did,[59] is not clear. Probably because the last stage–first stage theory was so glaringly inconsistent with the rest of his ideology, Haya de la Torre never stressed it in the early years of *aprismo*. To the contrary, *Aprista* leadership emphasized the need for the prompt anti-imperialist revolution and the introduction of socialism.[60]

Apologists of the APRA have often described it in such terms as to make it appear to have been in its early days a peaceful organization whose leaders intended to acquire power through non-violent means. The public pronouncements of *Aprista* leaders during the mid and late-1920's and the general tone of the 1931 minimum programme seem to justify this description, as does the fact that Haya de la Torre liked to be pictured as an admirer of the Indian statesman Mohandas K. Gandhi and his school of non-violence. Here again *aprismo* was not what it seemed to be. Like González Prada whose disciple he frequently proclaimed himself, Haya did not shy away from violence as the means of attaining political ends. His actual appraisal of Gandhi is revealing:

Time will continue to demonstrate that the non-violence of Gandhi is more apparent than real. . . . If Gandhi completes his task, then will come others who will initiate the second epoch with new methods and new tactics. The work of Gandhi will remain . . . as the firm base of revolutionary actions in India. It does not matter that his original programme bore the banner of peace. In its essence it is war, violence and forceful struggle.[61]

Haya went on to say that if a certain element of non-violence had been necessary in India because of British dominance, the situation was different in Indo–America.

European countries and the United States, in the opinion of Haya de la Torre, had often been able to avoid violence in their internal development because of a continuing integral evolution. No such evolution had occurred in Indo–America, where feudalism still existed beneath a superimposed and weak capitalist structure. Under these circumstances, with the institutions of different ages and civilizations existing side by side, violence might be inevitable.[62]

In a book published in 1926 Manuel Seoane, who until his death in 1963 was generally second only to Haya de la Torre in the *Aprista* high command, called the people of Indo–America to action and combat. He was clearly persuaded that reform could not come to Peru through democracy or peaceful means:

The task of governing a nation each day becomes more and more the work of science, of specialists, of men of high and solid culture. . . . It is ridiculous to think, therefore, of curing our ills by giving the vote to the person who has had one year of school . . . there is a difference between the quantitative criterion of elections and the qualitative criterion of Government. The two are mutually opposed. . . . To speak of a Peruvian transformation based on suffrage is laughable. . . . Our formula must be another. We should be interested in the end, not in the means. . . . When society has changed, then you can think of extending suffrage.[63]

Seoane believed that only a few, initiated intellectuals could lead the Peruvian transformation and this conviction was fully shared by Haya de la Torre. Inquiring if within the theory of economic determinism there was room for the hero, the strong man, the great man, Haya replied, 'all the room in the world. The hero interprets, intuits and directs the vague and imprecise aspirations of the multitude'.[64]

Notwithstanding the statements and implications of their official minimum programme, democracy had little to do with either the means whereby *Apristas* hoped to capture control of the government or with the methods they intended to use once in power. Certainly the party structure organized by *aprismo* was not of the type that would have been suitable for operation in a democratic environment. Learning probably both from the Communists and Fascists with whom he had contact during his European travels of the mid and late-1920's, as well as from the experience of the Mexican Revolution in developing a one-party system under the 'strong-man', Plutarco Elias Calles, Haya de la Torre insisted on iron-bound discipline for all *Apristas*. Membership cards were awarded only after a close scrutiny of the applicants and after party chiefs were satisfied that prospective members would follow party discipline and ideological pronouncements with the same blind loyalty of Communist Party cardholders. The attempt of the *Aprista* leader, Luis Heysen, to explain the rigours of APRA discipline is revealing: 'Its [the APRA's] internal life does not suffer in the slightest respect from the vicissitudes of other parties where the ideology and discipline are not shared unanimously.

With the APRA the accord of the militants is complete and the discipline is accepted with pleasure and responsibility'.[65]

Haya de la Torre's unstinting praise of the communist educational system after a visit to Russia in 1929 did not augur well for the future prospects of democracy if the APRA obtained power in Peru. Stating that the children in Russian schools were happy because they were receiving an integral education, Haya lamented that this type of instruction could not be introduced in Peru, at least not until the intellectual and manual workers had taken control of the government and displaced the classes that were presently ruling. How did Haya envision the ideal and integrated education?

To be integral, education must be reflected in every aspect of life: in the family, the Government, the political structure. You cannot teach children to be socialists in school unless the whole governmental and social structure are also socialistic. .... Education must be imparted in the school, the home, the street.[66]

The sort of educational pluralism usually associated with democracy obviously had no place in the plans of the APRA's supreme creator of ideology who wished to substitute indoctrination for instruction.

The non-democratic features of *aprismo* are not necessarily in themselves deserving of total condemnation. Revolutionary movements in the past had made worthwhile accomplishments and authoritarian governments had provided sound and enlightened government. Certainly it is possible that some of the reforms which the country required in the 1920's could not have been introduced through democratic processes. The truly serious consideration was that *aprismo*'s ambiguous position in regard to democracy, its apparent endorsement of it in some statements and its courting of pro-democratic elements on the one hand, and its contemptuous dismissal of democracy and appeal to partisans of totalitarianism on the other revealed what were the movement's basic flaws: rank opportunism, absence of candour, and lack of a solid moral foundation.

With one group of voluble intellectuals urging that a movement of violence emanating in the sierra should destroy all traditional social-economic-political patterns and eliminate the influence of and perhaps even the population of the coast, and with another group preaching, at least part of the time, the violent overthrow of the ruling sectors by the coastal bourgeoisie, it is little wonder that less and less was heard from the champions of moderate reform. Frightened by the mounting extremism of new reform movements, men from the directing classes who had previously said and actually done a great deal about gradually improving social and economic conditions were thrown increasingly on the defensive. To them there seemed little alternative to bracing for a defence of the existing structure, faults and all, against the violent attempts to introduce new and untried and vaguely defined expedients.

THE OVERTHROW OF LEGUÍA AND THE END OF THE 'ONCENIO'

A year before the inception of the *oncenio* Víctor Andrés Belaúnde had stated that the Peruvian military was not characterized by a greedy, heedless desire to seize political power. At the same time Belaúnde recognized that the disruption of the regular parties, the collapse of political responsibility and morality and the general loss of orientation could at some future time, should such lamentable circumstances arise, force the military to seize power from discredited civilians.[67] Midway through the *oncenio* parties were not only disrupted but had virtually disappeared; and signs abounded that responsibility and morality had been abandoned by those surrounding the dictator, especially by his son Juan. Still, the military did not strike, in part because the administration seemed even yet to have a policy, that of achieving prosperity and material progress. So long as this continued, Leguía was taken 'as a magician endowed with mysterious powers, and the public was willing to judge his administration by the tangible signs of progress'.[68]

Early in his third term Leguía felt sufficiently secure to relax some of the repressive features of his government, and a steady stream of political figures, among them Oscar R. Benavides, exiled earlier in the *oncenio* began to be welcomed back to the country, although *Aprista* leaders were not permitted to re-enter. The Prime Minister at this time, Pedro José Rada y Gamio,[69] was a man of moderation and a respected pillar of the Catholic Church who exhibited none of the cruelty that had characterized one of his predecessors in office, Germán Leguía, 'the Tiger'. The mildness and paternalism of Leguía began increasingly to be commented upon by observers of the Peruvian scene.[70]

The climate of opinion changed rapidly in late 1929 when the impact of the world depression came to be felt in Peru and the magician was no longer able to perform his tricks. The *oncenio* had lost its orientation and, in August 1930, Luis M. Sánchez Cerro in Arequipa led a military uprising against its faltering director. Twice before Sánchez Cerro, who had so conspicuously displayed his valour in the 1914 *coup* that overthrew Billinghurst, had tried and failed to overthrow Leguía. Both times he had been forgiven and, following periods of observation, allowed to return to the army. Newly promoted to lieutenant colonel in 1930, Sánchez Cerro foresaw little possibility of failure when he tried for the third time to destroy Leguía.

The revolution of Arequipa, which proclaimed the need to reintroduce morality and then normality into Peru's political processes and which promised to respect all political groups that did not threaten social morality or legal order, soon won the support of garrisons in Puno and Cuzco. As opposition quickly mounted against him in Lima itself, Leguía, his son Juan, and some friends left the national palace, proceeding to Callao where they boarded the warship *Almirante Grau* and put to sea. Meanwhile Sánchez Cerro arrived in Lima, flown there from Arequipa by Elmer Faucett, the pilot who had introduced commercial aviation in Peru. By the end of August, Sánchez Cerro was the presiding officer of a military junta that governed Peru and the *oncenio* had come to an inglorious end.

Whether Leguía voluntarily ordered the *Almirante Grau* to return to Callao so that he could defend himself against the charges he knew the junta would level, or was forced to turn back by bad health, or because the ship's commander was prevailed upon by the new government to set about, has long been debated by Peruvian historians.[71] Whatever the exact circumstances leading to Leguía's return, he was back in Callao shortly after Sánchez Cerro had assumed power. The junta ordered him and his son Juan to be confined for a time on San Lorenzo Island, and then transferred them to the penitentiary.

In the months ahead what the deposed dictator endured would have been enough to atone for the most heinous crimes, let alone for the always less than savage repressive measures and the often well-intentioned excesses and errors of judgement of which he had been guilty. Suffering from an excruciatingly painful prostate condition, Leguía was kept in an unsanitary cell and denied medical attention until it was far too late to save his life. Finally, after he had wasted away to sixty-seven pounds, the government permitted him to be attended by doctors and to undergo the long overdue prostate operation. He never recovered from it, dying on 6 February 1932.[72]

Shortly before his death Leguía stated to a priest that his only hope was that Peruvians would come to say of him that in his last days he had not maintained rancour towards anyone, that he had pardoned all who had tried to do evil to him, and that he had always desired happiness and prosperity for the Peru which he so deeply loved. A generation or so after Leguía's death most Peruvians would ungrudgingly concede him this much. In asking so little in the way of appreciation from his countrymen, Leguía had on his deathbed acquired the moderation which in life had generally eluded him.

The virtue of moderation was conspicuously absent in most of the figures who struggled for political power in Peru following the *oncenio*. Basically, the reason for this was that in the 1930's the analysis of middle-sector impoverishment made first by Belaúnde and later incorporated by Haya de la Torre into the APRA ideology was in accordance with reality. With their impoverishment a bitter fact in the early depression years, Peru's middle groups grew increasingly hostile towards the aristocracy with which they had been willing and eager to co-operate during the previous decade. At the same time they developed a sharp antagonism towards foreign capital. Once the depression had begun, strongly worded demands for repayment of loans, accompanied by tariff discrimination and worsening terms of trade, replaced large-scale capital inflow as the main feature of Peru's relationship to the world of foreign capital, especially the United States. Middle groups began to look on foreign capital not as the necessary source of economic development and opportunity, as it had appeared to be in the 1920's, but as an instrument of exploitation, as Haya de la Torre and other members of the Marxist–Leninist school of economics had described it.

More and more the whole sum and substance of APRA economic theory, except for the vague and largely ignored allusion to the need to co-operate with foreign capital in line with the last stage–first stage hypothesis, seemed vindicated. Not only was foreign investment synonomous with exploitative imperialism, but capitalism had as predicted collapsed in all parts of the world. If capitalism was moribund even in the great world powers, obviously Peru must reject the system and under the leadership of the hard-pressed middle sectors seek redemption through socialism, destroying in the process the aristocracy and all traditional institutions. As expounded by *aprismo*, moreover, socialist doctrines had been only mildly and superficially associated with *indigenismo* and Andeanism and thus did not terrify coastal, middle-group whites and *mestizos*. By 1930 Peruvians were divided into two uncompromisingly hostile camps of *Apristas* and anti-*Apristas* and preparing for one of the bitterest struggles in their country's history. For all practical effects this struggle was a civil war: the hatred and passion which it aroused would endure for a generation to come and the acts of violence which it occasioned spread from one end of Peru to the other and for over three years brought the processes of government nearly to a standstill.

The Changing APRA's Quest for Power, 1930–45

PRELIMINARY SKIRMISHES TO A VIRTUAL CIVIL WAR, AND THE ELECTION OF SÁNCHEZ CERRO, 1930–1

HAILED upon his arrival in Lima as Peru's liberator from the tyranny of the *oncenio*, the forty-year-old Sánchez Cerro from the very outset displayed an ability, previously unmatched by Peruvian political figures, in winning the adulation of the masses. In the course of his political campaigning in 1930 and 1931 he visited the populous urban centres as well as some of the most remote regions of the country. Almost wherever he went he gained the enthusiastic backing of the multitudes, presented for the first time with the spectacle of a politician who seemed to take them seriously, who personally carried his message to them, and explained his aspirations in easily understandable language.[1]

In the sierra the rapidly growing organization that called itself the Youth of Cuzco (*Juventud del Cuzco*) saw in Sánchez Cerro the man who would inaugurate the reforms that the Andean political leaders had been advocating for over twenty years.[2] Elsewhere in the Andean region and its approaches, in such departments as Puno, Junín, Ancash, Ayacucho, Apurimac and Arequipa, Sánchez Cerro also gained overwhelming popular support. It is true that in the northern coastal area surrounding Trujillo, the native city of Haya de la Torre, lower and middle sectors by and large ignored Sánchez Cerro and backed the APRA. Even in the 'solid *Aprista* North', however, Sánchez Cerro was by no means without his partisans. The residents of his native Piura and also those of Tumbes were in their great majority committed to the lieutenant colonel turned politician.

José Marías Manzanilla, the author of most of Peru's early

social legislation, summarized correctly the political situation of 1930 when he wrote that the great gift of Sánchez Cerro was his ability to attract and to direct the lower classes. 'He understood them and they understood him. He loved them and because of this he won their love'.[3]

Strictly speaking, Sánchez Cerro never formulated a political philosophy. Rationalization and philosophical analysis did not concern him. A man of action rather than reflection, his forte was his intuitive ability to grasp a situation and to respond energetically to its exigencies. Because he could not or did not choose to articulate his understanding of a situation, he was often contemptuously dismissed by intellectuals as ignorant, uncultured and shallow. Still, by means of his shrewd understanding, Sánchez Cerro had come to grasp conditions in Peru better than many intellectuals and had determined to play precisely the political rôle best suited to the times. Essentially, what he hoped to accomplish was the formation of a political party that would permanently bind together proletariat and aristocratic elements.

Success in the political rôle which he envisioned for himself, therefore, depended upon more than the support of the urban and rural masses. In addition it required the loyal backing of the upper ranks of society. Herein lay one of the grave problems that confronted Sánchez Cerro. The frail officer from Piura who seldom weighed as much as 120 pounds was regarded as too outspoken, too lacking in tact and concern for protocol, too moody, emotional, volatile and occasionally vulgar, to be taken seriously by the refined and gentlemanly elements of Peru's upper classes. Moreover, many aristocrats were still extremely colour conscious, and found it difficult to accept the dark-skinned *cholo* who was even suspected by some of having a few drops of Negro blood. While they might welcome him ecstatically as the deliverer from the obnoxious features of the *oncenio*, which from their point of view had sometimes paid too much attention to middle elements and not enough to the élite, the aristocrats tended to regard Sánchez Cerro as a social upstart and an unreliable maverick who must soon be replaced by a political leader who was a *bona fide* gentleman.

Shortly after his entry into Lima and his appointment as presiding officer of a military junta it became clear that Sánchez Cerro would have his difficulties with certain members of the upper classes. Several aristocratic political groups were formed with the

251

purpose of removing the popular militarist from the political scene and the electing to the presidency a member of their own class. In addition, a rival military figure appeared in the person of Gustavo A. Jiménez, known as 'the Fox'. In opposing Sánchez Cerro, Jiménez apparently was moved both by personal ambition and by the belief that the *Aprista* programme of class warfare directed against the upper social sectors represented the best hope for solving the problems then besetting Peru.

Apristas had at first welcomed the rise of Sánchez Cerro to power, had praised the lieutenant colonel inordinately, and had asserted that 'militarism plus *aprismo* equals the ideal government of the people'.[4] They soon learned, however, that they could not come to terms with Sánchez Cerro, who was rabidly hostile to their plans for the elimination of the aristocracy by middle-sector intellectuals with the support of the masses.

Unable to effect the hoped-for understanding with Sánchez Cerro and to use him as the instrument for coming to power themselves, *Aprista* leaders initiated revolutions in Cuzco and elsewhere. Sánchez Cerro promptly suppressed these movements and put their instigators in jail.[5] Infuriated by this course of events, *Apristas* by the beginning of 1931 directed appeals to the 'unstained and untainted young military officers' to defend with their arms the cause of the people and to overthrow Sánchez Cerro.[6]

With political leaders of the traditional aristocracy either refusing to take him seriously or else actually hostile, with rival military officers working to unseat him, and with the APRA engaging in revolutionary activity, Sánchez Cerro was unable to accomplish any significant results. Frustrated by this situation he summoned to the national palace on the first day of March political leaders of all persuasions, from Fascists to *Apristas* and Communists. To them he announced his resignation. Six days later, his act of 'political abnegation' fulsomely praised by the Apostolic Administrator, Monsignor Mariano Holguín, Sánchez Cerro went into voluntary exile in Europe.

A new junta presided over ostensibly by David Samánez Ocampo, a widely-respected, elderly political leader who had played an important rôle in the Arequipa uprising that had overthrown Leguía, assumed the task of governing Peru and of preparing for free elections. In reality, Samánez Ocampo was little more than a figurehead; the dominant figure in the junta was its minister of war, Gustavo Jiménez, the implacable foe of Sánchez Cerro and ever more overtly the friend of the APRA. With its leaders released from jail by the new government and enjoying a close relationship with the junta, the Peruvian *Aprista* Party (*Partido Aprista Peruano*, or PAP) began confidently to believe that it would win the presidential and constituent assembly elections due to be held in October.[7]

Outraged that their hero had apparently been forced to withdraw, the masses showed signs of increasing restlessness after the departure of Sánchez Cerro. As popular insistence mounted that the *cholo* officer be recalled and guaranteed the right to campaign for the presidency, a group of influential politicians sought desperately to prevent the eruption of violence and to provide for peaceful elections. After considerable deliberation they agreed that both Haya de la Torre, the announced *Aprista* candidate, and Sánchez Cerro should be urged to withdraw from the campaign. Initially Sánchez Cerro in Paris agreed to their suggestion, but then changed his mind when the APRA refused to withdraw its candidate and when it became altogether evident that the junta favoured the *Aprista* cause.

More than ever persuaded that *aprismo* was a dangerous movement that threatened Peru with chaos and ruin, Sánchez Cerro determined to return to his country. The junta tried to prevent this, instructing the Peruvian consular service in Europe not to supply him with the required re-entry visa. When Sánchez Cerro insisted he would return with or without the visa and when indications of massive popular support for his position became unmistakable, the junta retreated, removed legal obstacles and permitted him to land at Callao in early July.

With Peru's traditional parties having virtually disappeared during the *oncenio* and with politicians showing little interest in resuscitating them, a new party, the Revolutionary Union (*Unión Revolucionaria*, or UR), was organized to back the Sánchez Cerro campaign. Sánchez Cerro at once undertook an extensive tour that carried him to some of Peru's most remote hamlets to explain his party programme. Published shortly after his return to the country, the programme called for hard work and sacrifice and for the recognition of the capacity of all elements in the population, Indian, European, Negro and mixed blood, to contribute to the forging of a modern republic; it severely criticized those who sought to create cleavages among Peruvians and expressed the conviction that the country could be revitalized only through the co-operation of all social, economic and ethnic groups. In obvious reference to the APRA, the Revolutionary Union programme stated:

Nothing could be more prejudicial to the country than to elevate to its Government a closed group of narrow and sectarian spirit, especially now that we have scarcely begun the re-creation of ordinary political life and institutions following the dictatorship. If the direction of public affairs were entrusted to partisan intolerance, to the hatred of a sect, to demagoguery and violence, it would be impossible to prepare the way for democracy in Peru. With a régime of sectarian hatred in power, it would be impossible to re-establish public liberties after their long, eleven-year eclipse. If a group whose goal is exclusivism in politics governs the country, it will be impossible for diverse political parties to function; and it will be extremely difficult to accommodate the divergent tendencies and aspirations of organized social and economic groups to the extent that is always essential to the operation of a true democracy.[8]

In his campaign and in the Revolutionary Union platform of which he was the principal author, Sánchez Cerro by no means limited himself to vague assertions in favour of an integrated country, or to attacks against the more menacing aspects of the *Aprista* spirit. He called for administrative decentralization, for a sound currency and balanced budgets. He acknowledged the need for continuing foreign investment, but at the same time demanded new legislative guarantees that a high percentage of Peruvian nationals would be employed in all enterprises. The urgency of agricultural diversification was persuasively argued and a programme of colonization leading to the utilization of new lands was described in considerable detail. In addition, Sánchez Cerro in his party platform called for the expropriation, with compensation, of the unutilized portions of large agrarian holdings.

The Revolutionary Union programme was considerably ahead of the times in Latin America in its recognition that agrarian problems could not be solved just by land redistribution. The document stated:

In addition to increasing the number of small property holders . . . it is necessary to provide for agricultural credit, technological instruction, the formation of co-operatives and the undertaking of irrigation projects. . . . All redistributive programmes will fail and land reform will become a grave menace to the country if the peasant who is supposed to be benefited by the programme is not technically trained.

Acknowledging that the assimilation of the Indian was the fundamental problem in Peru, the Revolutionary Union programme in a section frequently stressed by Sánchez Cerro declared that 'so long as we do not consider all of our people, Indian and non-Indian, to be Peruvians, with the same rights and duties, there will never emerge the unity which is the indispensable element of the nation'. Sánchez Cerro and those who helped him to formulate the party platform, however, conceded that the 'spiritual evolution' which would lead Peru's directing classes to regard the Indians as human beings might require a very long time indeed. All the while that this evolution was taking place, abetted by an educational programme that emphasized the scientific findings of modern sociologists and anthropologists concerning the equal capacities of ethnic groups, the Indians were to be protected and provided with technological training and obligatory primary education. Indian communities were to be encouraged to establish arts and crafts industries and to construct roads that would facilitate the marketing of products. Thus the Revolutionary Union programme recognized that the spiritual change on the part of the non-Indian people which it advocated could be speeded by programmes aimed at helping the Indian to help himself and by so doing demonstrate to all observers that he possessed ability and virtue.

In opposing the eminently practical and at the same time idealistic Revolutionary Union programme, Haya de la Torre, who had returned in August 1931 to wage his campaign, offered solutions that were based on the jargon of Marxism–Leninism. He depicted the upper classes and the clergy as black-hearted knaves without exception and denounced capitalism and foreign investment while remaining vague on the specific policies of economic rehabilitation other than to recommend bi-metallism.

Lesser *Aprista* leaders, picturing themselves as the intellectuals of culture and dignity, resorted to tawdry methods in campaigning against Sánchez Cerro who, they said, was coarse and uncultured. Luis Heysen quoted St Thomas to the effect that a being whose very nature consigned it to an inferior grade could never raise itself, regardless of hopes and efforts, to a higher grade. 'The ass cannot aspire to become a horse; and Sánchez Cerro must always continue to be Sánchez Cerro, imprudent, irascible, explosive'. He was, concluded Heysen, illiterate and neurotic, the type of advanced paranoic who 'can only be studied with the books of Freud and Adler in hand'.[9]

As the campaign drew towards its conclusion, the Revolutionary Union rallies in Lima consistently outdrew those of the APRA. The *Apristas* responded to this situation with violence. In Lima alone some twenty Sánchez Cerro supporters were killed, frequently gunned down from cars. Fortunately the electoral process itself was not marred by violence. In October 1931, in fact, the governing junta presided over elections that were not only peaceful but undoubtedly the freest and most honest that Peru had known.[10] A recent electoral law had removed property qualifications and awarded suffrage rights to all literate male citizens of twenty-one years of age or over. For the first time in the country's history, moreover, the use of the secret ballot was provided by law. Because Gustavo Jiménez and the military junta enforced the new regulations, resisting what undoubtedly was a serious temptation to intervene, the elections provided an honest reflection of the will of the enfranchised citizens. Sánchez Cerro received 152,062 votes, and Haya de la Torre 106,007. Two minor candidates between them garnered some forty thousand ballots.

However much they had distrusted him as a wild and dangerous individual, 'the most rash and impetuous leader the country had known since the days of Gonzalo Pizarro',[11] Peru's aristocratic elements had come to accept the fact that, for the moment at least, they could not rid themselves of Sánchez Cerro. In the majority, then, they had supported him as a lesser menace than that represented by Haya de la Torre and *aprismo*. Much more important to his victory than the reluctant endorsement of the upper classes was the enthusiastic backing which Sánchez Cerro received from the masses. As Jorge Basadre has stated, it was the popular sectors, 'above all those of rural background, who determined that Sánchez Cerro would be President of Peru'.[12]

The impressive electoral victory by no means assured the new President a calm and fruitful term in office. Instead, the extremism that was rampant in Peru in the early 1930's with the resulting polarization of the country into rightist and leftist armed camps, a process that was accelerated by continuing economic difficulties, turned the span of the Sánchez Cerro administration into the sixteen most turbulent months in Peru's twentieth-century history.

PERUVIAN EXTREMES IN THE 1930'S

Responsible in part for the division of Peru into extremes of right and left was the emergence of a fascism as a powerful intellectual movement. Fascism in Peru was characterized by a disillusionment with liberal capitalism, which was pictured as a selfish, Godless, materialistic system concocted mainly by Protestants, Masons and Jews, and in total opposition to the Christian spirit of the middle ages.[13] The excessive individualism which inhered in and was nourished by the capitalist structure should give way, according to Peru's fascist spokesmen, to a system of economic regulations imposed and enforced by management-labour associations known as corporations. Within these corporations management would in effect enjoy a weighted ballot since a small managerial élite would cast the same number of votes as the large labourer membership. These same corporations were also to elect the national legislature, thereby dealing a fatal blow to the democratic, 'levelling' concept of one man, one vote, and facilitating the preservation of a hierarchical political structure.

Peruvian fascists delighted in identifying their cause with Catholicism. To them, the strengthening of 'political authority and Catholic dogmatism' had to proceed simultaneously, for the one depended upon the other.[14] Many Peruvian churchmen, from prelates to the humblest parish priests, moreover, embraced fascism as the one politico-economic system in harmony with the social teachings of the Church and the pronouncements of papal encyclicals.[15] In a way the clergy's favouring of fascism represented a renewed effort on its part to remake society in the authoritarian, hierarchical image of the Church; it was an effort that hearkened back to that of conservative nineteenth-century priests like Bartolomé Herrera, himself a pioneer advocate of the basic principles of the corporate state, to fashion a temporal world that reflected the internal organization of the Church.

Associated also with fascism in the minds of many Peruvians was the concept of *hispanismo*. Fascism was regarded as the means for restoring and safeguarding the aristocratic, centralized, authoritarian political structure, together with the paternalistic and carefully supervised economic order and the close Church–State relationship that Spaniards were said to have maintained in colonial

Peru. In their concern with glorifying the Spanish colonial traditions, some of Peru's fascist sympathizers contemptuously dismissed all vestiges of Indian civilization and suggested that the
only worthwhile cultural and ethnic elements in all the land were
those that were Spanish.[16] Thus they exacerbated the *indigenista-
hispanista* dispute and impeded the progress that some Peruvian
intellectuals had been making towards agreeing that *mestizaje* was
the ideal and inevitable goal for their country.

One of the most passionate champions of fascism in Peru was
José de la Riva Agüero, who with justification could write: 'I
enjoy the honour of having raised in Peru the cry against the
pseudo-democratic lies, the cry in favour of Fascist Italy and the
true concept of social and distributive justice'.[17] Having returned
to Peru from his self-imposed exile after the fall of Leguía, Riva
Agüero began in tones that were occasionally wild and ranting to
denounce capitalism which 'New York City, the revolting centre of
international Jewry', had helped impose upon the world.[18]
Democracy and liberalism, he asserted, led inevitably to communism. Announcing his return to the Catholic Church in 1932, he
began to proclaim that only Catholicism and fascism could contain
the communist menace. 'Up with Catholicism,' he wrote, 'up with
the corporate state and fascism, with order, hierarchy and authoritarianism.' Warming to his subject Riva Agüero, who by this time
preferred to be known as the Marquis of Aulestia, the noble title
of his Spanish ancestors, continued:

There can be no middle ground. Either to the right or to the left.
Democracy, capitalism, the liberal tradition, all represent a middle
ground which is really disguised communism or else the certain road to
it. Liberalism, capitalism and democracy, all based on utilitarianism and
materialism, destroyed the hierarchy of classes and values and led to the
reign of mediocrity, and in general so befouled human existence that
they spawned communism as a reaction and supposed remedy. The
only solution is to return to the medieval, Catholic, Hispanic tradition as
now embodied in fascism.[19]

Fascist extremism in Peru was matched on the left by that of the
Communists. In September 1930 Ricardo Martínez de la Torre,
who along with Eudocio Ravines had taken over the leadership
of the communist movement in Peru after the death of José
Carlos Mariátegui, published a significant article in the newly-
founded newspaper *La República*.[20] In it Martínez de la Torre

said that the time had come for Peruvian communism to drop the mask of secrecy and to agitate openly for the proletariat revolution. The Communist Party of Peru (formerly the Socialist Party which had been founded by Mariátegui), asserted the author, is not a party of the people, but of a single class, the exploited proletariat. He then described the primary objective of communism in Peru as 'the war to the death against the *bourgeoisie*, against the middle classes, and against all those who fight at their side'. Finally, in a song which he helped to compose at this time, Martínez de la Torre urged open warfare against all property owners, 'insatiable monsters, who suck the blood of the working classes'.[21]

Intensifying their activity in organized labour, Communists helped to form the General Confederation of Peruvian Workers (*Confederación General de Trabajadores Peruanos*) and by the end of 1930 were claiming for it a membership of over 56,000 industrial workers and an additional eight thousand of Peru's un-employed.[22]. The Confederation organized a number of 'José Carlos Mariátegui Worker and Peasant Schools', ostensibly to teach technological skills but actually to instruct the lower classes in revolutionary activity. Seeking also to recruit the natives of the sierra, the Confederation by the beginning of 1931 claimed a membership of thirty thousand Indians. This was in line with Mariátegui's conviction that communism in Peru should identify itself with the cause of the Indian. Throughout the 1930's Peruvian communism ever more stridently proclaimed the rights of the Indian communities to seize all privately held land which through the years had been plundered from them. Communist propaganda also claimed for the Indians the right to govern themselves in 'Quechua and Aymara republics'.[23]

In October 1930 the Socialist Party of Peru was founded by Luciano Castilla. A Marxian socialist party, its programme was virtually the same as that of communism except for its advocacy of gradualism and its insistence upon avoiding ties with the inter-national communist movement.[24] Socialists were just as con-vinced as Communists that in Indian usages and customs they would find many of the formulae for assuring Peru's future great-ness. Peruvian socialism, as expounded by one of its proponents in the pages of an influential Lima periodical, proclaimed: 'Peru will not emerge as a nation until power is transferred into the hands of the majority, the Indians of the sierra. Peru will not begin a genuine political life until the socialist *serranos* take the capital'.[25]

Conservative interests were duly impressed by the manner in which both communism and Marxian socialism in Peru took up the cause of protecting and glorifying the Indian and his customs. A characteristic editorial in the periodical published by the Catholic University made the point that a combination of international Jewry, communism and Protestantism was trying to take advantage of the Indian issue in order to force alien forms of life and culture on the Peruvian people. The editorial added that all *indigenista* movements in Peru were actually communist fronts.[26] Even more clearly, then, than in the previous decade, communism and Marxian socialism in the 1930's came to be identified both by advocates and detractors with the cause of *indigenismo*.

As the Catholic University publications and also its student body in general came to the defence of the values of fascism, hierarchy and *hispanismo*, students of San Marcos unfurled the banners of socialism, the proletariat revolution and *indigenismo*. Thus the intellectual cleavage between right and left came to involve university students, drawing them more decidedly into the arena of political dispute.

Almost at once after the fall of Leguía, the San Marcos student body went out on a prolonged strike. Ostensibly, the students were seeking reforms that affected only the university. They demanded, for example, the introduction of a genuine system of *cogobierno*. They called also for the military junta governing Peru to return to the student body the right to censure and remove incompetent professors, a right that had been first granted and then suppressed by Leguía. All the while, however, the students were interested in far more than what occurred on the campus. Urged on in some instances by outside agitators like Rómulo Betancourt of Venezuela who had recently been exiled from his native country and had become for the time being a member of the Communist Party, they concerned themselves more with transforming the political structure than with reforming the university. Attacking all defenders of conservative values, launching blistering attacks against the clergy and the military, the San Marcos students, organized in the Federation of Peruvian Students (*Federación de los Estudiantes del Perú*, or FEP), embraced the cause of the proletariat revolution and the socialist republic. The FEP, however, quickly dissociated itself from the Communist Party which had helped to instigate and had for a time supported the student strike.[27]

The leftist group most successful in gaining control over the San Marcos student body and using it as an instrument for advancing its essentially Marxian-inspired but highly eclectic programme of political reform was the APRA. Owing to the wide support it enjoyed among Peru's middle sectors, including many of the former partisans of Leguía, and among the urban proletariat of the northern coastal cities, the APRA was a more potent extremist movement than fascism, or communism, or Marxian socialism. The APRA, in fact, possessed and soon exercised the power to plunge Peru into a virtual civil war.

SÁNCHEZ CERRO FACES A CIVIL INSURRECTION AND A
FOREIGN WAR, 1931-3

In the early 1930's *aprismo* attacked foreign investment in Peru and capitalism in general.[28] It lashed out as well against the influence of religion and declared that it was necessary to destroy 'whatever Spain had introduced' in the country.[29] The Peruvian *Aprista* Party continued also to concern itself primarily with the middle sectors, assigning to them the leading rôle in bringing about a socialist revolution. And, at this time, Haya de la Torre seemed to be delighted by the attempt of *Aprista* leaders to develop a great man cult.

Alberto Hidalgo, beginning to acquire some notoriety in literary circles of Peru, published early in 1931 an article in which he praised Mussolini and Hitler as super-heroes, and affirmed that in Latin America Haya de la Torre more than any other was the man destined for greatness. 'He is the instrument that history has chosen,' declared Hidalgo, 'to move the air of all Latin America . . . He understands that he has been singled out for greatness, and that his actions will live forever. . . .'[30] In acknowledging the receipt of a copy of Hidalgo's article, Haya de la Torre from Europe wrote to his admirer:

> You understand me; there now exists between us the bond of faith, of faith and love. . . . To me your article is something sacred. Until today only my conscience has said to me, 'greatness calls you'. But now you have said it in words which only the great and the initiated men can hear. . . . You have spoken to me in the name of destiny. . . . After

hearing your voice, I now await only the sound of another that will announce to me the hour at which I should open my arms and deliver myself to destiny.[31]

In December 1931 Haya de la Torre evidently felt he had heard that other voice. The Lima daily *El Comercio* had published documents purportedly containing proof of *Aprista* plans to mount a revolution.[32] Apparently anticipating that the newly-elected administration would use these documents as an excuse for crushing the *Aprista* movement by force, Haya summoned a mass meeting in his native Trujillo on the night of 8 December. At this meeting, which took place just a few hours after the inauguration of Sánchez Cerro in Lima, Haya delivered an emotional harangue that was a clear invitation to his followers to arise and by force install him in the presidency:

Wait? Yes, we will wait, but not in repose and passivity in the false expectation that matters, unaided, will arrange themselves. We must wait in action. . . . Now more than ever we must be resolved to conquer. . . . Knowing that *aprismo* . . . is the cause of action, of struggle, of rebellion, of tenacious, perennial battle, I will not fear adversity. Rather, I fear easy victories, for they deceive. Companions, today begins for the *Apristas* a new chapter in the history of their party. The pages will be of glory or of shame. We will write them with blood or with mud. . . . We are the party of the people, and the cause of the people will triumph. . . . With the profound joy of strong warriors, with the conviction of our great cause, with the resolve to conquer, let us continue to move forward. Let us be worthy of the people and make them worthy of us. Only *aprismo* will save Peru.[33]

Thus did Haya de la Torre reject the results of the 1931 elections, which loyal *Apristas* had already begun unjustifiably to describe as fraudulent. By early 1932 he and the *Aprista* high command had repeatedly served notice that the party would not play the rôle of a loyal or constitutional opposition force to the triumphant Revolutionary Union. Instead, *Apristas* launched a war without quarter to overthrow the new régime. Sánchez Cerro, whose character may not have been without a certain streak of cruelty, fought back with furious abandon and soon the country was caught in the throes of the bitterest civil discord in its history.

On the very day of Sánchez Cerro's inauguration and of the *Aprista* rally in Trujillo the constituent assembly, elected at the same time as the President, began its sessions. At once it became apparent that the *Aprista* delegates, by the use of obstructionist tactics and by insistence upon revolutionary innovations which could only antagonize the large majority of the assembly, intended to pursue a policy of 'mischievious, relentless opposition'.[34] Sánchez Cerro, had he been willing to work towards the creation of an alliance of rightist and centrist representatives, could have formed a majority group in the assembly capable of defeating the manoeuvres and manipulations of the *Aprista* delegates. Instead, the President, over-reacting to the *Aprista* threat and temporarily abandoning his concern for broadly-based political support, sought to work almost exclusively with the delegates of the far right, some of whom at least had definite fascist leanings. Moreover, he displayed what may well have been undue haste in deciding to fight the *Apristas* with their own methods of illegality and violence. In January he ordered the police to enter the assembly quarters and arrest all of the twenty-three *Aprista* delegates who could be found on the premises. Following this the mutilated assembly, in which the rightists denied a significant rôle even to the centrists, lost the confidence of the people, who viewed with indifference the constitution that it completed in 1932 and that the government promulgated in January of the following year.[35]

One result of the rightist strength in the assembly after the arrest of its *Aprista* members was that the constitution which it produced called for a senate that would be elected by corporations representing the country's various functional groups. In actual practice, however, this feature of the constitution was never applied and the senate continued to be elected according to geographic regions and on the basis of non-weighted votes. Other features of the new constitution, many of which were likewise destined to be more ignored than honoured in the years since 1933, provided for a mixed presidential-parliamentary system, with the executive enjoying the right to appoint his ministers while the legislature was empowered to interpellate and remove cabinet members. Although the post of prime minister (*primer ministro*) was provided, its prerogatives pertained principally to ceremony, protocol and the supervision of ministerial work and did not endow the holder with actual powers to govern as in countries with genuinely parliamentary systems. The president, according to the provisions of the 1933 charter, was to be elected for a five-year term by the direct secret vote of all literate male citizens twenty-one years of age or over and not in the armed forces. Continuing the suppression of local autonomy begun in 1919, the new constitution stated that the president could appoint juntas of notables to govern municipalities. The legal personality as well as the inviolability of the property of Indian communities was proclaimed and the constitution further stipulated that communities which lacked sufficient terrain to support their members would receive land donations from the government.

A provision establishing the continued union of Church and State was passed unanimously by the constituent assembly, as was the usual long, and frequently meaningless, list of personal guarantees. The constitution framers also asserted the duty of the State to intervene in economic affairs so as to protect the labouring classes and enumerated the features of fairly comprehensive social security and public education systems.

Promulgation of the new instrument at the beginning of 1933 was an empty gesture, for a state of siege accompanied by the suspension of constitutional guarantees had long since been in effect, as Sánchez Cerro and the *Apristas* carried on their war to the death. After the arrest of the constituent assembly delegates, *Apristas* had understandably intensified the ferocity of their attacks against the administration. Indicative of the general level of their propaganda onslaught was a pornographic tract in which Alberto Hidalgo went into the most intimate details in describing the act of copulation performed by the President's mother and a pig that produced as its issue Luis M. Sánchez Cerro.[36] Thus did the self-styled defenders of national dignity and cultural and intellectual values attack the man whom they accused of being too uncouth to merit his high office.

Apristas did not limit themselves to verbal and written attacks against the Sánchez Cerro administration. By the end of December, 1931, *Aprista*-organized violence had become commonplace on the streets of Lima and preliminary plans were being formulated, apparently under the personal supervision of Haya de la Torre, for a revolutionary uprising in Trujillo.[37] On 6 March of the following year an eighteen-year-old *Aprista*, Melgar Márquez, attempted to assassinate Sánchez Cerro in the Church of Miraflores and succeeded in critically wounding the President. Beginning at this stage in some of his published pronouncements to pose as the foe of violence, Haya de la Torre sought to explain the act of the would-be assassin. The boy, said Haya, realizing that the strict discipline of the APRA did not permit violence, had temporarily separated himself from the party before attempting the assassination.[38]

Sánchez Cerro was not impressed by this explanation. To a visitor who came to see him in the hospital when he was recovering from his wounds, he remarked that the APRA was responsible for the fact that crime had assumed epidemic proportions in Peru. The President added that it was necessary to crush the APRA to prevent the country from falling into chaos. To another friend who advised him to put down the pistol at this point in his fight against the APRA, Sánchez Cerro replied: 'This is not the time to put the pistol down, but to have two. You don't know what the *Apristas* are.'[39]

Notwithstanding Sánchez Cerro's efforts to crush them,[40] *Apristas* persisted in their plans for a massive revolutionary uprising in Trujillo. On 7 July 1932, they were ready to act. With the help of some subverted military personnel, *Apristas* launched an attack at four in the morning against the powerful Trujillo garrison and after five hours of fighting succeeded in taking it. Soon all Trujillo was in the power of the insurgents and a high percentage of its overwhelmingly pro-*Aprista* civilian populace had been armed.

The government responded promptly, ordering the cruiser *Almirante Grau* to Salaverry and arranging to have troops from Cajamarca and other cities closer to the scene of trouble converge on Trujillo. By the afternoon of the eighth, the defeat of the rebels seemed certain and government airplanes began to drop pamphlets demanding the surrender of the besieged city. At nightfall, the top-level *Aprista* leaders decided to flee the city before the government troops began their all-out attack. Before departing they apparently gave orders for the cold-blooded assassination of some sixty military officers and enlisted men who had been taken prisoner and held as hostages. Not only were the soldiers killed, but the bodies of some were mutilated.

Even with the *Aprista* high command having fled, a large portion of Trujillo's citizens continued to fight and the government troops had to take the city house by house. Upon discovering the bodies of the massacred military personnel, the commanders of the finally triumphant government armies demanded a dreadful vengeance. According to the accounts of Trujillo residents who survived the events of the next few days, soldiers entered every house in the city and examined the shoulders and index fingers of male occupants. All men and boys whose shoulder bruises or finger irritations indicated that they might recently have fired weapons were removed to the nearby Indian ruins of Chan Chan and summarily executed by firing squads. *Aprista* spokesmen claimed that close to six thousand men were thus martyred in the environs of Trujillo. A more impartial estimate placed the number of victims at one thousand.[41]

It has often been assumed that the events of July 1932 created a permanent, unbridgeable gulf between the military and the APRA and thereby doomed the hopes of *Apristas* to acquire political power so long as the military remained a powerful institution. Actually, it was not long before at least some military officers began once more to co-operate with the revolutionary activities of *Apristas*. Meantime, however, before passions subsided somewhat, the military responded wholeheartedly and unitedly to the call to wage a war of extermination against the APRA. Simultaneously, moreover, Peru's armed forced prepared to take on a foreign foe, Colombia.

Peruvians had never been happy over the Salomón–Lozano Treaty, finally ratified in 1928, which ceded the small Amazonian port of Leticia, together with a large tract of jungle land, to Colombia. They were ready to applaud, then, when on the last day of August 1932, a group of heavily armed men crossed from Peru into Leticia, a community at the time of some three to five hundred inhabitants. Proclaiming that they had come to protect their persecuted fellow Peruvians and to reclaim the land that had improperly been granted Colombia, the invading forces proceeded to expel all Colombian officials.[42]

The high-handed actions of the invaders in the Leticia region constituted a patent violation of Peru's treaty obligations. Recognizing this, Sánchez Cerro at first condemned the act of aggression, attributing it to a handful of Communists. Other Peruvian politicians and diplomats, although lacking evidence to substantiate the charge, blamed *Apristas* for the armed trespass. According to their interpretation, *Apristas* hoped by this action to embroil Sánchez Cerro in a foreign controversy that might bring about his downfall.

While there is no evidence that *Apristas* planned or carried out the strike at Leticia, it is clear that they sought to take full advantage of the situation, regardless of how seriously they might thereby jeopardize the international standing and interests of their country. Posing as the only true defenders of their country's territory, *Apristas* organized an underground propaganda campaign against the President, accusing him of not backing the actions of the patriotic heroes in Leticia.[43]

Sánchez Cerro at this juncture still wanted to pursue a responsible policy and to reiterate his condemnation of the actions taken by a few impetuous, however patriotic, Peruvians. Above all else, though, he sincerely felt his mission in Peruvian history to be that of crushing the movement which he had ample grounds to regard as the most dangerous and subversive in the country's history. With alarm he witnessed the favourable response of the masses to the *Aprista* campaign in favour of engaging if necessary in an all-out war with Colombia in order to reclaim the surrendered Amazonian region. And he began to fear that he would lose the popular support necessary to suppress *aprismo* if he did not assume the strong stand against Colombia that the masses were coming to demand. As a result, Sánchez Cerro reluctantly decided to endorse the deeds of the Peruvian adventurers in Leticia. A statesman could have found a better solution. An unsophisticated, simple and direct military leader unaccustomed to dealing in subleties, who not only found popularity with the multitudes essential to achieve victory in the domestic war he was waging, but who also in almost childish fashion valued popular support as a supreme good in itself, could find no alternative to preparing for a military showdown with Colombia.

On 30 April 1933, while leaving the San Beatriz racetrack where he had reviewed some 25,000 men who had been mobilized for the impending war with Colombia, Sánchez Cerro was killed by the bullets of an *Aprista* assassin named Abelardo Mendoza Leiva. The assassination may well have been a tactical blunder on the part of the *Apristas*. They had already manipulated the President into a hopeless position by forcing him to stake his vast popularity upon waging and winning a war with a neighbour republic. The United States, however, as well as most Latin American nations, the League of Nations, and world opinion in general would probably have exerted sufficient pressure to prevent a Peruvian triumph.

Because he did not live to disillusion the masses by backing down in the struggle with Colombia, as surely he would have been forced to do, the *cholo* adventurer died secure in the devotion of the humbler elements of the Peruvian populace.

For sixteen violence-ridden months Sánchez Cerro had fought the *Apristas* to a standstill. He had done it in the only way he knew how, by being as nasty, vicious and bloodthirsty as the *Apristas* themselves. It is possible that more suave and moderate methods might in the long run have been equally or even more effective in keeping the *Apristas* from power. It is also possible that Sánchez Cerro, as he claimed, understood the true nature of *aprismo* in the early 1930's. The only way to have kept Peru out of the clutches of *aprismo* at this time may well have been by taking up not one, but two pistols.[44]

Oscar R. Benavides (1876–1945), who nearly twenty years earlier had ousted Guillermo Billinghurst from power succeeded Sánchez Cerro in the presidency, chosen by congress to serve out the unexpired term of the assassinated executive. Herein lay the final and most significant, however unintended and indirect, contribution that Sánchez Cerro rendered his country. Had it not been for him and his successful initial fight against the APRA, Benavides and the advisers who helped to shape his policy would never have had the opportunity to provide Peru with six years of remarkably efficient and constructive government. Instead, men of the phoenix approach would have had their fling at burning the country to the ground and there is no telling how grotesque the results of their attempts to rebuild it, according to an ideology that had become a strange mixture of Marxism and personalism, might have been.

THE BENAVIDES REGIME, 1933–9

Socially prominent himself and at home in the salons of the most wealthy and cultured Peruvian families, Benavides exhibited a certain aloofness in his dealings with most people. He lacked both the talent for campaigning at the grass-roots level and the obsession with gaining the adulation of the masses that had characterized his predecessor in office. Yet Benavides possessed a profound social consciousness.[45] Concerned not only with preserving order in Peru against the threat from the left, Benavides sought also to establish a government that was attentive to the needs of all classes.[46] Given the situation of virtual civil war that still prevailed in Peru, Benavides understood that genuine democracy was not at the moment the most suitable means for accomplishing his purposes. Still, he scrupulously avoided excesses in his authoritarian rule and was soon being criticized by certain extremists of the right for not imposing an iron-hand fascistic dictatorship in order to crush the forces of the left.[47] Benavides, moreover, proved to be the only twentieth-century Peruvian dictator who was not only personally honest but insisted that those associated with him in administering the country conduct themselves in accordance with the most stringent dictates of private and public morality.

Able because of his temperament and background to pursue policies which he felt to be in the country's best interests, regardless of how his actions might affect his popularity with the masses, Benavides proceeded quickly to resolve the dispute with Colombia. The president-elect of that country, Alfonso López, had become a close friend of Benavides when the two men had served their countries in high diplomatic posts in London. Benavides now invited López to Lima to confer over the Leticia crisis. As a result of the conversations, Peru and Colombia agreed to accept a cease-fire formula prepared by the League of Nations and to enter into negotiations in Rio de Janeiro aimed at a permanent settlement. The sessions in Rio lasted from October 1933 to May of the following year and produced an unrestricted Peruvian agreement to abide by the terms of the Salomón–Lozano Treaty. Peruvian forces were withdrawn from the Leticia region, mobilization was discontinued, and the minor war that had threatened to become a major conflict was settled by diplomacy.[48] Thereafter Benavides reduced the percentage of the budget allotted to the military,[49] but at the same time reorganized the armed forces and vastly increased their efficiency.

For the first few months of his rule, Peru's energetic President seemed on the verge of bringing an end to his country's civil discord. With Jorge Prado, the man who had conspired with Benavides to overthrow Billinghurst in 1914, serving as a moderate and conciliatory Prime Minister, Haya de la Torre and many other *Apristas* were released from prison and allowed to hold political rallies. Because of the *rapport* that seemed for a time to be developing between Benavides and Haya, rumours began to circulate, unfounded but persistent, that the new President had actually conspired with the *Apristas* to arrange the assassination of Sánchez Cerro.

The truce between the Government and the APRA was short-lived. Discord erupted over the matter of congressional elections. The constituent assembly, having completed its work in framing the 1933 charter, was continuing to function as the regular national legislature. APRA leaders demanded that Benavides call elections to fill the vacancies in that body created by the arrest of its *Aprista* representatives in 1932. Accounts differ as to whether Benavides had made a previous promise to the APRA that he would hold such elections.[50] However that may be, by the end of 1933 it was apparent that Benavides had no intention of permitting special elections. *Apristas* took to arms again and the President appointed as his new Prime Minister the leading spokesman of fascism, José de la Riva Agüero. Operating on his conviction that compromise with the left was not only impossible but sinful even to attempt, Riva Agüero launched an effort to return all *Apristas* either to jail or exile. Haya de la Torre managed to escape imprisonment by hiding in the house of President Benavides' brother-in-law. In 1934, when Riva Agüero resigned from the cabinet rather than sign a divorce law which had been passed by congress, the anti-*Aprista* repression eased slightly. Peru continued, however, to be an embattled country where violence and revolutionary plotting abounded.

One of the most notorious acts of violence in the APRA's struggle for power occurred on 15 May 1935, when Carlos Steer, a young *Aprista* fanatic, assassinated Antonio Miró Quesada, director for thirty years of *El Comercio*. When Señora Miró Quesada tried to come to her husband's aid, Steer killed her also. Failing then in his attempt to end his own life, Steer was imprisoned and tried by a military tribunal that sentenced him to a twenty-five year term. Furious that the assassin had not been given the death penalty, the Miró Quesada family launched through the editorials of *El Comercio* a bitter attack against Benavides, implying that he had reached a secret understanding with the monstrous *Apristas*.

Despite the turbulence of the times, Benavides had a solid record of accomplishment to describe to the Peruvian populace when his originally-announced term of office approached its end late in 1936.[51] Under him the universities had been reopened, and in a three-year span, from May 1933 to May 1936, eighty-eight new primary schools had been constructed and the number of teachers and students in the primary system had increased by some two thousand and 146,000 respectively.[52] Furthermore, the serving of free breakfasts to thousands of students in the public schools had been initiated. Impressive workers' housing projects had been undertaken and many of them completed; low-cost popular restaurants had been opened in Lima's slum areas; rural postal savings services had been introduced, and by December 1936 a law of compulsory social security had gone into effect. To administer the various government social projects, a new Ministry of Public Health, Labour and Social Security had been created.

Shortly after assuming power, Benavides had observed that most of the grave national problems, including the deterioration of the Indian communities, had their origin in the lack of a system of roads and communications.[53] To the improvement of this situation Benavides and his extremely able minister of development, Héctor Boza, one of the two engineers who had surveyed the petroleum lands of La Brea–Pariñas in 1914, dedicated their untiring efforts and achieved results that must have been surprising even to them. The number of men employed on highway projects was increased from two to thirty thousand and by mid-1936 some one thousand miles of new roads had been constructed, while additional thousands of miles had been surfaced or repaired.

A central highway (*carretera central*), to which Benavides and Boza attached particular importance, connecting Lima with La Oroya in the department of Junín in the central Andes had been completed and paved. From it a secondary road system branched off to the departments of Huánuco, Huancavelica and Ayacucho. Also in the sierra, between the towns of Cuzco and Abancay and between Huánuco and Tingo María, for example, additional roads had been completed. In the northern coastal area the port of Chimbote had been linked by modern roads to Huylas, while Trujillo and Lambayeque had been connected with their ports, Salaverry and Pimentel respectively. For the first time it had become possible to travel over asphalt highways between Lima and Ancón to the north; between Chorillos and La Herradura on the outskirts of the capital; between Lima and Cañete to the south; between the southern coastal port of Pisco, where San Martín had landed to begin the emancipation of Peru, and the inland town of Ica; between Arequipa and the more than twelve-thousand-foot-high Puno on the shores of Lake Titicaca.

By the end of 1936, Benavides had, in comparison to 1933 figures, increased social assistance outlays by 193 per cent., educational expenditures by 77 per cent. and development or public works appropriations by over 400 per cent.[54] Obviously, the Benavides projects were expensive but, under the skilful supervision of the President and his shrewd, knowledgeable advisers, the Peruvian economy had expanded enough to make possible the financing of the daring government programme. Leguía had begun to modernize Peru through the use of foreign loans and investments. The accomplishments of the Benavides administration were based largely upon internal capital formation.

Rejecting the temptation to resort to deficit financing and inflationary paper money, Benavides stabilized the *sol* throughout most of his term at a value, in comparison to the United States dollar, of between twenty-three and twenty-five cents. Under his administration Peru was one of the few Latin American countries that did not adopt exchange controls to regulate foreign commerce. Results seemed to justify the President's confidence in free-market foreign trade operations. The total value of foreign commerce, imports and exports, rose between 1933 and 1936 from 250 to nearly 500 million *soles*, in part because the value of mineral production increased better than 40 per cent.; government revenue originating in foreign commerce taxes rose from 24 to 54 million *soles*.[55]

During the same 1933–6 period revenue realized from direct internal taxes increased 60 per cent., evidence of the expansion and mounting success of the private sector of the Peruvian economy. Bank deposits increased from 94 to 221 million *soles*, while in the first seven months of 1936 alone 235 new business enterprises were established. With its confidence restored by the Benavides administration, the Peruvian business community demonstrated that notwithstanding the diatribes directed against it by intellectual prophets of reform, it was capable of contributing dramatically to the advance of the country.

Able to point to an amazing record of economic progress in 1936, Benavides proceeded to commit an egregious political error. With the unexpired term of Sánchez Cerro which congress had elected him to serve out coming to an end, Benavides began to groom Jorge Prado to succeed him in the presidency. For many years Prado had been fond of voicing empty platitudes about the need for social reform.[56] In his long career in politics, however, he had given almost no evidence of ever acting sincerely in the interests of social justice. He was also something of a political gadabout, willing to co-operate with socialists at one time and to flirt with fascists at another. Although his moderation and conciliatory attitudes as Prime Minister during the first five months of the Benavides régime had impressed some favourably, others had simply taken them as additional indications of Prado's opportunism and complete lack of political conviction and principle.

Benavides hoped that all political centrists in Peru would support the National Front (*Frente Nacional*), the party that was founded to advance Prado's candidacy, thus leaving extremists both of the right and left isolated and impotent. He miscalculated badly. Men who were seriously committed to social reform of an evolutionary nature and who regarded themselves as somewhat to the left of centre simply could not bring themselves to trust Jorge Prado. A typical political leader who found himself in this position was Luis A. Eguiguren. An historian and San Marcos professor of some distinction who in 1931 had been an outspoken partisan of Sánchez Cerro and critic of the APRA, Eguiguren tried for a time to co-operate with the National Front. Ultimately, he concluded that Prado was a hypocrite who by failing to support even the mildest reforms would drive the country once more towards chaos. Accordingly Eguiguren withdrew from the National Front and helped form a new political alliance, the Democratic Front (*Frente Democrática*), of which he was the presidential candidate. Not permitted at this time to enter their own candidate in the campaign, *Aprista* leaders instructed the faithful to vote for Eguiguren.

Jorge Prado was rejected by extreme rightist elements as well as by moderates of the left. Riva Agüero, for example, distrusted now by Benavides because of his fanaticism and head of a recently-formed fascist-sympathizing party known as the Patriotic Union (*Unión Patriótica*), feared that Prado in office might compromise with the left and thereby prepare the way, however unwittingly, for a communist take-over. Then there was Pedro Beltrán, leader of the new National Agrarian Party (*Partido Nacional Agrario*), who seemed primarily concerned with protecting vested interests through the establishment of a system of economic liberalism of the pure and classical variety based on the teachings of Adam Smith and David Ricardo. Beltrán was apprehensive that Prado would not be resolute enough in resisting the pressures of social reformers to introduce greater governmental supervision over economic affairs.

Fanatics of the right, such as Riva Agüero and Beltrán, together with many wise, balanced and restrained representatives of the political centre and the moderate right who had no faith in Prado's political integrity or competence, prevailed now upon the old intellectual, university man and politician Manuel Vicente Villarán to run for the presidency. Villarán, whose supporters formed the National Party (*Partido Nacional*), conducted the highest level campaign of any of the candidates,[57] but nevertheless compromised his reputation in the eyes of many Peruvians because of the unsavoury extremism of some of the political friends he accepted in his presidential bid.

With political fragmentation having already advanced to an alarming stage, still another candidate appeared upon the scene in the person of Luis N. Flores. The candidate of the Revolutionary Union, which after the death of Sánchez Cerro had begun to assume fascistic leanings, Flores hoped that some of the assassinated *cholo* President's mass popularity would pass to him. In addition Flores hoped to draw support, and did, from some of the fascistically inclined upper-class voters who for one reason or another disliked Riva Agüero and would not co-operate with him in backing the candidacy of Villarán.

Had Benavides chosen a candidate wisely, it would have been possible to form around him a political party that was a National Front in more than name, one that could have maintained the support of the centre and those slightly to its left and right. As it was, the centre and all those from the extreme to the near right of it suicidally divided their forces, thus guaranteeing electoral victory to Eguiguren, supported probably by almost as many moderate leftists as by extremist *Apristas*. Although apparently not gaining a majority of the votes, Eguiguren received more ballots than any of the candidates of the centre and right. In the popular vote he was followed by Flores, Prado and Villarán in that order.

At once the *Apristas* began to claim that it was their support exclusively which had been responsible for the Eguiguren victory and to assert that they and they alone would govern Peru. Quite obviously they regarded Eguiguren as a mere figurehead in a government which they would dominate. Understandably the political, social and economic leaders of Peru who for some six years, first under Sánchez Cerro and then under Benavides, had fought to keep the APRA out of power, and who in the process had made dramatic advances towards the modernization of Peru, decided that drastic actions had to be taken. The administration promptly cancelled the electoral results and announced that Benavides would serve for a full six years from the time he had assumed power (his supporters were already at work to modify the constitution to extend presidential tenure from five to six years), rather than simply completing the unexpired portion of the Sánchez Cerro term.[58]

In the second portion of his term, begun in this high-handed fashion, Benavides saw to it that Luis Flores and other high leaders of the Revolutionary Union were harried out of the country or else kept under surveillance in the jails of Peru. *Aprista* chieftains and some of their close collaborators were also forced into hiding, exile or jail. On the positive side, the President continued his public works projects. In addition, he granted recognition to the legal existence of some seven hundred Indian communities, and sent government agents to help various of them resolve their disputes over land ownership and to instruct their residents in modern methods of agriculture and livestock raising. In its last years of power the Benavides administration also provided for the organization of teaching brigades that went into some of the most remote regions of the sierra and gave instruction in reading, writing and hygiene to the natives.[59]

Towards the end of his sixth year in power Benavides in March 1939, after suppressing a well-planned *Aprista*-military *coup* against him,[60] announced that presidential elections would shortly be held and that a new administration would be installed on 8 December. At the same time that they chose a new president, proclaimed Benavides, Peruvians would elect a congress. The electorate would also be asked to approve certain constitutional amendments that the administration would propose, the main provisions of which would extend the presidential term to six years and limit the powers of congress in its relations with the executive. With *Apristas* forced somewhat more deeply underground than in 1936, and with the Revolutionary Union leader, Flores, still in exile, there was little chance that the candidate chosen by Benavides could fail to triumph. This time Benavides's choice fell on a banker, Manuel Prado (b. 1889), Jorge's brother. With only José Quesada, a weak and ineffectual candidate supported by remnants of the Revolutionary Union, opposing him, Manuel Prado triumphed easily in elections that were by no means a model of the proper functioning of democratic processes. At the same time the proposed constitutional amendments were overwhelmingly approved. In spite of consistent APRA denials, there are indications that before the elections Prado had reached a secret understanding with *Apristas*: in exchange for their promise to support him or at least not to oppose him at the polls, Prado agreed to legalize their party after coming to power.[61]

THE MANUEL PRADO ADMINISTRATION, 1939–45

If adequate government for Peru in the years between 1939 and 1945 had demanded no more than the skilful manoeuvring and manipulation of aristocratic and middle groups, if it had called only for shrewd compromises, accommodations and deals so as to avoid crises and political explosions, then Manuel Prado could properly be considered a great President. Apparently never allowing ideology or conviction to interfere with his actions, the tiny man with the aristocratic bearing and suave manners who so delighted in wearing his medals and in other ways indulging his considerable vanity, proved to be one of the most adept jugglers of men, factions and groups that Peru has produced. As a result the country remained on the surface calm, tranquil and orderly. Beneath the surface, however, profound problems such as the assimilation of the Indian were ignored and Peru advanced not one iota towards becoming a true, a modern nation.

Benavides had accomplished much, but much more remained to be done when he left office. A census completed in 1941 showed that only one out of every forty-one Peruvians had received secondary instruction, only one out of every 202 had been exposed to university education, and only one out of every 336 had received technical or commercial training. Barely 11 per cent. of the population had received education beyond the fifth-grade level; nearly 57 per cent. of all Peruvians were illiterate, while 35 per cent. could not speak or understand Spanish, being able to converse only in Indian dialects. Although he did surround himself with able economic advisers and carried ahead various public works projects, Prado largely ignored problems of the fundamental nature revealed by these statistics.

Still Prado was, by and large, a popular President. One reason for this was the moderate approach he used in dealing with the APRA. Although he did not legalize the Peruvian *Aprista* Party until the end of his term he was much milder in repressing its leaders than either Sánchez Cerro or Benavides had been. Prado's more tolerant attitude was in part the result of the fact that *aprismo* itself underwent a profound change in the early and late 1940's. *Apristas* favoured the unstinting support that the Prado régime gave to the United States and to the allied nations in general during World War II. The old diatribes against United States imperialism were dropped and the Good Neighbour Policy of Franklin D. Roosevelt's administration was accorded considerable praise.[62] More remarkable still, *aprismo* dropped its attacks against the capitalistic system. By the mid-1940's *aprismo* in its ideological pronouncements was beginning to sound as favourable towards capitalism as ever its foe of the 1920's, Augusto B. Leguía, had been. *Aprista* publications, in fact, began to pay tribute to the contributions of the *oncenio* in encouraging the development of Peruvian capitalism.[63]

Haya de la Torre tried to suggest that despite apparent changes, APRA ideology had remained constant after all. His theory that imperialism was the last stage of capitalism in the developed countries but the first stage in the underdeveloped, the doctrine which had been so glaringly inconsistent with the original APRA programme, was expanded and given an importance never attached to it in the 1920's. Peru, it was reasoned, had to welcome more foreign investment so as to hasten the advent of a genuine capitalist society which in turn would some day produce the reaction of a socialist revolution led by the middle sectors with the backing of the proletariat. As early as 1945, however, it was apparent that the utopian some day which they had proclaimed to be just around the corner in the 1920's had been postponed to such a dim, remote and nebulous future as no longer to be a concern of *Aprista* leaders.

They had come to see the advantage of not thinking beyond their present enjoyment of capitalism's benefits, except when it seemed to suit their purposes to make a few radical pronouncements intended to keep in tow the minority of APRA members still loyal to the movement's pristine ideology.[64]

Haya de la Torre and his subordinates in the command of *aprismo* seemed to be tiring of the bloody fight they had waged in the 1930's and to have decided to seek power henceforth by joining the established order rather than by trying to destroy it. Perhaps, however, another factor was even more important in causing the fundamental switch in *Aprista* attitudes. *Aprismo* had always been primarily concerned with winning middle-sector support. In the 1920's its leaders had badly miscalculated the mood of the rapidly rising middle groups and had failed to win them because of the radical extremism of *Aprista* ideology, extremism which had originated in and appealed only to small circles of intellectuals and students. Then, in the following decade, as they suffered from the effects of the world-wide depression, middle sectors had been attracted by the very extremism of *aprismo*'s Marxian-influenced radicalism. By the end of World War II, however, thanks to the sound economic policies begun by Benavides and also to the high prices which wartime demand had created for Peru's wide variety of exports, capitalism seemed to be functioning even more successfully than during the *oncenio*. Middle groups along the coast reacquired their optimism and their enchantment with the capitalist system. Obviously, if Haya de la Torre hoped to retain their support for the APRA, he had to change the movement's ideology.

During the same period the far right declined appreciably in Peru. As the outcome of the world conflict became apparent, fascism lost the popularity it had enjoyed in many circles. In 1944, moreover, its leading spokesman, Riva Agüero, died. With *aprismo* apparently tamed and with fascism becoming just a political memory, new possibilities of conciliation and co-operation seemed at hand. Tired of years of civil strife and vastly relieved by the likelihood of political peace, Peruvians accorded credit and gratitude to President Prado for developments that he had actually done very little to shape. Credit and gratitude, though, were nothing compared to the near adulation that Prado came to enjoy as a result of a brief war that flared with Ecuador.

A lengthy series of boundary disputes extending back to the

earliest days of independence had created a climate of bitter animosity between Peru and Ecuador. Matters reached a crisis stage in July 1941 when Ecuador, asserting territorial claims along both its south-eastern boundary with Peru in the region of the Marañón River and its south-western boundary around the town of Zarumilla, began an undeclared war against its old antagonist. Under the command of General Eloy G. Ureta the Peruvian army, profiting from the reorganization it had undergone during the Benavides régime, promptly scored a stunning victory in the battle of Zarumilla and the populace went wild with joy. Subsequent peace negotiations held in Rio de Janeiro at the beginning of 1942 produced a Pact of Peace, Amity and Limits, its provisions to be guaranteed by Argentina, Brazil, Chile and the United States. The pact, subsequently confirmed by negotiations in 1945, established Peruvian ownership over most of the region of some 120,000 square miles of land that had constituted the bone of contention with Ecuador.[65] The diplomatic victory, confirming the triumph of arms, produced more celebrating in Peru and President Prado was given much of the credit for what was regarded by many as the country's supreme moment of military glory in its entire republican history.

With his popularity at a high peak in late 1944 and early 1945, Prado may well have thought seriously about prolonging his term of office or amending the constitution to permit his immediate re-election. The Allied victory in the World War, however, gave considerable impetus to the cause of democracy in Peru, and Prado probably feared that public opinion might turn dangerously against him if he sought to establish a purely personalistic rule. The emergence of a powerful new political force, the National Democratic Front (*Frente Democrática Nacional*), could well have confirmed these fears. The new party's announced purpose was to end government by small circles of the Peruvian élite and transform the republic into a genuine democracy.[66] The rapidity with which the National Democratic Front won support forced Prado to recognize the need for democratic elections. Moreover, Oscar R. Benavides had returned to the country from his diplomatic post in Buenos Aires and appeared to be seriously considering running for the presidency himself. Prado both feared and respected his friend Benavides and abandoned any plans he might have entertained to extend his stay in power.

Perhaps feeling the weight of his sixty-nine years, Benavides ultimately decided not to become a candidate. Instead he began to co-operate with President Prado in persuading José Luis Bustamante y Rivero (b. 1894), a highly respected Arequipa attorney and professor of middle-class origins serving at the time as Peru's ambassador in Bolivia, to accept the proffered nomination of the National Democratic Front. At the same time Benavides approached Haya de la Torre, whose hiding place in Lima was not a secret to the administration, seeking his agreement to give *Aprista* support to the Front in the coming elections. In both of his missions Benavides scored notable successes. Bustamante agreed to accept the nomination and the *Apristas*, after an ill-fated attempt to seize power through an uprising led by military groups in Ancón,[67] decided to back the ticket of the National Democratic Front. Accordingly, the electoral tribunal hastily legalized the APRA under the name of the Party of the People (*Partido del Pueblo*).

The elections were held as scheduled in June and Bustamante defeated the rival candidate, General Eloy Ureta, hero of the war with Ecuador, by a vote of approximately 300,000 to 150,000. Ureta at once called upon the President-elect, offered his congratulations and promised his co-operation in the coming administration. For a moment it appeared that democracy had arrived and that Prado, 'having received a dictatorially governed Peru, had turned it over to his successor as a democratic country'.[68]

This appearance would prove to be deceptive, principally because Benavides and Prado in masterminding the strategy of the 1945 elections had made two serious errors. They had chosen as their favoured candidate a man who would have made a superb supreme court justice, head of a bank or legal firm, or rector of a nineteenth-century university. But the calm, reflective and lacklustre, the punctiliously honest, conscientious and responsible Bustamante had no stomach for the political in-fighting in which the President of Peru would, as it turned out, still have to engage. That the President in 1945 would have to be a master of no-holds-barred political combat was owing in large part to the second error in judgement committed by Benavides and Prado. This was the belief that the APRA, having undergone some changes including the discarding of much of its original extremist ideology, had become a safe and respectable political organization that would co-operate with other groups within a democratic framework. Events soon indicated that *Aprista* lust for unlimited power was undiminished and that the party's top leaders when motivated mainly by opportunism could be just as dangerous and subversive as when they had advanced an ideological programme.

The APRA Declines and New Forces for Change Emerge, 1945–65

BUSTAMANTE DUELS WITH THE APRA, 1945–8

PERU in 1945 stood on the threshhold of essential and all-encompassing change. To this belief José Luis Bustamante y Rivero was deeply and even enthusiastically committed. Throughout his distinguished career, Peru's fifty-one-year-old new executive had urged the need for greater morality in government, for reduction of the bureaucracy, for balanced budgets, and for decentralization. In addition he had advocated the need for social reform, arguing persuasively that unless Peru's upper and middle sectors dealt more generously with the masses, a Marxian-inspired social upheaval was inevitable. Born and brought up in Arequipa, on the fringe of Peru's vast Indian region of the sierra, and thus personally acquainted with Andean problems, Bustamante had also proclaimed the need for a concerted effort to assimilate the native into Peru's economy and society. When he assumed the presidency, he was satisfied that the time had finally come to proceed towards the changes which for years he had eloquently championed.

A deeply religious man, Bustamante had always hoped that the Catholic Church and closely affiliated organizations would provide the impetus, inspiration and leadership for transforming the republic. In 1945, however, Catholic influence, which had begun to rise in the 1920's when so many of the Arielists or Futurists had felt the need to turn to formal religion, had slipped to almost the low ebb of the turn-of-the-century period when neopositivism had held sway. Largely responsible for Catholicism's new decline as a temporal force had been the manner in which so many of its spokesmen had associated themselves with fascism, a cause that had been discredited and indeed disgraced by the events and outcome of World War II. Thus it was that in 1945 Bustamante reluctantly decided that *aprismo*, rather than the Church and Catholic Action groups, would have to provide much of the leadership for Peru's transformation. The newly-inaugurated President felt that the middle sectors, of which he was himself proud to be a member, must preside over the birth of a new Peru. At the time, the APRA seemed to be the only influential, well-organized middle-sector movement that, because of its ideological origins, was widely assumed to be change orientated.

According to his own testimony, Bustamante expected to turn his office over at the end of his six-year term to the *Apristas*, after having demonstrated by co-operating with them that their movement had matured, acquired responsibility, and shed its early Marxian extremism. So long as he was President, however, Bustamante was determined not to become the puppet of their party. Realizing that the *Apristas* had constituted only one segment of the electorate that had voted him into office, Bustamante was prepared to let them share in, but not dominate, his administration.[1]

Apristas had expected, as Manuel Seoane put it, that in helping to elect Bustamante they had brought to the Peruvian presidency a man who would serve not as the 'referee' in a competition among various political groups, but exclusively as the 'captain' of the APRA team.[2] When it became clear that Bustamante would pursue a somewhat independent policy, when he appointed Rafael Belaúnde, brother of Víctor Andrés, as his Prime Minister instead of Haya de la Torre and named a cabinet that was not dominated by the APRA, the party leadership began to plot trouble for him.

Shortly before the opening sessions of the newly-elected congress, the *Apristas* who had been elected to that body and who constituted a majority in it came together and swore fidelity to their chief, Haya de la Torre, thus serving notice that they 'were more concerned with sectarian loyalty than with service to the overall interests of the country'.[3] Then, when congress actually convened on 28 July 1945, its *Aprista* majority proceeded at once to revoke the constitutional amendments suggested by Benavides and approved by the electorate in 1939. As a result, the executive was stripped of certain prerogatives and congress won the right to over-ride presidential vetoes with a simple majority. Already the APRA strategy was becoming clear: the party would claim that Peru should be governed by congress and that the President was little more than a figurehead.

At the same time the *Apristas* intensified their campaign to gain control over labour organizations, wishing to use them more as a means of advancing party political interests than of bargaining effectively with management. *Apristas* sought also to infiltrate Peruvian teaching groups in order to turn the country's schools into their party's indoctrination headquarters. The Peruvian *Aprista* Youth Movement (*Juventud Aprista Peruana*, or the JAP) was organized to instil loyalty to *aprismo* among the age ten-to-eighteen populace. As a result not just the universities, but the high schools and primary schools were politicized. Both in the classroom and outside it, *Aprista* teachers led their pupils in singing the APRA hymn, set to the tune of 'La Marseillaise'; moreover, especially in the provinces, they established the custom of marching their students to political rallies.

With increasing frequence *Apristas* also resorted to violence. They bombed the houses of their enemies, burned the headquarters of the Revolutionary Union Party, assassinated the prefect of Cerro de Pasco, and in general created an atmosphere of terror in the country. When the two leading newspapers of Lima, *El Comercio* and *La Prensa*, undertook a concerted campaign to denounce these activities and began to publish various exposés of APRA terrorism that were embarrassing to the party, its congressional majority introduced a law calling for press censorship. Thereupon students assembled in the University of San Marcos Plaza on the night of 7 December 1945, to protest against the proposed legislation. *Aprista* thugs, the notorious *búfalos* who formed the party's strong-arm squads, attacked and seriously injured many of those participating in the demonstration.

All the while, Bustamante was also beset by economic problems. From the previous Prado régime he had inherited a troublesome inflationary spiral, indicated by the fact that between 1939 and 1945 the cost of living had increased 190 per cent. Immediately after World War II came to an end the United States had cut back its purchase of Peruvian commodities and thus export taxes collected by the Bustamante régime declined alarmingly. Not until

1951 did copper, cotton, lead and wool regain the export volumes they had enjoyed in the period at the close of the war. Coffee and sugar did not rise to their wartime export volumes until 1952 and 1953 respectively. Not until 1960 did petroleum exports climb to their 1945 level. Peru's major food producers, furthermore, taking advantage of the high world prices prevailing directly after the war's end, exported most of their crops and the country as a consequence was faced with a serious food shortage. This forced the Government to expand its already dwindling foreign currency on food imports. Even so the amount of food available was not adequate to meet demand. Prices soared and each day long lines formed early in the morning outside grocery stores as housewives sought in vain to procure sufficient dietary staples.

In this troubled economic situation Bustamante in 1946 found one issue on which he could agree with his *Aprista* tormentors. The President was desperately anxious to increase petroleum production so as to ease some of the country's financial difficulties. Accordingly his administration signed a contract with the International Petroleum Company, providing that this Standard Oil subsidiary, whose concessions at La Brea–Pariñas had since their early exploitation produced over 80 per cent. of Peru's crude petroleum and more than 90 per cent. of its natural gas, should conduct exploration for new deposits on lands in the northern coastal area around Sechura that had been set aside as a national reserve by the Benavides administration. *Apristas* warmly backed the agreement, known as the Sechura Contract, when it came before congress for approval, even claiming credit for having conceived it. Undoubtedly *aprismo*'s friendly attitude towards the IPC helped account for the fact that at this time the United States Department of State began to regard the APRA as its favourite Peruvian political party, a policy it would maintain at least through the mid-1960's.

In the Peruvian congress many friends of Benavides, who had died in 1945, fought to protect the national petroleum reserve lands that had been designated by the former President. In business circles as well a group of outspoken economic nationalists, among them some of Peru's wealthiest capitalists anxious to form their own petroleum company and hence desirous of preventing IPC expansion, denounced the Sechura Contract as a give-away to foreign interests. At the same time *El Comercio* and *La Prensa* united in condemning the contract. Both newspapers tended to hold the APRA exclusively responsible for the alleged attempt to betray national interests, dealing rather leniently with Bustamante on the issue. One of *La Prensa*'s editors, Francisco Graña Garland, was particularly harsh in the attacks that he published against the APRA because of its support of the Sechura Contract. On 7 January 1947, Graña was shot down in Lima. An apparently carefully conducted investigation, in which a respected Canadian police official participated, produced strong evidence that the APRA had planned and carried out the assassination. After a long judicial process two *Apristas*, Alfredo Tello Salavarria and Héctor Pretell Cobosmalón, were found guilty of actually firing the shots that ended Graña's life and were sentenced to lengthy prison terms.

Aristocratic and conservative elements took the Graña assassination as one final proof that Benavides and Prado had been wrong in assuming that it would be possible to co-operate with the ideologically transformed Peruvian *Aprista* Party. Returning from his post as Ambassador to the United States, Pedro Beltrán assumed a rôle of leadership in the efforts of Peruvian rightist elements to crush *aprismo*. Taking over the direction of *La Prensa*, Beltrán vowed to preside over a struggle that would not end until *aprismo* had been wiped out as a political force. He and his associates now urged Bustamante to declare the party illegal and to jail its leaders. Genuinely dedicated to the quest for democratic rule, the President refused and for approximately a year after Graña's assassination continued to search for some formula that would permit pacific dealings with *Apristas*.

Meantime Héctor Boza, leader of the senate group that by shrewd parliamentary manipulation had managed to prevent approval of the Sechura Contract, had come to agree with the majority of his fellow aristocrats that continuing co-operation with the APRA was absolutely impossible. For one thing he was tiring of the nearly daily *Aprista* threats against his life. Reading the constitution one day and proceeding to do a little arithmetic, Boza was impressed with the following facts: the senate's executive commission (*mesa directora*), chosen each year on 28 July, could not be elected unless at least two-thirds of the upper chamber's membership was on hand for the event; the senate could not function without an executive commission; the chamber of deputies could not meet unless the senate was functioning, for the constitution stated that there must be simultaneous sessions of the two houses; the *Apristas* lacked three of having a two-thirds majority in the senate. Acting speedily, Boza persuaded all save one of the senate's non-*Aprista* members to boycott the 28 July 1947 session. As a result, no executive commission could be elected and the senate and lower chamber were forced to suspend sessions.[4] In this manner *Aprista* hopes to govern the country through congress were frustrated and Bustamante was given the opportunity to rule through decree law.

The President persevered, however, in his endeavours to find some basis for co-operating with the APRA. Because of this, and also because they were becoming convinced that Bustamante simply lacked the capacity to govern Peru in a time of crisis when civil discord had again become rampant, the political leaders who had engineered the congressional suspension came to the conclusion that the President might have to be replaced. Their belief that Bustamante was not the man required by the times seemed to be confirmed by an incident that occurred in late 1947.

The leader of the so-called Senatorial Absentees, Héctor Boza, decided one day to call on the President. At the particular moment the country was in chaos, wracked by a series of *Aprista*-inspired strikes and gripped more than ever by acts of terrorism and vandalism. The wheels of government had virtually come to a standstill. Arriving at the national palace, Boza was informed that the President was engaged in important duties and could not be disturbed. After insisting, the senator was admitted into the President's private office where he discovered Bustamante feverishly at work typing with two fingers the text of an obviously very long manuscript. Upon inquiring as to the nature of the work, Boza was informed by Bustamante that he was engaged in a project which had occupied nearly all his time for the past two weeks, the preparation of a scholarly paper on legal theory which he was shortly to deliver to a lawyer's convention. As a consequence, the President did not have the time to discuss with Boza the country's grave problems.

Strangely enough, during the same troubled period two of Peru's greatest scholar-intellectuals, Jorge Basadre and Aurelio Miró Quesada Sosa, completed works that rank as masterpieces in the country's literature, *Meditaciones sobre el destino histórico del*

Perú, and *Costa, sierra, y montaña* (a preliminary version of which had been published in 1939 and 1940), respectively. Both books were calm and reflective in nature, indicating faith in the ultimate ability of Peru to surmount its problems and through a long-term process of *mestizaje* evolve into a true nation. It was one thing, however, for scholars to remain detached from the crises of 1947 and quite another for the President of the republic to attempt to do so.

With men of wealth and position clearly becoming ever more convinced that Bustamante had to be replaced, *Apristas* decided to strike first in the attempt to oust the President. Since mid-1947 they had been working assiduously, and with considerable success, to enlist support of lower-echelon officers of the army, navy and air forces in a revolution against Bustamante. Becoming aware of these activities, General José Marín approached Haya de la Torre with the warning that if the APRA persisted in these schemes the country would once again suffer a violent confrontation in which the higher-level, more conservative military officers, backed by Peru's anti-*Aprista* oligarchy, would inevitably triumph. Marín then held out an attractive alternative to the APRA leader. If Haya would co-operate with what was expected to be a bloodless *coup* that Marín and certain highly-placed military and civilian collaborators were planning against Bustamante, then *Apristas* would be allowed to participate in the free elections which would subsequently be held. According to most indications, Haya decided to back the course of action proposed by Marín.

Haya de la Torre's new plans to reach power in a safe and bloodless manner, in return for accepting an alliance of a type that probably would have prevented him from introducing even the mildest reform programme, went awry because of a collapse of APRA discipline. Certain 'Young Turks' of *aprismo*, loyal to the radical and Marxian origins of the movement, proceeded with the conspiracy among the lower-level military leaders. On 3 October 1948, the young and militant *Apristas*, both civilian and military, arose in Callao against the Bustamante government. The APRA high command was apparently taken by surprise and failed in its hastily undertaken endeavours to persuade Marín and his influential associates to side with the rebels. Instead, the generals for the moment backed the administration and, with the larger part of the armed forces following their orders, crushed the Callao uprising.

Bustamante promptly declared the APRA illegal, and launched a drive to apprehend and imprison its leaders.[5]

Even with the Callao insurrection effectively smashed, the beleaguered President still seemed unable to restore tranquillity to the country. *Aprista*-prompted student uprisings occurred not only in Lima but in the provinces as well. The problem of high food prices continued and Bustamante seemed as powerless as ever to curb the by-then notorious black market operations that had mushroomed throughout the country. Justifying their actions by charges that the President had demonstrated his incapacity to deal effectively with *aprismo* and the nation's economic problems, the military in Arequipa launched a revolution on 27 October. Christening their movement the 'Restorative Revolution', they proclaimed as its Supreme Chief General Manuel A. Odría, previously a member of one of Bustamante's cabinets. Once again as in the days of Manuel Vivanco, Arequipa supported the revolution of a conservative military caudillo who claimed that only he could restore order and respect for the law.

When General Zenon Noriega, commander of the troops in Lima and the man who had directed the suppression of the 3 October *Aprista* uprising, disobeyed the President's orders to advance against Arequipa, claiming he did not wish to immerse the country in a bloodbath, Bustamante realized he was powerless to deal with the insurrection. He withdrew from the national palace on 29 October. Manuel Odría quickly reached Lima and assumed the powers of provisional President.[6]

Bustamante had fallen primarily because he could not deal effectively with the APRA. The President's inability to do so resulted from the fact that during the transition period when Haya de la Torre was trying to impose a new ideology on his party, there was not one APRA in Peru; rather, there were two. The new-style, conservative APRA, led by the now cautious, original party chieftains, was obsessed with the desire to wield exclusive political power and not particularly interested in inaugurating even the moderate, gradual reforms that Bustamante felt the country required. The old-style element of the APRA, clinging to the pristine ideology and supported mainly by youthful elements, desired change far more drastic than anything Bustamante had in mind. Thus the sort of collaboration with the APRA which the unfortunate President had envisioned in 1945 was doomed to fail.

His futile three-year search for the means of reaching accord with the movement inevitably alienated the aristocracy which hated the old and distrusted the new-style APRA.

THE 'OCHENIO' OF ODRÍA, 1948–56

When Odría, a fifty-one-year-old Brigadier General from the central Andean town of Tarma, seized the presidency the economic recession which had plagued the Bustamante administration was about to lift. In a short time the Korean War would drive the prices of Peruvian exports sharply upward and the country would for a time savour a prosperity eclipsing even that of the late World War II days. Foreign investments increased at a dizzy rate, amounting to close to $800 million at the end of the *ochenio* (the eight-year period of Odría's rule), nearly double what they had been in 1948.[7] Stimulated by foreign investment, mining output and petroleum production soared, contributing thereby to the vast expansion of government revenue derived from export taxes. The 140 per cent. increase in industrial productivity between 1950 and 1955[8] was also due in large part to foreign investments. In a way Odría's economic accomplishments during the *ochenio* were reminiscent of Leguía's during the *oncenio*: they depended upon capital from abroad and did not stem from soundly conceived policies of domestic economic reorganization or from new and effective programmes of internal capital formation.

The at least apparent economic gains of the early *ochenio* resulted largely from Odría's success in restoring political stability and winning the confidence of foreign and local investors. Although his methods were sometimes excessively authoritarian, needlessly harsh, and easily open to criticism,[9] he did accomplish the by no means easy task of pulling Peru out of the anarchy into which it had sunk after 1945.

With congressional sessions already adjourned because of the action taken by the Senatorial Absentees in July of 1947, Odría and his military junta proved in no hurry to allow the legislature to reconvene. They governed instead for two years through a lengthy series of decree laws. Individual guarantees were suspended and the July 1949 Law of Internal Security gave to the Government power to adopt whatever means it deemed necessary, free from judicial interference and restraint, to defend public order. Through this law Odría and his governing associates, already immune from legislative checks, freed themselves from the supervision of the courts and effectively nullified the principle of *habeas corpus*.

Aprista leaders, meantime, were jailed or forced into hiding. Frequently when the Government discovered the hiding places of *Apristas*, it sent its agents to shoot them down. Haya de la Torre, who had found asylum in the Colombian Embassy, was not allowed to leave its premises until 1954. All the while the Embassy was kept under constant surveillance, a moat was built around it for the laying of a new sewer which actually was never installed and tanks were stationed outside the building. Inside, Haya devoted himself to studying, writing and refining some of his theories of history and philosophy.

In 1950 with both the APRA and the Communist Party forced underground, and with Bustamante and many of his more influential supporters in exile, Odría decided to stand for election to a regular six-year term. Running unopposed, he received some 500,000 votes. At the same time a new congress was elected and the military junta permitted several members of the Socialist Party to win seats despite their avowed Marxian orientation. Marxists were at this time a fairly subdued group in Peru, advocating a policy of gradualism and Odría eventually found it possible even to co-operate with certain Communists in his unrelenting battle against *Apristas*.

On 28 July 1950, after his forces had bloodily suppressed a student uprising and a general strike in Arequipa, both organized to protest against dictatorial methods and the travesty of democratic processes represented by the electoral campaign, Odría was duly installed as constitutional President. In his speech upon this occasion Odría, conscious of the growing discontent of the labouring masses, stated that he sympathized with the lower classes, suffered with them in their adversity, identified himself with their cause and promised them a bright new day of social justice.

In his announced concern with social justice and the plight of the masses, Odría was obviously seeking to borrow some of the methods that Juan Domingo Perón was finding so useful at the time in Argentina. The President's wife, María Delgado de Odría, was even groomed as the Peruvian counterpart of Eva Duarte de Perón. She presided over an expensive programme for distributing Christmas gifts to the children of poor families and dispensed charity on a lavish scale through the María Delgado de Odría Centre of Social Assistance. Founded in 1951, the Centre in its first year's operations provided medical attention to over two thousand persons and supplied medicines and even houses for additional hundreds of Lima's poor. Luis Antonio Eguiguren, a man sincerely interested in social reform who had been denied the presidency in 1936 when the Benavides administration decided to ignore the electoral results, was among the many Peruvians who praised the programme of the Odrías. Thanks to it, said Eguiguren, 'the masses now have medical and social assistance offered them in new and modern buildings; and they now have palaces as schools in place of the squalid quarters of other times'.[10]

At best, however, the Odría social programme was spotty. It was confined primarily to Lima and a few other coastal cities and virtually no attempt was made to improve the conditions of the truly destitute members of the population, the Indians of the sierra. Moreover, in spite of Odría's promises of reform, the tax structure remained regressive so that the rich were not called upon to contribute adequately to the social welfare of the country.[11] This was one reason why the school building programme which so impressed Eguiguren had to be confined essentially to Lima. At the end of the *ochenio*, a survey showed that 49·7 per cent. of the children enrolled for primary instruction throughout the country did not even have the use of a desk in their school buildings.[12] Outside of a few showplaces in Lima, Peru's schools had not after all become palaces.

Just as the building of new educational facilities was confined largely to Lima, so also Odría's vast public works projects in general did not extend beyond the capital city. There sky-scraper public buildings and needlessly ostentatious state banks were constructed with heedless abandon, as the more pressing building needs of the provinces were by and large ignored. Irrigation projects were also often of the type least needed, benefiting those who already owned large estates rather than creating new landowning groups.

By late 1953 Odría was increasingly hard-pressed to continue his public works projects even in Lima, for the economy had entered upon a serious recession. The prices of such goods as cotton and sugar declined appreciably after the Korean War, and 'Odría's prosperity collapsed like a house of cards'.[13] Although Odría was decorated by the United States government during the Dwight

Eisenhower administration because of his contributions to the 'free-enterprise system', the truth was that the system did not seem to be operating satisfactorily in Peru during the late years of the *ochenio*. Faced with an unfavourable trade balance that amounted to $70 million in 1953 alone[14] and with government revenue declining, Odría resorted more and more to the printing of paper money. Inflation became a serious problem: by 1956, the final year of the *ochenio*, the cost of living was 92·6 per cent. higher than when Odría had seized the presidency from Bustamante.[15] This development contributed to labour unrest which had first become a serious problem for Odría in late 1952.

To the crucial economic situation Odría responded, at least according to his critics, by becoming less attentive to administrative duties as he threw himself into the gay life of Lima society. The President was also accused of closing his eyes to the corruption of his associates. In particular, minister of the treasury Humberto Ponce Ratto was linked by increasingly persistent rumours with alleged acts of graft and malfeasance. Odría himself was widely criticized when he accepted as a token of esteem from some of his friends the tax-free gift of a mansion with swimming pool in the rich Monterico suburb of Lima.[16]

All the while new problems arose to confront the pleasure-seeking President. On 20 July 1955, Pedro Beltrán and his associate editors published in *La Prensa* a courageous document demanding that Odría suspend operation of the Law of Internal Security and take measures that would guarantee the honesty of the next presidential elections. Before the end of the year, Odría again had to confront a serious threat in Arequipa. Instigated in part by the newly-organized Christian Democratic movement, a huge civilian uprising occurred there in late December with the populace demanding a return to democratic processes and the removal from office of minister of government Alejandro Esparza Zañartu. The hated Esparza had been the principal agent in carrying out the administration's programme of political repression that frequently had degenerated into out-and-out terrorism. Not until he had removed Esparza from office and promised free elections did Odría succeed in calming the aroused Arequipeños.

As the time approached for the mid-1956 elections a hastily-formed National Coalition Party announced the candidacy of Manuel Prado. Absent in Paris throughout the *ochenio* and not intimately associated with either the supporters or foes of Odría, Prado was highly regarded in many circles, mainly because circumstances not of his making during his first term had resulted in a booming economy and because he was connected in the public fancy with Peru's 1941 victory over Ecuador. Prado had also dealt leniently with *Apristas* and quickly won their support for the 1956 campaign by promising to legalize their party immediately upon coming to power. Bustamante, recently returned to the country and received with vast popular acclaim, decided also to support the National Coalition. As a result of these circumstances the new party quickly acquired such strength that Odría, who undoubtedly had hoped to extend his own stay in office, felt powerless to stand in its way.

Another significant political development was the appearance of the National Front of Democratic Youth. Advancing a programme of rather sweeping reform with emphasis on decentralization and assimilation of the Indian, the Front was supported not only by much of the youth of Peru, but by established professional people and intellectuals, and also by Marxist elements who through the years had grown disillusioned with Peruvian *aprismo*, socialism, and communism. The Front backed the candidacy of the forty-four-year-old, University of Texas-trained architect, Fernando Belaúnde Terry. The son of Rafael, the first Prime Minister in the Bustamante régime, and the nephew of Víctor Andrés, the distinguished Catholic intellectual and diplomat, Fernando Belaúnde had held his first important political post in 1945 when elected to the chamber of deputies. Upon receiving the Front's nomination the handsome, dynamic Belaúnde virtually turned his back on Lima and conducted an extensive campaign in the provinces.

Concerned that Belaúnde and the Front represented a genuine menace to the established order, Odría and his advisers brought pressure to bear upon the National Electoral Jury which as a result refused to inscribe the new party on the electoral list. His candidacy thus disallowed, Belaúnde hastened to Lima and in the Plaza San Martín presided over what, according to witnesses, was one of the best attended political rallies ever held in the City of the Kings. At the end of an eloquent address that was notable for its spirit of moderation, Belaúnde led a procession towards the near-by headquarters of the Electoral Jury. Using tear gas and fire hoses, the police attempted to halt the procession. As the people fell back a dishevelled and roughed-up Belaúnde seized a Peruvian flag and clutching it tightly advanced alone to deliver his ultimatum to the representatives of the Jury who awaited him at *Calle la Merced* in the very centre of downtown Lima. If the candidate of renovation and youth was not officially inscribed on the electoral list, stated Belaúnde, then the dictator would have to face the consequences. The dictator backed down, the Jury reversed its decision and the Front was duly inscribed as a legal political party.

A third candidate in the 1956 election was Hernando de Lavalle, a respected lawyer of unimpeachable integrity whose cause was probably damaged by the announced backing of the Odría administration. Actually, just before the elections the incumbent President and his henchmen made a secret decision to throw their support to Prado. Apparently they received firmer promises from Prado than from Lavalle not to investigate the corruption of the Odría régime.

The elections were held without serious incident and the official count awarded the *Aprista*-supported Prado 568,000 votes, perhaps an over-generous count, Belaúnde 458,000, possibly an under-generous count, and Lavalle 222,000, probably an honest tally. On 28 July, Prado received from Odría the insignia of office and began his second term as constitutional President. The new congress, installed on the same day, proceeded in a matter of minutes to revoke the Law of Internal Security.

Shortly before the elections *Apristas* had been allowed to resume virtually normal political activities. On 14 June they had held their first public political rally in eight years and Ramón Prialé, a dedicated and thoroughly honest leader who had suffered years of imprisonment in the service of his party, delivered one of the more enlightened and memorable discourses in the history of *aprismo*. The APRA, however, seemed to have gone into decline. It had suffered serious defections, among them those of Alberto Hidalgo[17] who had earlier described Haya de la Torre as Peru's great man of destiny, of Magda Portal,[18] long the party's leading woman campaigner, and of Ciro Alegría, one of Peru's leading novelists. In the departments in which it had presented slates for the 1956 elections the APRA won some 27 per cent. of the ballots in contrast with 1945 when it had received some 50 per cent.[19] On the other hand, the Front that backed Belaúnde had made a remarkable showing. This fresh political force was given a more permanent basis when, immediately after the elections, Belaúnde formed a party that was christened Popular Action (*Acción Popular*, or AP).

Still another new political movement to be reckoned with had appeared in Arequipa. There the Christian Democratic Party (*Partido Demócrata-Cristiano*, or PDC), although not participating in the presidential elections, won a majority of the congressional seats, one of them going to the party's principal founder Héctor Cornejo Chávez. Although centred in Arequipa, Christian Democratic strength was not confined exclusively to that city. In the country as a whole thirteen Christian Democratic deputies and four senators were elected to office. In their campaign, Christian Democrats had denounced the social injustices prevailing in Peru and demanded that capitalism, allegedly cruelly exploitative in its very essence, be replaced by an imprecisely defined socialistic structure described as 'communitarian'.[20] Quite clearly, new forces for change were at work in Peru, even though Manuel Prado would choose to ignore the fact.

PRADO'S SECOND TERM AND A BRIEF PERIOD OF MILITARY RULE, 1956–63

Enjoying throughout his term the support of *Apristas*, who were chastened by the years of Odría's harsh suppression and anxious to enjoy life once again no matter what the price might be in the way of political compromise, and also by his own National Coalition Party, Prado was able to count upon a large majority in both houses of congress. While his collaboration with the APRA guaranteed automatically the constant and unsparing criticism of the influential *El Comercio*, it also meant that the President was free to appoint and dismiss from cabinet posts as he saw fit and did not have to suffer through ministerial crises occasioned by interpellation. Besides working with the *Apristas*, Prado allowed the Communist Party, technically illegal at the time, a fairly free hand in both political activity and labour organization. With *Apristas* and Communists tamed for the moment and finding it to their apparent advantage to co-operate with the administration, Prado was able to preside over a period of relative political stability.

Hailed during the World War II period for the economic progress which he had done little to bring about, Prado had the bad fortune to be criticized during his second term for an adverse situation which was not essentially of his making. He inherited from Odría a badly mismanaged economy, a virtually empty treasury, a problem of dwindling foreign currency reserves, plus an unrealistic commitment to the continuation of vast public works projects and to the expansion of the bureaucracy and the elevation of its salaries. Although annual per-capita income had risen in recent years, reaching nearly $123 in 1956, it was estimated that 75 per cent. of the population received less than this amount; moreover, Lima's fewer than 1,500,000 inhabitants out of the total Peruvian population of nearly ten million received 50 per cent. of the overall, annual national income. Per-capita food consumption, both in proteins and calories, had declined between 1947 and 1955. In the latter year agriculture, employing 60 per cent. of the active population, produced only 27 per cent. of the gross national product.[21] Finally, Peru's terms of trade had worsened appreciably in the years preceding the beginning of Prado's second term. Between 1950 and 1955 export tonnage had tripled but the value of exports had gone up only from $200 million to $330 million. Meantime, import tonnage had doubled – Peru was importing one-fourth of its consumer and one-half of its capital goods – but the value had increased from $186 million to over $400 million.[22]

To deal with the critical economic situation, Prado appointed José Pardo y Barreda, grandson of Peru's first *Civilista* President and son of the later two-term President whose given name he bore, as minister of the treasury. Pardo attempted to peg the *sol* artificially at the level of nineteen to the dollar. As a result dollar reserves in the Central Bank within a short time almost disappeared. *La Prensa* sharply criticized the fiscal policies of Pardo, demanding that the *sol* be allowed to fall to its actual open-market value and that the government's economic restrictions in general be removed. When a budget was proposed for 1959 with a deficit of nearly one billion *soles*, *La Prensa* intensified its attacks against the Government. Alarmed by the abuse he was receiving from the country's two leading newspapers, Prado, ever the shrewd politician, sought to win the support of *La Prensa* by offering to make its director Pedro Beltrán his Prime Minister with the specific cabinet post of minister of the treasury. After first refusing the offer, Beltrán finally yielded to Prado's pressure and was installed in the exalted cabinet position in July 1959. As was predictable,

La Prensa's principal rival, *El Comercio*, responded by augmenting the severity of its editorial assaults against the administration.

Insisting upon a free-market economy, an austerity programme, a balanced budget and a sound currency, Beltrán set about to win the confidence of the business community and to induce it to increase productive investment so as to accelerate the pace of economic development. He assured businessmen that rather than raising taxes, which he described as already so high that they stifled capitalist initiative, he would lower them. Many disagreed with the Beltrán analysis. They argued that maximum taxes of 35 per cent. on Peruvian industrial and commercial profits, 43 per cent. on profits of foreign firms and 53 per cent. on profits of cotton producers did not necessarily constitute initiative-stifling imposts, especially when, as was the case, tax regulations were not rigorously enforced.

Refusing steadfastly to consider a raise in taxes, Beltrán, with the full backing of the APRA,[23] decided to obtain the revenue that the Government desperately needed by authorizing a rise in the price of gas and petroleum products. *El Comercio* complained indignantly that this would benefit exclusively the International Petroleum Company, which had absorbed its principal rival, the British 'Lobitos' firm, in 1957 and now enjoyed a virtual monopoly in the field. Beltrán countered that the Government would share almost equally with the IPC in the gains resulting from the price increase, as the United States firm was required to pay 43 per cent. – the amount was later raised to 50 per cent. – of its profits to the Government.

Beltrán's policies did contribute to an approximately 4·5 per cent. annual increase in the gross national product during the time he served as minister of the treasury. Under his economic direction, moreover, the State began to replenish its foreign currency reserves. Still, Beltrán was not able to fulfil his promise to reduce Government expenditures. Nor did he accomplish a promised amelioration of Peru's social problems.

Originally Beltrán had stated that once he had restored the economy to a progressive rate of development, he would proceed to inaugurate a programme of 'Roof and Land' ('*Techo y Tierra*') that would provide housing and land for needy Peruvians. Actually, very little was accomplished along these lines. A few urban housing projects were initiated, but they were inadequate even to keep pace with the flow of migration into the cities. With the Government investing less than 3 per cent. of its income in agricultural programmes, the irrigation and colonization projects to which Beltrán was pledged were not carried out. The landless remained without land and per-capita agricultural production continued its decline.[24] Furthermore, although the gross national income rose appreciably during the Beltrán years, the rich gained disproportionately in relation to the poor, with the advance in income of Peru's entrepreneurial and managerial groups being some 50 per cent. greater than that of the labouring classes.[25] All in all the policies of the controversial Prime Minister and minister of the treasury, who with commendable honesty at least continued to flaunt his customary disdain for the lower classes, did not give a very convincing demonstration that what was good for a few Peruvians was necessarily good for the country as a whole. By 1962 among the general populace Beltrán had become one of the most disliked figures that Peruvian politics had produced in many years.

Beltrán planned to become a candidate for the presidency, but the political rally in Lima to launch his campaign at which he expected the attendance of thousands of enthusiastic supporters drew only a handful of supporters, many of them allegedly recruited and paid. Faced with this rebuff, the cabinet's most influential member renounced his presidential aspirations and watched from the sidelines as a total of seven candidates prepared for the 1962 elections. It soon became clear that only three of them had any real chance of victory: Haya de la Torre, backed by the Prado administration and described as 'the sort of conservative we need in Peru';[26] Fernando Belaúnde, supported by Popular Action; and Manuel Odría, trying to stage a political comeback through a hastily organized party known as the *Odrista* National Union (*Unión Nacional Odriista*, or UNO).

In the June elections none of the candidates received the third of the 1,689,618 votes cast which would have meant election. As a result the congress, in line with constitutional provisions, was called upon to choose between the three highest candidates: Haya de la Torre with approximately 557,000 votes, Belaúnde with slightly more than 544,000 and Odría with some 520,000. Popular Action reacted to the situation by renewing charges, originally made during the campaign in regard to registration procedures, of

Aprista fraud. These charges were later verified, at least in part, by an exhaustive military investigation the results of which, published in a massively documented *White Paper* of 1963, cannot be totally dismissed despite the well-known prejudice of armed forces officials against Haya de la Torre.[27]

Apparently worried both by the well-attended civilian demonstrations staged throughout the country in protest against alleged fraud and by the likelihood that the military would inevitably intervene to prevent him from reaching the presidency, Haya de la Torre met on 17 July with Odría, the man who had previously said the *Aprista* leader was not morally worthy of Peruvian citizenship and who had spilled more *Aprista* blood than any man since Sánchez Cerro. In their meeting Haya and Odría came to an accord which was publicized at once: when congress met to decide which of the three highest candidates to select as President, *Apristas* would support Odría. By preparing the way for Odría to become President, Haya de la Torre felt he had guaranteed the actual seating of the large bloc of *Aprista* senators and deputies elected to congress at the same time that Peruvians had gone to the polls to vote for a President. The military, he felt, would not prevent one of its own members, Odría, from occupying the presidency. Once Odría was in office, then *Apristas* could reduce him to a mere political figurehead and actually govern the country through the congress which they expected to dominate by means of already-planned alliances with other political groups. Pedro Beltrán, who on the grave of Francisco Graña had sworn unrelenting opposition to *aprismo*, promptly added his personal support and that of his paper *La Prensa* to the Haya–Odría alliance. Thus there were allied three of the most powerful defenders of Peru's established order.

At this juncture the widely-respected President of the joint chiefs of staff, fifty-seven-year-old General Ricardo Pérez Godoy, a man who in 1955 had turned his back on an opportunity to seize the presidency from Odría, decided after consulting with his colleagues that Peru should not be delivered to the tainted leader of the *ochenio* and his new *Aprista* collaborators. Pérez Godoy sincerely believed that Peru required the fresh approach of an administration genuinely aiming towards reform. Past political events had persuaded him that neither Odría in the presidency nor Haya de la Torre's followers in the congress could be expected to govern

Peru in any interest other than opportunism. Accordingly, Pérez Godoy and his military colleagues prepared to take drastic actions which they felt could be justified on the grounds that the least popular of the three main contenders did not deserve to come to the presidency through a pact that had shocked and disgusted even the more sophisticated and cynical of the Peruvian electorate.

In the national palace, Manuel Prado may have pondered whether to turn the Government over to Odría and Haya de la Torre, satisfied that they would pose no threat to the *status quo* of which he had been so adroit a defender, or to use the charge of electoral fraud as an excuse to continue in power himself. If indeed Prado had a dilemma of this sort, it was resolved for him on the dawn of 18 July, ten days before the legal end of his constitutional term, when a tank crashed through the gates of the national palace and a few military men in a bloodless *coup* seized control of the Government. Although some officers recommended that Prado be jailed, the moderate Pérez Godoy, who had masterminded the military takeover, pronounced in favour of exile. Thus Prado returned to Paris, where he had already learned to feel as much at home as in Lima.

Installed as the President of a military junta of government, Pérez Godoy wisely refrained from pursuing a vindictive policy. Individual guarantees were respected, as was the freedom of the press; labour organizations were allowed to function freely; and political parties, including the APRA and even the Communist Party, were permitted to engage in normal activities. Promising that honest and free elections would be held the following June, Pérez Godoy set himself to the task of making Peru's year of military government one of impressive accomplishments.

Under his leadership the military junta established an institute of development planning (*Instituto de Planificación*), a bank to extend low-interest credit for the purchase of inexpensive houses (*Banco de la Vivienda*), and a new housing agency to carry out slum-clearance projects (*Junta Nacional de la Vivienda*), all of which performed valuable services during the period of military rule and afterwards. The junta also instituted several pilot land-reform projects, resulting in the opening of new regions to colonization. Technical training was given to rural labourers expected to benefit from the planned land redistribution and colonization projects and new agrarian credit facilities were provided. Many of the plans and concepts developed during the period of military rule and tried out in pilot projects became the basis of Peru's first major law of agrarian reform passed in 1964.

Inexplicably abandoning its original respect for political freedom, the military junta in January 1963 imprisoned a large number of persons accused of being Communists or having communist affiliations. Critics of the junta, making exaggerated estimates that two thousand persons had been involved in the round-up, claimed that this was the price the junta had to pay for the resumption of United States recognition which had been suspended immediately after the military *coup* by the John F. Kennedy administration, owing perhaps in part to the poor advice of its notoriously pro-*Aprista* Ambassador in Lima. Early in March Pérez Godoy, who it seemed had permitted the political jailings only with reluctance and against his better judgement, was overthrown by the other members of the military junta, direction of which then passed to General Nicolás Lindley. Although various of his colleagues urged him to take advantage of his popularity among many military and civilian elements to fight to retain power, Pérez Godoy accepted his deposition with outward calmness, apparently not wishing to take actions that might have led to the further politicization of the military.[29]

According to their own accounts, the associates of Pérez Godoy in the military junta deposed him because he was drifting towards personalistic rule and planning to establish a dictatorship. Pérez Godoy partisans attributed his ousting to his insistence upon reform and to the alarm he caused United States interests by his talk of nationalizing some of the International Petroleum Company holdings.[30] Whatever the true cause of the political change may have been, the reshuffled military junta of government did slow down the rate at which reform programmes were inaugurated and did not insist upon the scrupulous accounting for the use of public funds that had characterized the administration of the deposed general.[31]

To its credit, the junta abided by the original pledge to hold free elections and so in June 1963 Peruvians prepared once more to go to the polls to elect a President and congress. The outcome of the elections was largely determined by social and political developments of fundamental importance that had been occurring during the previous several years.

NEW FORCES FOR CHANGE IN PERU AND THE 1963 VICTORY
OF POPULAR ACTION

By the early 1960's middle sectors, accounting for probably more than 15 per cent. of the population, had come to hold the balance of political power in Peru.[32] A continuing demographic shift in the country had contributed to this development. In the years between 1940 and 1961, more than 15 per cent. of the rural population moved to the cities. A census conducted in 1961 revealed that urban inhabitants had come to make up nearly 48 per cent. of Peru's population.

Once in the cities many of the new arrivals simply swelled the ranks of the urban proletariat. Some, however, within a fairly short period succeeded in entering the lower ranks at least of the middle sectors. The rapid expansion of industry vastly facilitated their entry. By 1963 industry was producing 19·5 per cent. of the gross national product, almost matching agriculture which accounted for 19·9 per cent.[33] One particularly dramatic example of expansion was presented by the fish meal industry. Begun only some ten years earlier, the Peruvian fish meal industry in 1963 seemed ready to pass Japan and gain chief status in the world production of that commodity. Gains in certain sectors of mining were almost as spectacular. By 1962 with its annual production having climbed to 167,000 tons, Peru was the world's sixth largest producer of copper; and marked increases in annual tonnage extracted had placed Peru in fifth place among the world's producers of lead and zinc.[34]

Unlike other Latin American countries where the new middle sectors were almost exclusively urban, in Peru rural middle groups were also coming into existence. On the scientifically-run haciendas along the coast agricultural labourers had come, by and large, to live in reasonably attractive houses equipped with electricity, radios and sometimes television sets. They enjoyed fairly adequate medical services, belonged to effective unions and earned wages sufficient to place them definitely within the money economy and to allow them considerable choice in the acquisition of consumer goods. Their children received an education, occasionally extending through secondary and even the university level. In Peru's selva or Amazonian region there were also signs by the early

1960's of a burgeoning middle sector. Not yet as well established as its coastal counterpart, its members, mainly fishermen who owned their meagre equipment or proprietors of small farm plots (*chacras*), nonetheless earned an income adequate to enable them to enter the market economy and to acquire far more goods than their fathers had dreamed possible.

Contributing to the emergence of middle sectors was the rapid expansion of higher education facilities. By the early 1960's university training in Peru had long since ceased to be the exclusive privilege of the aristocracy and had begun to extend to social groups of humble origins – so much so that families of any social prestige hesitated to send their children to San Marcos or other national universities where they would have to mingle with an essentially low-born student body. In 1940, 3,839 students were enrolled in Peru's seven universities. In 1964, some 48,000 students were attending the country's thirty universities[35] and many of them came from backgrounds of genuine poverty.

Before the end of World War II the members of Peru's tiny middle sectors could hope without an entire lack of reality to find accommodation ultimately in the upper classes. Enough instances of upward social mobility of this sort existed to give at least some substance to this hope which traditionally constituted an important ingredient of the value system of Peruvian middle sectors. By the 1950's and 1960's, however, in part because of the dramatic increase in their numbers, it was not realistic or feasible for the majority of middle-sector Peruvians to look forward to an eventual rise to aristocratic status; circumstances were forcing them to realize that they were destined in all probability to remain permanently in a position between the lower and upper classes. As this realization became clearer, middle-sector members, acquiring self-consciousness and self-awareness as part of a stable social group and discarding the notion of being in a state of flux and about to rise appreciably in the social hierarchy, emerged as a genuine middle class.

Not only were realistic members of Peru's emergent middle class unable to aspire to aristocratic status, they were presented with overwhelming evidence that it would be necessary for them to wage a concerted struggle as a class unit to maintain for their children the economic and social level they had attained themselves. In many ways economic opportunities were not keeping pace with the increase in population. Between 1940 and 1961, the Peruvian population rose from seven to nearly eleven million. In general, employment possibilities in industry, mining, commerce and services rose at a far less spectacular rate. As of 1963, in fact, the Peruvian economy was supplying only some ten thousand new job opportunities per year, while most economists agreed that within ten years if the country hoped to avoid staggering unemployment problems and economic stagnation the annual number of new employment openings would have to rise to at least 100,000.[36] Moreover, notwithstanding the remarkable expansion of higher-education facilities, Peru's universities in 1964, because of lack of space and inadequate preparation of secondary students, admitted only 13·6 per cent. of the applicants.[37] As a result of the insufficient increase of employment and higher education opportunities, accompanied by an inflation which though mild in comparison with most other Latin American countries still placed a strain on all save the wealthiest classes, many Peruvians felt desperately insecure in their middle-class status.

Where might men in these circumstances turn for political leadership? The APRA could exercise little appeal to them, for Haya de la Torre, campaigning for the presidency in 1962 and again in 1963, spoke as if there was no reason for grave apprehensions among the Peruvian electorate. He called for patience and maintained that Peru's social and economic problems were not really terribly pressing.[38] It was altogether clear that the APRA had become primarily the party of the small group of higher middle sectors whose members had already found a place of security in their country's economic and social life and who could not be regarded as psychologically belonging to a true middle class because of their continued hope for assimilation into the upper classes.

Some Peruvians who felt that all was not so well within their country as pictured by Haya, turned towards communism as the means of resolving national problems. Among converts to communism or closely affiliated front groups were many *Aprista* defectors, men who had originally entered the APRA because its ideology had been based principally on the theories of Marx and Lenin. When the APRA changed, its members in not a few instances felt that they could best remain consistent by taking up the Communist cause. In 1960 one fairly substantial group defected and organized the Communist-front APRA *Rebelde*, subsequently rechristened the Revolutionary Leftist Movement (*Movimiento de Izquierda Revolucionaria*, or MIR).

Although benefiting to some extent by APRA deserters, communism in Peru was unable to capitalize upon the restlessness and apprehension of proletarian and lower middle-class sectors. In part this was because the movement began to splinter badly in the 1960's, with its leaders expending more energy in vying with each other than in fighting their mutual foes, the defenders of the capitalist system. Peking Communists bitterly assailed Moscow Communists[39] and the latter through their position of control in the Peruvian Communist Party fought back without scruple or restraint.[40] In addition various Trotskyists,[41] especially in Arequipa, and even alleged Stalinists advanced their versions of orthodoxy and thus intensified the internal cleavages within communism. In Lima during the early 1960's Communists and far-left fellow travellers consistently failed dismally in their endeavours to stage political rallies, attracting at best only a few hundred unenthusiastic observers. Those attending the rallies were apt to be confused as the rival tracts of Peking and Moscow Communists were pressed upon them. Their confusion might well have been compounded by the fact that proceedings occasionally began with recitation of the Lord's Prayer and 'Hail Mary', led by the Communist-leaning unfrocked Catholic priest, Father Salomón Bolo,[42] who defied ecclesiastical authorities by wearing his clerical garb at Communist meetings and other public events.

In addition to its internal dissensions, communism and all Marxian-inspired socialist movements have faced another obstacle to winning converts among the all-important populace of the coast. Since the time of Mariátegui, and going back even to the socialist period of González Prada, communism and socialism in Peru have been inseparably identified with *indigenismo* and the concept that the Indians as the superior Peruvians should spread their customs throughout the country, completely destroying in the process the coastal institutions, ways of life and perhaps even the population itself. Peruvians of the coastal region have been constantly admonished by Marxian-inspired reformers that 'Peru will not emerge as a nation until power is transferred into the hands of the majority, the men of the sierra. Peru will not begin a genuine political life until the socialist *serranos* take the capital'.[43]

The consensus among coastal Peruvians, regardless of ethnic and social origins, who dismissed as ridiculous and dangerous the far left's traditional adulation of Indian, sierra culture,[44] contributed for years to the ability of a small, coastal capitalist class to resist change and reform. Because change and reform as advocated by leftist spokesmen had invariably been associated with *indigenismo*, the middle sectors and proletariat of the coast, no matter what their difficulties and problems, had decided to struggle along with the *status quo*. If in the early 1960's they were to be enlisted in a drive to introduce certain long overdue changes, it would be necessary to present them with a programme that, however advanced in its ideas of reform, was still one of compromise. A programme was needed that could establish the basis for co-existence and co-operation between the coast and the sierra, between capitalism, individualism and the westernized way of life on one hand, and socialism and Inca traditions of communal labour and landownership on the other.

Fernando Belaúnde in his Popular Action campaigns, especially that of 1963, found a formula for a compromise programme of this type. He found it because he was the first significant reform-minded political leader of the twentieth century who did not insist, in his zeal for change, either on forcing the coastal way of life on the sierra or on imposing the sierra cultural patterns on the coast. He envisioned a genuinely pluralistic country in which the coast could advance with its westernized, capitalist traditions while the sierra progressed through its at least semi-socialistic Inca customs.

In addressing the campaign message of Popular Action to the sierra, Belaúnde, who personally travelled indefatigably to even the most remote Andean communities, sounded much like a socialist *indigenista* of the Mariátegui tradition. Unstintingly praising Inca traditions, including those of communal landownership and labour, Belaúnde called upon the native communities to advance themselves through the energetic use of the same methods employed by their distant ancestors, trying like Mariátegui to instil among the Indians, as the mystique of progress, a pride in the achievements of their pre-conquest predecessors.

Unlike Mariátegui and his direct successors in Peru, Belaúnde did not call upon the Indians to spread their way of life, by force if necessary, throughout the land. Instead, he recognized the many accomplishments of Peru's coastal capitalism. While he spoke of the need for greater planning to integrate future efforts towards economic expansion, he also indicated a willingness to allow room for the free exercise of initiative by businessmen themselves. However much he was convinced that free-enterprise capitalism could not solve the agrarian problems of the sierra with its Indian population, he was equally persuaded that Indian-style socialism would not contribute to bringing about the required prodigies of economic expansion in the industrial, commercial and mining enterprises of the coast, or in its scientifically managed and technologically advanced privately owned farms.

Instead of urging an Indian expansion towards the coast and even its complete takeover, Belaúnde seemed to feel that with its natural potential for growth, the coastal population was already nearly sufficient to provide for the immediate needs of industrial growth. His great desire was to have the Indians migrate towards the East and colonize the fertile eastern slopes of the Andes, thereby bringing new land under cultivation through the communal landownership and farm labour system to which the natives had clung tenaciously ever since the conquest. In this manner Belaúnde hoped to solve the problem of the country's chronic food shortage while not threatening with redistribution into small-sized food producing farms the large estates of the coast that produced such valuable export products as sugar and cotton.

With these goals in mind, Belaúnde proposed the building of a *carretera marginal de la selva*, a highway along the edges of the jungle in the eastern Andean foothill country. The intended highway would open up new land for colonization and food production, and would integrate the population settled along it with the rest of the country. The inspiration would be the marvellous Inca roads that had united the Indian confederation politically, economically and religiously. By building the road, Belaúnde argued, the State could bring together the land, the materials and the workers of the country, thus enabling Peru to increase agricultural production and amount of land under cultivation in proportion to the rise in population as had been done during the time of the Incas.[45]

An advocate of decentralization, Belaúnde realized that the country could never escape the overweening influence of Lima unless the inhabitants of the provinces began on their own to initiate self-help programmes, even though the programmes would inevitably be humble in inception. Throughout Peru, he emphasized, progress had to be made by people at the local level. He was fond of noting that wherever he travelled in the provinces, whether in the Indian sierra or elsewhere, the really promising developments and accomplishments he observed had been undertaken and executed not by the Government but by the local people themselves. One of the favourite slogans employed in his campaign was 'El pueblo lo hizo' ('The people did it') as opposed to the concept of 'El gobierno lo hizo'. To give greater impetus to genuine decentralization by trying to provide local regions with incentives for self action, Belaúnde promised that municipal elections would be restored and that some degree of local autonomy, crushed since the beginnings of the *oncenio*, would once more be permitted in Peru.

In his advocacy of decentralization, Belaúnde differed from past partisans of this reform. He did not insist that centralization had come about because of the blackhearted selfishness of a Lima oligarchy and bureaucracy. He implied instead that it had arisen largely because of the apathy of the people in the provinces. The way to correct the evil, therefore, was not to punish the oligarchy and bureaucracy of Lima and even to threaten their very existence, as earlier decentralization champions had delighted in doing, but to call upon the people of the provinces to take by their own display of initiative and leadership capacity the first vital steps towards correcting the ills of excessive centralization. Just as his espousal of *indigenismo* did not threaten the existence of the coastal populace or discredit and jeopardize their accomplishments, Belaúnde's message of decentralization did not menace the immediate interests or endanger the achievements of the power-wielding groups in Lima. *Indigenismo* and decentralization, as expounded by Belaúnde, served to infuse new vitality into groups long somnolent and ignored without threatening with catastrophe the classes that had traditionally directed Peru. Himself a member of the aristocracy and able to sympathize with some of its fears and apprehensions, Belaúnde felt the directing classes if not confronted with reform-mongers' threats of violent retribution could be persuaded through enlightened self interest to co-operate with the efforts of once ignored geographic, social and ethnic groups to make a better place for themselves in their country.

The Popular Action programme, because it offered a compromise solution to old issues that had pitted the coast against the sierra, Lima against the provinces, whites and *mestizos* against Indians, continued to win adherents among the populace. Exhausted by years of irreconcilable disunion, Peruvians apparently were ready to reanimate the spirit of moderation and of willingness to seek a middle way between extremes that had characterized their actions at crucial moments in the past.

Campaigning almost without respite between July 1962 and June 1963 when the military junta of government, true to its word, permitted new elections, Belaúnde gained ever-widening approval for Popular Action's programme of reform within a framework of moderation and compromise. His programme appealed to hard-pressed, lower-echelon members of the middle class who found nothing to hope for in the APRA's satisfaction with the *status quo*; it appealed to many *Apristas* who had deserted their party when its high command entered into a pact with the odious Odría; it aroused vast enthusiasm among the masses throughout Peru, especially because many had for the first time an opportunity to see, to shake hands with and to listen to a presidential candidate as the ubiquitous Belaúnde carried his message to the most remote regions; and it won the endorsement of some well-to-do members of the middle and upper sectors who had enough idealism, patriotism and also realism, to appreciate the need for reform and change within their country.

Belaúnde benefited also in 1963 from the support of the Christian Democratic Party which did not, as it had the previous year, run its own presidential candidate, and from the backing, obvious but reasonably discreet, of the military junta. The Catholic clergy and hierarchy, moreover, which had tended to enlist under Odría's banners in 1962, switched by and large to Fernando Belaúnde in 1963, assured by Víctor Andrés Belaúnde, possibly Peru's most respected Catholic layman, that his nephew's flirtation with the far left and Communist elements in the quest for votes had no deep significance and that Popular Action would at all times seek the collaboration of the Church in its endeavours to achieve reform and social justice.

All these factors contributed to Belaúnde's handy victory in 1963 over the same two main contenders he had faced in the previous year's election, Haya de la Torre and Odría. Receiving more than the required third of the ballots cast, Belaúnde was inaugurated for a six-year term on 28 July 1963.

THE BEGINNING OF THE BELAÚNDE ADMINISTRATION: PROBLEMS AND SOURCES OF HOPE

As Belaúnde began his term, the presence of diverse and mutually antagonistic ethnic and cultural background groups still posed one of Peru's major problems, one of the most significant obstacles to its becoming integrated and a true nation. A leading Peruvian journalist did no more than state a sad fact when he wrote in 1963: 'To be white constitutes an indescribable advantage that does not come from merit or talent . . ., but merely from the biological factor. Against this advantage the *mestizo*, the Indian, the mulatto will continue to rebel. . . .' His conclusion was: 'Only after the process of *mestizaje* has at last absorbed all whites will social tensions be eased in Peru'.[46]

Many factors combine with racial and cultural prejudices in contributing to the Indian problem in Peru. There is, for example, according to many observers, an increasing tendency towards drunkenness and excessive reliance upon mastication of the coca leaf among the *serranos*. There is also the fact of a rapid population increase. Throughout Peru the population is mounting at a rate of close to 3 per cent. each year. In the sierra this means that each year more and more people are born who seem destined to fall prey to the debilitating effects of alcohol and addiction to the coca leaf,[47] and also to be denied the opportunity of education because the slow expansion of school facilities is falling behind population increases. The burgeoning sierra population may only provide more examples to convince society's fortunate elements that the Indians are indeed a hopeless 'race', undeserving of attempts to uplift them.

Problems attendant upon land, its use and division, had assumed staggering proportions by the time Belaúnde came to power. Only approximately 1·5 per cent. of Peru's territory was under cultivation. As a result the number of persons per square kilometre of cultivated land was 480, one of the highest concentrations in the world. This meant that land under cultivation came to only half an acre per capita, an amount deemed woefully inadequate to furnish Peruvians with a satisfactory diet. The country urgently required expensive irrigation and colonization programmes, not just the redistribution of land. Even with the most lavish irrigation projects, however, there remained a question as to just how much of Peru's land, in part bleak and barren, in part tropical and jungle, could support agriculture or livestock raising.[49] Along the coast at least, a high percentage of territory best suited to cultivation under currently available techniques was already being productively utilized.

While distribution was by no means the major land problem in 1963, it was serious in its proportions. On the coast *minifundia* was an impediment to efficient farming, with some forty-thousand landholders owning estates of less than twenty-five acres, while 27,000 claimed plots of less than five acres. In contrast, 181 proprietors held estates of more than 1,250 acres each. In the sierra there were nearly 33,000 landowners. Over 27,000 of them held farms of seventy-five acres or less. Within this category more than a third, or nearly ten thousand proprietors, held property that was five acres or less in extension. Many labourers, known as *yanaconas*, were virtual serfs, being given the right to use tiny plots of land, often no more than a furrow or two, in exchange for contributing a specified number of days of labour throughout the year to the estate owner. On the other hand, the 1,233 sierra landowners who held property of more than 2,500 acres each controlled nearly 80 per cent. of the land under cultivation or used for pasture. Both on the coast and in the sierra the absence of medium-sized farms was conspicuous.[49]

The 1961 Peruvian census pointed to other striking problems. Even though the population had increased markedly since the previous census of 1940, the infant mortality rate continued to be amazingly high with 50 per cent. of the children in some regions dying before reaching age one.[50] Children who lived, moreover, continued to encounter serious obstacles in obtaining education. Approximately a million children over five years of age had not received primary instruction and over 40 per cent. of the population above seventeen was illiterate.[51]

As the charismatic Belaúnde assumed the burdens of office and confronted his country's staggering problems, he benefited enormously from the new and dynamic spirit of progress exhibited by groups and institutions previously characterized by inertia and antagonism towards change. The new spirit was particularly evident in the attitudes of the Catholic Church. With its 2,300 priests, with its religious vocations increasing at a rate nearly double that of the population growth, and with its educational facilities providing instruction for 135,000 of Peru's 1,700,000 school children, the Catholic Church was one of the most influential institutions in Peru.[52] It was also one of the most popular in a land where spiritual fervour, some might call it fanaticism, has always been a national trait. Significantly, Church leaders no longer contended, as had Lima's Archbishop Pedro Pascual Farfán in 1937 that 'poverty is the most certain road to eternal felicity. Only the State which succeeds in making the poor appreciate the spiritual treasures of poverty can solve its social problems'.[53]

Churchmen of a later era assumed a vital interest in trying to improve the material lot of the Peruvian masses, apparently convinced that only when enjoying surroundings of reasonable comfort could man develop fully his spiritual potential. A 1958 pastoral letter of the Peruvian prelates lamented the increasing concentration of wealth in the hands of the few and maintained that if the inequitable distribution of goods continued, ever more serious social conflicts would be inevitable.[54] In addition, the Cardinal–Archbishop of Lima, Juan Landázuri Ricketts, stated in a 1959 discourse marking the conclusion of the First Peruvian Catholic Social Week:

The Church sees that the present economic and social order must be reformed and improved. . . . A living wage must be paid to workers and there must be a better distribution of wealth; private selfishness must be curbed, for there is no longer an excuse of the miserable conditions in which rural labourers and the urban proletariat live.[55]

Churchmen by no means restricted themselves to words in their campaign for social justice. In the archdiocese of Cuzco the Church had by 1956 divested itself of much land, selling it at approximately half its market value to rural labourers with low-interest, ten-year credit provisions.[56] Especially in the sierra, moreover, Peruvian clergymen co-operated with the efforts of the United States Maryknoll priest Daniel McClellan to establish credit and consumer co-operatives among the natives. In the past it had always been assumed that the Indian possessed no money and was therefore hopelessly outside the market of economy. Father McClellan and his associates proved dramatically that once the Indian's confidence was won, he could after all produce money to deposit in co-operatives. As a result, throughout the sierra Indians began in the mid-twentieth century to have access for the first time to credit facilities and to find the means of acquiring, often at below market cost, the goods vitally necessary for the improvement of living standards. Largely owing to the activities of churchmen, the credit co-operative movement in Peru as from 1964 was established on a larger scale than in any other Latin American country. By the beginning of that year, primarily in the sierra and other poverty-stricken rural regions, the total of 365 Peruvian credit co-operatives boasted a membership of 130,000 with a combined savings of 130 million *soles*, the equivalent of approximately thirty-five million United States dollars.[57]

A radio school established in Puno in 1963 by Maryknoll priests with the enthusiastic backing of the Peruvian hierarchy was within a year reaching thousands of Indian inhabitants of the region. In broadcasts beamed in Spanish, Aymara and Quechua, it offered its listeners lessons in reading and writing, general culture, hygiene and sanitation, and modern farming methods. Indians who were interested in some of the advanced agricultural methods and implements described in the radio-school programmes could visit a model farm maintained on the outskirts of Puno and if impressed by what they saw, purchase on credit through a Church-initiated co-operative tools, seeds, livestock or virtually anything else required to improve their farms and homes. Assisted by projects of this type, Indians by the mid-1960's, travelling about on lightweight bicycles rather than the traditional horses and burros and with their transistor radios never far from reach, were beginning to change the face of the sierra.

The Church's new-found interest in social justice was not without its drawbacks. In their zeal for reform, some churchmen were apt to ignore economic realities as they voiced to the masses promises of immediate material betterment that could not possibly be met. At the same time, the oversimplified analysis in which some churchmen attributed Peru's social problems exclusively to the selfishness and viciousness of the wealthy fomented a purely negative form of class animosity.[58] Finally, in spite of the fact that very little in the way of social and economic betterment for the lower classes can be expected if the population continues to expand at its present rate, Archbishop Landázuri has been adamant in advancing the Church's traditional position on birth control:

In the problem of demographic growth, the Church confides in the Providence of God who will not permit the lack of material necessities for His creatures ... and to those who propose radical remedies contrary to the natural law, the Church insists upon the Christian solution to the problem based upon an international sense of responsibility and a spirit of solidarity.[59]

The military represented another institution often accused of being a bastion of conservative interests. Ever since the appearance of early nineteenth-century liberalism, various champions of reform had advocated its elimination. Upon assuming the presidency, however, Belaúnde was obviously prepared to accept the appraisal of Jorge Basadre that because of historical considerations and owing to the domestic and international exigencies of troubled times, the elimination of the military could not be seriously contemplated.[60] It seemed that Belaúnde also subscribed to the appraisal of the Peruvian military made by historian Luis Humberto Delgado: 'Our army continues to be the hope of our still unachieved restoration, regeneration and purification. With all its defects and errors, our army has always remained a hope'.[61]

Even before the one-year rule of the military junta, the armed forces of Peru had demonstrated a desire and an ability to take a part in achieving social and economic betterment throughout the country. A Centre of High Military Studies (*Centro de Altos Estudios Militares*, the CAEM), established during the Odría administration and staffed by military and civilian professors of a broad variety of subjects, had begun to study scientifically the vast problems confronting Peru and to devise possible means for their alleviation. Particularly impressed by the demands which the rapidly increasing population would shortly place upon the economy, the Centre recognized that internal stability and order could not be preserved unless all technically qualified Peruvians were enlisted at once in an integrated effort to plan for an era of greater material progress than the country had ever experienced. Acting upon its conviction that 'the armed forces must consider its mission to be that of facilitating the achievement of social welfare and collective well-being',[62] the Centre has been responsible for some of the most careful studies of social and economic conditions ever carried out in Peru, as well as for not a few of the most scientifically and expertly prepared plans for future development.

The allegedly antimilitarist President Manuel Pardo remarked in 1876 that it was his mission to democratize the army.[63] Since taking office in 1963 President Belaúnde has co-operated with the officers of the armed forces to achieve what in one sense can only be described as the democratization of the military. With the President's constant encouragement, the armed forces have begun to establish contact with the people and to work with them on a basis of equality towards the development of national resources, both material and human. No longer does the military stand as an aloof, isolated institution whose principal relations with the people take place when it must impose discipline upon them. In dozens of areas throughout Peru, army officers are engaged in community development projects, persuading local residents to supply the labour while the engineering corps contributes the technological expertise needed to construct new educational and recreational facilities, clinics and roads. There is scarcely an area where military men, co-operating with local residents, are not at work on road construction programmes. Thanks to the new rôle of the military, the Benavides dream of eventually connecting the coast, sierra and *selva* through an adequate system of communications has never been so close to the possibility of realization. Moreover, the constructive contact of the armed forces with humbler civilian elements seems certain to increase, for since 1963 many military officers have been sent abroad at government expense to carry out studies that will equip them to participate in the agrarian reform programmes of the new administration. And in the slums of Lima armed forces personnel have already begun work, frequently in collaboration with Peace Corps volunteers from the United States, on a variety of projects aimed at improving standards of living.[64]

Belaúnde's renovation attempts were supported not only by the Church and the military, but also by many neoliberal business groups recognizing the need for government economic planning and for greater management concessions to labour.[65] Still, the President was confronted by many serious political problems as he launched his administration. The APRA and the *Odriísta* National Union, continuing to honour the pact that Haya de la Torre and Odría had celebrated in July 1963, formed an opposition that controlled a clear majority both in the senate and chamber of deputies. Additional trouble seemed to be in store when Belaúnde, true to his campaign promises, scheduled municipal elections for

December 1963. Most observers expected that the combined forces of Haya and Odría would score a victory over the candidates presented by the Popular Action–Christian Democratic alliance. *Apristas* began openly to boast that with the control they enjoyed in congress, where they regarded their *Odriísta* collaborators as little more than the tail on the kite, and with the domination over the municipalities which they thought the elections would assure them, they could in effect govern Peru and virtually ignore the man in the national palace.

Aprista hopes were shattered when Popular Action–Christian Democratic candidates scored a stunning victory over their rivals for municipal offices. Even in the one-time 'solid *Aprista* North', the APRA–*Odriísta* ticket was defeated in many locales, while in the election for the mayor of Lima María Delgado de Odría, backed by *Apristas* and thought to be extremely popular because of her charitable activities during the *ochenio*, was overwhelmingly defeated by Belaúnde's close friend Luis Bedoya Reyes, an important leader of the Christian Democratic Party.

Prior to the municipal elections of December, Belaúnde had dramatically broken with the Communist and far-left elements that had supported his bid for the presidency. The outcome of the local elections suggested that he had enhanced his popularity by doing so and also indicated that by their pact both *Apristas* and *Odriístas* had hurt themselves politically.

Although *Apristas* and *Odriístas* continued publicly to abide by their pact after their December setback at the polls, Haya de la Torre may have decided in behind-the-scenes negotiations to relax his party's opposition to the administration, at least upon certain occasions. Certainly many *Apristas* in congress co-operated with the administration in gaining the passage of an agrarian reform bill,[66] although the multiple exceptions and restrictions they insisted upon may have unduly impaired the effectiveness of the legislation. As finally approved the agrarian reform law protected the highly productive, scientifically managed estates of the coast against expropriation, but did provide, perhaps unwisely, for the possibility of ultimately converting them into workers' co-operative enterprises. The law devoted much attention to irrigation and colonization projects and to establishment of training programmes and credit facilities for rural labourers expected eventually to become landowners. Idle land of sierra estates, according to the 1964 law, would be confiscated, with the owner receiving what was judged by a government agency to be adequate compensation.

Perhaps the project dearest to Belaúnde's heart in the early days of his administration was the establishment of contact with Indian communities of the sierra and initiation of community development projects in them. By the end of 1965 well over two thousand of the estimated five thousand Indian communities had been surveyed and in many instances persuaded by agents of the Government to undertake, largely on their own efforts and with only the modest support of the financially hard-pressed administration, the building of roads, clinics and schools. Throughout the sierra more and more projects to which Belaúnde could point and say, 'El pueblo lo hizo' were reaching completion.

Frequently sierra community development projects were aided by volunteers in a programme known as Popular Co-operation. Volunteering for service in this programme, scores of young Peruvians left the comforts of life on the coast in order to work with the Indians. In the summer of 1964 alone, some 550 university students, most of them far advanced in medical, engineering, dental, veterinary and agronomy studies, gave up their usual vacations and went to the sierra to share their labour and knowledge with the Indians.

Peru's problems, though, admit of no easy solutions and attempts to resolve them frequently only lead to new problems. The bureaucratic administration of Popular Co-operation soon came to be, according to many observers, graft-riddled. This situation was cited by the *Aprista–Odriista* congressional majority when in mid-1965 they refused to appropriate funds to support the programme. Although there may have been some justification for this action, there were mounting indications that it heralded a decision to abandon the rôle of responsible opposition and to take up a policy of narrow, sectarian and mischievious obstructionism. Certainly the majority bloc in congress seemed to be proceeding in this fashion when it voted a drastic reduction of funds for the agrarian reform programme at about the same time it was acting to cripple the operation of Popular Co-operation.

Other developments in the same period made it necessary to temper optimism somewhat in assessing the ultimate chances for success of the Belaúnde administration. A serious obstacle to the dynamic President was the relative hostility of the United States and the obvious intention of its State Department to wring from him guarantees to maintain the favoured treatment which the Peruvian government has accorded the International Petroleum Company. This firm, whose original claims were acquired under questionable circumstances and which long benefited from one of the most favourable concession contracts to be found in any place in the world – a fifty-fifty profit-sharing agreement with Peru at the inception of the Belaúnde régime, when governments of some other countries received more than 70 per cent. from foreign oil concerns – was by the mid-1960's subjected to mounting criticism from a wide cross-section of Peruvian politicians and intellectuals. As a result Belaúnde was under considerable internal pressure to win for his Government a far more advantageous relationship with the IPC or, failing that, to nationalize its holdings. Apparently feeling that continuation of the conspicuous privileges of United States oil interests takes precedence over matters of internal Peruvian reforms and renovation projects, the pristine spirit of the Alliance for Progress to the contrary notwithstanding, the Lyndon Johnson administration declined to co-operate with the Belaúnde administration unless it would give the desired assurances of following an indulgent policy towards the IPC. This Belaúnde refused to do and, as a result, by late 1965 was still not receiving the share of Alliance for Progress funds that his Government had earned the right to expect.

By late 1965 Belaúnde was further handicapped by the operation of some extreme leftist guerrilla bands in the sierra which were rumoured to be supported by Cuban and perhaps other Communist countries. Though small in number of enlistees, these bands, because of the rugged terrain in which they operated, were extremely difficult to apprehend and possessed a considerable nuisance potential which appeared to be more immediately useful to reactionaries than to revolutionists. Extreme rightist groups and their favourite organ of the press, *La Prensa*, began to delight in maliciously exaggerating the significance of the guerrilla threat, hoping thereby to discredit Belaúnde and by bringing about his fall end the threat of reform which he posed.

Whether in the long run Belaúnde makes notable advances against his country's problems or is forced to bow to them, it is significant that in its early stages his administration did succeed in creating a climate of opinion that was favourable to reform and in directing Peru towards the partial solution of at least a few problems, no small human achievement. Under the Belaúnde régime 'a variety of changes began to take place, not forced or forcefully, but with vigour; not necessarily for the best, but at least for the better'.[67] Thanks in large part to Belaúnde and the forces that brought him to power, Peruvians had been given another chance, however ephemeral it may prove to be, to show that they are at their best when circumstances permit compromise and moderation to triumph.

In the mid-nineteenth century Ramón Castilla was the key figure in finding a compromise which spared the country a devastating civil war and liberal revolutions dedicated to the really hopeless purpose of stamping out all vestiges of the past. Then in 1895 Nicolás de Piérola was instrumental in devising a compromise that was no less important in avoiding the dismemberment of the country by rival extremist groups and in preparing the way for more than twenty years of stability and progress. Some sixty-five years later Fernando Belaúnde was the principal architect of a new compromise: a programme of moderation, practicality and pragmatism, but also of vitality and daring. To some it appeared that Belaúnde's compromise might be as consequential as those fashioned by the two titans of the past in permitting Peruvians to advance towards the creation of a nation. Only the future will tell whether Peruvians themselves in adequate numbers will want to take advantage of a new opportunity for nation-making and whether they will be permitted to do so by outside forces exercised from Russia, China, Cuba or the United States.

Bibliographical Essay

THE 'civil war' that Jorge Basadre maintains has long been waged by those concerned with the writing and teaching of Peruvian history has centred principally upon the matter of *indigenismo* versus *hispanismo*. The issues involved in the historiographical civil war were exacerbated during the 1920's when *Indigenistas* often aligned themselves with communism or Marxian socialism and *Hispanistas* just as frequently embraced fascism. Authors including José Carlos Mariátegui in *Siete ensayos de interpretación de la realidad peruana* (Lima, 1928), Hildebrando Castro Pozo in *Nuestro comunidad indígena* (Lima, 1924) and Luis E. Valcárcel in *Tempestad en los Andes* (Lima, 1927), glorified both the Indian and socialism. On the other hand such intellectuals as José de la Riva Agüero in *Por la verdad, la tradición y la patria*, 2 vols (Lima, 1937–8) and Alejandro O. Deustua in *La cultura nacional* (Lima, 1937) sang the glories of European contributions to Peru and urged the adoption of fascism as the only means of preserving the country's best traditions and highest values.

In a much more restrained and moderate fashion than either Riva Agüero or Deustua and always avoiding advocacy of fascism, Víctor Andrés Belaúnde sought to refute *Indigenista*–Marxist interpretations of Peruvian history while at the same time praising Spanish and Catholic contributions to his country's formation. These are the central themes expressed in his *La Realidad nacional*, published originally in 1929 and 1930 as a series of articles in the Lima periodical *Mercurio Peruano*. Belaúnde in particular challenged the interpretations advanced by Mariátegui in the *Siete ensayos* and touched off one of the most significant debates in the intellectual history of Peru.

Since World War II many intellectuals have at last shown willingness to abandon the *Indigenista–Hispanista* dispute, at least in its old terms, and to agree that both the past and future greatness of their country rest upon *mestizaje*, the biological blending of Indians and Europeans and the cultural mixing of their ways of life. A few of the more important works advocating *mestizaje* as the great national goal of Peru include Jorge Basadre, *Meditaciones sobre el destino histórico del Perú* (Lima, 1947), Aurelio Miró Quesada Sosa, *Costa, sierra y montaña* (Lima, 1947), and Raúl Porras Barrenechea, *Mito, tradición e historia del Perú* (Lima, 1951).

Even in the 1960's, however, exaggerated forms of *indigenismo* and *hispanismo* could still be found in certain intellectual circles. In 1963 the young San Marcos history professor Juan José Vega published *La guerra de los Viracochas*, a study glorifying the Inca empire and implying that the conquest was a tragedy in which the noble and virtuous Indian civilization was crushed by the villainous hordes from Spain. The book sparked off one of the bitterest polemics in recent years among Peruvian intellectuals, being defended by some historians but roundly condemned by César Pacheco Vélez and José Agustín de la Puente Candamo. In denouncing *La guerra de los Viracochas*, Pacheco, Puente Candamo and other historians often became as extreme in their *hispanista* protestations as Vega was in proclaiming his *indigenista* sentiments.

Associated with the *indigenista–hispanista* debate has been the sharp disagreement over interpretation of the colonial period. In the years immediately following the attainment of independence and even as late as the early twentieth century it was quite the fashion for intellectuals to attribute all the ills of Peruvian society to the benighted Spanish colonial system. Works exemplifying this spirit include Felipe Barreda y Laos, *Vida intelectual del virreinato del Perú* (Lima, 1909, San Marcos University thesis, and Buenos Aires, 1937), Pedro M. Oliveira, *La Política económica de la metrópoli* (Lima, 1905), and Javier Prado y Ugarteche, *Estado social del Perú durante la dominación española* (Lima, 1894). In recent years the careful and diligent research of more objective historians has placed the colonial period in a comparatively favourable light. Of primary importance in this revisionist movement are the works of Guillermo Lohmann Villena which include *El arte dramático en Lima durante el virreinato* (Lima, 1945), *El Conde de Lemos, Virrey del Perú* (Madrid, 1946), and *El corregidor de indios en el Perú bajo los Austrias* (Madrid, 1957).

For many years Peruvian historians have also disagreed heatedly over the contributions which local intellectuals and political leaders made to the cause of independence. The prolific nineteenth-century historian Mariano Felipe Paz Soldán, whose works are characterized by careful and even exhaustive research and also by a dull and dry style and lack of analysis and interpretive insight, asserted that Peruvians made virtually no contribution to the independence movement. This is the essential thesis in the first volume of his *Historia del Perú independiente* which appeared in 1868. Infuriated by the Paz Soldán treatment, Francisco Javier Mariátegui who as a young man had participated in the events of independence published a refutation in *Anotaciones de la 'Historia del Perú independiente' de Mariano Felipe Paz Soldán* (Lima, 1869). Mariátegui felt that liberal Peruvian intellectuals, influenced by Enlightenment ideology, together with local guerrilla military leaders had made a major contribution to the attainment of independence. Later Peruvian historians have remained equally far apart in their interpretations of the period although the most prolific author on the independence movement and its background, José M. Vargas, *La gesta emancipadora del Perú*, 12 vols (Lima, 1940–3), favours the Mariátegui viewpoint.

In the mid-nineteenth century liberals such as Francisco de Paula González Vigil strove to introduce political democracy and to remove Church influence from temporal society, while conservatives led by Bartolomé Herrera asserted that authoritarian institutions of government and some degree of ecclesiastical direction of the body politic were providentially ordained. How the liberal–conservative debate could influence the writing of history is revealed by Ricardo Cappa, *Historia del Perú* (Lima, 1886), the work of a conservative Italian Jesuit who had lived for some time in Peru, and the furious rejoinder to it by the country's leading nineteenth-century man of letters Ricardo Palma, *Refutación a un compendio de historia del Perú* (Lima, 1869).

Largely owing to the bitterness of the liberal–conservative split, Peru's great statesman of the mid-nineteenth century, Ramón Castilla, seldom received adequate appreciation from contemporary historians. Castilla laboured to effect a compromise between liberalism and conservatism and as a result was criticized by advocates of both causes. Only in recent years have Peruvian historians begun to recognize Castilla as the great national hero of his century. This revisionist viewpoint is apparent in what is probably the best of several new biographies of Castilla, Miguel A. Martínez, *La vida heróica del Gran Mariscal don Ramón Castilla* (Lima, 1952).

The ideological dispute triggered off by the liberal–conservative debate has not received adequate coverage, for intellectual history has been relatively neglected in Peru, although Alberto Tauro has begun increasingly to focus his interest on that field. Useful preliminary studies of nineteenth-century intellectual currents have been written by Raúl Ferrero Rebagliati, *El liberalismo peruano* (Lima, 1958) and Jorge Guillermo Leguía, *Estudios históricos* (Lima, 1939). Both men show commendable objectivity and are able to deal sympathetically with Vigil as well as with Herrera.

Indispensable nineteenth-century works describing some of the political struggles precipitated by the liberal–conservative issue include Modesto Basadre (an uncle of Jorge Basadre), *Diez años de historia política del Perú, 1834–44* (Lima, 1953 edition), with prologue and notes by Félix Denegri Luna, José Rufino Echenique, *Memorias para la historia del Perú, 1808–78*, 2 vols (Lima, 1952 edition), with a prologue by Jorge Basadre and notes by Denegri Luna, and Juan Gualberto Valdivia, *Las revoluciones de Arequipa* (Arequipa, 1956 edition), with a prologue by Francisco García Calderón. Also useful is Nemesio Vargas, *Historia del Perú independiente*, 9 vols (Lima, 1903–42). Vargas, a somewhat eccentric humanist and translator of Shakespeare who turned to history rather late in life, dealt in this massive work with the period from independence to 1839 – the same period covered by Mariano Felipe Paz Soldán in his identically-titled study. Until the appearance of the Jorge Basadre general history, the Vargas work was generally considered to be the most satisfactory treatment of the early years of the republic.

Various aspects of the liberalism versus conservatism debate, often modified by the rise of positivism as an intellectual influence, coloured the writings of history until well into the twentieth century. Mariano Amezaga in *Los dogmas fundamentales del catolocismo ante la razón* (Valparaíso, Chile, 1873) presented a spirited, positivist-inspired attack against the Church and its historical rôle in Peru; but Manuel González Prada was always the most bombastic and outspoken critic of the Church's historical influence. Two of his works, *Horas de lucha* (Lima, 1908) and

Páginas libres (Lima, 1894), were published during his lifetime. Since his death in 1918 his son Alfredo has collected and published many more of the works of Peru's fulminating iconoclast. On the other hand, the historical rôle of the Church is defended by Pedro García y Sanz, *Apuntes para la historia eclesiástica del Perú* (Lima, 1876) and Manuel Tovar, the Archbishop of Lima from 1897 until his death in 1907, *Obras*, 4 vols (Lima, 1904–7).

Among Peruvian intellectuals of the present era anticlericalism has passed relatively out of vogue. In part this is because in an increasingly secular age the Church no longer is capable of wielding the vast influence of bygone days and thus attracts less criticism. In the past, moreover, the Church was attacked as a bastion of the *status quo* by champions of change, whether they were liberals, positivists, or Marxists. By the 1960's many important Catholic spokesmen in Peru had themselves joined in the quest for sweeping social, economic and political reform and were seeking to identify the ecclesiastical institution with the forces of modernization. Reform-seekers in Peru therefore found less justification for assailing the Church. The spirit of reform in the post-World War II Church is revealed in the collection of essays by leading Catholic intellectuals, *Política deber cristiano* (Lima, 1963). In the changing climate of opinion it may become possible for an objective history of the Church to be written. So far no work has appeared on this topic which is even partially satisfactory, although the organ of the Archdiocese of Lima *El Amigo del Clero*, founded in 1891, is often a valuable primary source.

The attempt to assess the rôle of the military in history has produced almost as much discord as the endeavour to evaluate the Church. A classic defence of the military and of militarism is found in Fernando Casós, *La revolución de julio en el Perú* (Valparaíso, 1872). Peru's outstanding military historian Carlos Dellepiane in his *Historia militar del Perú*, 2 vols (Lima, 1943 edition) and prolific historian Luis Humberto Delgado in his short study *El militarismo en el Perú, 1821–1930* (Lima, 1930) also extol the rôle of the Peruvian military. On the other hand González Prada and subsequent champions of drastic change and social revolution have been as outspoken in condemning the military as they have in censoring the Church. In this vein of writing is Víctor Villanueva Valencia, *El militarismo en el Perú* (Lima, 1962) and *Un año bajo el sable* (Lima, 1963).

Just as the Church, so also the military in the years since World War II has given some indications of wishing to participate in the quest for modernization and reform. If military leaders prove sincere and consistent in playing such a rôle, the anti-military animus characteristically demonstrated by reform-minded intellectuals may subside and the climate of opinion could become conducive to the writing of an adequate history of the Peruvian military.

Already the intensity of the anti-military bias among some intellectuals has diminished and this has been an important factor contributing to widening acceptance of a new interpretation of nineteenth-century Peruvian history. Traditionally historians tended to disparage the military caudillos. However, a revisionist movement led most notably by Jorge Basadre has been gaining ground in recent years, with the virtue, idealism and enlightenment of many caudillos being stressed. In particular Agustín Gamarra, killed in 1841 during an attempted invasion of Bolivia, has come to be recognized as a statesman of stature. This revisionist approach is apparent in Dante Herrera Alarcón, *Rebeliones que intentaron desmembrar el sur del Perú* (Lima, 1961). The same revisionist theme was evident even in the much earlier works of Miguel A. Martínez, *El Mariscal de Piquiza, don Agustín Gamarra* (Lima, 1946) and Luis Alayza y Paz Soldán, *El Gran Mariscal José de la Mar* (Lima, 1941). Unfortunately, as Peruvian historians come increasingly to appreciate Gamarra and other local caudillos, their animus against Bolivian caudillo Andrés Santa Cruz seems to intensify. This fact may help explain why no objective Peruvian account of the Santa Cruz-dominated Peru–Bolivia Confederation (1835–9) has been written, although Félix Denegri Luna, particularly in his superb annotations for Manuel de Mendiburu, *Biografías de generales republicanos* (Lima, 1963), demonstrates talents and impartiality of judgement which decidedly qualify him to undertake the task.

The disputes which originated in the 1870's between Nicolás de Piérola and his Democratic Party on one hand, and Manuel Pardo and his *Civilista* Party on the other, often prevented Peruvians from co-operating in waging the War of the Pacific against Chile. Passions awakened by these disputes also prevented historians for many years from dealing objectively with the period from 1870 to the turn of the century. Then, during the 1920's both the

Democratic and *Civilista* Parties virtually disappeared and the issues over which they had contended were largely forgotten. Historians have subsequently begun to find it possible to write with detachment on Piérola and Pardo. Thus Piérola's most successful biographer Alberto Ulloa Sotomayor, *Don Nicolás de Piérola: una época de la historia del Perú* (Lima, 1949), deals objectively with Pardo while one of Pardo's principal biographers. Evaristo San Cristóval, *Manuel Pardo y Lavalle, su vida y su obra* (Lima, 1945), is eminently fair to Piérola.

The period from 1895 to 1919 brought notable economic development to Peru and produced a group of important intellectuals who advocated considerable transformation and reform of the established order. Intellectuals in this mould, each of them a prolific author and active also in politics, included Joaquín Capelo, Mariano H. Cornejo, José Marías Manzanilla, Luis Miró Quesada, Javier Prado and Manuel Vicente Villarán. Something of the spirit of the progressive 1895–1919 period is captured in V. A. Belaúnde, *Mi generación en la universidad* (Lima, 1961), Ventura García Calderón, *Nosotros* (Paris, 1946), and José Carlos Martín, *José Pardo y Barreda* (Lima, 1948). The last work, dealing with the son of Manuel Pardo who was twice President of Peru in the early twentieth century, is one of the more successful biographies of modern political leaders.

In the decade following World War I a group of energetic, persuasive and talented writer-politicians who advocated total revolutionary change rose to prominence. These men, among whom the young Víctor Raúl Haya de la Torre and his *Aprista* followers were prominent, maligned the statesmen of the 1895–1919 era. A typical example of this approach is found in the work of the *Aprista* politician-*pensador* Luis Alberto Sánchez, *Balance y liquidación del novecientos* (Santiago, 1941). If the history of modern Peru is to be placed in proper perspective the contributions of the early twentieth-century statesmen must be recognized. Fortunately by the 1950's some of the animosity aroused in a previous generation between *Apristas* and their opponents was beginning to diminish and it seemed possible that the time might be near when a balanced history of the early part of the century could be written.

The time may even be approaching when Peruvians can deal objectively with Haya de la Torre and the *Aprista* movement. It is true that *Aprista* leaders such as Haya himself, Luis Alberto

Sánchez, Carlos Manuel Cox and Luis Heysen continue to publish works which uncritically glorify the movement. It is also true that intemperate denunciations of *aprismo* continue to be published, among them Luis Eduardo Enríquez, *Haya de la Torre, la estafa mas grande de América* (Lima, 1951) and Víctor Villanueva Valencia, *La tragedia de un pueblo y de un partido* (Santiago, 1954). However, at least an occasional flash of impartiality in dealing with the APRA is apparent in Alfredo Hernández Urbina, *Los partidos y la crisis APRA* (Lima, 1956). More detached still is Enrique Chirinos Soto, *El Perú frente a junio de 1962* (Lima, 1962), a valuable survey of Peruvian politics since 1895 written by a skilful journalist who may be classified as a neo-*Aprista*.

Unhappily, Peruvians seem nearly as far as ever from an objective evaluation of the eleven-year rule of Augusto B. Leguía (1919-30). Works dealing with this period of history either glorify or vilify the dictator. Glorification is found in Manuel A. Capuñay, *Leguía: vida y obra del constructor del gran Perú* (Lima, 1952), who does little more than repeat the apologies for Leguía made by sycophantic contemporary authors. Vilification characterizes the work of Marxist-influenced Abelardo Solís, *Once años* (Lima, 1934). In contrast, Luis M. Sánchez Cerro, the man who succeeded Leguía in the presidency in 1931 following a brief period of government by a junta, has received, in addition to much vilification at the hands of *Aprista* writers, a relatively satisfactory biographical treatment. In *Sánchez Cerro y su tiempo* (Lima, 1947), Carlos Miró Quesada Laos has produced a work which although criticized by some as excessively sympathetic to the *cholo* officer–politician is actually quite penetrating and surprisingly free from prejudice. No acceptable biographical study has been written on any Peruvian President who has served since Sánchez Cerro. In *Tres años de lucha por la democracia en el Perú* (Buenos Aires, 1949), however, José Luis Bustamante y Rivero provides much useful information on his 1945-8 presidential term, cut short by the Manuel A. Odría military *coup*.

Several multi-volume studies of Peru's republican history have been written. One of the more useful is Pedro Dávalos y Lissón, *La primera centuria: causas geográficas, políticas, y económicas que han detenido el progreso moral y material del Perú en el primer siglo de su vida independiente*, 4 vols (Lima, 1926). Although avoiding interpretive analysis and frequently resorting to interminable quotations from newspapers and other sources, amateur historian Dávalos y Lissón included in this work much material that would otherwise be difficult to locate. Without question, though, the best and most comprehensive treatment of Peruvian history from independence to 1930 is Jorge Basadre, *Historia de la República del Perú*, fifth edition, enlarged and corrected, 10 vols (Lima, 1961–4). Basadre's work is always carefully researched and notable for objectivity. As a younger man Basadre was outspoken in his social criticism, but in recent years has assumed a somewhat more optimistic viewpoint on Peruvian development. A fourth edition of his history (the first was published in 1939 in a single volume) appearing in two volumes in 1949 was quite forthright in presenting value judgements. In the newest and expanded version of his history, however, Basadre seems inclined to avoid assessment and appraisal and to quote the opinions of others when evaluating controversial figures and occurrences. Undoubtedly, between 1949 and 1961 he discovered the difficulties of expressing opinions about contemporary Peruvian history while still maintaining his residence in the country.

A highly useful survey of Peruvian political history, despite the pro-*Civilista* label which critics have attached to it, is Carlos Miró Quesada Laos, *Autopsía de los partidos políticos* (Lima, 1961). Although criticized in some circles for being excessively conservative in viewpoint, José Pareja Paz Soldán, *Las constituciones del Perú* (Madrid, 1954) is a distinguished constitutional history. Pareja Paz Soldán is also an authority on diplomatic history and the editor of *Visión del Perú en el siglo XX*, 2 vols (Lima, 1962), an excellent collection of lengthy articles by the country's leading intellectuals dealing with economic, political, religious, social, military and cultural history of twentieth-century Peru. Another useful compilation of high-quality studies on contemporary Peru is Darío Sainte Marie S., editor, *Perú en cifras* (Lima, 1945). Many valuable insights into various aspects of Peruvian development from independence to approximately 1930 are found in fairly recently published anthologies of two of the country's leading men of letters: Francisco García Calderón Rey, *En torno al Perú y América* (Lima, 1952), with a preliminary essay by Jorge Basadre, and Manuel Vicente Villarán, *Páginas escogidas* (Lima, 1962), with a prologue by Basadre.

Although its appraisals often reveal a partisan *Aprista* approach, the standard literary history of Peru is Luis Alberto Sánchez, *La literatura peruana*, 6 vols (Lima and Buenos Aires, 1946–51). In many ways more objective but not so comprehensive in treatment are several studies on Peruvian literature by Estuardo Núñez. A helpful but poorly organized and by no means exhaustive history of Peruvian journalism is Carlos Miró Quesada Laos, *Historia del periodismo peruano* (Lima, 1957).

Two of the more important works in the generally neglected field of nineteenth-century Peruvian diplomatic history are Arturo García Salazar, *Historia diplomática del Perú* (Lima, 1928), and Pedro Ugarteche, *El Perú en la vida internacional americana* (Lima, 1927). An excellent synthesis of twentieth-century Peruvian diplomatic history is Alberto Wagner de Reyna, *Historia diplomática del Perú*, 2 vols (Lima, 1964), while a modest study of one facet of contemporary Peruvian diplomacy is James Carey, *Peru and the United States, 1900–62* (Notre Dame, Indiana, 1964).

The pioneering economic history of Peru is César Antonio Ugarte, *Bosquejo de la historia económica del Perú* (Lima, 1926). Having received part of his training in the United States, Ugarte in the early 1920's introduced courses on economic history at San Marcos University. A more recent attempt at a survey of the country's economic history is Emilio Romero, *Historia económica del Perú* (Lima, 1949). Romero is also the author of the highly regarded *Geografía económica del Perú* (Lima, 1961 edition). Unfortunately, the economic historian of Peru is severely handicapped by a lack of reliable statistics and carefully-researched monograph materials. As a result, the writing of economic history has not yet reached a distinguished level. It is also regrettably true that social factors have been neglected even more than economics in the writing of Peruvian history. No work that is even remotely satisfactory has appeared on the social history of Peru since independence.

Perceptive studies dealing with Peruvian historiography, its major strengths and weaknesses, include Jorge Basadre, 'Notas sobre la experiencia histórica peruana', *Revista Histórica* (Lima), XIX (1952), pp. 5–140, César Pacheco Vélez, 'La historiografía peruana contemporánea', in Pareja Paz Soldán, editor, *Visión del Perú*, II, pp. 527–80, Raúl Porras Barrenechea, *Fuentes históricas peruanas* (Lima, 1963 edition), Alberto Tauro, *Historia e historiadores del Perú* (Lima, 1957), and José de la Riva Agüero, *La historia en el Perú.* Originally written as a San Marcos doctoral thesis in 1910, this last work was republished in Lima in 1952. It is generally acknowledged as the point of departure for all subsequent analyses of Peruvian historical literature.

An invaluable bibliographical guide is Alberto Tauro, *Bibliografía peruana de historia, 1940–53* (Lima, 1954). The work abounds in reliable criticial analysis. A *Primer suplemento* to the *Bibliografía*, published in 1958, deals with books and pamphlets that appeared from 1940 to 1953 and are not treated in the original study as well as with works published between 1935 and 1939 and between 1954 and 1957. Other bibliographical aids include the *Anuario Bibliográfico Peruano*, published at irregular intervals by the Biblioteca Nacional de Lima, and the *Boletín Bibliográfico de la Biblioteca Nacional de Lima* which appeared first in 1919 and 1920, was then suspended, and finally resumed publication in 1943. In addition the Biblioteca Central de la Universidad Nacional Mayor de San Marcos has published at irregular intervals since 1923 the *Boletín Bibliográfico*. The classic nineteenth-century bibliographical work is Mariano Felipe Paz Soldán, *Biblioteca peruana* (Lima, 1879), which comments upon some seven hundred Peruvian publications, including a great number of newspapers and periodicals.

Since the mid-1940's a new impetus to historical studies has been evident in Peru. A promising group of young historians has appeared and the Institute Histórico del Perú has been revitalized. It has lent its efforts to those of the Instituto Sanmartino, the Centro de Estudios Histórico–Militares, and the Centro Universitario de Investigaciones of San Marcos University in stimulating the training of historians and the production of solid historical works. In addition the Sociedad Peruana de Historia, founded in 1945 through the efforts of Ella Dunbar Temple and other distinguished historians, has brought together various specialists whose hope is to produce through mutual co-operation a fresh synthesis of Peruvian history. Before these efforts can lead to sustained accomplishments, however, the disciplines that are ancillary to the study of history must be developed. Furthermore, much remains to be done to carry forward the pioneering efforts of José de la Riva Agüero, of Raúl Porras Barrenechea, and of the Jesuit historian Rubén Vargas Ugarte, whose main concentration has been on the colonial period, in assessing the weaknesses and strengths of previous historical writing and in organizing and cataloguing public and private collections of sources. Only with this accomplished will life and vitality be infused into the libraries which have tended to remain, in the terms González Prada once applied to the Biblioteca Nacional, cemeteries of books and documents.

Notes

CHAPTER I

1 When he discovered the ruins of Machu Picchu in 1911, Hiram Bingham thought he had come upon the fabled Vilcabamba, as he explains in his *The Lost City of the Incas: the Story of Machu Picchu and its Builders* (New York, 1948). Subsequently, however, most authorities have concluded that Machu Picchu was not Vilcabamba. For an insight into the grandeur and awe-inspiring difficulties of Peruvian geography see Isaiah Bowman, *The Andes of Southern Peru* (New York, 1916), G. R. Johnson and R. R. Platt, *Peru from the Air* (New York, 1930), and Christopher Sanderson, *A Wanderer in Inca Land* (London, 1949).

2 Víctor Andrés Belaúnde, *Peruanidad* (Lima, 1957), p. 491. Unless otherwise specified, all books and periodicals cited hereafter are published in Lima.

3 Basadre, *Meditaciones sobre el destino histórico del Perú* (1947), p. 48.

4 Riva Agüero, *Afirmación del Perú* (1960), quoted in José Pareja Paz Soldán, editor, *Biblioteca de cultura peruana contemporánea* (1964), I, pp. 266–7.

5 Bailey W. Diffie, *Latin American Civilization: Colonial Period* (Harrisburg, Pennsylvania, 1947), pp. 381–5.

6 For a succinct summary of the main features of the empire of Tahuantinsuyo see Luis Eduardo Valcárcel, 'Sumario del Tahuantinsuyo', *Amauta*, Año III, No. 13 (March, 1928). Through a long career Valcárcel has written prolifically on Peru's pre-Columbian past, tending romantically to glorify the accomplishments of the aborigines. In 1964 he published his monumental *La historia del Perú a través de las fuentes escritas*, 3 vols (Buenos Aires), based on writings of the sixteenth, seventeenth and eighteenth centuries dealing with pre-conquest and colonial Peru. For valuable non-Spanish language studies of the Inca and pre-Inca civilizations see Louis Baudin, *L'Empire Socialiste des Inca* (Paris, 1928); Wendell C. Bennett and J. B. Bird, *Andean Culture History* (New York, 1949); G. H. S.

Bushnell, *Peru* (New York, 1957); Paul Kosok, *Life, Land and Water in Ancient Peru* (Brooklyn, 1965); J. Alden Mason, *The Ancient Civilizations of Peru* (Penguin Books, Harmondsworth, Middlesex, 1957); Philip Ainsworth Means, *Ancient Civilizations of the Andes* (New York, 1931); Sally Falk More, *Power and Property in Inca Peru* (New York, 1958); Harold Osborne, *Indians of the Andes: Aymaras and Quechuas* (London and Cambridge, Massachusetts, 1952); Julian H. Steward, editor, *Handbook of South American Indians*, Vol. II, *The Andean Civilizations* (Washington, DC, 1946), containing excellent articles on the Inca and pre-Inca civilizations by John H. Rowe, Luis Valcárcel and others; Max Uhle, *Kultur und Industrie der Sudamericanischen Völker*, 2 vols (Berlin, 1889–90); Victor W. von Hagen, *Highway of the Sun* (New York, 1955) and *Realm of the Incas* (New York, 1957).

7 For a masterful and sympathetic treatment of the colonial chroniclers see Raúl Porras Barrenechea, *Los cronistas del Perú, 1528–1650* (1945).

8 See Belaúnde's review of J. Basadre, *La multitud, la ciudad y el campo en la historia del Perú* (1929) in *Mercurio Peruano*, Año XIII, Vol. XX, Nos 137–8 (January–February 1930).

9 Quoted in Dora Mayer de Zulén, *El oncenio de Leguía* (Callao, 1932), II, p. 2.

10 Espinosa, *Diccionario para el pueblo: republicano, democrático, moral, política, y filosófico* (1855), pp. 609 ff.

11 Romero, *Perú por los sendros de América* (México, DF, 1955), pp. 133–5.

12 Mariátegui, *Siete ensayos de interpretación de la realidad peruana* (1959 edition of the work originally published in 1928), p. 9.

13 Javier Pulgar Vidal, *La Gea, el hombre y la historia del Perú: visión Aprista del congreso económica nacional en función de nuestra realidad* (1947: pamphlet), p. 11.

14 Miró Quesada, *Pueblo en crisis* (Buenos Aires, 1947), pp. 66 ff.

15 See Sarmiento de Gamboa, *History of the Incas*, translated and edited by Sir Clements Markham (Cambridge, England, 1907).

16 See Raúl Porras Barrenechea, *Mito, tradición e historia del Perú* (1951), pp. 47–8.

17 Carranza, *Artículos publicados por . . ., segunda colección de artículos* (1888), II, pp. 48–53.

18 Prado, *Estado social del Peru durante la dominación española* (1941 edition of the work originally published in 1894), pp. 168 ff.

19 Deustua, *Ante el conflicto: problemas económico-sociales y morales del Perú* (1931), p. 11.

20 A balanced and impartial English-language history dealing especially with the colonial period is by Sir Clements Markham, *A History of Peru* (Chicago, 1892).

21 Rafael Cubas V., *Hacia una auténtica concepción de la realidad peruana: hispanismo, única y verdadera forma de peruanismo* (1955: pamphlet), p. 30.

22 See *Letras: Organo de la Facultad de Filosofía, Historia, y Letras de la Universidad Mayor de San Marcos*, No. 6 (first quarter, 1937), p. 819.

23 Hidalgo, *Diario de mi sentimiento, 1922–36* (Buenos Aires, 1937), pp. 340–41.

24 See Francisco Gil de Taboada y Lemos, 'La población del Perú, 1796', and José Fernando de Abascal, 'El virreinato del Perú, 1812', reproduced in José Agustín de la Puente Candamo, editor, *El estado del Perú* (1959), I, pp. 8–9, 16.

25 Herrera, 28 July 1846 sermon in his *Escritos y discursos* (1929–30), II, p. 91.

26 Arenas y Loayza, *Visión de nuestro tiempo: ensayos* (1956), pp. 46–7.

27 Deustua, review of Javier Prado, *El estado social del Perú*, published originally in the newspaper *El Callao* (Callao), 28 March 1894, and included in the 1941 edition of the Prado work, p. 15.

28 *Ibid.*, pp. 16 ff.

29 Aníbal Maúrtua, *El porvenir del Perú* (1911), pp. 2–3.

30 Belaúnde, *Palabras de fé* (1952), pp. 44–5.

31 Barreda Laos, *Vida intelectual del virreinato del Perú* (Buenos Aires, 1937 edition of a 1909 San Marcos doctoral thesis), pp. 380, 382.

32 Porras, *Mito, tradición e historia*, p. 12.

33 For English-language studies of the effect of the conquest on the Indians see Charles Gibson, *The Inca Concept of Sovereignty and the Spanish American Administration in Perú* (Austin, Texas, 1948), and P. A. Means, *Fall of the Inca Empire and the Spanish Rule in Peru 1530–1780* (New York, 1932). The latter work suffers somewhat from an *indigenista* bias. See also William H. Prescott, *History of the Conquest of Peru*, 2 vols (New York, 1947), which although a recognized masterpiece may not do justice to the figure of Francisco Pizarro.

34 Belaúnde, *Palabras*, pp. 42–3.

35 See *Revista de la Universidad Católica del Perú*, Año VI, Vol. V, No. 32 (June 1937), pp. 236–8.

36 García Calderón, *Diccionario de legislación perúana* (1879), II, pp. 1104 ff.

37 Lorente, *Pensamientos sobre el Perú* (1875), p. 43.

38 Quoted in Prado, *Estado social del Perú*, p. 164.

39 *Ibid.*, p. 165.

40 Deustua, review of Prado, p. 20.

41 Varallanos, *El cholo y el Perú* (Buenos Aires, 1962), pp. 232–45.

42 Ugarte, *Bosquejo de la historia económica del Perú* (1926), p. 50.

43 Deustua, *Ante el conflicto*, p. 49.

44 Orrego, *El pueblo continente: ensayos para una interpretación de América Latina* (Santiago de Chile, 1939), p. 29.

45 Varallanos, *El cholo*, pp. 209, 112.

46 Solari Swayne, 'Los paises se levantan sobre afirmaciones', *El Comercio* (a leading Lima daily), 24 March 1964.

47 Varallanos, *El cholo*, pp. 120, 176.

48 Puente Candamo, 'Sobre Juan José Vega y *La guerra de los Viracochas*', *El Comercio*, 12 January 1964. Of outstanding importance on the topic is 'Sumario del Congreso Sobre Mestizaje', *Revista Histórica*, Vol. XXVIII (1965).

CHAPTER 2

1 See Bailey W. Diffie, *Latin American Civilization: Colonial Period* (Harrisburg, Pennsylvania, 1945), pp. 366–81.

2 See the excellent study by Arthur P. Whitaker, *The Huancavelica Mercury Mine* (Cambridge, Massachusetts, 1941).

3 Diffie, *Latin American Civilization*, p. 590.

4 Clarence H. Haring, *The Spanish Empire in America* (New York, 1947), pp. 281–2.

5 See the penetrating study of John Howland Rowe, 'The Incas Under Spanish Colonial Institutions', *The Hispanic American Historical Review*, XXXVII, No. 2 (May 1957), 155–99.

6 This thesis is developed by the Peruvian Jesuit historian, Rubén Vargas Ugarte in Vol. IV of his *Historia de la Iglesis en el Perú* (Burgos, Spain, 1961).

7 Two of the best studies on castes and discrimination in colonial Peru are José Varallanos, *Legislación indiana republicana* (1947), which in spite of what the title seems to indicate contains much material on the colonial period, and the same author's *El derecho indiano a través de 'Nueva Crónica' y su influencia en la vida social peruana* (1946).

8 See John Lynch, *Spanish Colonial Administration, 1782–1810: The Intendant System in the Viceroyalty of the Rio de la Plata* (London, 1958), and F. B. Pike, 'The Cabildo and Colonial Loyalty to Hapsburg Rulers', *Journal of Inter-American Studies*, II, No. 4 (October 1960), 405–20.

9 Haring, *The Spanish Empire*, p. 72.

10 Jorge Cornejo Bouroncle, *Túpac Amaru, la revolución precursora de la emancipación continental* (Cuzco, 1949), and B. Lewin, *La rebelión de Túpac Amaru y los origines de la emancipación americana* (Buenos Aires, 1957), argue that the goal of the uprising was independence. Carlos Daniel Valcárcel, *La rebelión de Túpac Amaru* (México, DF, 1947), is more persuasive in viewing the movement as one seeking reform within a continuing colonial structure.

11 A large section of the Baquíjano discourse is reproduced in Felipe

Barreda Laos, *Vida intelectual del virreinato del Perú* (Buenos Aires, 1937), pp. 317–26.

12 For an excellent analysis of the address see Joss de la Riva Agüero y Osma, 'Don José Baquíjano y Carillo', in Raúl Porras Barrenechea and Riva Agüero, *Precursores de la emancipación* (1957), pp. 22–6. See also Carlos Deustua Pimentel, *José Baquíjano y Carillo* (1963).

13 Quoted in Barreda, *Vida intelectual*, pp. 62–3.

14 On Rodríguez de Mendoza see Jorge Guillermo Leguía, *El precursor: ensayo biográfico de D. Toribio Rodríguez de Mendoza* (1922), Pedro García y Sanz, *Apuntes para la historia eclesiástica del Perú* (1876), and two works of José Toribio Polo, *Apuntes biográficos del Doctor Don Toribio Rodríguez* (1886), and 'Don Toribo Rodríguez', *El Tiempo* (a Lima daily), 19 September 1864. See also the monumental biographical work on colonial and early independence figures compiled by Manuel de Mendiburu (1805–80), *Diccionario histórico biográfico del Perú*, 11 vols (second edition, 1931–4), with additions and biographical notes by Evaristo San Cristóval. Vol. VII, pp. 134 ff, contains material on Rodríguez de Mendoza. Also useful is Oscar N. Zevallos, *Toribio Rodríguez de Mendoza* (1963). Information on Cisneros is contained in the above works, especially in Mendiburu, *Diccionario*, II, p. 381.

15 See Carlos Miró Quesada Laos, *Historia del periodismo peruano* (1957), pp. 25 ff. for a good account of Peruvian journalism during this period. On Unánue see Luis Alayza y Paz Soldán, *Hipólito Unánue* (1952), Percy Cayo, *Hipólito Unánue* (1963), and José Miguel Vélez Picasso, *Unánue periodista* (1955).

16 On Sánchez Carrión see Alfonso Pérez Buonanni, *José Faustino Sánchez Carrión* (1963), Luis León Pezutti, *El prócer olvidado* (1935), dealing with the rôle of Sánchez Carrión in freemasonry and in the emancipation period in general, and Raúl Porras, 'José Faustino Sánchez Carrión, el tribuno de la república peruana', in Porras and Riva Agüero, *Precursores*.

17 Jorge Guillermo Leguía, *Manuel Lorenzo de Vidaurre: historia y biografía* (Santiago de Chile, 1936), p. 41. On Vidaurre see also Leguía, *Vidaurre: contribución a un ensayo de interpretación sicológica* (1935), Estuardo Núñez, *Manuel Lorenzo de Vidaurre, ciudadano de América* (1945), and Raúl Porras, 'Semblanzas de Manuel Lorenzo de Vidaurre', *Boletín del Museo Bolivariano* (1929).

18 Vidaurre, *Plan del Perú* (Philadelphia, 1823), pp. 164 ff.

19 As late as 1820 Vidaurre was still arguing for reform of Peru within the colonial framework. In that year he published *Votos de los americanos a la nación española, y nuestro amado monarca el Señor Don Fernando VII: verdadero concordato entre españoles, europeos y americanos* . . . .

20 Prologue of Jorge Fernández Stoll to J. G. Leguía, *Manuel Lorenzo de Vidaurre*, p. v.

21 Raúl Porras, *Mariano José de Arce* (1927), p. 36. See also Francisco Mostajo, *Eulogio de prócer Arequipeño Mariano José de Arce* (Arequipa, 1931).

22 See Luis Alberto Sánchez, *Los poetas de la revolución* (1919), esp. p. 53.

23 On the Pumacahua uprising see Luis Antonio Eguiguren, *La revolución de 1814* (1914), and José Manuel Valega, *La gesta emancipadora del Perú*, 12 vols (1940–44), esp. III. This massive study by a Peruvian historian born in 1887 covers the period from 1770 to 1826, giving detailed information about a great number of Peruvian insurrections prior to the arrival of San Martín.

24 Basadre, 'Conferencia en la Escuela de Ingenieros de la Universidad Nacional de San Marcos', *Letras*, Año I, Vol. II, No. 2 (1929), p. 581.

25 Raúl Porras was one of several Peruvian historians who took pride in the number of abortive revolutions that occurred within the viceroyalty between 1810 and 1820. He argued that the failure of Peruvians to achieve outstanding results was not due to lack of effort but to the presence on their soil of massive royalist armies. See his *Arce*, pp. 81–9.

26 See *Segunda edición del discurso presentado al soberano congreso por D. Francisco Javier Moreno, aumentada con un discurso preliminar e ilustrado con notas* (1823).

27 See prologue of Alberto Tauro to Luna Pizarro, *Escritos políticos* (1959), p. xii. Tauro includes a valuable bibliography of works on Luna Pizarro, pp. xxxix–xl.

28 Julio Valdez Garrido, *De Bolívar a Haya de la Torre* (Piura, 1945), p. 40.

29 A description made by a contemporary of Luna Pizarro and quoted in V. A. Belaúnde, *Peruanidad* (1957), p. 309.

30 Raúl Ferrero Rebagliati, *El liberalismo peruano* (1958), p. 89.

31 Peruvian historians are divided in their evaluation of San Martín. The nineteenth-century liberal Santiago Távara, *Historia de los partidos*, published in Lima's *El Comercio* in instalment form and finally as a book in 1951 with notes by Jorge Basadre and Félix Denegri Luna, criticizes San Martín for his monarchical leanings. A San Martín partisan among more recent historians is conservatively-inclined J. A. de la Puente Candamo, *San Martín y el Perú* (1948). Quite objective in treating the matter is César Pacheco Vélez, *Sobre el monarquismo de San Martín* (Seville, 1952). See also José M. Vélez Picasso, *San Martín y el periodismo peruano* (1950), containing a good account of the polemic over the suitable form of govern-

ment that raged in Peru at the time of San Martín's protectorate.
32 For a summary of the main political views expressed in the assembly that framed the 1823 constitution see *Bases de la constitución: política del Perú* (1822), signed by Francisco Javier de Lúna Pizarro, Hipólito Unánue, José de Olmedo, Manuel Pérez de Tudela and Justo Figuerola.
33 José Pareja Paz Soldán, *Historia de las constituciones nacionales* (1943), pp. 32–3.
34 Villarán, *Páginas escogidas* (1962), p. 42.
Additional Bibliographical Suggestions. The following are works of basic importance dealing with the independence period which were not specifically cited in this chapter's notes: Jorge Basadre, *La iniciación de la república* (1929) and *La promesa en la vida peruana y otros ensayos* (1958); Seminario de Historia del Instituto Riva Agüero, *La causa de la emancipación del Perú: testimonios de la época precursora* (1960), an important compilation of documents and articles prepared by some of Peru's leading historians; Rómulo Cuneo Vidal, *Historia de las insurrecciones de Tacna por la independencia del Perú* (1961 edition), with a prologue by Jorge Basadre; Pedro Dávalos y Lissón, *Historia republicana del Perú*, 8 vols (1931–8), dealing with the period from independence to 1870; A. Nieto Vélez, *Contribución a la historia del fidelismo en el Perú, 1808–10* (1960); Manuel de Odriozola, *Documentos históricos del Perú*, 10 vols (1863–77), an important collection of primary source material pertaining to the 1800–1830 period; César Pacheco Vélez, 'La idea del Perú en la independencia,' *Mercurio Peruano*, Año XXXVII, No. 324 (1954), one of several important articles in this and immediately succeeding numbers of the periodical in which eminent Peruvian historians consider the emancipation era; J. A. de la Puente Candamo, *La idea de la comunidad peruana y el testimonio de los precursores* (1956); Vicente Rodríguez Casado and Guillermo Lohmann Villena, *Memoria de gobierno del Virrey Joaquín de la Pezuela* (Seville, 1947), on the 1816–21 period when Pezuela, the Marquis of Viluma, served as viceroy; Humberto Ugolotti Dansay, *La cultura como causa determinante de la independencia de América* (1963), a somewhat misleading title as only the first of three essays in the work deals with the announced subject; Nemisio Vargas, *Historia del Perú independiente*, 9 vols (1903–42), covering the period from the independence movement to 1839; Rubén Vargas Ugarte, *Historia del Perú: emancipación, 1809–1825* (Buenos Aires, 1958); and Benjamín Vicuña Mackenna, *La revolución de la independencia del Perú, 1809–1819* (Lima editions of 1860 and 1942), a valuable treatment of the period by one of Chile's most renowned nineteenth-century historians, included originally in his massive study of San Martín. Finally, on the general question as to what factors were most important in influencing the emancipation movement in Latin

America as a whole, see R. A. Humphreys and John Lynch, editors, *The Origins of the Latin American Revolutions, 1808–1826* (New York, 1965).

CHAPTER 3

1 On the life of Eléspuru see Felipe A. Barreda, *Eléspuru* (1957).

2 Olmedo's poem celebrating the triumph of Bolívar at Junín is especially famous. See Olmedo, *Poesías completas* (México, DF, 1947 edition), with a valuable preliminary study by the Ecuadoran Jesuit Aurelio Espinosa Polit.

3 On these events and on the subsequent participation of Riva Agüero in Peruvian politics see his *Memorias y documentos para la historia de la independencia del Perú y causas del mal éxito que ha tenido esta*, 2 vols (Paris, 1858), published under the pseudonym of Pruvonena. For a general description of 1823–45 events, stressing military aspects, see the standard military history of Peru, Carlos Dellepiane, *Historia militar del Perú*, 2 vols (1943 edition) and Manuel de Mendiburu, *Biografías de generales republicanos* (1963), with an introduction by Manuel Moreyra Paz Soldán and edited by Félix Denegri Luna. Prepared by nineteenth-century historian Mendiburu, this work was never published during his lifetime. When it finally appeared it benefited from the superb editing and annotation of Denegri Luna.

4 On these events see Luis Alayza y Paz Soldán, *Hipólito Unánue, San Martín, y Bolívar*, 2 vols (1952) and Víctor Modesto Villavicencio, *Sánchez Carrión: ministro general de Bolívar* (1955).

5 Quoted by M. V. Villarán in *Páginas escogidas* (1962), p. 13. On Bolívar's political ideology see also V. A. Belaúnde, *Bolívar and the Political Thought of the Spanish American Revolution* (Baltimore, 1938).

6 On the constitution see José Pareja Paz Soldán, *Historia de las constituciones nacionales* (1943), pp. 11, 37–46.

7 See the 6 April 1826 letter of Bolívar to La Fuente, quoted by Denegri in his notes to Mendiburu, *Biografías*, p. 197.

8 For a typical expression of Peruvian resentment against Bolívar because of the creation of Bolivia as an independent republic see José C. Ulloa, 'La cuestión boliviana', *Revista de Lima*, No. 10 (15 February 1860), pp. 561–2.

9 Pareja Paz Soldán, *Historia de las constituciones*, p. 46.

10 See Antonine Tibesar, 'The Shortage of Priests in Latin America: A Historical Evaluation of Werner Prompter's *Priesternot in Lateinamerika*', *The Americas*, XXII, No. 4 (April 1966), 413–20.

11 See Watt Stewart, *Chinese Bondage in Peru* (Durham, North Carolina, 1951).

12 Part of the material on treatment of Indians in nineteenth-century Peru is based on the third chapter of a book-length study of the development of the Peruvian industrial labour force written by the University of Wisconsin sociologist David Chaplin. Professor Chaplin was kind enough to make his manuscript available to the author prior to its publication. See also Thomas R. Ford, *Man and Land in Peru* (Gainesville, Florida, 1955) and George Kubler, *The Indian Caste of Peru, 1795–1940* (Washington, DC, 1952).

13 Quoted in Mendiburu, *Biografías*, p. 147.

14 *Ibid.*, p. 147.

15 On La Mar see Luis Alayza y Paz Soldán, *El Gran Mariscal José de la Mar* (1941), sometimes uncritically favourable to the officer-politician, and Pío Jaramillo Alvarado, *El Gran Mariscal José de la Mar: su posición histórica* (Quito, 1950), written by an Ecuadoran and perhaps the best study of La Mar.

16 See Miguel V. Merino Schroeder, *El Portete de Tarqui: victoria peruana* (Callao, 1950).

17 See Gamarra, *Epistolario* (1952), edited by Alberto Tauro who shows considerable sympathy for the general, and Miguel A. Martínez, *El Mariscal de Piquiza, don Agustín Gamarra* (1946), a well-documented work of Peruvian historical revisionism presenting Gamarra in a favourable light.

18 See the intriguing study by historian and psychiatrist Juan B. Lastres, *Una neurosis celebre: el estraño caso de 'La Mariscala' Francisca Zubiaga Bernales de Gamarra, ensayo de interpretación histórico-psicológico-psiquiátrico* (1945).

19 On Orbegoso see *Memorias del Gran Mariscal Don Luis José de Orbegoso* (1939) and *Colección de documentos del Gran Mariscal Don Luis José de Orbegoso,* 3 vols (1908–29).

20 Manuel Mújico Gallo, *Nuestro Castilla* (1955), pp. 62–3. On Nieto see Pedro Ruiz Bravo, *Apuntes históricos sobre la vida militar del Gran Mariscal Don Domingo Nieto* (1942).

21 An excellent account of this period is Modesto Basadre y Chocano, *Diez años de historia política del Perú, 1834–1844* (1953 edition). See also N. A. M. Cleven, 'The Dictators of Peru', in A. C. Wilgus, editor, *South American Dictators during the First Century of Independence* (Washington, DC, 1937).

22 See Jorge Basadre, *La multitud, la ciudad, y el campo en la historia del Perú* (1929), pp. 221–9.

23 Echenique's memoirs, written with a certain dignity and detachment, are a valuable source for nineteenth-century Peruvian history: *Memorias para la historia del Perú,* 2 vols (1952 edition).

24 Jorge Basadre, 'Los hombres de traje Negro', *Letras,* Año I, Vol. 1 (1929), p. 38.

25 Luna Pizarro expressed these ideas in an important 1832 discourse contained in his *Escritos políticos* (1959), pp. 195–6.

26 On Vigil see Carlos Alberto González, *Francisco de Paula González Vigil, el precursor, el justo, el maestro* (1961), a glowingly favourable account, and Rubén Vargas Ugarte, 'Algunos datos para la biografía de don Francisco de Paula González Vigil', *El Amigo del Clero*, Nos. 1610–12 (July–September 1959), and Nos. 1613–14 (October–November 1959), a prejudiced, at times almost slanderous attack against Vigil. Unfortunately, there is no satisfactory biography of the great Tacna liberal.

27 Luna Pizarro revealed his disillusionment and implied that only a moral regeneration based on the teachings of Catholicism could save Peru in an 1833 discourse contained in his *Escritos políticos*, p. 303.

28 Editorial, almost certainly written by Pando, in *La Verdad*, No. 22, 13 February 1833.

29 *Ibid.*, No. 1, 5 December 1832, and a quotation of Pando in Villarán, *Páginas escogidas*, pp. 64–6. See also Pando, *Pensamiento y apuntes sobre moral y política* (Cadiz, 1835). Then in exile in Spain and destined never to return to Peru, Pando in this book bitterly assailed every aspect of liberal ideology.

30 On Pardo see the prologue written by his son, Manuel, President of Peru 1872–76, to *Poesías y escritos en prosa de don Felipe Pardo* (Paris, 1869), and Evaristo San Cristóval, *Manuel Pardo y Lavalle, su vida y su obra* (1945), esp. pp. 11 ff.

31 The quotation of Pando is in Villarán, *Páginas escogidas*, p. 66.

32 J. Basadre, 'Los hombres de traje Negro', p. 29.

33 See Manuel Bilbao, *Historia del Jeneral Salaverry* (1853). This interesting work by the brother of Chile's fiery nineteenth-century liberal Francisco Bilbao appeared in a useful 1936 edition with notes and a prologue by Evaristo San Cristóval.

34 A generally reliable work on Santa Cruz is Alfonso Crespo, *Santa Cruz, el Condor Indio* (México, DF, 1944). See also Agustín Iturricha, *Historia de Bolivia bajo la administración del Mariscal Andrés Santa Cruz*, 2 vols (Sucre, Bolivia, 1920).

35 On Chile's intervention directed against the Peru–Bolivia confederation see Robert N. Burr, *By Reason or Force: Chile and the Balancing of Power in South America, 1830–1905* (Berkeley and Los Angeles, 1965), pp. 33–57.

36 Fortunately Valdivia has written on many of the Arequipa revolutions and his rôle in them: *Memorias sobre las revoluciones de Arequipa desde 1834 hasta 1866* (1874). See also José de la Riva Agüero y Osmo, 'El dean Valdivia y la confederación Peru–Boliviana', *El Comercio*, 1 May 1936.

37   On the confederation see Dante Herrera Alarcón, *Rebeliones que intentaron desmembrar el sur del Perú* (1961). Useful but with less thorough research is Carlos Neuhaus Rizo–Patrón, *El estado sud-peruano* (1948).

38   E. San Cristóval, 'El primer buque vapor que llegó al Callao', *El Comercio*, 10 March 1964.

39   Mendiburu, *Biografías*, p. 283.

40   J. Basadre quoted by J. Pareja Paz Soldán in *Historia de las constituciones*, p. 84.

41   See Clements Markham, *Cuzco: a Journey to the Ancient Capital of Peru* ... (London, 1856), p. 351. See also E. San Cristóval, *Manuel Ignacio Vivanco* (not dated). On events in Peru during the rule of Vivanco see the excellent account of the French traveller Max Radiquet who was in the country in 1844: *Souvenirs l'amerique espagnole* (Paris, 1856).

42   J. Basadre, 'El Regenerador': contribución al estudio de los caudillos y de los partidos en el Perú', *Mercurio Peruano*, Nos. 75–6 (September–October 1924).

43   Jorge Guillermo Leguía, *Estudios históricos* (1939), p. 201.

CHAPTER 4

1   Some of the useful Peruvian works on Castilla not cited elsewhere in the notes include: Luis Alayza y Paz Soldán, *He aquí Ramón Castilla* (1955), consisting of judgements on Castilla made by his contemporaries and liberally sprinkled with revealing quotations of the soldier-president; *Archivo Castilla* (1956–63), a work of funda-mental importance made up of Castilla's manifestos, messages, pro-clamations and letters and edited by such distinguished historians as Alberto Tauro, Félix Denegri Luna, Evaristo San Cristóval, and Pedro Ugarteche, and which by 1963 had grown to four volumes; F. Mario Bazán, *Comentario en torno a Castilla* (1958); Víctor Andrés Belaúnde, *El Libertador Mariscal Castilla* (1951); Félix Denegri Luna, *Ramón Castilla* (1963); Jorge Dulanto Pinillos, *Ramón Castilla* (1944), a perceptive historical-novel approach to the life of Castilla that has gone through several editions; Sara Patiño Ráez, 'Ensayo de una bibliografía Castillista', *Fenix*, No. 10 (1954), an important bibliographical study; Perú, Escuela Militar, *El Libertador Mariscal Castilla: aspectos de su obra; homenaje al* ... (1951), con-sisting of essays by some of Peru's leading intellectual figures; Rogelio Toro Díaz, *Castilla, libertador y guerrero, 1854–1954* (1955); Rubén Vargas Ugarte, *Ramón Castilla* (Buenos Aires, 1962); Carlos Wiesse, *Biografía en anecdotas del Gran Mariscal don Ramón Castilla* (1924), a warm portrayal of Castilla based on anecdotes and the

testimony of other writers, prepared by a man who was one of Peru's most eminent early twentieth-century historians.

2 Miguel A. Martínez, *La vida heróica del Gran Maríscal don Ramón Castilla* (1952), p. 130. This is one of the most valuable Castilla biographies.

3 V. A. Belaúnde, *Peruanidad* (1957), p. 514.

4 Castilla, *Ideología* (1948), pp. 40–41. This useful work consists of excerpts from the writings and speeches of Castilla, selected, annotated and with a prologue by Alberto Tauro.

5 See J. J. von Tschudi, *Travels in Peru during the Years 1838–1842* (London, 1847), esp. pp. 194–201, and José Varallanos, *Bandoleros en el Perú* (1937).

6 See Manuel Mújica Gallo, *Castilla, soldado de la ley* (1952).

7 Martínez, *Vida heróica*, p. 133.

8 Martínez, *Vida heróica*, p. 116.

9 *Ibid.*, p. 135.

10 See Castilla, *Ideología*, pp. 19–20, and Pedro Dávlos y Lissón, *La primera centuria: causas geográficas, políticas, y económicas que han detenido el progreso moral y material del Perú en el primer siglo de su vida independiente* (1926), IV, p. 11. Valuable works dealing with Castilla's continentalism and other aspects of Peruvian foreign policy include Oscar Barrenechea y Rayaga, *Congresos y conferencias internacionales celebrados en Lima, 1847–1894* (Buenos Aires, 1947); Arturo García Salazar, *Historia diplomática del Perú* (1928); José Pareja Paz Soldán, *Para una bibliografía diplomática del Perú: publicaciones oficiales de la Cancillería peruana* (1950), a helpful bibliographical guide; Alberto Ulloa Sotomayor, *Congresos americanos de Lima*, 2 vols (1938), consisting mainly of documents pertaining to the American Congress of 1847 and its antecedents; the Continental Treaty of 1856; the Congress of 1864 aimed at achieving a solid South American front against the threat of Spanish imperialism; and the American Council of Jurisconsults, 1877.

11 Martínez, *Vida heróica*, p. 138.

12 See Raúl Porras, *Fuentes históricas peruanas* (1963), p. 490.

13 Castilla, *Ideología*, p. 33.

14 Emilio Romero, *Historia económica del Perú* (1949), p. 148. For good accounts of Castilla's first-term economic policies see in addition César Antonio Ugarte, *Bosquejo de la historia económica del Perú* (1926), pp. 107–20, and Alberto Ulloa, *Don Nicolás de Piérola: una época de la historia del Perú* (1949), p. 63. See also A. J. Duffield, *Peru in the Guano Age* (London, 1877).

15 Félix Denegri Luna, note in Manuel Mendiburu, *Biografías de generales republicanos* (1963), p. 419.

16 For an accurate appraisal of the Herrera position see Raúl Ferrero,

El liberalismo peruano (1958), p. 152, and Raúl Porras, *Fuentes*, p. 276. For a very favourable account see Oscar Barrenechea y Rayada, *Bartolomé Herrera: educador y diplomático peruano, 1808–1864* (Buenos Aires, 1947) and *La primera legación del Perú en los estados pontíficos y en las cortes de Italia en 1852* (1940), a study of the mission Herrera made to Rome in the attempt to negotiate a concordat between the Vatican and Peru. Bartolomé Herrera, *Escritos y discursos*, 2 vols (1929–30), annotated and with a prologue by Jorge Guillermo Leguía, includes an adulatory biography written by Gonzalo and Rodrigo Herrera.

17 The Peruvian *sol* at the time was worth some forty cents. in comparison to the United States dollar.

18 Note of Denegri Luna in Mendiburu, *Biografías*, p. 421. For adverse appraisals of the Echenique administration see also Felipe Barriga Alvarez, *El gobierno del General Echenique* (1864). In his *Memorias para la historia del Perú, 1808–1878*, 2 vols (1952), Echenique makes a restrained and at times convincing defence of his administration.

19 Some of the Elías letters were collected and published in 1855 as *Manifesto de D. Domingo Elías a la nación.*

20 See Alberto Tauro, 'El conflicto Peru–Boliviano de 1853 como causa de la revolución de 1854', *Letras*, segundo cuatrimestre (1936), pp. 294–9.

21 See Távara, *Abolición de la esclavitud* (1955).

22 Manuel Mújica Gallo, 'Pasión libertaria de Ramón Castilla', *Revista Fanal*, No. 39 (1954) argues that humanitarian idealism motivated the decrees emancipating the slaves and freeing the Indians from tribute. Emilio Romero, *Historia económica*, pp. 288–9, is among the historians attributing the decrees to expediency.

23 See Manuel Labarthe, *Pedro Gálvez y la abolición del tributo indígena* (1954), a highly informative pamphlet.

24 See Alfonso Benavides Correa, *Herrera y Gálvez en la trayectoria política de la vida republicana del Perú* (1944).

25 See Escudero, *Exposición que hace el diputado Ignacio Escudero ante la nación i la provincia de Piura de sus tareas parlamentarios en la convención nacional de 1855* (Piura, 1858), and Carlos Chávez Sánchez, *Ignacio Escudero: tribuno de la convención nacional de 1855* (1950).

26 See Tejeda, *Libertad de la industria* (1948), prologue and notes by Alberto Tauro.

27 On the stormy debates of the constituent assembly out of which arose the 1856 Constitution see Perú, Congreso 1855–57, *Actas oficiales y extractos de las sesiones en que fue discutido la constitución de 1856* (1911).

28 See José Pareja Paz Soldán, *Historia de las constituciones nacionales* (1943), pp. 100–101.

29 Castilla, *Ideología*, p. 39.

30 See *Breve noticia de la fundación y transformación de la Facultad de Filosofía y Letras por los alumnos de historia del Perú bajo la dirección de Carlos Wiesse* (1918).

31 In addition to the works cited in note 11 on diplomatic history see *Correspondencia cambiada con la legación del Perú en la república Argentina sobre el Tratado Continental celebrado en Santiago de Chile, 15 de setiembre, 1856* (Buenos Aires, 1856).

32 Castilla, *op. cit.*, pp. 48–50.

33 Manuel Mújica Gallo, *Nuestro Castilla* (1955), p. 41.

34 See César Antonio Ugarte, 'La política agraria de la república', *Mercurio Peruano*, Año VI, No. 59 (May, 1923), pp. 673–6, and Watt Stewart, *The Chinese Bondage in Peru* (Durham, North Carolina, 1951).

35 See, for example, José Casimiro Ulloa, 'La hacienda pública', *Revista de Lima*, No. 6 (1 December 1859), 224–9.

36 Ugarte, *Bosquejo de la historia económica*, pp. 119–22.

37 Ulloa, 'La hacienda pública', *Revista de Lima*, No. 8 (15 January 1860). For other adverse appraisals of Castilla's economic programme see Carlos Barroilhet, *Grandeza ó decadencia del Perú* (Paris, 1858); Manuel Atanasio Fuentes, *Biografía del Excmo. e Ilustrísimo Señor Don Ramón Castilla, Libertador del Perú, escrito por el mas fiel de sus adoradores* (Valparaíso, Chile, 1856), a satirical pamphlet; Felipe Masías, *Curso elemental de economía política* (1860); and José Manuel Osores, *Conferencia dada en el Ateneo de Lima: causas económicas de la decadencia de la república y medidas que podian adoptarse para mejorar la situación* (1856).

38 Dávalos y Lissón, *Primera centuria*, IV, p. 135. A similar appraisal of Castilla's economic policy was made earlier by Francisco García Calderón, *Diccionario de legislación peruana* (1879), I, p. 220.

39 Denegri Luna, note in Mendiburu, *Biografías*, p. 327.

40 Reference to the allegedly monarchical leanings of Vivanco is found in William Columbus Davis, *The Last of the Conquistadores: The Spanish Intervention in Peru and Chile, 1863–1866* (Athens, Georgia, 1950), pp. 108, 118–9. The fact that other conservatives at the time entertained monarchical aspirations is revealed in Felipe Masías, *Examen comparativo de la monarquía y de la república* (1867).

41 A favourable biography of Prado is by Luis Humberto Delgado, *Mariano Ignacio Prado, caudillo y prócer del Perú* (1952).

42 For information on the 1867 constituent assembly and the heated debates which its preparation of a constitution provoked see Perú, Comisión de la Constitución de 1867. *Proyecto de constitución que la*

comisión de esta nombre presenta al congreso constituyente de 1867 (1867), signed by J. M. Quimper, Francisco García Calderón, Modesto Macedo, and others; and Perú, Congreso, *Diario de debates del congreso constituyente de 1867* (1867).

43 Dávalos y Lissón, *Primera centuria*, IV, pp. 210–12.

44 Martínez, *Vida heróica*, p. 229, and Mújica Gallo, *Nuestro Castilla*, p. 45.

45 Martínez, *op. cit.*, pp. 139–40.

CHAPTER 5

1 The best biography of Balta is Geraldo Arosemena Garland, *Coronel José Balta* (1945).

2 Luis Alayza y Paz Soldán, *Mi país: Peruanidad; Ricardo Palma; Flora Tristán; la viborita de Mahoma; recurso de fuerza; vandalismo* (1962), p. 272.

3 See Jorge Guillermo Leguía, *Hombres e ideas en el Perú* (Santiago de Chile), pp. 105 ff.

4 Alberto Ulloa, *Don Nicolás de Piérola, una época en la historia del Perú* (1949) is the standard biography of Piérola. A brief but useful work is Enrique Chirinos, *Nicolás de Piérola* (1963). Somewhat distorted and based primarily on the sensationalist newspaper accounts of the period is Jorge Dulanto Pinillos, *Nicolás de Piérola* (1947).

5 On the mining resources of Peru during this period see Carlos Jiménez, *Evolución histórica de la minera en el Perú* (1924).

6 For the economic thought of Luis Benjamín Cisneros see his *Cuestiones económicas del Perú* (1866).

7 See Raúl Porras Barrenechea, *Luciano Benjamín Cisneros, abogado representivo del siglo XIX: 1832–1906* (1956).

8 See Jorge Basadre, *Meditaciones sobre el destino histórico del Perú* (1947), pp. 121–2; Pedro Dávalos y Lissón, *La primera centuria:* ... *Perú en el primer siglo de su vida independiente* (1926), IV, pp. 234–308; Raúl Ferrero Rebagliati, 'Visión de la república', *Revista Fanal*, No. 45 (1955); Luis Alberto Sánchez, *El Perú, retrato de un país adolescente* (1963), p. 21; and Ulloa, *Don Nicolás de Piérola*, pp. 73–194.

9 See Francisco García Calderón R., *En torno al Perú y América* (1954), pp. 57–8; José Carlos Mariátegui, *Siete ensayos de interpretación de la realidad peruana* (1959), p. 17; and Manuel Vicente Villarán, *Páginas escogidas* (1962), p. 461.

10 See Basadre, 'El Perú republicano', in Darío Sainte Marie, editor, *Perú en cifras* (1945), pp. 645 ff. For an excellent biography of Meiggs see Watt Stewart, *Henry Meiggs, Yankee Pizarro* (Durham, North Carolina, 1946).

11 See Pardo, 'Estudios sobre Jauja', *Revista de Lima*, esp. No. 1 (1 October 1859).

12 Quoted in Ulloa, *Don Nicolás de Piérola*, p. 70.

13 The anticlerical spirit that sometimes animated the Beneficence Society is revealed by José Antonio García y García, *Memoria presentada a la sociedad de beneficencia pública de esta capital sobre el colegio* ... *de nuestra Señora de O, por el inspector del turno* (1875).

14 See Pardo's 16 November 1871 discourse, extensively quoted in Evaristo San Cristóval, *Manuel Pardo y Lavalle: su vida y su obra* (1945), pp. 283–5. The San Cristóval work is a highly useful biography. Other valuable studies are Nicanor Camino, *Rasgos característicos del Ilustre Manuel Pardo* (1886), Jacinto López, *Manuel Pardo* (1947), a monumental work by a Venezuelan historian that carries the story of Pardo up to 1866, and the broadly-ranging collection of opinions dealing with Pardo compiled by Alfredo Moreno Mendiguren, *Manuel Pardo y Lavalle* (1961).

15 García Calderón R., *En torno al Perú*, p. 58.

16 See Guillermo J. Guevara, 'Origin de los partidos en el Perú', *Revista de Filosofía y Derecho*, Nos. 4–6 (January–May 1939), 43–8, and Alejandro Revoredo, *La obra nacionalista y democrática del Partido Civil* (1931). Although partial to *Civilismo*, both works are valuable.

17 Basadre, 'El Perú republicano', pp. 646–7.

18 Julio Valdez Garrido, *De Bolívar a Haya de la Torre* (Piura, 1945), p. 8.

19 Joaquín Capelo, *Sociología de Lima* (1895–1902), III, p. 296.

20 See 16 November 1871 address of Pardo quoted in San Cristóval, *Manuel Pardo*, p. 47, and Villarán, *Páginas escogidas*, p. 461.

21 Basadre, 'Las elecciones y las jornadas multitudinarias de 1872', in José Pareja Paz Soldán, editor, *Biblioteca de cultura peruana contemporánea* (1963), III, pp. 566–7, 591. See also Alayza y Paz Soldán, *Mi país*, p. 271, Faustino Silva, *La revolución de los Gutiérrez en julio de 1872* (1927), and Fernando Casós, *La revolución de julio en el Perú* (Valparaíso, Chile, 1872), in which the principal civilian supporter of the Gutiérrez brothers attempts to justify their revolution.

22 See Angélica Palma, *Pancho Fierro, acuarelista limeño* (1935).

23 See Pardo's 21 September 1872 speech quoted in San Cristóval, *Manuel Pardo*, pp. 322–3, and Dávalos y Lissón, *Primera centuria*, IV, pp. 312–14. See also Perú: Congreso, *Diario de los debates, 1872–75* (1872–75), which includes the messages of President Pardo.

24 Pardo described the benefits he had hoped would be derived from the nationalization of the nitrate industry in his 28 July 1876 address to congress. See Perú: Presidentes, *Mensajes de los presidentes del Perú,*

selection and notes by Pedro Ugarteche and Evaristo San Cristóval (1943), II, pp. 105 ff. For a favourable account of Pardo's conduct of economic affairs see Alejandro Revoredo, *Apuntes de historia política y financiera* (1939). For a highly critical account see Mariano Amezaga, *Perú, galería financiera* (1873).

25 Dávalos y Lissón, *Primera centuria*, IV, p. 369, and Aníbal Maúrtua, *El porvenir del Perú* (1911), p. 6.

26 David Cornejo Foronda, *D. Manuel Pardo y la educación nacional*, with a prologue by Evaristo San Cristóval (1953), p. 13. See also Felipe Barreda Laos, *Las reformas de instrucción pública* (1919), and J. A. García y García, *La escuela primeria* (1878). An influential senator during the Pardo régime, García y García was one of the leading supporters of the move to reform primary education so as to give it a practical orientation.

27 Francisco García Calderón, *Diccionario de legislación peruana* (1879), I, p. 901.

28 San Cristóval, *Manuel Pardo*, pp. 286–90.

29 Cornejo Foronda, *Manuel Pardo*, p. 93.

30 *Ibid.*, esp. pp. 11–14.

31 Carlos Miró Quesada, *Autopsía de los partidos políticos* (1961), p. 58. Although sometimes showing a pro-*Civilista* bias, this is a valuable study in Peruvian political history.

32 *La Sociedad*, 18 October 1875.

33 William Clarke, *Peru and its Creditors* (London, 1877), gives a colourful account of these events.

34 14 and 15 November 1878 address of Manuel Pardo before the Peruvian Senate, Perú: Congreso, *Diario de los debates de cámara de senadores, 1876–79* (1879), III, pp. 189 ff.

35 See Carlos Camprubí Alcázar, *Historia de los bancos en el Perú* (1957), and Emilio Pruge, *Protección a la industria nacional: a los honorarios representantes del congreso de 1878* (1878).

36 See Pedro Irigoyen, *La alianza Peru-Boliviana–Argentino y la declaratoria de guerra de Chile* (1921).

37 See Basadre, *Historia del Perú republicano* (1962), III, pp. 128 ff.

38 José de la Riva Agüero, *Por la verdad, la tradicion, y la patria* (1937–38), II, p. 59.

39 Miró Quesada, *Autopsía*, p. 145.

40 Some of the standard works dealing with the War of the Pacific from the Peruvian point of view include: Andrés A. Cáceres, *La guerra entre el Perú y Chile, 1879–1883* (Buenos Aires, 1924); Carlos Dellepiane, *Historia militar del Perú*, 2 vols (1943); Clements Markham, *The War Between Peru and Chile, 1879–1882* (London and New York, 1883), published in Lima in a Spanish version as *La guerra entre el Perú y Chile* (1922); Luis Felipe Paz Soldán, *Páginas*

históricas de la guerra del Pacífico (1942); and Mariano Felipe Paz Soldán, *Naración histórica de la guerra de Chile contra el Perú y Bolivia* (Buenos Aires, 1884).

41 Letters of Palma to Piérola, 4 March, 8 April, 29 May and 27 June 1881, in Carlos Milla Batres, editor, *Cartas inéditas de Ricardo Palma* (1964).

42 See Fredrick B. Pike, *Chile and the United States, 1880–1962* (Notre Dame, Indiana, 1963), pp. 45–58.

43 On García Calderón's resentment against the United States see his *La intervención americana en la guerra del Pacífico* (1884). Other expressions of Peruvian resentment over United States policy are found in Mariano Amezaga, *El proceso del civilismo* (Panamá, 1882); Luis Humberto Delgado, *Nuevo Perú* (1945), pp. 189, 227; and Evaristo Gómez Sánchez, *Memorandum sobre la actitud del gobierno de los Estados Unidos de Norte América en el Pacífico* (Buenos Aires, 1882).

44 Ulloa, *Don Nicolás de Piérola*, p. 239.

CHAPTER 6

1 Raúl Porras, quoted in Alfredo Moreno Mendiguren, *Repertorio de noticias breves sobre personajes peruanos* (Madrid, 1956), pp. 274–5.

2 See Emilio Romero, *Historia económica del Perú* (1949), p. 379, and César Antonio Ugarte, *Bosquejo de la historia económica del Perú* (1926), pp. 193–7.

3 See Jorge Guillermo Leguía, *Hombres e ideas en el Perú* (Santiago de Chile, 1941), pp. 45–7. An excellent bibliography on Cáceres is included in this work, pp. 47–53.

4 Enrique Chirinos Soto, *El Perú frente a junio de 1962* (1962), p. 19.

5 For the political ideas of Mariano Nicolás Valcárcel see his *Discursos parlamentarios* (1906), and the anonymous *Rasgos biográficos del Dr Mariano Nicolás Valcárcel* (1890).

6 Alberto Ulloa Sotomayor, *Don Nicolás de Piérola: una época de la historia del Perú* (1949), p. 276.

7 See Luis Humberto Delgado, *El militarismo en el Perú, 1821–1930: la hora suprema de su encubramiento para salvar al país* (1939), p. 17; Leguía, *Hombres e ideas*, pp. 72–80; Carlos Miró Quesada Laos, *Autopsía de los partidos políticos* (1961), pp. 233–40, and *Historia del periodismo peruano* (1957), pp. 185–6; Romero, *Historia económica*, pp. 365 ff.; and Víctor Villanueva Valencia, *El militarismo en el Perú* (1962), pp. 29–33.

8 The anti-Indian bias that characterized much, but by no means all, of Peru's original positivism is reflected strongly in Luis Carranza, *Artículos publicados por Luis Carranza*, 3 vols (1887–88), and Juan

Francisco Pazos Varela, *Tesis sobre la inmigración en el Perú* (1891).

9 See Luis Alberto Sánchez, 'Nuestro año terible', *Letras: Órgano de la Facultad de Letras de San Marcos*, Año I, Vol. I, No. 1, pp. 210–12, and *Breve noticia de la fundación y transformaciones de la facultad de filosfía y letras por los alumnos de historia del Perú bajo la dirección del Catedrático Doctor Carlos Wiesse* (1918), pp. 24 ff.

10 Lissón, *Breves apuntes sobre la sociología del Perú en 1886* (1886), p. 45.

11 *Ibid.*, p. 25.

12 *Ibid.*, pp. 12–13.

13 Quoted in Benvenutto Neptalí, *Bosquejo biográfico de Javier Prado* (1940), p. 18. See also Javier Prado, *Estado social del Perú durante la dominación española* (1941), p. 189. This 1941 edition of Prado's work, which was published originally in 1894, contains interesting reviews of the first edition by two important intellectuals, Alejandro O. Deusuta and Pablo Patrón, as well as an excellent biographical sketch of Prado by Manuel Vicente Villarán.

14 M. V. Villarán, 'Elogio de Prado', in Prado, *Estado social*, p. 2.

15 Prado, *Estado social*, p. 206.

16 *Ibid.*, p. 196.

17 See José Mejía Valera, *Comentarios a la sociología de M. H. Cornejo* (1958), pp. 1–2.

18 Report on 22 September 1928 speech of Cornejo in *La Prensa*, 23 September 1928, and Cornejo, *Sociología general* (Madrid, 1908), I, p. 305.

19 Quoted in José Albino Ruiz, *Biografía del Sr Dr Mariano H. Cornejo* (1942), p. 41.

20 Cornejo, *Sociología*, I, pp. 455–8.

21 *Ibid.*, pp. 349, 379. Cornejo's views on race underwent an evolution. In his *Discurso pronunicado por* ..., *en apertura del año universitario de 1899 sobre los principios generales de la sociología* (1899), there are strong indications of belief in the racial inferiority of Indians. By 1908, however, when he published the first volume of his *Sociología general*, Cornejo had completely repudiated this viewpoint.

22 Capelo, *Sociología de Lima* (1900), III, pp. 322–33.

23 *Ibid.* (1897), II, p. 25.

24 *Ibid.*, III, p. 164.

25 See the sketch of Villarán written by Jorge Basadre in his prologue to a collection of Villarán's writings, *Páginas escogidas* (1962), p. viii.

26 Villarán in *ibid.*, pp. 337–8. For Villarán's ideas on education see also Raúl Porras, 'El Maestro Manuel Vicente Villarán', *La Prensa*, 9 November 1945. The same edition of *La Prensa* contains appraisals of Villarán by Víctor Andrés Belaúnde, José Gálvez Barrenechea, Jorge Basadre, and others.

27 Villarán, *Los profesiones liberales en el Perú, con especial referencia a abogados* (1900), pp. 9, 27–8.
28 Villarán, *Páginas escogidas*, pp. 339–40.
29 *Ibid.*, pp. 329–30.
30 See Eduardo Rada Benavides, *Homenaje del Colegio de Abogados de Lima al Dr José Matías Manzanilla, precursor de la legislación social en el Perú en el acto académico en celebración del día del abogado, 3 abril de 1961* (1961).
31 Manzanilla, 11 October 1912 discourse 'La libertad política y el intervencionismo económico', in *Discursos parlamentarios, 1912–1913* (1915), pp. 171–90.
32 Valuable studies dealing at least in part with the mature Piérola include: Carlos Arenas y Loayza, *Visión de nuestro tiempo: ensayos* (1956), pp. 107 ff.; Rafael Belaúnde, 'Piérola y la juventud', *La Prensa*, 23 July 1956; V. A. Belaúnde, 'Democracia y despotismo en Hispano–América', *Mercurio Peruano*, Año VI, Vol. X, No. 60 (June 1923), pp. 638 ff.; Alfonso Benavides Correa, *Reflexiones sobre el sentido de historia peruana* (1949), pp. 73 ff.; Enrique Chirinos Soto, *Nicolás de Piérola* (1962) and 'La política peruana en el siglo XX', in *Visión del Perú en el siglo XX* (1962), pp. 48 ff.; Raúl Ferrero Rebagliati, 'Visión de la república', *Revista Fanal*, No. 45 (1955); Federico More, *Una multitud contra un pueblo* (1934); Buenaventura Seoane, *Biógrafo americano* (1901), dealing with the principal figures of the *Civilista* and Democratic Parties of the 1895–1901 period; and Alberto Ulloa Sotomayor, *Escritos históricos* (Buenos Aires, 1946).
33 Julio Valdez Garrido, *De Bolívar a Haya de la Torre: estudio de las diferentes ideologías de nuestra historia* (Piura, 1945), p. 70.
34 See *La Prensa*, 12 February 1939.
35 Piérola adopted the gold standard for government fiscal operations, but his recommendation that the country return completely to this standard in all economic transactions was not approved until 1901.
36 See Chirinos Soto, *Perú frente a junio de 1962*, p. 19. See also Ugarte, *Bosquejo*, p. 94, and Villanueva, *Militarismo*, p. 35. Contemporary accounts of Peru's economic rehabilitation under Piérola include Carlos B. Cisneros, *Reseña económica del Perú* (1906), and Waldo Díaz U., *Desde el Perú* (Chiclayo, 1906).
37 Abel Ulloa Cisneros, *Escombros* (1934), p. 34.
38 Emilio Romero, 'El proceso económico del Perú en el siglo XX', *Visión del Perú*, I, p. 99.
39 See Alejandro Garland, *Política externa del Perú: la cuestión de Tacna y Arica* (1898).
40 Partido Democrático, *Declaración de principios* (1912), third edition, with notes by Piérola and others, p. 179. See also J. Basadre, 'El

Perú Republicano', *Historia del Perú desde sus orígines hasta el presente* (1962), III, pp. 132–5.

41 Miró Quesada, *Autopsia*, p. 249.

42 Ulloa Sotomayor, *Piérola*, p. 267.

43 See Joaquín Capelo, *Sociología de Lima*, II, pp. 124–6; Juan Mendoza R., 'El ejército', *Visión del Perú*, I, pp. 294–9; and Villanueva, *Militarismo*, pp. 34–8.

44 J. C. Mariátegui, *Siete ensayos de interpretación de la realidad peruana* (1959), p. 100.

45 Ulloa Sotomayor, *Piérola*, p. 333.

46 For biographical accounts that are highly favourable to González Prada see the semi-novel treatment by Luis Alberto Sánchez, *Don Manuel* (1931), Eugenio Chang-Rodríguez, *La literatura política de González Prada, Mariátegui, y Haya de la Torre* (México, DF, 1957), and the work of his widow, Adriana de González Prada, *Mi Manuel* (1947). Representative of the anti-Prada literature is Ventura García Calderón, *Semblanzas de América* (Madrid, 1920).

47 See F. Bernardino González, *Páginas razonables en oposición a las 'páginas libres'* (1895), II, p. 72.

48 This is the central theme developed in Prada's *El tonel de Diógenes*, published posthumously in 1945.

49 Prada's 'Discurso en el Teatro Olimpo', reproduced in his *Páginas libres* (1894).

50 Prada, 'Propaganda y ataque', in *ibid*.

51 Leguía, *Hombres e ideas*, p. 80.

52 *Ibid*., p. 79.

53 Prada's 'Discourso en el Teatro Politeama', in his *Horas de lucha* (1908).

54 Selections of Prada written in 1906 and 1908, in *Anarquía* (1936, posthumous), pp. 74–5, 93.

55 Selections of Prada written in 1908 in *ibid*., pp. 105–9.

56 Prada, *Nuevas páginas libres* (Santiago de Chile, 1937, posthumous), pp. 55–60.

57 V. A. Belaúnde quoted by Raúl Porras in *Fuentes históricas peruanas* (1963), p. 522.

58 Luis E. Valcárcel, *Tempestad en los Andes* (1927), p. 179.

59 See in particular Prada's 'Nuestros Indios', in *Horas de lucha*.

60 Selection of Prada written in 1906 and included in *Anarquía*, p. 63.

61 *Horas de lucha*, p. 321. For more material on the anti-*cholo* bias of Prada see José Varallanos, *El cholo y el Perú* (1962), p. 239.

62 Quoted in *La Sierra*, Año I, No. 4 (April 1927), p. 38.

63 *Ibid*., p. 34.

64 Carlos Miró Quesada, *Pueblo en crisis* (Buenos Aires, 1946), p. 63.

CHAPTER 7

1 Enrique Chirinos Soto, 'La política peruana en el siglo XX', in José Pareja Paz Soldán, editor, *Visión del Perú en el Siglo XX* (1962), II, pp. 45-6.
2 Emilio Romero, 'El proceso económico del Perú en el Siglo XX', *ibid.*, I, p. 102.
3 José Carlos Mariátegui, *Siete ensayos de interpretación de la realidad peruana* (1959), p. 17.
4 José Pareja Paz Soldán, 'Evolución constitucional del Perú en el siglo XX', in *Visión*, II, p. 3.
5 An important work by Elvira García y García in which she discusses some of her views on feminism is *Tendencias de la educación feminina correspondiente a la misión social que debe llenar la mujer en América* (1908).
6 One of García y García's more significant studies on education is *Educación moderna* (1907).
7 Contemporary works dealing with general social and economic problems include Alejandro Garland, *Artículos económicos publicados en 'El Comercio'* (1901); Santiago Giraldo, *Cuestiones sociales: reforma electoral* (1900); Aníbal Maúrtua, *El porvenir del Perú* (1911); and Sixto Silva Santisteban, *¡Perú adelante!* (1900).
8 See the various studies of Pedro Dávalos y Lissón, especially *La salubridad pública* (1908); *El problema sanitario del Perú* (1910); *La prostitución en Lima* (1908); and *Mortalidad y natividad en el Perú* (1904).
9 See Juan Antonio Portella, *El regimen de las casas de vecindad: necesidad de construir casas higiénicas para obreros* (1903).
10 See Carlos Sutton, 'Irrigation and Public Policy in Peru', in *Proceedings*, Second Pan American Scientific Congress (Washington, DC, 1915-16), III, pp. 840-54; Abraham Rodríguez Dulanto, *El primer problema de la agricultura nacional* (1907), and *Agricultura nacional: primera conferederencia dada en la Sociedad Nacional de Agricultura por Abraham Rodríguez Dulanto* (1904).
11 Contemporary works urging protection of the Indians included: Alberto Ballón Landa, *Estudios de sociología arequipeña* (Arequipa, 1909) and *Los hombres de la selva: apuntes para un ensayo de sociología aplicada* (1917); Ricardo Bustamante Cisneros, *Condición jurídica de las comunidades de indígenas en el Perú* (1919); Félix Cossio, *La propiedad colectiva del ayllu* (Cuzco, 1915); José Antonio Encinas, *El alcoholismo en la raza indígena* (1915), *Causas de la criminalidad indígena en el Perú: ensayo de psicología experimental* (1919) and *Contribución a una legislación tutela indígena* (1918); and Masías

Sánchez, *La raza indígena y los medios de promover su evolución* (Trujillo, 1916).

12 See Víctor Andrés Belaúnde, *Memorias* (1962), III, pp. 94 ff.

13 See Mariano Ibérico Rodríguez, 'Homenaje al Doctor Deustua', *Mercurio Peruano*, Año VI, Vol. XI, Nos 61–2 (July–August 1923), pp. 55–7, and Deustua, *El problema nacional de la educación* (not dated, apparently published between 1901 and 1905), pp. 1–18.

14 See Deustua, *El problema*, esp. pp. 15–18, and 'A propósito de un cuestionario sobre la reforma de la ley de instrucción', in his *Colección de artículos* (1914), esp. p. 56.

15 Alberto Ungaro Cervantes, *Grandes rasgos de un bohemio lírico político soñador: remembranzas de medio siglo* (1947), p. 89.

16 Manuel Vicente Villarán, *Discurso en homenaje a Federico Elguera, al celebrarse el cuarto centenario de la fundación de Lima, 31 de enero, 1935* (1935).

17 Carlos Miró Quesada, *Autopsía de los partidos políticos* (1961), p. 315.

18 J. Guillermo Guevara, 'El origen de los partidos políticos en el Perú', *Revista de Filosofía y Derecho* (Cuzco), Nos 4–6 (January–May 1939), pp. 46–8. See also Aníbal Maúrtua, *Ideales de un constituyente* (1931), p. 6.

19 Luis Antonio Eguiguren, *Recordando a Manuel Candamo, el hombre, el estadista* (1909), p. 67. See also Candamo, *Política peruana* (1903), for a good insight into the political thought of the short-term President.

20 *La Prensa* was founded by Pedro de Osma. Its most influential early editorial writers included the staunch Democrats Alberto Ulloa Cisneros and Enrique Castro Oyaguren.

21 Jorge Basadre, quoted in Alfredo Moreno Mendiguren, compiler, *Repertorio de noticias breves sobre personajes peruanos* (1956), p. 419. See also Germán Arenas, *Algo de una vida, para después de mi muerte* (no date), the valuable reminiscences of a man who served in the Pardo cabinet, and José Carlos Martín, *José Pardo y Barreda* (1948), a very competent biography. Two English-language books which contain useful information on Peru at the time of the first Pardo administration are C. R. Enock, *Peru, Its Former and Present Civilization* (London, 1908), and P. F. Martin, *Peru of the Twentieth Century* (London, 1911).

22 Víctor Villanueva, *El militarismo en el Perú* (1962), pp. 38.

23 See *Mensaje de S. E. José Pardo, Presidente de la República, a congreso ordinario, 28 de julio, 1916* (1916), p. xxxi and the 24 February 1964 editions of *La Prensa* and *El Comercio*, observing the hundredth anniversary of Pardo's birth.

24 On the social legislation proposals which he prepared see

THE MODERN HISTORY OF PERU

Manzanilla, *Accidentes del trabajo* (1907), *El contrato de trabajo* (1907), and *Discursos parlamentarios* (1939, fourth edition).

25 Some of the writings of Luis Miró Quesada on the need for social reform include: *El contrato de trabajo* (1901); *El socialismo intervencionista y su influencia en América* (1908); *La moderna crisis social* (1900); and *La cuestión obrera en el Perú* (1904).

26 See James Carey, *Peru and the United States, 1900–1962* (Notre Dame, Indiana, 1964), pp. 21–3, and Darío Sainte Marie, editor, *Perú en cifras* (1945), pp. 217–20.

27 See Dante Cussato, 'Arana, el hombre que defendió al Perú con su propio ejército', *Dominical*, the Sunday supplement of *El Comercio*, 17 May 1964, and 'Que su padre fue un patriota afirman hijas de Julio Arana', *La Prensa*, 21 May 1964.

28 Emilio Romero, *Historia económica del Perú* (1949), p. 437.

29 See Juan Pedro Paz Soldán, *El golpe de estado de 29 de Mayo de 1909* (1914 edition).

30 Alberto Ulloa Sotomayor, *Don Nicolás de Piérola* (1949), p. 378.

31 The extremely pro-Leguía historian Manuel Capuñay, *Leguía: vida y obra del constructor del Perú* (1952), pp. 177–8, is not convincing when he maintains that a mild, moderate Leguía was forced against his will by a small faction of the *Civilista* oligarchy to pursue a policy of harsh repression against the 1909 plotters.

32 See Jorge Basadre, 'Un fragmento de la historia peruana en el siglo XX: la primera crisis de la república aristocrática hace cincuenta años, la época de Billinghurst', in *Visión del Perú*, II, p. 436.

33 Luis Alberto Sánchez, *Perú, retrato de un país adolescente* (1963), pp. 134–5.

34 Basadre, 'Un fragmento', p. 387.

35 V. A. Belaúnde, *Memorias* (1962), II, p. 19.

36 Villanueva, *Militarismo*, pp. 39–40. Basadre, 'Un fragmento', p. 411, denies that Billinghurst reduced military expenditures.

37 Capuñay, *Leguía,* p. 106.

38 Carlos Miró Quesada, *Sánchez Cerro y su tiempo* (1947), pp. 37 ff.

39 See José Urdanivia Ginés, *Una revolución modelo del ejército peruano* (1945), p. 65, and Villanueva, *Militarismo*, pp. 44–7.

40 A grossly unfair attack on the rule of Benavides is found in Manuel González Prada, *Bajo el oprobrio*, written in 1914 and published posthumously in Paris, 1933.

41 *Mensaje de S. E. Oscar Benavides, el Presidente de la República, al congreso ordinario, 28 de julio de 1914* (1914), p. 16, refers to the Indian violence.

42 Belaúnde, *Memorias*, III, p. 54.

43 Edwin Elmore, editorial in *Mercurio Peruano*, dealing with the generation of 1900, Año VI, Vol. X, No. 56 (February 1923), p. 471.

Elmore was one of the more talented literary figures of Peru who was a spokesman for many of the values of the generation of 1900. *Mercurio Peruano*, founded in 1918 largely owing to the efforts of V. A. Belaúnde, was dedicated principally, though by no means exclusively, to spreading the views of this generation.

44 Belaúnde, *Memorias*, III, p. 31.

45 Riva Agüero, prologue to Oscar Miró Quesada, *Problemas ético-sociológicos* (1907), pp. iv-v.

46 Riva Agüero, *Historia del Perú* (1953), II, p. 409.

47 Raúl Porras Barrenechea, *Fuentes históricas peruanas* (1963), pp. 172–89. Led on by his interest in traditions and the past, Riva Agüero became the outstanding historian produced by Peru in the early twentieth century. On Riva Agüero see the massive and superbly done 'Bio-Bibliografía de José de la Riva Agüero', in *Documenta*, Año III, No. 1 (1951-5), pp. 186–346, prepared by many of Peru's leading historians and men of letters.

48 Belaúnde's 1908 university thesis was entitled *El Peru antiguo y los modernos sociólogos*.

49 Belaúnde, *Memorias*, III, p. 10. See also his *Mi generación en la universidad* (1961).

50 See the Belaúnde editorial, *Mercurio Peruano*, Año I, Vol. 1, No. 1 (July 1918), pp. 50 ff.

51 Belaúnde's ideas on the middle class and other crises in Peru are expressed in *La crisis presente* (1914). See also his *Meditaciones peruanas* (1917).

52 A useful study is Luis Humberto Delgado, *La obra de Francisco García Calderón* (1934).

53 See Ventura García Calderón, *Acerca del generación literaria peruana de 1905* (Paris, 1946). Some Peruvians refer to the generation under discussion as that of 1905 rather than of 1900.

54 See J. G. Llosa, 'La cultura peruana en el siglo XX', *Visión del Perú*, II, pp. 155-7.

55 Porras, *Fuentes*, p. 523.

56 See Jorge Basadre, *Materiales para otra morada* (Buenos Aires, 1960), p. 29.

57 V. García Calderón, *Nosotros* (Paris, 1945), pp. 94–6. This book was written primarily to reply to a series of articles and editorials published in the *Aprista* newspaper *La Tribuna* in 1935, vigorously attacking the allegedly reactionary attitudes of the men of the generation of 1900.

58 See F. García Calderón, *El Perú contemporáneo*, the Spanish translation of his work originally published in 1907, *Le perou contemporain* (Paris) and contained in his *En torno al Perú y América* (1954), pp. 141 ff.

59 Belaúnde, *Palabras de fe* (1952), p. 166. See also pp. 279 ff.

60 See editorial in *Estudios*, Año I, No. 1 (July–August 1928); pp. 1–2, commenting on the founding of the Catholic University.

61 An unduly harsh appraisal of the generation of 1900 is Luis Alberto Sánchez, *Balance y liquidación del novecientos* (Santiago de Chile, 1941).

62 See Carey, *Peru and the United States*, pp. 28–31.

63 *Mensaje de S. E. José Pardo, Presidente de la República, al congreso ordinario, 28 de julio de 1918* (1918), p. iii.

64 See Belaúnde, *Nuestra cuestión con Chile* (1919). Federico More, *La próxima conflagración sudamericana* (1918), took the United States severely to task at the time for not adequately rewarding Peru's wartime policies by energetically supporting the country in its dispute with Chile.

65 See F. B. Pike, *Chile and the United States, 1880–1962* (Notre Dame, Indiana, 1963), pp. 155–8.

66 Basadre, *Historia del Perú desde sus origenes hasta el presente* (1962), III, pp. 151–2.

67 On the university reform in Peru see José Luis Bustamante y Rivero, *La crisis universitaria* (Arequipa, 1918); José Jiménez Borja, 'La universidad peruana en el siglo XX', *Visión del Perú*, II, pp. 127–47; Gabriel del Mazo, *La reforma universitaria: documentos relativos a la propagación del movimiento en América Latina, 1918–1927* (Buenos Aires, 1927); Pedro M. Oliveira, 'Discurso de apertura del año universitario de 1910, la reforma universitaria', *Estudios sociales* (Bogotá, Colombia, 1921), pp. 81–146; Augusto Salazar Bondy, *Mitos dogmas, y postulados en la reforma universitaria* (1957); and Julio C. Tello, *Reforma universitaria: ensayos y discursos* (1928).

68 *Mensaje de S. E. José Pardo . . ., 28 de julio de 1916* (1917), p. xxxii.

69 See Paz Soldán, *De la inquietud a la revolución: diez años de rebeldías universitarios, 1909–1919* (1919).

70 *Mensaje de S. E. José Pardo . . ., 28 de julio de 1916*, pp. xxvi–xxvii.

71 See Julio Vargas Prada, *La universitaria en el Perú* (1943), p. 10.

72 See José Macedo Mendoza, *¡ Nacionalicemos el petroleo !* (1960), pp. 7–24.

73 Villarán, 'Discurso en el sepelio de José Pardo, 6 de agosto de 1947', in his *Páginas escogidas* (1962), pp. 461–3.

CHAPTER 8

1 Quoted in Manuel A. Capuñay, *Leguía: vida y obra del constructor del Perú* (1952), p. 151. Other favourable works on Leguía include: José E. Bonilla, compiler, *El siglo de Leguía, MCMIII–MCMXXVIII* (1929); Pedro Dávalos y Lissón, *Leguía* (Barcelona, Spain, 1928);

Clemente Palma – son of Ricardo Palma – *Había un hombre: artículos políticos* (1935); Abel Rodríguez R., *El Perú social y político* (1924); Abel Ulloa Cisneros, *Leguía: apuntes de cartera, 1919–1924* (1933), by a man who served as Leguía's secretary and remained steadfastly loyal to the dictator.

2 For one of the more recent restatements of the old assertion that the main positive contribution of Leguía's rule was the fostering of a new middle class, see Luis Alberto Sánchez, *Perú, retrato de un país adolescente* (1963), p. 135.

3 Highly critical treatments of Leguía which invariably launch this charge include Víctor Andrés Belaúnde, *Meditaciones peruanas* (1933 and 1963 editions), and *Memorias* (1962), III, esp. pp. 160–2; Jacinto López, the prominent Venezuelan historian who was a long-term resident of Peru, *La caida del gobierno constitucional en el Perú* (New York, 1927); Abelardo Solís, *Once años* (1934); Pedro Ugarteche, *La política internacional peruana durante la dictadura de Leguía* (1930); and Manuel Vicente Villarán, *El momento político y la opinión pública* (1924).

4 On constitutional and general legislative provisions favourable to labour during the Leguía rule see Enrique Ravago Velarde, *Legislación del empleado dictada en el gobierno de don Augusto B. Leguía* (1928).

5 José Pareja Paz Soldán, *Historia de las constituciones nacionales* (1943), p. 165.

6 On the 1920 constitution see also Alberto Arca Parro, 'Tendencias constitucionales en la América Latina', *Mercurio Peruano*, Año VI, Vol. XI, No. 65 (November 1923), 224–37, Aníbal Maúrtua, *Ideales de un constituyente* (1931), pp. 173–5, and G. H. Stuart, *The Governmental System of Peru* (Washington, DC, 1931).

7 For the ideas of Erasmo Roca on the Indian problem see his *Por la clase indígena* (1935); for those of José Antonio Encinas see his *Contribucion a una legislación tutela indígena* (1918).

8 For the thinking of Castro Pozo on the Indian and related social problems see his *Legislación del trabajo y previsión social* (1925), *Nuestra comunidad indígena* (1924), and *Renuevo de peruanidad, novela precedida de un prólogo polémico sobre cuestiones sociales* (1934).

9 For the landowners' point of view see *Memoria relativo a la cuestión indígena que la Liga de Hacendados eleva al Supremo Gobierno* (1922).

10 See the prologue by Manuel Seoane to Enrique Chirinos Soto, *El Peru frente a junio de 1962* (1962), pp. 8–9.

11 See *Mercurio Peruano*, Año III, Vol. IV (March 1920), pp. 311–12.

12 See Víctor Raúl Haya de la Torre, *Ideología aprista* (1961), p. 94; Jorge Jiménez Borja, 'La universidad peruana en el siglo XX', in *Visión del Perú en el siglo XX* (1962), II, pp. 127–46; and José Carlos

Mariátegui. 'La reforma universitaria', *Amauta*, Año III, No. 12 (February 1928).

13   Carlos Miró Quesada Laos, *Autopsía de los partidos políticos* (1961), p. 458.

14   According to Sánchez, *Perú*, p. 69, the counter-demonstration was moved primarily by political opposition to the Leguía government. Dora Mayer de Zulén, *El oncenio de Leguía* (Callao, 1932), II, p. 88, believed that the event was staged primarily because of the anti-clerical and anti-religious sentiments of Haya de la Torre.

15   The Cornejo quotation is found in Alfredo Moreno Mendiguren, compiler, *Repertorio de noticias breves sobre personajes peruanos* (1956), p. 291. See also Cornejo, *Significación del regimen político inaugurado el 4 de julio de 1919: la filosofía de la 'Patria Nueva'* (1928), an uncritical eulogy of the Leguía régime.

16   Chocano, *Apuntes sobre las dictaduras organizadoras y la gran farsa democrática* (1922).

17   Abel Ulloa Cisneros, compiler, *Escombros, 1919–1930* (1934), pp. 32–3. The work is uncritically favourable to Leguía.

18   Emilio Romero, *Historia económica del Perú* (1949), pp. 438–45.

19   See Manuel Irigoyen Puente, *Bosquejo sobre empréstitos contemporáneos en el Perú*, a 1928 San Marcos thesis highly critical of foreign-loan policy, published in instalments in *El Comercio* beginning 2 December 1930.

20   Alarm over United States economic penetration during the *oncenio* is expressed in Manuel E. Ríos, *El Perú libre* (1922), and *La verdadera democracia* (1925), as well as in Benjamín Chirinos Pacheco, *El imperialismo yanqui y la dictadura bolchevique* (Arequipa, 1929). On United States economic relations with Peru during the *oncenio* see James Carey, *Peru and the United States* (Notre Dame, Indiana, 1964), pp. 51–80.

21   Mayer de Zulén, *El oncenio*, II, p. 7.

22   *Ibid.*, I, p. 3.

23   See Carey, *Peru and the United States*, pp. 94–7, and Arthur P. Whitaker, *The United States and South America: the Northern Republics* (Cambridge, Massachusetts, 1948), esp. p. 178. Capuñay, *Leguía*, p. 3, justifies Leguía's policies, but attacks the United States. Pedro Ugarteche, *El Perú en la vida internacional americana* (1927) is harshly critical both of Leguía and the United States. A balanced and dispassionate account of Peruvian foreign policy is Arturo García Salazar, *Historia diplomática del Perú* (1930).

24   See Clemente Palma, *La cuestión de Tacna y Arica y la conferencia de Washington* (1922), pp. 24–5.

25   See Alberto Ulloa, *El fallo arbitral del presidente de los Estados Unidos de América en la cuestión de Tacna y Arica* (1925), esp. p. 68,

and the review of the book by Carlos Neuhaus Ugarteche, in *Mercurio Peruano*, Año IX, Vol. XV, No. 91 (January 1926), pp. 74-6.

26 Ulloa, *Posición internacional del Perú* (1941), p. 239.

27 Ugarte, 'El proceso de Tacna y Arica', *Mercurio Peruano*, Año IX, Vol. XV, Nos 95-6 (May-June 1926).

28 See W. J. Dennis, *Tacna and Arica* (New Haven, Connecticut, 1931), and F. B. Pike, *Chile and the United States* (Notre Dame, Indiana, 1963), pp. 214-9, 228-31.

29 Villarán, *Páginas escogidas* (1962), pp. 293-6.

30 See Orrego, '¿Cual es la cultura que creará América?' *Amauta*, Año IV, No. 14 (April 1928), and *El pueblo continente: ensayos para una interpretación de la América Latina* (Santiago de Chile, 1939), pp. 19-25.

31 Valcárcel, *Tempestad en los andes* (1927), p. 116.

32 See Valcárcel, *Ruta cultural del Perú* (México, DF, 1945), and the prologue by J. C. Mariátegui to *Tempestad en los andes*.

33 See Mariátegui, 'El proceso del gamonalismo', a 1927 supplement to *Amauta*.

34 *La Sierra*, Año I, No. 1 (January 1927), p. 3.

35 *Ibid.*, Año I, No. 5 (May 1927), editorial by J. Guillermo Guevara.

36 See Manuel J. Gamarra, *Orientación y organización: población y decentralización; programa de reconstrucción nacional* (Cuzco, 1926).

37 *La Sierra*, Año I, No. 6 (June 1927), pp. 22-3.

38 Mariátegui, 'Indigenismo y socialismo', *Amauta*, Año II, No. 7 (March 1926), p. 37.

39 Castro Pozo, *Renuevo del peruanidad*, pp. 20-23.

40 Carlos Manuel Cox interview of Valcárcel in *Libros y Revistas*, Año II, No. 8 (February 1927). *Libros y Revistas* was an occasional supplement to *Amauta*.

41 See Julián Huanay, *Mariátegui y los sindicatos* (1956), p. 15.

42 In pre-conquest times Amauta was the title for members of an Inca élite of wise men charged, among other functions, with preserving and passing on to their successors knowledge of Inca traditions and history.

43 See Alberto Tauro, '*Amauta*' *y su influencia* (1959).

44 For the ideas of Ravines, one of Peru's consummate opportunists, during his communist period see his 'El etapa del monopolio en la economía capitalista', *Amauta*, Año III, No. 16 (July 1928), 29-32.

45 For the ideas of Martínez de la Torre see his *Apuntes para una interpretación marxista de historia social del Perú*, 4 vols (1947-9). Considerable portions of this work were written in the 1920's and published originally in *Amauta*.

46 See Mariátegui, 'La crisis mundial y el proletariado peruano', *Amauta*, Año V, No. 30 (April-May 1903), pp. 7-9.

47 See *Amauta*, Año II, No. 7 (March 1927), p. 38.
48 See *Ibid.*, Año III, No. 17 (July 1928), pp. 11–13.
49 Mariátegui, prologue to Valcárcel, *Tempestad*, pp. 33–4.
50 Mariátegui, review of Miguel de Unamuno, *L'agonie du Christianisme*, in *Libros y Revistas*, Año I, No. 3 (September 1926), p. 3.
51 Mariátegui, *Ediciones Populares de Obras Completas, primera etapa* (1959), III, p. 22.
52 Mariátegui, 'Defensa del marxismo', *Amauta*, Año III, No. 19 (November 1928), pp. 10 ff.
53 Mariátegui, review of Unamuno, p. 4. For works that depict Mariátegui as a genuine Marxist–Leninist, and the founder of communism in Peru, see: Armando Bazán, *Biografía de José Carlos Mariátegui* (1951 edition), Jorge del Prado, *Mariátegui y su obra* (1946), and the articles by Ricardo Martínez de la Torre and Eudocio Ravines in *Amauta*, Año V, No. 30 (April–May 1930). Antonio San Cristóbal–Sebastián, *Economía, educación, y marxismo en Mariátegui* (1960), stresses the spiritualism in the ideology of Mariátegui, and tends to regard him as the precursor of a Catholic social justice movement. Favourable appraisals of Mariátegui are found in Eugenio Chang–Rodríguez, *La literatura política de González Prada, Mariátegui, y Haya de la Torre* (México, DF, 1957), Raúl Porras, 'Homenaje a José Carlos Mariátegui', *Variedades*, 23 April 1930, and María Wiesse, *José Carlos Mariátegui, etapas de su vida* (1959 edition). An exhaustive listing of the literature pertaining to Mariátegui as well as an invaluable sketch of his life is Guillermo Rouillón, *Bio-bibliografía de José Carlos Mariátegui* (1963).
54 See William S. Stokes, 'Democracy, Freedom and Reform in Latin America', in F. B. Pike, editor, *Freedom and Reform in Latin America* (Notre Dame, Indiana, 1959), pp. 117–49, for a perceptive if unsympathetic account of early APRA ideology. The frequently unreliable Eudocio Ravines sets forth an adverse account of the early *Aprista* movement in *The Yenan Way* (New York, 1951). For highly favourable accounts that in many instances do not concur with the conclusions reached in the present book see Robert J. Alexander, *Prophets of the Revolution* (New York, 1962), pp. 75–108, Germán Arciniegas, *The State of Latin America* (New York, 1952), pp. 79–94, and Harry Kantor, *The Ideology and Program of the Peruvian 'Aprista' Movement* (Berkeley, California, 1953).
55 See Haya de la Torre, *Construyendo el aprismo: artículos y cartas desde el exilio, 1924–31* (Buenos Aires, 1933), pp. 93–8, 104–13, and *Indoamérica* (1961: Vol. I of *Pensamiento político de Haya de la Torre* a five-volume set made up mainly of extracts from earlier writings by the APRA leader), pp. 70–71.
56 Haya de la Torre, *Construyendo*, p. 121.

57 Julio Antonio Mella, 'La lucha revolucionaria contra el imperialismo: ¿qué es el APRA?' *Amauta,*[Año IV, No. 31 (June–July 1930)-
41–8, contended that communism was the only authentic and effective
anti-imperialist movement. Luis Heysen, at the time Secretary General of the *Comité Central de la Sección de APRA* in Paris, and Director, *Centro de Estudios Anti-Imperialistas*, in a November 1929 letter
to Mariátegui set forth the claims of the APRA as the only true
voice of anti-imperialism. See *Amauta*, Año IV, No. 29 (February–
March 1930), pp. 95–8.

58 1928 writings of Haya de la Torre reproduced in his *Ideología
Aprista* (1961), esp. pp. 72–108, 129, 148.

59 Haya de la Torre, *Construyendo*, pp. 29–34.

60 See Haya de la Torre, *El anti-imperialismo y el APRA* (Santiago de
Chile, 1936 edition), Luis Heysen, *El abecé de la peruanización del
Perú* (Cuzco, 1931), and Salomon Wapnir, *La sombra imperialística:
a propósito de 'Por la Emancipación de la América Latina' de Víctor
Raúl Haya de la Torre* (Buenos Aires, 1928).

61 1930 writings of Haya de la Torre reproduced in his *Nuestro
América y el mundo* (1961), p. 183.

62 Haya de la Torre, *Ideología*, pp. 65–6.

63 Seoane, *Mirando a Bolivia con ojo izquierdo* (Buenos Aires, 1926),
p. 79.

64 Haya de la Torre, *Ideología*, pp. 66.

65 November 1921 letter of Heysen to Mariátegui, cited in note 57.

66 Haya de la Torre, *Construyendo*, pp. 167–70.

67 Belaúnde, 'El militarismo', *Mercurio Peruano*, Año I, Vol. I, No. 1
(July 1918), p. 54.

68 Mayer de Zulén, *El oncenio*, II, pp. 51–2.

69 On the political ideas of Rada y Gamio, see his *Discursos* (1924).
See also J. A. Belaúnde, *El Dr Pedro José Rada y Gamio: los variados
aspectos de su mentalidad* (1927).

70 See Percy Mac-Lean y Estenós, *Historia de una revolución* (Buenos
Aires, 1953), p. 29.

71 On this matter see in particular the interview of Dr Belisario Sosa
Artola by Abel Ulloa Cisneros in the latter's *Escombros*, pp. 113 ff.
See also Federico More, *Zoocracia y canibalismo* (1933), pp. 12–14.

72 See Víctor Larco Herrera, *Leguía, el martir de la penitenciaría*
(Santiago de Chile, 1934).

CHAPTER 9

1 For the type of address delivered by Sánchez Cerro in the early
stages of campaigning see his *Manifiesto a la nación* (1930).

2 See *Juventud Revolucionario del Cusco a los pueblos del Perú* (1930).

3 Manzanilla, quoted in Alfredo Moreno Mendiguren, compiler, *Repertorio de noticias breves sobre personajes peruanos* (1956), p. 523.

4 See the single-sheet tract by *Aprista* militant Gamaliel Churata, *Corad, Sapos* (Puno, 24 September 1930), in the *Colección de Ojas*, 1930–2, Sala de Investigaciones, Biblioteca Nacional del Perú.

5 For the viewpoint of *Apristas* on the repressive measures taken against them by Sánchez Cerro when serving as head of the junta see Luis Eduardo Enríquez, *Sánchez Cerro al desnudo* (Santiago de Chile, 1931), Luis Heysen, *El comandante del Oropesa* (1931), and Manuel Seoane, *Con los trabajadores estamos los Apristas* (Santiago de Chile, 1931), and *Nuestros fines* (Buenos Aires, 1931).

6 See the one-page tract of 6 March 1931, signed by the Comité Ejecutivo del Partido Aprista Peruano, in the above-cited *Colección de Ojas*.

7 Heysen, *El comandante del Oropesa*, p. 42.

8 See *Programa de gobierno del Comandante Luis M. Sánchez Cerro, candidato a la presidencia de la República del Perú* (1931). Subsequent material in the text on the 1931 programme and campaign of Sánchez Cerro is also taken from this important document.

9 Heysen, *El comandante*, pp. 22–5.

10 One of Peru's best political analysts and writers in the second half of the twentieth century, Enrique Chirinos Soto, a decided *Aprista* sympathizer, concedes the honesty of the 1931 elections. See his *El Perú frente a junio de 1962* (1962), p. 47, and 'La política peruana en el siglo XX', *Visión del Perú en el siglo XX* (1962), II, p. 59. The highly respected historian and constitutional authority José Pareja Paz Soldán, 'Evolución constitucional del Perú en el siglo XX', *ibid.*, II, p. 32, also remarks on the honesty of the elections. See also the careful analysis of these elections published in the lively and frequently valuable Lima magazine *Caretas*, Año X, No. 211 (22 December 1960 –15 January 1961), p. 11, and Carlos Miró Quesada, *Sánchez Cerro y su tiempo* (1947), pp. 167–74. Although partial to Sánchez Cerro in this work, Miró Quesada gives what appears to be an objective account of the elections.

11 Ventura García Calderón, quoted in Moreno Mendiguren, *Repertorio*, p. 522.

12 Basadre, quoted in *ibid.*, p. 522.

13 See Raúl Ferrero Rebagliati, *Marxismo y nacionalismo: estado nacional corporativo* (1937), p. 51. A similar spirit is revealed in Carlos Radicati de Primeglio, *De las antiguas a las modernas corporaciones* (1937). Both works were written as doctoral theses at the Catholic University in Lima.

14 Luis Alberto Sánchez, *Balance y liquidación del novecientos* (Santiago de Chile, 1941), p. 19.

15 See, for example, José Rosell Ríos, 'Introducción al estudio de la doctrina social de la Iglesia', *Revista de la Universidad Católica del Perú*, IX, Nos. 2–3 (May–June 1941), and Monsignor Fernando Cento, the Apostolic Nuncio who encouraged the cause of fascism in Peru, 'Los pactos Lateranses', *ibid.*, VIII, No. 1 (April 1940).

16 One Indian-disparaging fascist sympathizer was the old philosopher Alejandro O. Deustua. See his *La cultura nacional* (1937), *Cultura política* (1936), and his prologue to José de la Riva Agüero and Carlos Miró Quesada, *Dos estudios sobre Italia contemporánea* (1937).

17 Riva Agüero, 'Sobre dos recientes opúsculos de Jorge del Vecchio', *Dos estudios*, p. 53.

18 Riva Agüero's comments in *Revista de la Universidad Católica del Perú*, IX, Nos 8–9 (November–December 1941), p. 466.

19 'La última conferencia de Riva Agüero', *ibid.*, XIII, No. 1 (April 1945).

20 See *La República* (Lima), 14 September 1930.

21 See *Amauta*, No. 32 (August–September 1930), p. 7.

22 On Peruvian labour organization at this time see Alberto Bolognesi, *Sindicalismo: apuntes de historia, crítica, doctrina y organización sindical* (1945).

23 *Amauta*, No. 32 (August–September 1930), p. 10. Further information on Peruvian communism at this time is found in Manuel Seoane, *Comunistas criollos* (1933), and Eudocio Ravines, *The Yenan Way* (New York, 1951).

24 See Luciano Castilla's prologue to the work of the French Socialist Paul Louis, *Doctrina socialista* (1954), pp. iv–viii.

25 César Góngora P., 'La geografía humana del Perú', *Letras*, primer cautrimestre, 1936, p. 124. See also *Primer manifiesto y programa de revindicaciones inmediatas, aprobadas por la primera conferencia nacional del Partido Socialista del Perú* (1933).

26 *Revista de la Universidad Católica del Perú*, XIII, Nos 4–5 (July–August 1940), pp. 439–40.

27 See Tomás Escajadillo, *La revolución universitaria de 1930* (no date), a valuable work by one of the FEP leaders at the time, and José Jiménez Borja, 'La universidad peruana en el siglo XX', *Visión del Perú*, II, pp. 135–42.

28 See Haya de la Torre, *Teoría y táctica del aprismo* (1931), and the *Aprista* newspaper *La Tribuna* which began publication at this time under the direction of Manuel Seoane.

29 Haya de la Torre, *Ideología Aprista* (1961), p. 24.

30 Hidalgo, *Diario de mi sentimiento, 1922–1936* (Buenos Aires, 1937), pp. 45–7. Similar thoughts were expressed by Hidalgo in his pamphlet *Haya de la Torre en su víspera* (1931).

31   11 March 1931 letter of Haya de la Torre to Hidalgo, reproduced in the latter's *Diario*, pp. 314–6.

32   In a 1932 interview published in *Construyendo el aprismo: artículos y cartas desde el exilio, 1924–1931* (Buenos Aires, 1933), pp. 84–92, Haya de la Torre did not directly deny the authenticity of these documents. He merely stated they were of questionable authenticity.

33   *Ibid.*, pp. 172–5.

34   José Paraja Paz Soldán, *Historia de las constituciones nacionales* (1943), p. 32.

35   One of the best analyses of these events is found in V. A. Belaúnde, *Meditaciones peruanas* (1933).

36   Hidalgo, *Diario*, pp. 150 ff.

37   See Víctor Villanueva, *El militarismo en el Perú* (1962), pp. 75 ff.

38   Haya de la Torre, *Construyendo*, p. 90.

39   Miró Quesada, *Sánchez Cerro*, pp. 29–30, 245.

40   See Federico More, a colourful but not always reliable journalist, *Zoocracia y canibalismo* (1933), who estimated that in early 1932 five hundred citizens suspected of *Aprista* sympathies were deported and close to two thousand jailed. *Aprista* works dealing with the Sánchez Cerro repression include: Rómulo Meneses, *Por el APRA: en el cárcel, al servicio del PAP* (1933), with a prologue by Luis Heysen; Samuel Ramírez Castilla, *La tiranía se desencadena* (1932: pamplet); and Juan Seoane, *Hombres y rejas* (Santiago de Chile, 1937), with a prologue by Ciro Alegría.

41   More, *Zoocracia*, p. 57.

42   See Arnold Toynbee, *Survey of International Affairs, 1933* (London, 1934), pp. 439 ff., and United States Department of State, *Foreign Relations of the United States, 1932* (Washington, DC, 1948), pp. 272 ff.

43   See the pamphlet of the Editorial Clandestino APRA, *Saber gobernar es saber prever* (1932), in which the APRA claims credit for the initial Peruvian invasion of Leticia and maintains that only it knows how properly to defend national interests. On the Leticia affair see also José A. Vallejo, *El conflicto Perú–Colombiano* (1934).

44   For an excellent collection of tributes to Sánchez Cerro written by many of Peru's leading figures of literature and politics see *Homenaje a Sánchez Cerro, 1933–1953* (1953).

45   See Emilio Romero, 'El proceso económico del Perú en el siglo XX', *Visión del Perú*, I, p. 101.

46   See Chirinos Soto, *Perú frente a 1962*, p. 156.

47   See Alejandro O. Deustua quoted in Luis Humberto Delgado, *Nuevo Perú* (1945), p. 232.

48   See Alberto Ulloa, *Posición internacional del Perú* (1941), and

Manley Hudson, *The Verdict of the League: Colombia and Perú at Leticia* (Boston, 1933).

49 Villanueva, *El militarismo*, p. 90.

50 *Aprista* Luis Alberto Sánchez, *Haya de la Torre y el APRA* (Santiago de Chile, 1955), p. 344, claims Benavides had promised Haya to hold the special elections.

51 Favourable accounts of the accomplishments of the Benavides administration include J. L. Basombrio, 'Estado comparativo de la situación comercial, financiera, y económica del país de 1888 a 1938', *Boletín de la Cámara de Comercio de Lima* (March, 1938), and *Progreso del Perú 1933–38 durante el gobierno del Presidente de la República General Oscar R. Benavides* (Buenos Aires, 1945). A very unfavourable brief account is Partido Aprista Peruano, *Autopsía de las finanzas de la tiranía del Gral. Benavides* (1940).

52 30 May addresses of Benavides, reported in the Lima newspaper *Las Derechas*, 4 June 1936. See also *El Comercio*, 26 March 1939.

53 See *Las Derechas*, 4 June 1936.

54 See *Cinco años de labor gubernativa, 1933–1938* (1938).

55 8 December address of Benavides quoted in *Las Derechas*, 19 December 1936.

56 See Prado's *Artículos políticos* (1916).

57 On the issues stressed by Villarán in the campaign see his *Páginas escogidas* (1962), pp. 269–87.

58 On the 1936 elections, as well as the background and aftermath, see Luis Antonio Eguiguren, *La usurpador: para la historia* (1939); Fernando León de Vivero, *El tirano senil* (Paris, 1937), a bitter attack against Benavides; Elías Lozado Benavente, *Vaivenes de la política* (1938), a view of political happenings in Peru, 1930–38, that is generally favourable to Benavides; and Luis Velázquez, *Contra la amenaza civilista* (1936), a strong attack by a well-known poet against the candidacy of Villarán, unfairly describing him as an arch reactionary.

59 25 March address of Benavides, quoted in *La Prensa*, 26 March 1939.

60 For an anti-*Aprista* view of the party's rôle in this conspiracy see Eduardo Sierralta, *El APRA y la sombra* (Mexico, DF, 1957), with a prologue by David Alfaro Siqueiros.

61 See L. A. Sánchez, *Haya de la Torre*, p. 368.

62 See for example, L. A. Sánchez, *Historia general de América* (Buenos Aires, 1943), II, pp. 474–5, and Haya de la Torre, *Ideología Aprista*, pp. 72–108. See also Thibaldo González, *Haya de la Torre: trayectoria de una ideología* (Caracas, 1958).

63 See *La Tribuna*, 18 December 1945.

64 A very unfriendly account of Haya's changing ideology is Luis

THE MODERN HISTORY OF PERU

Eduardo Enríquez, *Haya de la Torre, la estafa política mas grande de América* (1951).

65 See Bryce Wood, *The United States and Latin American wars* (New York, 1966), and David Zook, Jr, *Zarumilla–Marañón: The Ecuador–Peru Dispute* (New York, 1964).

66 See José Luis Bustamante y Rivero, *Tres años de la lucha por la democracia en el Perú* (Buenos Aires, 1949), pp. 11–22.

67 See *Caretas*, Año XIII (24 May–6 June 1963), pp. 8 ff.

68 Chirinos Soto, *Perú frente a 1962*, p. 62.

CHAPTER 10

1 See Bustamante y Rivero, *Tres años de la lucha por la democracia en el Perú* (Buenos Aires, 1949), pp. 14–18.

2 Quoted in Enrique Chirinos Soto, *El Perú frente a junio de 1962* (1962), p. 67.

3 Bustamante, *op. cit.*, pp. 30–31.

4 In dealing with the late Bustamante period, the author has relied frequently on information obtained from a 25 June 1964 interview with Héctor Boza.

5 Two books by Víctor Villanueva Valencia, although not always impartial, provide an extremely valuable coverage of the 3 October uprising: *El militarismo en el Perú* (1962), and *La tragedia de un pueblo y de un partido: páginas para la historia del APRA* (Santiago de Chile, 1954). Claiming initially to have enjoyed Haya de la Torre's backing, Villanueva was instrumental in planning this uprising. He feels top-level *Aprista* leaders betrayed the party by failing firmly to back the Callao uprising once it began.

6 Bustamante, *op. cit.*, pp. 250–70 gives an understandably unfriendly account of the Odría-led Arequipa revolution. Percy Mac-Lean y Estenós, an advocate of authoritarian rôle, praises the revolution in almost ecstatic terms in *Historia de una revolución* (Buenos Aires, 1953), pp. 92–101.

7 See Comisión Económica para América Latina, *Desarrollo industrial del Perú* (México, DF, 1959), pp. 21–2, and Erich Egner, 'El crecimiento económico del Perú y sus obstáculos', *Revista de la Facultad de Ciencias Económicas y Comerciales de la Universidad Mayor de San Marcos*, No. 66 (January–June 1963), pp. 66–7, an outstanding study by a West German who conducted research in Peru in 1958 and 1959. For additional information on economic aspects of the *ochenio* see: *Anuario Estadístico del Perú, 1956–1957* (1959); Banco Central de Reserva del Perú, *Renta nacional entre 1942 y 1958* (1961); and Manuel A. Odría, *La política económica y financiera del regimen*,

expuesto por el Presidente al Congreso Nacional, el 28 de julio, 1954 (1954).

8   Baltazar Caravedo, Humberto Rotondo, and Javier Mariátegui, *Estudios de psiquiatría social* (1963), p. 379. Although containing much information on the economy, this work is primarily a sociological study and easily among the most valuable to appear in Peru.

9   One of the strongest denunciations of Odría's alleged political terrorism was written by *Aprista* leader Fernando León de Vivero, *El tirano quedó atrás* (México, DF, 1951). Twelve years after publication of the book, León de Vivero was in the forefront of *Apristas* actively collaborating with Odría.

10   Eguiguren quoted in Alfredo Moreno Mendiguren, compiler, *Repertorio de noticias breves sobre personajes peruanos* (Madrid, 1956), p. 368.

11   On the tax structure of 1952, see Raúl Ferrero, *Estudio comparado de los impuestos a la renta en el Perú y los demás paises de América* (1952), especially pp. 29–69.

12   See *Caretas*, Año XIII, No. 267 (24 May–6 June 1963), pp. 8 ff.

13   See the work by the Peruvian Marxist Genaro Carnero Checa, *El águila rampante: el imperialismo yanqui sobre América Latina* (México, DF, 1956), pp. 308–9.

14   Lugo Perea, 'Comercio exterior del Perú', *El Comercio*, 4 May 1964, p. 105.

16   See Héctor Cornejo Chávez, *Nuevos principios para un nuevo Perú* (1960), pp. 44–56.

17   See Hidalgo, *Porqué renuncí al APRA* (1954).

18   See Portal, *¡Quienes traicionaran al pueblo!* (1948). A valuable work dealing in part with defections from the APRA in the 1940's and 1950's is Alfredo Hernández Urbina, *Los partidos y la crisis APRA* (1956). See also César Guardia Mayorga, *Reconstruyendo el aprismo; exposición i refutación de la doctrina política y filosófica hayista* (Arequipa, 1945).

19   *Caretas*, Año X, No. 211 (22 December–15 January 1961), p. 11.

20   See Cornejo Chávez, *Nuevos principios*, p. 185. For additional material on Christian Democracy in Peru see the same author's *Con los pobres de América* (1962) and *Que se propone la democracia cristiana* (1962), and Alfonso Benavides Correa, *Rumbos contemporáneos del pensamiento político* (1957).

21   Egner, 'El crecimiento económico del Perú', pp. 26–7. See also Rómulo Ferrero, 'La historia monetaria del Perú en el presente siglo', *Visión del Perú en el Siglo XX* (1962), I, pp. 125–43, and *El problema de la tierra en el Perú* (1958); Food and Agricultural Organization, and International Bank for Reconstruction and Development, *The Agricultural Development of Peru* (Washington, DC, 1959); and

Thomas R. Ford, *Man and Land in Peru* (Gainesville, Florida, 1955).

22 Egner, 'El crecimiento económico', p. 46.

23 See Hernando Aguirre Gamio, *Liquidación histórica del APRA y del colonialismo neoliberal* (1962).

24 See Banco Central de Reserva del Perú, *Actividades productivas del Perú* (1961).

25 See 'Crecimiento sin desarrollo tuvo economía del Perú entre los años 1950–1962', *El Comercio*, 6 September 1963, a carefully prepared article based on statistics compiled by the Instituto Nacional de Planificación. See also Manuel Montero Bernales, *Crisis en el Perú: conjunto de artículos sobre política, economía, y finanzas* (1961).

26 Pedro Rosselló quoted in Hernando Aguirre Gamio, *Liquidación histórica del APRA*, p. 10.

27 See Humberto Ugolotti Dansay, *Las elecciones de 1963 y las elecciones de 1962* (1963), and Enrique Chirinos Soto, *Cuenta y balance de las elecciones de 1962* (1962).

28 See, for example, the Lima weekly *Aquí Está*, 15 October 1963.

29 See *ibid.* and *Lea, Revista Peruana de Actualidad*, Año III, No. 39 (August 1963).

30 See interview with Víctor Villanueva in *Aquí Está*, 15 August 1963.

31 For an unfavourable account of the military junta's administration, especially following the fall of Pérez Godoy, see Villanueva, *Un año bajo el sable* (1963).

32 On the Peruvian middle sectors and/or class see Luis Alayza y Paz Soldán and Alberto Ruibal, *Problemas nacionales: la evolución social* (1962); Jorge Basadre, *Materiales para otra morada* (Buenos Aires, 1960), esp. p. 26; José Luis Bustamante y Rivero, 'Las clases sociales en el Perú', *El Amigo del Clero*, Nos 1610–12 (July, August, September 1959), 234–75; José Mejía Valera, 'Estratificación social en el Perú', in Universidad Nacional y Mayor de San Marcos, *Cultura Peruana* (1962); Francisco Miró Quesada Cantuarias, *Las estructuras sociales* (1961); and J. Zuzunaga Flores, 'El nacimiento de la clase media en el Perú', *La Prensa*, 2 March 1964.

33 See Alejandro Desmaison, 'El desarrollo de la industria peruana en los últimos 125 años', *El Comercio*, 4 May 1964. As of 1961 agriculture and livestock raising employed 62 per cent. of the active population, industry 17·5 per cent., services 3·4 per cent., government 3·4 per cent., commerce and finance 4·9 per cent., mining 2 per cent. and diverse occupations 6·1 per cent. See *Caretas*, Año XI, No. 218 (14–28 April 1961), p. 218.

34 See Mario Samame Boggio, 'La minería en el Perú, 1839–1964', *El Comercio*, 4 May 1964.

35 See Honorio Delgado, 'El panorama de nuestra cultura', *ibid.*, 4 May 1964.

36 See *La Prensa*, 8 September 1963.

37 See the 3 May 1964 editions of *El Comercio* and *La Prensa*.

38 See *Caretas*, Año XII (30 January–14 February 1962), p. 18, and *La Tribuna*, the Aprista daily published in Lima, 22 January 1962.

39 The Peking Communists in 1963 published as one of their main propaganda vehicles the periodical *Voz Obrera* (Lima).

40 One of the most eloquent defenders of Moscow-oriented communism is the poet Gustavo Valcárcel. See his *La prisión* (1960), a gripping novel dealing with the persecution of Communists and leftists in Peru, and *Reportaje al futuro: crónicas de un viaje a la URSS* (1963), a glowing account of conditions encountered in Russia during a tour of the country.

41 One Trotskyist organization in the early 1960's was the Partido Obrero Revolucionario, which published the periodical *Obrero y Campesino*. In its Año III, September 1963 edition, it gave a good resumé of the cleavages among different Communist groups in Peru. For additional material on this matter see Comité Ejecutivo Nacional de la Frente de Liberación Nacional, *Frente de Liberación Nacional: el FLN, el PCP, y la revolución peruana* (9 May 1964).

42 See Salomón Bolo, *Cristianismo y liberación nacional* (1962).

43 César Góngora P., 'La geografía humana del Perú', *Letras*, primer cuatrimestre, 1936, pp. 124–5.

44 See Caravedo, Rotondo, and Mariátegui, *Estudios de psiquiatría social*, and Humberto Rotondo, *Estudios sobre personalidad básica en mestizos* (1960).

45 See Robert E. McNicoll, 'Recent Political Developments in Peru', *Inter-American Economic Affairs*, XVIII, No. 1 (Summer, 1964), p. 85. On the Popular Action programme see Fernando Belaúnde, *La conquista del Perú por los peruanos* (1958) and *Pueblo por pueblo* (1960); Acción Popular, *Ideario, principios, programa de Acción Popular* (Miraflores, 1962); Leonidas Castro Bastos, *Geohistoria del Perú; ensayo económico–político–social* (1962), esp. pp. 231 ff.; Edgardo Seoane, elected as Belaúnde's vice-president in the 1963 elections, *Surcos de la paz* (1963) and interview in *Caretas*, Año XII, No. 236 (30 January–9 February 1962). The soundness of the Popular Action programme has, of course, been questioned from many quarters. One of the most significant criticisms comes, at least by inference, from observers who feel it is highly romantic to regard semi-socialistic Indian usages as constituting still a vital factor of life patterns in the sierra. Men of this persuasion incline to regard programmes based on the assumption of the survival of pre-conquest patterns as having little chance of success. See Henry F. Dobyns, *The Social Matrix of Peruvian Indigenous Communities* (Ithaca, New York, 1964), esp. pp. 1–22.

46   Eudocio Ravines, *La gran promesa* (1963), pp. 107–8.
47   See Caravedo, Rotondo and Mariátegui, *Estudios*, p. 3, and United Nations, Economic and Social Council, *Official Records:* Fifth Year, Twelfth Session, Special Supplement No. 1, *Report of the Commission of Enquiry on the Coca Leaf* (Lake Success, New York, 1950).
48   On Peru's land problem see Miguel A. Armestar V., *La tierra y el hombre: visión panorámica del problema agrario-social del Perú y su estrecha relación con el capital* (1964); Pablo S. de la Jara, *Desarrollo agrícola y reforma agrícola* (1963); Jorge Guillermo Llosa P., *Visión sintética del Perú* (1959); Carlos M. Paz Soldán and Carlos Derteano Urrutia, 'Evolución de la agricultura nacional en el siglo XX', *Visión del Perú* (1962), I, pp. 147–80; and Mario Polar, *La economía peruana y el capital extranjera* (1954). See also Perú: Comisión para la Reforma Agraria y la Vivienda, *La reforma agraria en el Perú: explicación de motivos y proyecto de ley* (1960), urging a very moderate agrarian reform, and Octavio Diez Bernales, *La falsa reforma agraria* (1961), with a prologue by Fernando Belaúnde, arguing in favour of more sweeping changes.
49   See Perú: Comisión para la Reforma Agraria y la Vivienda, *Documentos* (1962), I, p. 39.
50   *El Comercio*, 2 April 1964.
51   In addition to the census, see two studies by Enrique Torres Llosa, 'La educación católica en el momento actual', *El Amigo del Clero*, Año XLIX, Nos 1626–7 (November–December 1960) and *La educación: problema social en el Perú* (1961). Other works dealing with the problems of the educational structure include the following: Mario Alzamora Valdez, *La educación peruana: crisis y perspectivas; erores de una política educativa* (1961); Carlos Cueto Fernandini, *Problemas fundamentales de la educación nacional* (1955), and editor, *La universidad en el siglo XX* (1951); Julio Durán Benavides, *Perú: hombre, técnica, y educación* (1961); Josè Antonio Encinas, *Un ensayo de escuela nueva en el Perú*, 2 vols (1959); Carlos Salazar Bondy *Informe sobre los estudios secundarios en el Perú* (1960), and *La realidad educacional del Perú* (1945); and Emilio Vázquez, *Pedagogía* (Huancayo, 1963).
52   See *Anuario Eclesiástico del Perú* (1964), and *Actualidad*, a Catholic weekly published in Lima, 22 December 1963.
53   *Carta pastoral de Pedro Farfán, con motivo de la próxima festividad de Santa Rosa de Lima* (1937).
54   *Carta pastoral del episcopada peruana sobre algunos aspectos de la cuestión social en el Perú* (1958).
55   'Discurso ... de ... Monsignor Juan Landázuri Ricketts', *El Amigo del Clero*, Nos 1610–12 (July, August, September 1959), 213–14. See also Primera Semana Social, *Exigencias sociales del*

Catolicismo en el Perú (1959), Monsignor Luis Lituma P., 'La Iglesia Católica en el Perú durante el siglo XX', *Visión del Perú*, II, pp. 473–523, and *Política deber cristiano* (1963), a collection of essays by V. A. Belaúnde, Carlos Cueto Fernandini, Raúl Ferrero, Ernesto Alayza Grundy, and Rev. Felipe McGregor, SJ.

56 See *Vanguardia*, a Lima weekly, 15 April 1963.

57 Statistics of the Federación Nacional de Cooperativas del Crédito del Perú, in *El Comercio*, 18 September 1963.

58 An example of the perhaps irresponsible extremism of certain Catholic reformers in demanding the overnight solution of all social problems is Ricardo Talavera Campos, 'El pensamiento católico acerca de la propiedad', *Mensajero Agrícola* (Lima), No. 161 (August–September 1963), esp. pp. 14 ff.

59 'Discurso del Excmo. Sr Arzobispo . . . para la Asamblea Arquidiocesana de Acción Católica con motivo de conmemorarse el 25 aniversario de la fundación de la Acción Católica Peruana', *El Amigo del Clero*, Año XLIX, Nos 1626–7 (November–December 1960), p. 324.

60 Basadre, 'Un fragmento de la historia peruana en el siglo XX', *Visión del Perú*, II, p. 445.

61 Delgado, *Nuevo Perú* (1945), p. 234. For a highly critical treatment of the rôle of the Peruvian military see Alfredo Hernández Urbina, *Nueva política nacional* (1962).

62 See Gen. Juan Mendoza Rodríguez (r), 'El ejército en el siglo XX', *Visión del Perú*, I, pp. 335–49, and 'El ejército y la aviación en 1964', *El Comercio*, 4 May 1964.

63 See Evaristo San Cristóval, *Manuel Pardo* (1945), p. 293.

64 Many of the military civic action programmes are described in *Actualidad Militar*, a twice-monthly publication of the Peruvian Army's Department of Publications, appearing for the first time in 1962. Also valuable in this regard are the periodicals *Revista de la Escuela Superior de Guerre* and *Revista Militar del Perú*.

65 For evidence of a new approach on the part of Peruvian businessmen see 'La empresa privada reclama la libertad económica', *El Mundo* (a Lima monthly), Año XIV, No. 176 (1 August 1963), p. 13; Emilio Castañón Pesquel, 'La reforma de empresa', *ibid.*, Año XIV, No. 177 (1 September 1963), p. 27; and *La Prensa*, 30 April 1964, containing information on Acción para el Desarrollo, a reform-minded group of businessmen and army officers.

66 For the land-reform concepts of *aprismo*, see Víctor Graciano Maita, *Política agraria: bases para una ley agraria y un estatuto de comunidades de indígenas* (1963), with a prologue by Luis Heysen.

67 Lima, 18 March 1964 letter of the young Bolivian intellectual Guillermo Vivado M. to the author.

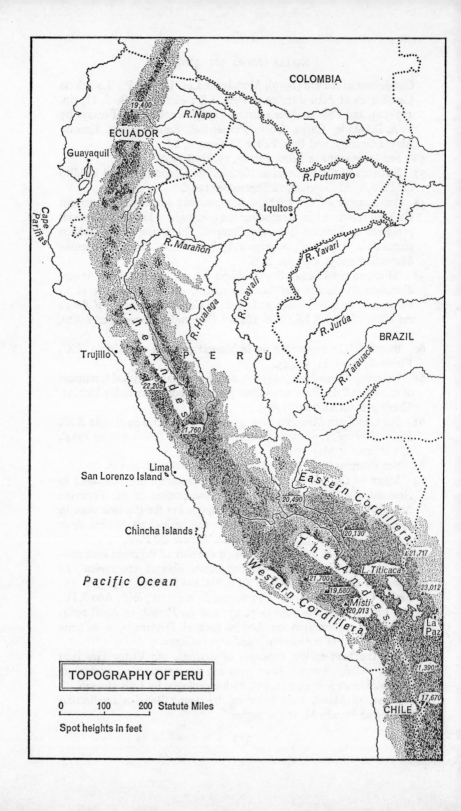

COLOMBIA

R. Napo

ECUADOR

Guayaquil

19,400

R. Putumayo

Iquitos

R. Marañon

Cape Pariñas

R. Yavari

R. Hualaga

R. Ucayali

R. Jurúa

P   E   R   Ú

BRAZIL

Trujillo

R. Tarauacá

The Andes

22,205

21,760

Lima

San Lorenzo Island

Eastern Cordillera

20,490

Chincha Islands

20,130

T h e   A n d e s

21,717

Pacific Ocean

21,700

L. Titicaca

23,012

19,680

▲ Misti
20,013

Western Cordillera

La Paz

21,390

TOPOGRAPHY OF PERÚ

0   100   200 Statute Miles

Spot heights in feet

17,670

CHILE

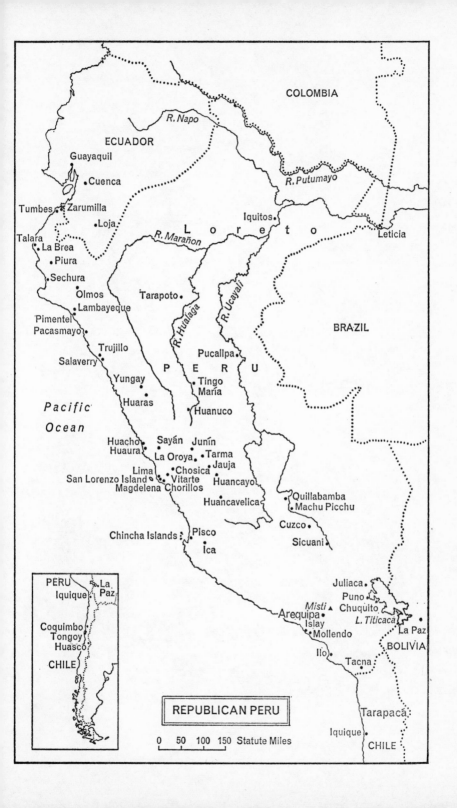

REPUBLICAN PERU

0   50   100 150 Statute Miles

Index